D1000803

Shirley Jackson

# Shirley Jackson

## Essays on the
## Literary Legacy

*Edited by* Bernice M. Murphy

McFarland & Company, Inc., Publishers
Jefferson, North Carolina, and London

DISCARDED

LIBRARY OF CONGRESS CATALOGUING-IN-PUBLICATION DATA

Shirley Jackson : essays on the literary legacy / edited by
Bernice M. Murphy.
    p.     cm.
    Includes bibliographical references and index.

    **ISBN 0-7864-2312-9** (softcover : 50# alkaline paper)

    1. Jackson, Shirley, 1916–1965—Criticism and interpretation.
2. Women and literature—United States—History—20th
century.   I. Murphy, Bernice M.
PS3519.A392Z853   2005
818'.5409—dc22                   2005011460

British Library cataloguing data are available

Front cover: Justin Kempton, Shirley Jackson, original hand cut block
print on paper, 7" × 9" (www.writersmugs.com)

Manufactured in the United States of America

*McFarland & Company, Inc., Publishers*
  *Box 611, Jefferson, North Carolina 28640*
   *www.mcfarlandpub.com*

For John and Majella Murphy

# Acknowledgments

I would like to thank the School of English at Trinity College Dublin, and acknowledge the invaluable support that the Trinity Trust provided for this project. Thanks are also due to Dr. Stephen Matterson for his advice and help, and to my colleagues in Foster Place and room 3160 for their encouragement and support. I am also deeply grateful to all of my contributors for agreeing to take part in this project. Permission to reproduce the "The Armada Portrait," by George Gower, was generously granted by His Grace the Duke of Bedford and the Trustees of the Bedford Estates.

# Table of Contents

# Introduction: *"Do You Know Who I Am?"* Reconsidering Shirley Jackson

During an episode of *The Simpsons* entitled "Dog of Death," Springfield's frequently fad-crazed citizenry succumb to a particularly virulent bout of gambling fever when the state lottery jackpot reaches an all-time high. The town's resident anchorman, Kent Brockman, begins the local news bulletin by announcing that people hoping to pick up tips on how to win the big prize have checked every copy of Shirley Jackson's *The Lottery* out of the local library. However, as Kent helpfully points out, "Of course, the book does not contain any hints on how to win the lottery. It is, rather, a chilling tale of conformity gone mad"—at which point a disgusted Homer Simpson tosses his copy into the fire.[1]

I begin by referring to this witty scene not only because it is very funny, but also because I believe that it illustrates, in suitably ironic form, some of the most contradictory things about Jackson. It says a lot about the visibility of Jackson's most notorious tale that more than 50 years after its initial publication it is still famous enough to warrant mention in the world's most famous sitcom. The fact that Springfield's citizenry also miss the point of Jackson's story completely (after all, no one in their right mind would ever want to win *her* lottery) can perhaps be seen as an indication of a more general misrepresentation of Jackson and her work—a process that as we shall see, was well underway even before her death in August 1965.

A great early success, of the type that Jackson had with first "The Lottery" and later with the short-story collection of the same name, can be both a blessing and a curse for a writer. A blessing because of course every fledgling writer dreams of achieving the type of visibility that Jackson attained in the months following the story's publication in June 1948. However troubled Jackson was by the many disapproving letters she received following the tale's publication in *The New Yorker*, a part of her must have delighted in the fact that something she had written had provoked such strength of feeling—what writer of any real ambition would not have to some extent have relished this kind of attention? The downside to this type of early success is the danger that this early effort will overshadow the writer's every subsequent effort in the popular and critical mindset. It's a problem that Jackson was all too aware of: as she noted in her essay "Biography of a Story," her witty account of the genesis and aftermath of "The Lottery,"

> It was not my first published story, nor would it be my last, but I have been assured over and over that if it had been the only story I ever wrote or published, there would be people who would not forget my name [*Come Along with Me* 210].

There have long been those who have acted as though "The Lottery" was the only story Jackson ever wrote. Along with her classic novel of supernatural horror, *The Haunting of Hill House* (1959), it did in fact make her name and seal her reputation as a writer of elegant, allusive, literary horror fiction. But Jackson was much more, as this collection will illustrate. Long revered by enlightened readers of horror and the gothic, and fêted for her masterful contribution to the ranks of the classic ghost story, readers can be forgiven for not realizing that *Hill House* was actually among the very few supernatural stories that Jackson ever wrote. Even then, much of the allegedly "supernatural" incident in the novel is as likely to have a psychological as a ghostly cause: neurotic outsider Eleanor Vance is the focus of the novel and the likely catalyst for the many of the incidents that take place within its pages. Similarly, those expecting the rest of Jackson's many short stories to resemble "The Lottery" will be disappointed. While unmistakably Jackson both thematically and stylistically, the story is by no means typical of her *oeuvre*.

So who was Shirley Jackson? A conventional biographical summing-up would, as in the case of most writers, appear fairly unremarkable, save for her obvious literary talent, and, because of Jackson's sudden death in early middle age, poignantly brief. Born in San Francisco in 1916 (although some accounts erroneously state 1919) to comfortably middle-class parents, Jackson moved with her family to Rochester, New York, when she was in her teens. She attended college there for a while, but was unhappy and dropped out for a year, during which she worked on her writing and took on a number of temporary jobs. Jackson then enrolled in Syracuse University, with better results: she helped edit *The*

*Spectre,* the college literary magazine, with her future husband, the academic and critic Stanley Edgar Hyman, graduated, got married, had four children in fairly rapid succession, and eventually settled in rural New England.

Like so many women of her class and generation, Jackson seemed absorbed in a life of apparently conventional domesticity: she raised her children, tolerated life as a faculty wife in a small, insular campus town, kept the family home running smoothly, and died at the age of 49 from heart failure. But of course, there was a great deal more going on in Jackson's life than the bare biographical facts would seem to suggest. Whatever she may have claimed in her family stories, Shirley Jackson was never just an "ordinary" housewife and mother: the importance of so much of her writing lies in the fact that she suggested so strongly that it was doubtful whether such a creature ever really existed at all.

It is no overstatement to say that Shirley Jackson was one of the most prominent female writers of the 1950s, so much so that one literary critic has even gone so far as to say that the "1950s became the decade of Jackson" (Wagner-Martin 107). Between 1948 and 1965 she published one best-selling short story collection, six novels, two popular volumes of her family chronicles, and many stories, which ranged from fairly conventional tales written for the women's magazine market to the ambiguous, allusive, delicately sinister and more obviously literary stories that were closest to Jackson's heart and were destined to end up in the more high brow end of the market. It is an impressive body of work for anyone to have produced in just over a decade and a half; when one considers that Jackson was also raising a family of four young children at the time it seems all the more notable.

Jackson was not alone in being able to find an audience for her work in both serious and popular outlets. As Joan Wylie Hall has observed, several of Jackson's contemporaries also published not only in *The New Yorker,* but also in mass market magazines—John Cheever featured in *Mademoiselle* and Ray Bradbury in *Charm,* while fellow writer of domestic humor Jean Kerr was a successful playwright whose work had been produced on Broadway. However, Jackson was "unusual for publishing so regularly in many of the magazines directed exclusively at a female readership ... her name is the only one that is now at all familiar in issue after issue of *Good Housekeeping* and *Ladies' Home Journal*" (Hall xiii). Jackson's ability to prosper in both highbrow and popular markets was admired by none other than Sylvia Plath, who, as biographer Linda Wagner-Martin has noted, hoped to meet Jackson in June 1953 during her summer internship at *Mademoiselle,* and aspired towards a similar career.

By anyone's standards, Jackson's career was a successful one. After making her first national publication in 1941 with the semi-autobiographical story "My Life with R.H. Macy," Jackson's work began to appear regularly, with the first of her many appearances in *The New Yorker* occurring in 1943.[2] She came to public prominence with the publication of "The Lottery" in 1948, and published *The Road Through the Wall* in the same year (it was generally liked by critics but not a great commercial success) and her first collection *The Lottery and Other Stories, or The Adventures of James Harris* in 1949. Her second novel, the unconventional Bildungsroman *Hangsaman* was published in 1951; like her follow-up, 1954's *The Bird's Nest*, it features a troubled young woman who suffers from a severe mental illness (schizophrenia and multiple personality disorder, respectively). The first (and most successful) of her so-called family chronicles, *Life Amongst the Savages* also appeared in 1954; the first of her "house" novels, *The Sundial*, appeared in 1956. The sequel to *Savages, Raising Demons*, was published in 1957, and Jackson's most famous novel, *The Haunting of Hill House*, appeared in 1959. Jackson's final completed novel, *We Have Always Lived in the Castle*, was published in 1962, though she was working on a new novel, *Come Along with Me*, at the time of her death three years later.

It is important to note that a surprising lack of critical work has been done on Jackson. I say surprising because at first glance, one would assume that she represents an obvious case for scholarship. In a revisionist academic climate in which some scholars have devoted entire careers to the rediscovery of marginalized writers—and from which a wealth of valuable feminist criticism has emerged—Jackson, a talented writer who focused on female anxieties and the contradictory pressures of domesticity and whose work has latterly been ignored, seems like a perfect choice for further study. And yet, an anecdotal biography, two book-length studies, around 40 or 50 critical papers and roughly the same number of dissertations represent the sum total of Jackson scholarship to date. Obviously, Jackson had not been entirely forgotten, but she has not been treated with the respect that her undeniable talent deserves.

Significantly, the vast majority of specific work on Jackson centers around just two specific works: the influential supernatural novel *The Haunting of Hill House* and the classic short story "The Lottery," both of which have invited more attention individually than the rest of her work combined. Indeed, aside from the three book-length studies I have previously mentioned, virtually nothing at all has been published about Jackson's first three novels and the vast number of her stories. While contemporaries such as Flannery O'Connor, Sylvia Plath, Eudora Welty and Carson McCullers have long been recognized as vitally important midcentury female voices, what little attention Jackson has received generally had a very narrow focus. Most of this critical work approaches Jackson from either an overtly feminist or psychoanalytic angle, or in the case of "The Lottery," has hinged upon the symbolism of the notorious tale. Despite the efforts of recent critics such as Darryl Hattenhauer and Joan Wylie Hall to establish her importance, there still persists the view in some quarters that Jackson, though unquestionably talented, was at heart a minor writer. It's a perspective that was first given prominence in the earliest (and for a long time, only) full-length critical study of Jackson's work, *Shirley Jackson* by Lenemaja Friedman (1973). In her concluding overview of Jackson's work, Friedman chose to damn her subject with faint praise:

> Miss Jackson is not, however, a major writer; and the reason she will not be considered one is that she saw herself primarily as an entertainer, as an expert storyteller and craftsman. She has insights to share with her readers; but her handling of the material—the surprise twists, the preoccupation with mystery and fantasy, her avoidance of strong passions, her versatility, and her sense of sheer fun—may not be the attributes of the more serious writer who wishes to come to grips with the strong passions of ordinary people in a workaday world, who prefers to deal directly with the essential problems of love, death, war, disease, poverty and insanity in its most ugly aspects.... Despite the lack of critical attention, her books continue to be popular with those people who are sensitive, imaginative, and fun-loving; and perhaps, in the long run, that popularity will be what counts [Friedman 161].

Friedman's reservations seem to hinge upon two (rather predictable) characteristics that she isolates in Jackson's work: the first of which being the fact that Jackson was an entertainer, i.e. a popular writer who tailored much of her output towards the desires of a particular audience, and whose work could often be considered fun. Alongside this damning knowledge of what the public wanted to read, Jackson's work, according to Friedman, has another significant flaw: "the preoccupation with mystery and fantasy" and the use of gothic devices such as surprise twists—in other words, the fact that Jackson was not afraid to venture beyond the boundaries of strictly realist fiction. The fact that Jackson reconfigured the stock devices and settings of the gothic form in order to skillfully reflect contemporary fears and anxieties is not mentioned. Jackson did not deal with the problems of the world "directly" (which according to Friedman seems to be one of the defining characteristics of a "major" writer), and so the best one can hope for in the future, Friedman concludes, is that ultimately "popularity will be what counts."

Friedman's rather condescending attitude towards Jackson's writing is one that has persisted even to this day: as recently as 2002, in the introduction to a guide on Jackson meant for American high school students, Harold Bloom wrote that "Jackson always had too palpable a design upon her readers—her effects are as calculated as Poe's" and concludes by saying that although Jackson "aspired to be more than an entertainer ... her art of narration stayed on the surface and could not depict individual identities" (Bloom 10). A rather more positive approach to Jackson's work can be found in Joan Wylie Hall's valuable *Shirley Jackson: The Short Fiction* (1993), and most recently in Darryl Hattenhauer's *Shirley Jackson's American Gothic* (2003), which argues that Jackson was an important precursor to postmodernism. Other useful texts for those interested in Jackson are Paul N. Reinsch's exhaustive bibliography and the biography *Private Demons* by Judy Oppenheimer (1988). The admittedly small but steadily growing body of criticism on Jackson and her works over recent years seems to suggest that interest in her work is increasing and indicates that at last her significant contribution to American literary culture in the postwar period will be recognized. It is hoped that this collection will aid that process. As I have indicated, while critics have long neglected Jackson, it would be wrong to suggest that she has been overlooked entirely. The texts most frequently written about even today are "The Lottery" and *Hill House*, with *Castle* probably coming in third. Outside of the two full-length studies of Jackson's work, very little has been written on *The Road Through the Wall*, *Hangsaman*, *The Bird's Nest* and *The Sundial*, and while Friedman's book devotes a chapter to the family chronicles, they are otherwise largely overlooked.

Consequently, there are two main aims for this collection: first of all, to provide a forum for the re-publication of some of the most significant existing examples of Jackson scholarship. This is the first time that a general, multi-author collection of Jackson criticism has ever been assembled, and it is hoped that it will provide an invaluable resource for both newcomers and those already familiar with her work. The second, and probably most important aim, is to widen the currently rather narrow scope of Jackson scholarship. Many of the existing articles on Jackson focus on only a small proportion of her writing. While such texts merit attention, interest in them has not necessarily translated into critical interest in the rest of her *oeuvre*, which is equally deserving of attention. It is a hoped that by giving equal attention to the typically overlooked areas of Jackson's writing, this collection will help redress the current imbalance in Jackson studies and help stress the unity and cohesiveness of her work.

Perhaps it is a good idea to pause here for a moment to consider the significance of Jackson's overlooked early novels. After all, certain authors and literary texts are neglected by dint of the fact that they simply aren't that good, or interesting. As I hope this collection will help prove, this is not the case with Jackson. Moreover, knowledge of her early novels shows just how many of Jackson's most prominent themes and preoccupations were present from the very beginning, as was her elegant prose and morbid wit.

Take Jackson's debut novel, *The Road Through the Wall* (1948). In general, this novel has been sorely overlooked by both readers and critics, and woefully mismarketed by publishers hoping to cash in on Jackson's reputation as a gothic writer. The hilariously over-the-top cover of my own 1970s paperback edition of the novel melodramatically proclaims "Welcome Wagon for evil" and tries, unsuccessfully, to convince the reader that the novel is part of that decade's horror boom. The reality is quite different. Evil—or rather the capacity of human beings to commit evil acts upon one another—is of course one of Jackson's most prominent themes (as contributor John G. Parks notes), but her exploration of this theme is of the subtle, allusive variety rather than symptomatic of the rather more graphic excesses that characterized 1970s horror. *Road* differs in several ways from the rest of Jackson's novels: it is her most obviously naturalistic text (all the more striking when one considers that *Hangsaman*, Jackson's next novel, would, like *The Bird's Nest*, attempt to replicate the cadences of the disturbed mind in the rhythms of her prose). *Road* is Jackson's most panoramic narrative, flitting from household to household as she outlines the events of the summer of 1936, when the wall separating the selfish, self-absorbed residents of Pepper Street from the wealthier suburb beyond is removed. Featuring a large cast of largely dislikeable characters, *Road* is by no means Jackson's most accomplished novel, nor was it particularly successful in a commercial sense (in a letter to her parents, Jackson called the book her "poor little stepchild"). Yet for all that, the novel deserves much more interest than it has hitherto received, and not least because it anticipated the most prominent themes and settings of the wave of suburban-related fiction that appeared during the postwar period by several years. Though *Road* suffers from a lack of focus, Jackson would evoke the self-absorption and casual cruelty of the middle-class suburbs in a manner that would seldom be bettered, particularly because her focus is mostly upon the children of the neighborhood, who in their petty rivalries, snobbishness and strict hierarchy are mirror images of their self-satisfied parents. Inevitably, it is the children who suffer because of the neglect and narcissism of the adults on the street. When a little girl, Caroline Desmond, goes missing after a garden party, Jackson expertly portrays the callousness and self-interest that define the residents of Pepper Street. They are connoisseurs of other people's misery:

> No one really wanted Caroline Desmond safe at home, although Mrs. Perlman said crooningly behind Marilyn, "The poor, poor woman" and Mrs. Donald said again, "If only we'd known in time." Pleasure was in the

feeling that the terrors of the night, the jungle, had come close to their safe
lighted homes, touched them nearly, and departed, leaving every family
safe but one [*Road* 206].

On a superficial level, Jackson's second and third novels, *Hangsaman*
and *The Bird's Nest*, seem to have a great deal in common. After all, both
texts have as their protagonists isolated young women suffering from
severe mental illness. Of course, one of Jackson's most prominent recurring themes is that of troubled women who find themselves unable to
distinguish between what is real and what is imagined. One of the most
disturbing things about her fiction is the fact that so many of her heroines find themselves crossing the lines between fantasy and reality, sanity and madness, so swiftly that it suggests that for all of us these
boundaries are dangerously unmarked and perilously easy to traverse. It
takes a writer of considerable skill and originality to write two novels in
rapid succession that seem to deal with almost the same concerns and
yet avoid repetition and a feeling of familiarity: yet this is what Jackson
achieves here.

*Hangsaman* tells the story of 17-year-old Natalie Waite, a disturbed
young woman who has just started her freshman year at college. The narrative details her gradual descent into madness so subtly that the reader,
like those around Natalie, is at first scarcely aware of the extent of her
delusional state. Indeed, the shocking revelation of the final pages—that
Natalie's friend Tony is actually a figment of her own troubled imagination and a likely symptom of schizophrenia—is so subtly and allusively
signposted that many contemporary reviewers found it a complete shock.
*Hangsaman* is a delicate, impressionistic novel, the first of Jackson's books
to explore at length the mindset of kind of troubled young woman who
would become her trademark. It is also a book ahead of its time, a clear
influence upon Plath's much more famous text *The Bell Jar* (1963), for
it clearly suggests that Natalie Waite is as constrained by the expectations placed upon her by society as she is by her own fractured psyche.
Indeed, her relationships with the other (real) women in the novel suggest that her unwillingness to enter adulthood is as significant from a feminist perspective as from a psychological one.

Elizabeth Richmond of *The Bird's Nest* is initially a less interesting
protagonist than the more obviously disturbed Natalie. Her life, Jackson
tells us, is one of dutiful routine and lifeless stoicism: "She had no friends,
no parents, no associates and no plans beyond that of enduring the necessary interval before her departure with as little pain as possible" (*TBN*
8). However, it soon becomes clear that something is badly amiss. She
suffers from constant, crippling headaches. She arrives at her boring
desk job (in the museum whose foundations have begun to "sag") to find
a nasty, puzzling note—"dear lizzie," the letter read, "your fools para-

dise is gone now for good watch out for me lizzie watch out for me..."
(*TBN* 8)—which we later find is only one in a series of such missives.
Much to her Aunt Morgen's displeasure Elizabeth has been sneaking out
of the house late at night yet claims not to remember a thing. At a social
gathering she arrives, blacks out, drinks far too much and causes several
embarrassing scenes, then comes to her senses with no idea of what has
transpired. At this point, it is decided that Elizabeth should receive professional help: she is referred to the affable, pompous Dr. Wright, who,
having placed his patient under hypnosis, soon discovers the real reason
for her odd behavior: multiple personality disorder.

Interestingly, unlike the single, highly subjective viewpoint of
*Hangsaman*, *The Bird's Nest* presents a multiplicity of viewpoints and
narratives, thus paralleling the mental state of its protagonist, to whom
the phrase "I don't quite feel myself today" has a rather unique resonance. The novel again provides a showcase for Jackson's considerable
interest in psychology and mental illness: it is both a pastiche of the real-
life psychiatric case studies that were to become so popular during the
1950s and a shrewd fictionalization of a famous real-life case. *The Bird's
Nest* also provides ample evidence of Jackson's wit, and several sections
of the text are blackly comic, particularly in the latter half of the novel
when Elizabeth's four personalities constantly vie for control and, in one
memorable instance, take four baths in a row while the increasingly exasperated Aunt Morgen watches in amazement. The novel further shows
Jackson's talent for capturing in a single paragraph the sense of a life that
has suddenly slipped out of gear: the opening lines describe the manner
in which the foundations of the museum in which Elizabeth works have
begun to sag. The extent to which her skewed surroundings parallel the
workings of her disturbed mind is soon made obvious:

> It is not proven that Elizabeth's personal equilibrium was set off balance
> by the slant of the office floor, nor could it be proven that it was Elizabeth
> who pushed the building off its foundations, but it is undeniable that they
> began to slip at about the same time [TBN 8].

Although *Hill House* was famously filmed in 1963, and again, rather
less successfully, in 1999, *The Bird's Nest* was actually the first Jackson
novel to be turned into a movie: it was filmed as *Lizzie* and released in
1957. However, the film was by all accounts not a particularly distinguished adaptation and was inevitably overshadowed by the similarly
themed and much superior *The Three Faces of Eve*. What *Hangsaman*
and *The Bird's Nest* (as well as *Hill House, Castle,* and many of the short
stories) demonstrate is that Jackson had as keen an interest in the fictional possibilities of the disturbed psyche as any American writer since
Poe.

Jackson tackled a different subject entirely in *The Sundial*, the first, and least known, of her three "house" novels. Simply put, *Sundial* is the story of 12 disagreeable people holed up in a large country house while they await the end of the world—but the synopsis only provides a hint of the depths of this remarkable tale, Jackson's most cynical and obviously satirical text. A knowing homage to eighteenth century gothic fiction, a satire of millenarian religious beliefs, and a reflection of contemporary Cold War anxieties, the interpretative possibilities of this rich text have for too long been ignored. Jackson obviously relished the chance to satirize the self-righteousness and narcissism of those who consider themselves to be chosen by a higher power. Following her encounter with a higher power (as represented by the booming voice of her late father) for the first time in her life, repressed maiden Aunt Fanny Halloran is the center of attention. Her new spiritual dispensation means that she can behave in any manner she likes and attribute it to her visions—while the family watches her sleep, she astonishes them by uttering the foulest of swear words. Self-satisfaction and arrogance soon follows: Jackson suggests that this is an inevitable by-product of serving as a messenger to some "greater power":

> When Aunt Fanny awakened she was perfectly aware of all that had happened, including her own revelations, and—probably resembling in this all souls who have been the vehicle of a major supernatural pronouncement—her first reaction of shivering terror was almost at once replaced by a feeling of *righteous commonplace....* She was completely subject to some greater power and, her own will somewhat buried in what controlled her, she could only become autocratic and demanding [*Sundial* 35; italics added].

With her next novel, *The Haunting of Hill House*, Jackson wrote the most influential ghost story since *The Turn of the Screw*. Informed by her keen understanding of psychology, in *Hill House*. Jackson brought the traditional tale of supernatural terror right up to date. About an ill-prepared group of would-be ghost hunters exploring a supposedly haunted house, the novel is (as has often been noted) one of the most beautifully written horror novels ever published. It is impossible to resist reprinting that famous first paragraph, surely one of the most elegantly atmospheric openings in all of modern American literature:

> No live organism can continue for long to exist sanely under conditions of absolute reality; even larks and katydids are supposed, by some, to dream. Hill House, not sane, stood by itself against its hills, holding darkness within; it had stood so for eighty years and might stand for eighty more. Within, walls continued upright, bricks met neatly, floors were firm, and doors were sensibly shut; silence lay steadily against the wood and stone of Hill House, and whatever walked there walked alone [HH 1].

While, as that opening establishes, the inherent malevolence of the monstrous Hill House is never in any doubt, it is also worth noting that this is a ghost story in which no ghosts actually appear. The dark heart of the novel lies in the manner in which Jackson so carefully portrays the relationship between lonely, disturbed outsider Eleanor Vance (who, like so many of Jackson's heroines, has "waited all her life for something to happen") and Hill House, which so readily exploits her obvious vulnerabilities and overwhelming desire for a home of her own. The book has all the familiar trappings of the traditional haunted house tale—unexplained noises in the middle of the night, a disorientating layout, strange occurrences—but the real horror lies perhaps in the fact that a lonely, unmarried woman like Eleanor is so out of place in a society that can only project one particular path for a young woman—that of wife and mother—that she becomes the perfect victim.

Jackson's final completed novel, *We Have Always Lived in the Castle* (1962), is the only first-person novel she ever completed. The heroine, 18-year-old mass murderess Merricat Blackwood, is perhaps one of the most beguilingly deranged protagonists a reader will ever meet. The novel had a long and difficult gestation period (and was written while Jackson was in a state of some considerable psychological and physical distress herself) but it is nevertheless the work of a writer operating at the very peak of her powers, a book that has scenes of both great tenderness and chilling horror. Given the fact that Jackson's fictional output was maturing in such an interesting fashion, her next novel, the unfinished *Come Along with Me* (1965), would no doubt also have been particularly interesting, not the least because it too was written in the first person, and in the form of Mrs. Angela Motorman, features a protagonist more like Jackson herself than we would have seen before.

Given Jackson's obvious talents, one might well ask why such a writer has until recently been denied the critical attention her writing would seem to warrant. Jackson's neglect can be attributed to a number of factors. Foremost among these is the fact that critics have not quite known what to make of her, a problem caused by the fact that she operated in two popular and yet frequently marginalized genres: those of horror and the gothic and the so-called domestic humor that appeared in women's magazines during the 1950s. As Lynette Carpenter has suggested in an important essay, Jackson's popularity, commercial success, and ability to simultaneously operate in two faintly disreputable genres has resulted in critical marginalization:

> Traditional male critics could not, in the end, reconcile genre with gender in Jackson's case: unable to understand how a serious writer of gothic fiction could also be, to all outward appearances, a typical housewife, much less how she could publish housewife humour in *Good Housekeeping*, they dismissed her [Carpenter 29].

Jackson's refusal to conform to conventional mores was complicated by the manner in which she was popularly depicted during her lifetime. Publicists and reviewers tended to focus upon two rather disparate but revealing representations of Jackson—either as "New England's only practicing amateur witch" or as matronly housewife. There was a grain of truth in each depiction, but ultimately neither revealed the true Jackson, and each would diminish the writer and her work. The polarization of Jackson's public personae began in 1948 with the publication of her first novel, the modestly successful *The Road Through the Wall*. The blurb on the dust jacket irreverently described Jackson as being "perhaps the only contemporary author who is a practicing amateur witch, specializing in small scale black magic and fortune telling with a tarot deck." As biographer Judy Oppenheimer notes, they were Jackson's husband Stanley's words and presumably it was also his idea to use this description— and, at "the time, since the book sold only moderately, it did no harm" (Oppenheimer 126). Stanley Hyman and Jackson had no way of knowing that in just over a year's time, this tongue-in-cheek publicity squib would come back to haunt them.

Jackson's relative anonymity ended on June 26, 1948, when *The New Yorker* published "The Lottery." Amidst the ensuing controversy, Jackson herself naturally became the object of much curiosity and speculation. Her stories were much in demand as a result of her newfound infamy, and now readers wanted to know more about the author of this all too memorable tale. With the hurried publication of the short-story collection of the same name in April of the following year, the publicity machine surrounding Jackson moved into high gear. It did not take long for publishing house Farrar Straus to rediscover Hyman's blurb for *Road*; and "Jackson herself had contributed biographical notes that could hardly have failed to pique interest" (Oppenheimer 139). The notes, which were perhaps just a little naive and revealing, outlined Jackson's unorthodox attitudes towards convention and the supernatural:

> My children and I believe wholeheartedly in magic. We do not any of us subscribe to the pat cause-and-effect rules which so many other people seem to use.... I have a fine library of magic and witchcraft and when I have nothing else to do I practice incantations [Oppenheimer 139].

There was an element of truth in Jackson's claims. As Oppenheimer notes, she did consider herself an expert on magic; she did have an extensive library of books on the subject; and she did make charms and mutter incantations to herself, as both family and friends testified (Oppenheimer 140); but it is also likely that Jackson was poking fun at the whole business of publicity and promotion, and most of all those who would be so gullible as to believe such a statement was said with an entirely straight face—no doubt the same rather impressionable section of the reading public who, a year earlier, had sent her angry letters demanding to know the name and location of the New England village whose arcane rites she had chronicled in "The Lottery."

However, there was something else there as well: deep-seated frustration towards the role she felt that a woman writer was supposed to adopt, and a genuine desire to evade conventional categorization. It was a desire that emerges strongly in the unpublished notes she made for that fateful biography:

> I am tired of writing dainty little biographical things that pretend I am a trim little housewife in a Mother Hubbard stirring up appetising messes over a wood stove.... I live in a dank old place with a ghost that storms around in the attic.... The first thing I did when we moved in was to make charms in black crayon on all the door sills and window ledges to keep out the demons [Oppenheimer 139].

This piece highlights the essential duality of Jackson's life and work—her consistent conflation of the domestic with the uncanny, the natural with the unnatural. What comes through most powerfully of all is Jackson's desire to resist imprisonment within the ideological norm, and a willful eccentricity and defiance that characterizes many of her finest fictional creations. The extract suggests that along with her faith in charms and incantations, Jackson had much in common with Merricat Blackwood, her most deeply felt character, of whom it could also be said, as it has been of Jackson, that "she would not be cubby holed, no matter how much easier it would make things for others" (Oppenheimer 139).

It did not take Jackson long, however, to realize that her mention of "witchlike" powers had badly backfired, for "rare was the interviewer who could resist asking her about black magic." At first, Jackson tended to respond to such questions truthfully. The result, as Oppenheimer puts it, "was the elbow nudging that surrounded her answers in print." Typical of such reports was one filed by Associated Press interviewer W.G. Rogers: "She says she can break a man's leg and throw a girl down an elevator shaft. Such things happen, she says! Miss Jackson tells you all this with a smile but she is not joking: she owns a library of two hundred books" (Oppenheimer 139).

Rogers was also responsible for saying that "Miss Jackson writes not with a pen, but with a broomstick"—an awkward but lasting description. It didn't help matters that Jackson's publishers went out of their way to enhance their client's occultist reputation, though given the fact that such stories "brought Jackson nearly as much publicity as the short stories themselves" they can hardly be blamed for their efforts. It was Farrar Straus who helped circulate the rumor that Jackson had, by means of

Voodoo, managed to break the leg of rival publishing magnate Alfred J. Knopf. Whether or not Jackson herself believed this is difficult to gauge (Oppenheimer 140).

Jackson's standing as a witch soon became a critical commonplace in reviews and interviews: an easy way of snidely explaining the disparity between her matronly outer appearance and the frequently otherworldly, ruthless nature of her fiction. As one rather hyperbolic review of *The Bird's Nest* put it: "Once more Shirley Jackson the wife and mother has yielded to Shirley Jackson the literary necromancer who writes novels not much like any other since the form was invented" (Wickenden). It is interesting that the reviewer of a novel about multiple personality disorder should phrase his praise of the author so as to suggests that she suffers from a literary form of this disorder herself—"wife and mother" "yielding" to "literary necromancer"—sorcerer, practitioner of the dark arts; as though one could not be all at once a wife, mother, and a writer of gothic fiction; as though a form of personality splitting, of uncanny transformation, was necessary before anything of that nature could be written by a woman.

Jackson soon learned to be more guarded while taking part in interviews. Speaking to *New York Times Book Review* interviewer Harvey Breit, she warily dismissed the by-now rather embarrassing and damaging issue of her "otherworldly" reputation (Breit 15). Jackson admitted that she believed in magic, but quickly added, "It was a silly thing to talk about." Perhaps in response to this dismissal, Breit instead focused on another theme that was becoming popular in critical dealings with Jackson: her "amazingly wholesome, motherly exterior" (Oppenheimer 143). Jackson, Breit stated, "looks notably wholesome but very much on the dayside. She is neat, detached and impersonally warm. She subtly radiates an atmosphere of coziness and comfort, and appears to be of a tranquil disposition." Breit's sentiments are similar to those expressed by Dan Wickenden in that in both instances, Jackson is presented as the image of an idealized '50s housewife—her matronly appearance seen as a surprise when contrasted with the nature of her writing. It reflects the expectation that writers of gothic fictions should be suitably gothic looking themselves—and if they do not conform to these expectations, then due attention is drawn to their lack of adhesion to preconceived ideas.

It was an issue that Jackson's husband tackled in his introduction to *The Magic of Shirley Jackson* (1966), a collection released after her death. Hyman discussed the reaction of critics who had been puzzled by the disparity between his wife's outward appearance and her most famous work:

> People often expressed surprise at the difference between Shirley Jackson's appearance and manner, and the violent and terrifying nature of her fiction. Thus many of the obituaries played up the contrast between a

"motherly-looking" woman, gentle and humorous, and that "chillingly horrifying" short story "The Lottery" and similar works. When Shirley Jackson, who was my wife, published two light hearted volumes about the spirited doings of our children ... it seemed to surprise people that the author of her grim and disturbing fiction should be a wife and mother at all, let alone a gay and apparently happy one [Hyman vii].

Critics who had been taken aback by Jackson's appearance and apparently conventional home life, Hyman continued, had displayed an "elementary misunderstanding of what a writer is and how a writer works, on the order of expecting Herman Melville to be a big white whale." While entirely reasonable, Hyman's remarks had neglected to mention the extent to which, as with the earlier "witch" label, Jackson herself had, intentionally or otherwise, encouraged this depiction of herself as an everyday housewife who just happened to write in her spare time. Slightly later on in Breit's interview, Jackson made some rather self-deprecating and revealing comments about the nature of her writing:

I can't persuade myself that writing is honest work. It is a very personal reaction, but fifty percent of my time is spent washing and dressing the children, cooking, washing dishes and clothes and mending. After I get it all to bed, I turn around to my typewriter and try to—well, to create concrete things again. It's great fun, and I love it. But it doesn't tie shoes [Oppenheimer 141].

The implication here is clear: writing for Jackson is just a pastime, fun, but the real work in Jackson's life is that of a hardworking, thoroughly domesticated wife and mother, for whom the creation of fictional, "concrete" worlds is a secondary occupation, something to be sandwiched between cooking dinner and tying shoe laces. Jackson's statement is partially true, for she was a busy wife and mother, who produced almost as many children as she did novels. However, such cozy sentiments and modest self-deprecation are sorely at odds with the more realistic depictions of Jackson the writer; who, in her late teens, had spent a year writing a thousand words of fiction a day, already convinced that her future lay in writing; the college magazine editor, frequent contributor to magazines both prestigious and popular; a woman who, from an early age, had been filled with determination, pragmatism, and above all, fierce ambition, and who, as her husband put it, "always regarded herself as a professional writer ... and did not see that vocation as being incompatible with being a wife and mother: did not see her art as being incompatible with producing art in saleable forms" (Hyman viii).

Hence Jackson's remarks to Breit can also be seen as the adoption of a calculated pose by Jackson, her way of presenting herself in a manner that the innately conservative world in which she lived would accept—

a kind of reassuring buffer between the writer and the entirely unexpected nature of her fiction.

Jackson was all too aware of the problem the figure of the writer/housewife presented, and or the fact that she lived in a society that was quite often unwilling to accept that a married mother could also have a successful, creative career outside the home. It is a preoccupation that comes to the fore in her writing on several occasions, most particularly in the essay "Fame" (first published in *The Writer* magazine two months after "The Lottery" appeared) and the story "The Third Baby's the Easiest" (1949) later integrated into *Savages*. "Fame" humorously recounts the purported details of a conversation that took place a week after her first novel, *Road*, was published. The essay begins with a ringing phone and a caller who abruptly demands, "Hello, who's this?" before brusquely introducing herself as the local society columnist. It is an exchange that, as Joan Wylie Hall notes, "precipitates an uncommon dialogue" (75):

> "This is Shirley Jackson," I said, a little soothed because my name reminded me of my book. "Well," she said vaguely, "is Mrs. Stanley Hyman there, please?" I waited for a minute, and then, "This is Mrs. Hyman," I said reluctantly. Her voice brightened. "Mrs. Hyman," she said, pleased. "This is Mrs. Sheila Lang of the Newspaper. I've been trying to get in touch with you for days" ["Fame"].

Soliciting announcements for "North Village Notes," Mrs. Lang "is more interested in Jackson's house and children than in the author's attempts to discuss her book and the publication party to be hosted by Farrar Straus." The next day's society column reads: "Mrs. Stanley Hyman has moved into the old Thatcher place on Prospect street. She and her family are visiting Mr. and Mrs. Farrar Straus of New York City this week." Jackson's attempts to assert her separate, distinct identity as a successful writer have been completely ignored by the local woman who conducts the interview: "Shirley Jackson" is completely overridden by "Mrs. Hyman," the name that Jackson only "reluctantly" admits to, because it negates her independent writerly persona, which, significantly, is conducted under her maiden rather than married name.

A similar identity crisis is depicted in "one of Jackson's most memorable family stories, 'The Third Baby's the Easiest'" (Hall 76). Checking into the hospital in order to give birth to her third child, the anonymous narrator (ostensibly Jackson herself), while asserting her readiness for the child's arrival, also refuses to limit her self-definition to the proscribed role of wife and mother (Hall 76). Before she can give birth, however, she must first unexpectedly prove herself to the hospital receptionist, who, like the interviewer in "Fame" is unable to accept that the narrator has an existence beyond that of wife and mother:

"Name?" the desk clerk said to me politely, her pencil poised.
"Name," I said vaguely. I remembered and told her.
"Age?" she asked. "Sex? Occupation?"
"Writer," I said.
"Housewife," she said.
"Writer," I said.
"I'll just put down housewife," she said [*Savages* 61].

Even though suffering the pangs of childbirth, the narrator still insists upon identifying herself as a writer, even before she lists her name or age. It is clearly the most important element of her self-definition. The exchange between the protagonist and the receptionist is both comical and significant, as the narrator futilely attempts to be heard but is mercilessly overruled by another woman. It is she, not the heroine, who has a pencil in her hands. Writing can both empower and dispossess, depending upon who is in charge, and therefore the refusal of a minor bureaucratic figure to accept that the narrator might be something more than she seems is indicative of a more widespread societal attitude.

Both stories also significantly contradict Jackson's assertions in the (already cited) interview with Harvey Breit, for they suggest that Jackson saw her occupation as that of a writer, almost before anything else, albeit a writer who was constantly trying to assert her unique identity in the face of limiting and oppressive societal expectations. However, despite the fact that the narrators in both "Fame" and "The Third Baby's the Easiest" succumb to the stony logic of their opponents, the last laugh will ultimately be on the Jackson/writer figure, who triumphs in the end because she recounts these exchanges in print, thereby asserting her own authorial status and power even as the words of the story themselves suggest she has been defeated. In the end it was always Jackson the writer who got to have the last word.

In the essays that follow, we shall see that just as Jackson herself resisted conventional categorization, so too does her writing, which is open to a wide range of critical and interpretive opinion. In the opening essay, "Fallen Eden in Shirley Jackson's *The Road Through the Wall*," Joan Wylie Hall discusses Jackson's sorely neglected debut novel in light of her relationship with the state of her birth, California, and suggests that the novel contributes to "a prominent theme of much California literature: the loss of innocence in the Eden of the final American frontier." James Egan's new essay, "Comic-Satiric-Fantastic-Gothic: Interactive Modes in Shirley Jackson's Narratives," begins by noting the "unintended but definite" compartmentalization of her writing, discusses the primary narrative modes used in her work, and argues that we should move towards a "renewed sense of the sophisticated totality of Jackson's canon."

Marta Caminero-Santangelo's contribution, "Multiple Personality and the Postmodern Subject *Theorizing Agency*," is an extract from her 1998 book *The Madwoman Can't Speak: Or Why Insanity Is Not Subversive*, which discusses Jackson's third novel, *The Bird's Nest*, in relation to the postwar redefinition of femininity and accompanying fascination with the female multiple personality. The essay that follows, "New World Miniatures: Shirley Jackson's *The Sundial* and Postwar American Society" by Rich Pascal, also explores one of Jackson's more neglected texts in light of the post–World War II historical and cultural context. Pascal also relates the novel's preoccupation with the possibility of annihilation and the promise of utopian renewal to America's originating image of itself as a New World. Both essays employ a perspective rarely used by earlier Jackson critics—that of historicism—and their readings suggest that this avenue of critical exploration may well prove one of the most rewarding critical approaches to Jackson in the future.

Bernice M. Murphy's essay, "'The People of the Village Have Always Hated Us': Shirley Jackson's New England Gothic," discusses the depiction of New England and New Englanders in Jackson's *oeuvre*, while "House Mothers and Haunted Daughters: Shirley Jackson and the Female Gothic" by Roberta Rubenstein argues that Jackson's resonant representation of family relationships (and in particular the ambivalent mother-daughter bond) deserves wider recognition. Rubenstein goes on to pay particular attention to such relationships in Jackson's three final novels and places Jackson's work within the wider context of the female gothic. In "'Whose Hand Was I Holding?': Familial and Sexual Politics in Shirley Jackson's *The Haunting of Hill House*," Tricia Lootens traces the origins and developments of Jackson's most famous novel, and by examining early notes and drafts of the text from the Library of Congress, finds proof that despite the ambiguous, complex nature of Jackson's masterpiece, "she seems to have set out to write a fairly standard ghost story, not a story about the way in which people, especially women, are destroyed by the nuclear family, sexual repression, and romantic notions of feminine self-sacrifice."

Judie Newman undertakes a psychoanalytic reading of the novel in "Shirley Jackson and the Reproduction of Mothering: *The Haunting of Hill House*," which analyzes the text in light of feminist psychoanalytic theorist Nancy Chodorow's book *The Reproduction of Mothering*—an approach to which *Hill House* seems particularly receptive. We find a different approach to domesticity in the next essay, an extract from S.T. Joshi's *The Modern Weird Tale* (2001). Here, perhaps the most overlooked aspect of Jackson's *oeuvre*—her family chronicles—is discussed in light of her more obviously literary achievements. Joshi begins by declaring Jackson one of the "leading writers of weird fiction since Lovecraft" and goes on to discuss the "strain of quasi-autobiography" present in her work from the later 1940s onwards.

In "The Establishment and Preservation of Female Power in Shirley Jackson's *We Have Always Lived in the Castle*," Lynette Carpenter reads Jackson's final completed novel from a feminist perspective, arguing that the text predates later critiques of the institution of patriarchy and that it is "her most radical statement on the causes and consequences of female victimization and alienation, a theme that runs through her work." In "King of the Castle: Shirley Jackson and Stephen King," Dara Downey and Darryl Jones discuss the profound influence Jackson's fiction has had upon the world's most successful writer of horror. John G. Parks' essay, "Chambers of Yearning: Shirley Jackson's Use of the Gothic," suggests that Jackson's effective use of gothic conventions allows her to "reveal and chronicle the outrage, at times tempered with laughter, which stems from the violation of the self by a broken world," while in "Stephen Spielberg's *The Haunting*: A Reconsideration of David Self's Script," Darryl Hattenhauer argues that the script upon which the much-reviled 1999 adaptation of *Hill House* was based was originally a much more accomplished and respectful piece of work than has previously been acknowledged. The collection concludes with Diane Long Hoeveler's essay, "Life Lessons in Shirley Jackson's Late Fiction: Ethics, Cosmology, Eschatology," which suggests that a kind of "highly coded gothic ethics" begins to emerge most prominently in Jackson's later work, and argues that she was at heart "a gothicist with a personal agenda."

As I have already noted, Shirley Jackson was one of the most prominent female writers of the 1950s and early '60s, someone whose work attracted both commercial success and critical acclaim. Her prominence, however, has not been as enduring as it deserves to be: while contemporaries Flannery O'Connor and Sylvia Plath (with whom her work has much in common) have long been elevated to the status of important American writers, Jackson has more often been sidelined as too commercial, too generic or too popular. Yet as this collection demonstrates, Jackson's work has a great deal to offer beyond her obvious mastery of generic material. Her writing provides a fascinating portrait of American womanhood during a period of significant change. She excelled at dramatizing the anxiety and claustrophobia experienced by so many (particularly middle class) American women during the postwar period. Her critique of the era's domestic ideology may not seem particularly overt at first, but it is almost always present, perhaps most strikingly apparent in that terrible, pervasive sense of indefinable longing and gnawing dissatisfaction that infects many of her female characters. Like *Hill House*'s Eleanor Vance, most of Jackson's women "held fast to the idea that someday something would happen" (*HH* 8). It's a longing for change that is in itself a powerful indictment of the decade's oppressive promotion of conservative domestic ideology: a nagging reminder of the unfulfilled potential and low-grade despair that frequently afflicted the many women who found themselves living bland, restricted lives. It says a lot about Jackson's work that the only character in her fiction who openly declares herself to be happy is a teenage girl who has burnt down the family home and poisoned almost all of her close relations.

However, Jackson's awareness of contemporary preoccupations and anxieties was by no means restricted to the problems facing American women. As we shall see, Jackson's work was influenced by a wide range of historical and cultural issues. Her ability to write for a wide array of commercial and literary outlets was paralleled by the diverse range of contemporary anxieties and preoccupations that appear in her work. Encouragingly, there are definite signs that the critical neglect Jackson has been faced with for so many years is coming to an end: in the past two years, Darryl Hattenhauer's full-length study which makes the case for Jackson's status as a key proto-postmodernist has appeared, as has an extremely useful critical bibliography by Paul N. Reinsch, while a much more general guide to her work intended for American high school students has also been published.

There is a rather surreal moment in one of Jackson's domestic volumes when her youngest daughter Sally repeatedly chants the question that has been asked by nearly every Jackson heroine at some point, if only of herself:

> "Do you know who I am?" Sally was singing on her head in the backseat, "Do you know who I am?"

In this case the childish answer is surreal and baffling:

> "I'm a rat and you're a fish," Sally said, "and now you know who I am" [Raising Demons 149].

It is a phrase that almost every Jackson protagonist could utter: for rare is the Jackson heroine who knows who she truly is. It's also a statement that Jackson herself could have asked of those who for so long have taken her versatility and efficiency to mean that her work is unworthy of truly serious consideration. Far from being a liability, Jackson's varied achievement should instead be considered one of her greatest strengths. Unlike so many of her own characters, Jackson knew exactly who she was. I can only hope that by airing the work of those who are examining her work from a fresh perspective, this collection has gone some way towards satisfactorily answering her question.

# *Notes*

1. "Dog of Death." *The Simpsons*. Fox. March 1992.
2. "My Life with R.H. Macy" appeared in *The New Republic* on December 22, 1941, "After You, My Dear Alphonse" was printed in *The New Yorker* on January 16, 1943.

# *Works Cited*

Bloom, Harold, ed. *Shirley Jackson*. Bloom's Major Short Story Writers. New York: Chelsea House, 2001.

Breit, Harvey. "Talk with Miss Jackson." *New York Times Book Review*, 26 June 1949.

Carpenter, Lynette. "Domestic Comedy, Black Comedy, and Real Life: Shirley Jackson, a Woman Writer." In *Faith of a Woman Writer*. Eds. Alice Kessler-Harris and William McBrien. New York: Greenwood Press, 1988.

Friedman, Lenemaja. *Shirley Jackson*. Boston: Twayne's U.S. Authors Series, 1975.

Hall, Joan Wylie. *Shirley Jackson: The Short Fiction*. New York: Twayne Publishers, 1993.

Hattenhauer, Darryl. *Shirley Jackson's American Gothic*. New York: State University of New York Press, 2003.

Hyman, Stanley Edgar. Introduction to *The Magic of Shirley Jackson*, by Shirley Jackson. New York: Farrar Straus, 1966.

Jackson, Shirley. *The Bird's Nest*. 1954; New York: Farrar, 1954.

_____. *Come Along with Me*. 1966; New York: Penguin, 1996.

_____. "Fame" *Writer*, August 1948.

_____. *The Haunting of Hill House*. 1959; New York: Penguin, 1987.

_____. *Life Among the Savages*. 1953; London: Michael Joseph, 1954.

_____. *The Lottery and Other Stories*, or *The Adventures of James Harris*, 1949.

_____. *The Masterpieces of Shirley Jackson*. London: Raven, 1996.

_____. *Raising Demons*. London: Michael Joseph, 1957.

_____. *The Road Through the Wall*. 1948; New York: Farrar Straus, 1975.

_____. *The Sundial*. 1958; New York, Ace Books, n.d.

_____. *We Have Always Lived in the Castle*. 1962. In *The Masterpieces of Shirley Jackson*. London: Robinson, 1996.

Oppenheimer, Judy. *Private Demons: The Life of Shirley Jackson*. New York: G.P. Putnam's Sons, 1988.

Reinsch, Paul N. *A Critical Bibliography of Shirley Jackson, American Writer (1919–1965): Reviews, Criticism, Adaptations*. Lewiston, N.Y.: Mellen, 2001.

Wagner-Martin, Linda. *The Mid-Century American Novel 1935–1965: Critical History*. New York: Twayne, 1997.

_____. *Sylvia Plath: A Literary Life*. Basingstoke: Macmillan, 1999.

Wickenden, Dan. *New York Herald Tribune* book review, 20 June 1965.

# 1

# Fallen Eden in Shirley Jackson's *The Road Through the Wall*

## JOAN WYLIE HALL

Shirley Jackson was born in San Francisco in 1916, descended on her mother's side from architects who had designed several of the city's more impressive homes. Her biographer, Judy Oppenheimer, suggests that the family's move to Rochester, New York, when she was in high school, left her with a sense of California as a lost paradise (18, 31).[2] A diary entry for April 1, 1933, four months before the move, sentimentally records the end of a yearly tradition: "This is the last time I shall ever press the first rosebud of spring that comes off my rosebush."[3] Displaced from the familiar world her grandfather and great-great-grandfather had literally helped to build, she wrote on September 2, "Damn Mimi [the grandmother who had moved with the Jacksons] and Rochester." Because her grandmother, her parents, and her brother Barry eventually returned to California, Jackson carried on a lifelong correspondence with her childhood home. Her books were enthusiastically reviewed in *The San Francisco Chronicle*, and the University of California at Berkeley was eager to add her papers to its archives.[4] Jackson wrote to her parents that Berkeley must have confused her with Helen Hunt Jackson, who described Mission Indians and greedy Americans in southern California. Amused at the request, she added: "I told them that the

---

*This essay first appeared in* Renascence: Essays on Values in Literature, *volume 46.4 (summer 1994): 261–70, and is reprinted with that journal's permission, slightly expanded.*

next time I cleaned my filing cabinet they were welcome to anything I
found. If they could make any sense out of my first drafts in the interest of scholarship they should be wasting their time on something else"
(letter to Geraldine and Leslie Jackson, late April 1955, SJP, Box 3).

Although five of Jackson's six novels and most of her short stories
with identifiable settings are situated in the Eastern states where she spent
the rest of her life, the Bay Area provides an important backdrop for an
early story and for her first novel, *The Road Through the Wall*.[5] Both
works contribute to a prominent theme of much California literature: the
loss of innocence in the Eden of the final American frontier. David Wyatt
has sought to find "the gain in the loss" in the writing of such California novelists as Jack London and John Steinbeck, both of whom suggest
possibilities of married love and other strong human ties. But, as Wyatt
acknowledges, "the old archetype is hard to shake" (207). In Shirley
Jackson's case, the archetype is reinforced. She has no place in the "alter-
nate tradition" of visionary romance that Charles L. Crow opposes to
the usual California "literature of disillusionment" (3).[6] In fact, Jackson's focus on the destruction of innocence not in adults but in several
children and adolescents makes her California novel among the most
disillusioned in the genre.

Contemporaneous with *The Road Through the Wall* is a short story
that provides a lighter treatment of the same theme of a lost Eden.[7]
"Dorothy and My Grandmother and the Sailors," which appeared in the
highly publicized collection *The Lottery*, or *The Adventures of James Harris* (1949), opens in a nostalgic mood that is rare in Jackson's fiction:
"There used to be a time of year in San Francisco—in late March, I
believe—when there was fine long windy weather, and the air all over the
city had a touch of salt and the freshness of the sea" (135). Reminiscent
of the young diarist who preserved a final rosebud, the unnamed narrator describes the last of her annual childhood visits to the fleet of battleships that once brought large numbers of sailors to town every spring.
Though escorted by her mother and grandmother, the girl and her friend
Dorothy—both at the impressionable age of "about twelve" (136)—
undergo a sequence of misadventures that comically but irrevocably
transforms their earlier innocent fascination with the sailors into an attitude of caution and even fear.

At the beginning of the story, the two eager girls, made "more
aware" by the spring winds, can feel the pull of the ships from their suburban home as they look toward the ocean, "almost able to see across
thirty miles and into a sailor's face" (135). But the narrator is frightened
when she is briefly lost on shipboard: nightmarishly, her relatives act as
if she has compromised her virtue during the separation. The grandmother's response is "I'm glad we found her in time," while the mother

shakes the girl's arm, demanding, "Aren't you ashamed?" (139). On boarding, the mother had done her fruitless best to avert disaster by warning her protégées to "Keep your skirts down" (138). No wonder both girls become panic-stricken when, later the same day, a pair of sailors sit beside them in a San Francisco movie theater. Rushing down the aisle, they are rescued by the two older women, who hurry them home to the safety of the suburb. "Because of what happened that evening, that was the last year we were allowed to see the fleet," the narrator explains (139).

Desire is linked to danger throughout the story, even in matters of eating. Dinner at the Merry-Go-Round restaurant always followed the visit to the fleet. In a scene worthy of a Marx Brothers comedy, "the food came along on a moving platform and you grabbed it as it went by" (140). The girls ate there, the narrator says, because they "loved it, and next to the battleships it was the most dangerous place in San Francisco, because you had to pay fifteen cents for every dish you took and didn't finish, and Dot and I were expected to pay for these mistakes out of our allowances" (140). This "last evening," she notes, they lost 45 cents. Thus the two are thwarted in all their customary arenas of springtime pleasure: on board ship, at the Merry-Go-Round, and at the movie theater. The only successful venture of the day is the purchase of identical coats, "with princess lines ... and warmly interlined" (141): cold comfort for adolescents who had "dropp[ed] our voices when we talked" about the fleet full of sailors, "out around the Golden Gate, unbridged at that time" (135). The final loss is that of this splendid open vista, forfeited at the end of the story for the small world of Burlingame, and barred subsequently to all viewers by the imposition of the iron bridge, whose completion in 1939 visibly marked the end of the prewar era in California.

Published in 1948, *The Road Through the Wall* similarly evokes a period before the war. Again the setting contains elements of a golden age, but the Eden of the novel is on its way to being lost from the opening page. In none of her later books is Shirley Jackson as explicit about the time and the geographical location as she is here. A prologue describes Pepper Street and adjacent Cortez Road in the San Francisco suburb of Cabrillo at 2:30 in mid-June, 1936. The afternoon is "very quiet and pleasant, with the California sunlight of early summer almost green coming through the trees, almost painful straight from the sky" (11). Like the sunlight, the pink blossoms newly fallen to the sidewalks from the trees are painfully beautiful. The narrator remarks that they will be underfoot only a few days before dying (12). The melancholy aspect of the setting anticipates the many sufferings of the families in the neighborhood. Thelma J. Shinn believes that the "violence and disintegration"

Jackson portrays in the small society of Pepper Street "clearly reflect" the crises of the war years that preceded the writing of *The Road Through the Wall* (49). Yet any correspondence between the action of the novel and world events is indirect. As Michael Nardacci points out, because the rise of Hitler and the aggression of Japan are never mentioned, the reader is inclined to conclude that, in depicting the cruelties of Cabrillo, "Shirley Jackson was after something more universal" than an allegory of recent history (37).

Raymond Miller suggests that Jackson's object is "a very broad-based descriptive attack on life in the United States" (33–34). Her allusions to Cortez and Cabrillo, sixteenth century Spanish explorers and exploiters of California, could add weight to Miller's claim, but his view shares the limitations of Shinn's reading. Although *The Road Through the Wall* is to some extent a critique of middle-class materialism and prejudices in a walled-off suburb, Jackson's social criticism has as much in common with Nathanael West's surreal satire as it does with realistic exposes like Steinbeck's. She was familiar with both writers. In one of her cartoon-like sketches of famous authors preserved at the Library of Congress, she pictures a blank-eyed Steinbeck clutching his stomach and standing next to a fish's skeleton; her caption explains: "Mr. John Steinbeck discovers a new—and poisonous—variety of marine life" (SJP, Box 36).[8] Nardacci notes that *The Road Through the Wall* is unusual among Jackson's works for its naturalism, a characteristic that links the book with much of Steinbeck's writing (36). She also shares his sympathy for the outcast. Tod Donald, whose suicide by hanging brings the action to a depressing conclusion akin to many of Steinbeck's, is introduced as a quiet boy without friends: "No one ever chose him for a side in a game; he was always allowed to merge himself undesired into one team or another, never allowed to bat in the baseball game" (*Road* 47).

Tod has affinities not only with Steinbeck's lone young males, whose loneliness can often be linked to society's abuse, but also with another fictitious Tod who inhabits 1930s California, the existentially alone Tod Hackett of West's *The Day of the Locust* (1939). Both Tods are death-haunted, as the name reveals in German. Tod Donald kills himself because he is accused of crushing the skull of a three-year-old girl with a heavy stone. He disappears from a neighborhood party at about the same time as little Caroline Desmond, and he behaves oddly after the discovery of her body, so Tod is the prime suspect; but a couple of characters express doubts that the boy could have committed the crime, and the reader never learns what really happened. Tod's suicide is especially horrifying if he is innocent of the murder. Mr. Perlman, a Jewish neighbor, complains that "the whole thing was too hasty. Far too hasty. Everyone jumping to conclusions" (266). In contrast to Tod Donald, Tod

Hackett survives the violent ending of *The Day of the Locust*, but he is injured by a mob that charges against a man who viciously attacks a child star. The boy provokes the attack by hitting the man in the face with a stone, and Tod tries unsuccessfully to defuse the man's angry response.

In both novels, the atavistic weapon of assault recalls traditional depictions of Cain's attack on his brother Abel, a postparadisal story that Steinbeck more explicitly echoes in his *East of Eden*. Nardacci's remark that, in Jackson's novel, "a steadily building atmosphere of decadence and moral decay" makes the final violence "logical and inevitable" (38) is also appropriate to West's account of a fantastically degraded Hollywood. Tod Hackett's masterwork, a painting he calls "The Burning of Los Angeles," depicts a huge crowd—not unlike the one that sweeps him up in the final chapter—whose frustrations erupt in fury: "For the faces of its members, he was using the innumerable sketches he had made of the people who come to California to die; the cultists of all sorts, economic as well as religious, the wave, airplane, funeral and preview watchers—all those poor devils who can only be stirred by the promise of miracles and then only to violence" (420). Tod and his friends occupy the lower foreground of the big canvas, running from the dancing mob, and Tod picks up a stone to cast before hurrying on. His tantalizing neighbor Faye, a would-be movie star, flees naked from a woman who is about to strike her down with a rock (321).

This scene of sudden mass rage inflicted on convenient victims is much like the conclusion of Jackson's most famous story, "The Lottery," where Tessie Hutchinson is stoned by her fellow villagers in a ritual whose significance remains unclear.[9] But the excitement of West's mob is also related to the behavior of Pepper Street, where the "prevailing mood" after Caroline's disappearance is "one of keen excitement: no one there really wanted Caroline Desmond safe at home" (253–54). The sad events that follow only titillate some of the characters. Mrs. Merriam, who nags her husband and spies on her daughter's private writings, insinuates that Tod raped the dead child: "'Mark my words,' Mrs. Merriam said, 'even if that killing was an accident, there were other things about it that *were not* accidental.' She tightened her lips and looked triumphant" (268).

In a monograph on Nathanael West, Jackson's husband, Stanley Edgar Hyman, says his genius is "to have found objective correlatives for our sickness and fears: our maimed and ambivalent sexuality, our terror of the idiot mass, our helpless empathy with suffering, our love perverted into sadism and masochism. West did this in convincing present-day forms of the great myths: the Quest, the Scapegoat, the Holy Fool, the Dance of Death" (45–46). The observation anticipates Hyman's similar comment on Jackson in a preface to a collection of her works: "Her fierce visions of dissociation and madness, of alienation and withdrawal, of cruelty and terror, have been taken to be personal, even neurotic, fantasies. Quite the reverse: they are a sensitive and faithful anatomy of our times, fitting symbols for our distressing world of the concentration camp and the Bomb" (viii).

Jackson herself avoided making such direct connections between her work and current events, but her short stories, novels, and even some of her drawings embody the same myths that Hyman identifies with West. Hyman could have added the Garden and the Fall to his list. In *The Day of the Locust*, Maybelle Loomis, a studio mother who describes herself as an "old settler" of six years, laughs at the thought that anyone might dislike California: "Why, it's paradise on earth!" (360). When the lascivious Mrs. John Schwartzen drags Tod Hackett into a garden of this paradise, the air smells of flowers, but the beauty is grotesquely marred by the life-size rubber reproduction of a dead horse that the hostess has set afloat in the sunken pool (274).

Jackson echoes the Edenic myth in *The Road Through the Wall* in her references to many such ruined gardens. Old Mr. Martin worries that the dust raised by the construction equipment that is tearing down the wall at the end of Pepper Street will "reach as far as his flowers, penetrate the sealed greenhouses, dirty the roses" (185).[10] He fears that not only the greenhouses but also the "sacred enclosed place which harbored the main house" of his employer's adjoining estate will be "exposed to intrusions from the outside world, perhaps small boys with stones, perhaps curious trespassers gathering flowers, perhaps all those people with large feet who trample down tiny growing things" (185). In his dreams, he sees "the broken glass, the crushed roots" (186). Two apple trees grow by Mr. Martin's own back door, and another in the back yard bears "wry unpalatable fruit" (64). He has no time to cultivate the wilderness of his garden or to tend his barren plum trees. Another old resident of the neighborhood, Mrs. Mack, also lives in a ruined landscape; her boarded-up windows are screened by a hedge and an orchard of "battered" apple trees (87).

The more prosperous gardens of Pepper Street are also liable to destruction. In the second chapter of the novel, Tod Donald lies on the grass at the end of the Desmonds' garden. In the family's absence, he has just wandered casually through the house. The furnishings of Mrs. Desmond's bedroom, where she sleeps apart from her husband, are in gardenlike shades of green and yellow. The scene is heavily sensuous as Tod pours perfume from a bottle on the dresser into his hand and pushes his way past Mrs. Desmond's dresses and negligées to "the most hidden part of the closet," where he sits with the perfumed hand over his face. Obviously repressed, the boy speaks, "quite loudly, all the dirtiest words he knew, all the words he had heard his brother James ever use, all the words George Martin [grandson of the gardener] taught the kids secretly and knowingly" (95).

When Tod leaves the Desmonds' house for their garden, Jackson's imagery becomes very sexual. Tod intently examines a blade of grass: "Against the sky it was long and straight, but it moved a little because his hand was shaking.... He twisted it around his finger, and moved it back to its straight stand; he tied it in a loose knot, and it eased back straight again." Dropping the bruised spear, Tod sees it lie "limp and dark" on the lawn as he turns from a phallic symbol to a female one. From a bush, he pulls a yellow blossom that he studies as carefully as he had scrutinized the grass. In a gesture that may lend credibility to Mrs. Merriam's malicious gossip about a probable rape, Tod destroys the flower: "Its petals were precise and neat, so soft he could hardly feel them against his fingers; annoyed at its soft pliability, he crushed it flat with his fingers and rolled the petals cruelly, until the flower was a little damp ball and he dropped it" (96).

A large gathering in the Ransom-Joneses' garden near the end of the book reinforces this early scene of lost innocence. Raymond Miller describes the garden party as the "ritual climax" of *The Road Through the Wall* (48). The less attractive members of the neighborhood, including the Jewish Perlmans and the eccentric Mrs. Mack, are not invited, and the polite group that gives "dutiful homage to the garden" (233) attacks each other in small ways as Caroline, dressed all in yellow—an obvious allusion to the crushed flower—strays off to her death. Mrs. Ransom-Jones's attractive but unbalanced sister, Miss Tyler, wounds Harriet Merriam deeply by telling the girl how lucky she is that she will never be pretty: "Harriet knew that this would keep her heartsick for months, perhaps the rest of her life, and she said thickly, 'I'm losing weight right now'" (238). Married couples wander apart and realign with new partners, sometimes to the irritation of their spouses. Miss Tyler distracts her brother-in-law from his duties as a host by observing that Mrs. Ransom-Jones is "acting up" with some of the guests (239). Since the garden is an untamed wilderness that the two sisters have been tending carefully for the length of the couple's marriage, the insinuation of betrayal achieves mythic resonance. The mood of corruption extends to the young. Tod Donald's sister Virginia, who has "never been officially at an adult party before" (239), flirts with a married man and asks for a drink while her mother "coquettishly" disclaims that she has a daughter.

The final image of the fallen garden is the murder site. Ironically, the overgrown creek bed earlier provides a special place of refuge for most of the Pepper Street children. Pat Byrne and Art Roberts lie in the deep grass, experiencing "a sort of pleasant comfort" that comes mainly from "the feeling of ground and grass under them and trees and sky overhead, with no houses to be seen" (73). Looking up at the steep banks, they feel free to criticize the fathers to whom they customarily act so respectful. The self-conscious Harriet and the Jewish Marilyn are "safe even from their friends" (150) in this setting. They create a secret spot by digging a hole and burying brief accounts of their hopes for the future. When Pat Byrne helps to guide two policemen to the creek in the nighttime hunt for Caroline, he does not giggle contentedly as he did with Art. Now he "walk[s] with long strides, putting his feet down manfully just as the other men did, and he talk[s] using words he would never have dared use before" (257). The daytime sanctuary has become dark, unfamiliar, and profaned. Caroline Desmond is "horribly dirty," and the stone that lies next to her "should have been left alone" (258). Darryl Hattenhauer suggests that, "for Jackson, all subjects are fallen, and evil violates not only the garden but everything in it" (95).

As in West's *The Day of the Locust*, the story of paradise lost in *The Road Through the Wall* attains prophetic urgency. Although Tod Hackett reminds himself that he is not a prophet but an artist, he refuses to abandon "the role of Jeremiah" (335). His masterpiece warns of a repressed violence that will not be contained in California: "The Angelenos would be first, but their comrades all over the country would follow. There would be civil war" (335). Mrs. Mack, whom the Pepper Street children shun as a witch, has her own vision of destruction, which she relates to her dog at three points in the novel (122–23, 169, 213). The dismantling of the neighborhood wall becomes symbolic as Mrs. Mack reads from her book that "the steep places will fall, and every wall shall fall to the ground. And I will call for a sword against him throughout all my mountains, saith the Lord God: every man's sword shall be against his brother" (212). She smiles at the dog, remarking that the passage reminds her of the Old Testament prophet Micah.

Because the narrator of *The Road Through the Wall* sometimes reveals future events, it is indeed surprising that he makes no connection between Mrs. Mack's readings in 1936 and the disasters of World War II. In chapter 1, we learn that nine-year-old Hallie Martin's future husband lives on the wealthy road beyond the wall, and the final page of the book seems to speak from some even more distant time—beyond the 1948 date of composition: "Harriet Merriam kept house for her father after her mother's death; she never married" (271). Among the several other glimpses of the future, the reader looks in vain for any reference to the boys of Pepper Street, some of whom must surely have journeyed westward to war. It is as if, with Tod Donald's suicide, Jackson turns her attention from the deeds of boys and men to the more outwardly placid lives of the women, who are the protagonists of her other five novels.

The uncertain object of the implied allegory in *The Road Through the Wall* may help to explain why the book became the "poor little stepchild" Jackson described in a letter to her parents.[11] With some justice, Michael Nardacci complains about the confusing array of characters and the constant juxtaposition of unrelated events in this obviously experimental work (37–39), possibly influenced by John Dos Passos (Miller 35).[12] What unity the novel possesses inheres chiefly in the related symbolism of the protective wall and the sheltering garden. Early in her career, Jackson abandoned California settings, but the image of a fallen Eden is one to which she returned repeatedly. In the short story "Flower Garden" (c. 1948), a New England village's cruel rejection of a kind newcomer coincides with the destruction of the woman's carefully tended garden by a storm. A college student's sexual innocence is violated at a garden party in *Hangsaman* (1951). The tyrannical Mrs. Halloran presides over a gathering on her lawn the night before the end of the world in *The Sundial* (1958). And in Jackson's final book, *We Have Always Lived in the Castle* (1962), a town's reluctance to put out a fire brings "ugliness and ruin and shame" to the Blackwood sisters' secluded house, and ashes to the vegetable plants. As Mary Katherine explains: "No fire had come this way, but everything, the grass and the apple trees and the marble bench in Constance's garden, had an air of smokiness and everything was dirty" (167).

Jackson's long series of wounded landscapes affirms a theme John G. Parks regards as central to all of her fiction: the possibility of evil. In *The Road Through the Wall*, however, evil is more than a possibility; it is a powerful presence. As Parks observes, the Pepper Street community becomes "so fragile and sick" that everyone is implicated in the deaths of the two children: "no one is innocent" (38). The dying flowers and the crushed grass of this first novel speak unmistakably of the loss of the innocence of Eden.

## Notes

ACKNOWLEDGMENT: Thanks to volume editor Bernice M. Murphy for allowing me to expand this reprinted essay slightly, especially in the bibliography and endnotes. In the decade since the piece originally appeared in *Renascence*, little has been published on *The Road Through the Wall*. Hattenhauer goes far to remedy the neglect in his recent chapter on the novel in *Shirley Jackson's American Gothic* (83–97). His comments will surely turn more attention to the Jackson book that, as Hattenhauer says, "comes closest to expressing her political themes about gender, ethnicity, and class explicitly" (83). Reinsch's annotations of early reviews of *The Road Through the Wall* verify that Jackson's contemporaries were well aware of her social critique (41–43).

1. See also Oppenheimer's discussion of Samuel Bugbee, Jackson's great-great-grandfather, who designed the Grand Opera House and mansions on Nob Hill, and her comments on Jackson's grandfather, Maxwell Greene Bugbee (12).

2. Diary for 1933, Shirley Jackson Papers, Special Collections, Library of Con-

gress, Box 1. Two pressed flowers survive between pages of Jackson's 1932 diary, also in Box 1. I am grateful to the staff of the Manuscript Reading Room at the Library of Congress for providing access to the Jackson collection, hereafter cited as SJP. My research was made possible by a travel grant from the National Endowment for the Humanities.

3. See letters from James D. Hart of the Berkeley English Department, dated 2 May 1955 and 24 October 1955, in SJP, Box 7.

4. The only other obvious California setting I have located in Jackson's fiction is in "My Uncle in the Garden," SJP, Box 17, posthumously published as the final selection in "Part One: Unpublished Stories" in *Just an Ordinary Day*. The female narrator makes annual trips from San Francisco to San Rafael to see Uncle Peter Duff and Uncle Oliver Duff, who are actually not uncles but family friends she has known since childhood. During the visit she describes in detail in this story, Uncle Oliver blames a tomato blight on Uncle Peter's recent meetings with the devil in the garden. Peter subsequently explains that the devil promised to protect the fruit trees if he would offer something else from the garden "for tribute" (190). "My Uncle in the Garden" is a good example of Paul N. Reinsch's discussion of the "haunting" nature of Shirley Jackson's fiction. "Jackson's texts," says Reinsch, "present fantastic narrative events in concrete reality" (6).

5. Crow discusses Jack London's *The Valley of the Moon*, Ernest Callenbach's *Ecotopia*, and Ursula K. LeGuin's *Always Coming Home*. Jean Hegland's post-holocaust California novel, *Into the Forest* (1996), published after these studies by Wyatt and Crow, does not fit comfortably into either of the two traditions; but her protagonists' entry into the dark woods on the final page of the book appears to be a return to Eden.

6. For a brief discussion of "Dorothy and My Grandmother and the Sailors" in the context of *The Lottery* collection, see Joan Wylie Hall, *Shirley Jackson: A Study of the Short Fiction* (32–33).

7. Jackson's other sketches of authors include Milton, Wordsworth, Byron, Walter Scott, Oscar Wilde, Flaubert, George Sand, Cotton Mather, and Theodore Dreiser (SJP, Box 36).

8. Fritz Oehlschlaeger compares "The Lottery" to *The Road Through the Wall* (261–62).

9. Wyatt (161) comments on the penetration of another California greenhouse in Raymond Chandler's *The Big Sleep* (1939). A fan of detective and mystery fiction, Shirley Jackson may have been influenced by Chandler's novel. Darryl Hattenhauer says that, in *The Road Through the Wall*, Jackson "has written a detective story that exposes the detective story; she frustrates the genre that relies most on the expectation of rational explanation" (91).

10. See Jackson's letter to Geraldine and Leslie Jackson, 4 October 1956, SJP, Box 3. She complains that a Pyramid reprint of *The Road Through the Wall* has changed her title [to *The Other Side of the Street*] and "put a vivid series of untruths on the cover." She reports that she enjoys receiving royalty statements "because it is so nice to find that, for instance, *Hangsaman* sold 11 copies in the last 6 months, *Bird's Nest* sold 22, and *Road Through the Wall*, poor little stepchild, sold 5."

11. Lenemaja Friedman discusses the ambiguity of the ending and the symbolism of the wall (82–85).

12. "Flower Garden" was first published in *The Lottery* collection (103–34). See Hall (29–31) on the story's theme of betrayal.

## Works Cited

Crow, Charles L. "Homecoming in the California Visionary Romance." *Western American Literature* 25 (1989): 3–19.

Friedman, Lenemaja. *Shirley Jackson*. Twayne's United States Authors Series. Boston: G. K. Hall, 1975.
Hall, Joan Wylie. *Shirley Jackson: A Study of the Short Fiction*. Twayne's Studies in Short Fiction Series. New York: Twayne, 1993.
Hattenhauer, Darryl. *Shirley Jackson's American Gothic*. Albany: SUNY Press, 2003.
Hyman, Stanley Edgar. *Nathanael West*. University of Minnesota Pamphlets on American Writers. Minneapolis: University of Minnesota Press, 1962.
_____. Preface to *The Magic of Shirley Jackson*, by Shirley Jackson. Ed. Stanley Edgar Hyman. New York: Farrar, Straus & Giroux, 1966. [vii]-ix.
Jackson, Shirley. "Dorothy and My Grandmother and the Sailors." *The Lottery, or The Adventures of James Harris*. New York: Farrar, Straus, 1949, 135–41.
_____. "Flower Garden." *The Lottery, or The Adventures of James Harris*. New York: Farrar, Straus, 1949, 103–34.
_____. "My Uncle in the Garden." *Just an Ordinary Day*. Eds. Laurence Jackson Hyman and Sarah Hyman Stuart. New York: Bantam, 1997, 186–92.
_____. *The Road Through the Wall*. New York: Farrar, Straus, 1948.
_____. The Shirley Jackson Papers. 41 boxes. Special Collections. Library of Congress, Washington, D.C.
_____. *We Have Always Lived in the Castle*. New York: Viking, 1962.
Miller, Raymond R., Jr. "Shirley Jackson's Fiction: An Introduction." Dissertation, University of Delaware, 1974.
Nardacci, Michael L. "Theme, Character, and Technique in the Novels of Shirley Jackson." Dissertation, New York University, 1980.
Oehlschlaeger, Fritz. "The Stoning of Mistress Hutchinson: Meaning and Context in 'The Lottery.'" *Essays in Literature* 15 (1988): 259–65.
Oppenheimer, Judy. *Private Demons: The Life of Shirley Jackson*. New York: Putnam, 1988.
Parks, John G. "The Possibility of Evil: The Fiction of Shirley Jackson." Dissertation, University of New Mexico, 1973.
Reinsch, Paul N. *A Critical Bibliography of Shirley Jackson, American Writer (1919–1965): Reviews, Criticism, Adaptations*. Studies in American Literature. Vol. 45. Lewiston, N.Y.: Mellen, 2001.
Shinn, Thelma J. *Radiant Daughters: Fictional American Women*. Contributions in Women's Studies. New York: Greenwood, 1986.
West, Nathanael. *The Day of the Locust: The Complete Works of Nathanael West*. New York: Farrar, Straus and Cudahy, 1957, 257–421.
Wyatt, David. *The Fall into Eden: Landscape and Imagination in California*. Cambridge Studies in American Literature and Culture. Cambridge: Cambridge University Press, 1986.

# 2

# Comic-Satiric-Fantastic-Gothic: Interactive Modes in Shirley Jackson's Narratives

## JAMES EGAN

Critical reaction to Shirley Jackson's work has divided itself into several familiar, appropriate camps. Recently her fantastic mode has been linked with the weird tradition of H.P. Lovecraft and Ramsey Campbell, and her adaptations of "female gothic" have been contextualized more carefully than they had been earlier (Joshi 13; Rubinstein 311). Ample attention has been paid to Jackson's comedy and satire, where the range of response has been wide, with S.T. Joshi calling Jackson a "horrific satirist" and Carol Cleveland pointing to Jackson's "scathing moral analysis of American society," while Nancy Walker traces her relationship to "women's humor ... [and its] critique of American culture" (Joshi 49; Cleveland 199; Walker 35). This analysis has been locally quite sensitive to Jackson; yet, when one assesses the scholarship as a whole, it is apparent that an unintended but definite compartmentalization of her writing has occurred. In this essay I want to move toward a renewed sense of the sophisticated totality of the Jackson canon, a body of material where the whole often exceeds the sum of its parts, by proposing that her most subtly crafted fictions draw upon interactive narrative modes. As a first step, it will be necessary to characterize the primary structures: the comic, the satiric, the fantastic, and the gothic. To examine interacting narrative structures in Jackson's work is to discover how expertly she manipulates rhetorical and genre conventions to achieve rich thematic permutations and tonal effects ranging from domestically comic scenarios like those of Jean Kerr and Erma Bombeck; to mainstream, conventional satires of manners such as Sinclair Lewis might have written; to the metaphysically fantastic idioms of Nathanael West and Franz Kafka.

# I

The primary sources for the study of Jackson's comic mode are the family chronicles, *Life Among the Savages* (1953) and *Raising Demons* (1957), where comic parameters and their attendant devices are fully established. In the domestic tales, Jackson simultaneously develops and undercuts, or at least qualifies, a normative environment. Several core strategies and circumstances can be identified, one of which appears in the following passage from *Life Among the Savages*:

> Ninki's [one of the family cats] supper, a full-grown and horribly active bat, was sweeping magnificently down the length of the living room. For a minute I watched it with my mouth open and then, still yelling, buried my head under the blanket....
> "Is it on the *blanket*?" I insisted hysterically, "On *Me*?" I do not know what the official world's record might be for getting out from under a blanket, flying across the room, opening a door and a screen door, and getting outside onto a porch with both doors closed behind you, but if it is more than about four seconds I broke it [406].

Frenetic physical movement, exaggerated into a type of slapstick, defines this scene. Jackson achieves comedy by playing off of rapid movement and confusion, all of which has been juxtaposed, for burlesque or lowering effect, with the bat's "sweeping magnificently down the length of the living room." In her domestic writings, farcical slapstick and nearly-falling-down movement seem omnipresent, so much so that the normative environment itself appears haphazard, topsy-turvy, on the verge of collision. The cumulative effect of repetition and magnification of such domestic detail qualifies as comic—a narrative environment has been undercut but not presented as malignant or aggressive. Because *Life Among the Savages* and *Raising Demons* have as their main characters the narrator's young and adolescent children, she need only reproduce some of the familiar activities of children to create another tonality of comedy. The "Baby-Ate-a-Spider Episode" would be a typical instance:

> Sally peered at me curiously through the bars of her crib and grinned, showing her four teeth. "What did you eat?" I demanded. "What do you have in your mouth?" Laurie shouted triumphantly. "A spider," he said. "She ate a spider." I forced the baby's mouth open; it was empty. "Did she *swallow* it?" "Why?" Jannie asked, wide-eyed. "Will it make her sick?" "*Jannie* gave it to her," Laurie said. "*Laurie* found it," Jannie said. "But she ate it herself," Laurie said hastily [*LS* 436].

We notice discrepancy: an anxious mother and curious, inventive children, whose innocence melts into mischief as they quickly transfer blame to one another with a rapid succession of one-liners. The scene appears chaotic, with no two characters in complete agreement, a sort of verbal collision, yet one without apparent damage to the baby, her siblings, or the beleaguered mother. Nonsense conversations, many of them at the dinner table, are frequent in both domestic collections, and they parallel the cross-purposed dialogue of the spider tale.

Miscellaneous tactics supplement the compounded clutter, confusion, and mistaken identity that are the mainstays of Jackson's comic mode. Lists and inventories are part of the narrator's housekeeping ritual, a ritual well represented by her habit of "picking things up":

> Every time I picked up something I put it down again somewhere else where it belonged better than it did in the place I found it. Nine times out of ten I did not notice what I was picking up or where I put it until sometime later when someone in the family needed it; then, when Sally said where were her crayons I could answer at once: kitchen windowsill, left [*RD* 726].

The order presumably involved in this process of categorizing and redistributing proves inseparable from the disorder it intends to control, yet the process works, perhaps very well; an improbability that sets the comic tenor of the episode.

The last example brings to the foreground the most important comic tactic of Jackson's domestic works, the device that unifies and coordinates the others: the role of the narrator. Anne Lecroy has called attention to the "pervasive conversational tone" of *Life Among the Savages* and *Raising Demons* (66). Jackson achieves that conversational tone primarily through the use of the first-person narrator, who characterizes herself as fallible and ordinary, to say the least:

> I am not of a mechanical turn of mind. I am wholeheartedly afraid of fuses and motorcycles and floor plugs and lightning rods and electric drills and large animals and most particularly of furnaces. Laboriously, over the space of years of married life, my husband has taught me to use such hazardous appliances as a toaster and an electric coffee pot, but no one is ever going to get me to go down cellar and fool around with a furnace [*LS* 475].

As in this passage, the narrator invariably seems self-effacing, even inept (having taken a long time to learn how to use a toaster), and prone to burlesque her own weaknesses by exaggerating them. She resolutely forgives the errors and shortcomings of her family because they are part and parcel of her own. Generally, the narrator conveys what Morton Gurewitch describes as the "comic rhythm," the affirmation of life (15).

In contemporary theory, comedy involves "rebirth or transcendent reconciliation or ... social harmony," of which Jackson's domestics provide frequent illustrations (Gurewitch 17). Consider the freshly repaired house the family will rent for several years in Vermont, after nervously moving from New York:

> [The house] had been literally scraped clean, down to the wood in the walls. Mr. Fielding had put on new wallpaper, rich with great gorgeous patterns, the windows had been washed, the pillars straightened, the broken step repaired, and a cheerful man in the kitchen was putting the last touches of glittering white paint to the new shelving [*LS* 394].

The house becomes a metaphor of security, warmth, welcome and nurturing, the dominant themes of *Life Among the Savages* and *Raising Demons*. The repair presents a legitimate cause for celebration, a happy ending. In the comedies, the normative world is reassuringly predictable, the family a closed, protective circle. Fallibility in this environment has been widely distributed enough to be normalized, while clutter, confusion, mishaps of communication, or periodic bouts of discomfort are the greatest threats to family harmony.

## II

Jackson's satires are very much the opposite of her domestic tales, a relentless, unnerving display of disharmony. Some of the rhetorical strategies and devices of the comic mode reappear in the satires. Like the comedies, the satires diminish the normative, yet in a profoundly harsher fashion, along different thematic lines. The definition of satire in this essay draws upon several components, both formalist and neoformalist. The most essential quality would be the "systematic exploitation, with aggressive intent, of what are, or are made to seem, deviations within the norm within a context" (Nichols 27). The norms implicit in satiric assessment may be treated as vantage points from which to evaluate the satiric portrayal; they are derived from the "general attitudes which most readers [presumably] share" (Nichols 26). Satire, of course, can be direct or insinuated. Several reductive strategies, primarily invective, caricature, burlesque, and irony, have long been associated with the medium. Formalist criticism of the 1960s isolated the primary characteristics of satiric fictions (one of which will be discussed in some detail) "through which the satirist conveys his subject matter: the corruption of an ideal and the behavior of fools, knaves, dupes, and the like" (Paulson 9). Dustin Griffin's recent evaluation of satire as a rhetoric of "inquiry and provocation" that teases "readers with the play of 'contraries,'" rather than as a medium that presupposes "a world of clear standards and boundaries," would allow for the flexibility generally absent from formalist criteria (4, 60, 35). Jackson's satires are the epicenter of the darkest, most misogynistic themes readers have found in her canon. Surely "human cruelty and the precariousness of life" are significant satiric concerns, along with the "pointless violence and general inhumanity in [human] lives" (Sullivan 1031; Friedman 64).

Jackson's satiric temperament manifests itself early and seems especially active during the 1940s. Her centerpiece is *The Road Through the Wall* (1948), a display of the full range of rhetorical devices and fictions of diminution at Jackson's command. The novel studies the manners and mores of selected residents, young and old, of Pepper Street, a small community in Cabrillo, California, in 1936. From the outset, the reader can easily discern that the narrator aims to expose the malaise and menace that infect many of the street's inhabitants at the same time that she details their everyday routines, concentrating on a core group of families and individuals (the Donalds, the Perlmans, the Byrnes, the Merriams, Mrs. Mack, Miss Fielding, and several others) and their occasional social gatherings, the play habits of their children, their parenting styles, and their attitudes toward gender roles, social status, marriage, and jobs. *The Road Through the Wall* reads as a twentieth century *novel* of manners, wherein Jackson determines Pepper Street's identity through the sum total of its occupants' behaviors, behaviors that are moral and ethical measuring devices for their incidental successes and their far more frequent failures, which are exposed by the narrator's satiric strategies.

Many of her most effective means of diminution are rhetorical forms of denunciation, whether direct, literal attacks by the narrator or subtle combinations of omission, association, or understatement meant to expose a deficiency. Describing the Donald home, the narrator observes that it was "made of bricks put together in a square, ample enough for Mr. and Mrs. Donald and their three children, and pretentious enough for Mr. Donald's wife and daughter to feel at home" (8). Again describing Mrs. Donald, the narrator notes "her whole naïve childishness [which was] a deliberate denial of the years of experience she had had and Virginia [her daughter] was still entitled to" (142). Such characterizations as "pretentious" and "childishness" leave no doubt of the narrator's disdain for what she describes. Jackson's invective often turns on a careful arrangement of language that suggests as much as it denotes, for example, her hostile description of Mrs. Merriam: "She sat in the long light living room with the basket of sewing on the floor beside her, unaware that with her tall thin body silhouetted against the big window, and her narrow severe head bent slightly to the sewing, she looked bleak and menacing" (14). Here, terms such as "bleak and menacing," and especially the combinations of three ("tall thin body," "narrow severe head") not only diminish Mrs. Merriam literally and directly, but implicitly compare her to an unpleasantly angular bird (14). In these instances, Jackson's plain, precise style intensifies her attack, often epitomizing characters in a word or phrase, and sometimes diminishing them in several ways simultaneously. Particularly at the verbal level of satire, the third-person narrator becomes a powerful means of conveying the narrative's doubt, skepticism, or lack of sympathy for the normative world of Pepper Street. Invariably the narrator appears distant, cool, detached and censorious, emphatically distant from what she narrates, not complicit in or forgiving of the events under scrutiny.

A second level of attack, more fictively intricate than invective and overt denunciation, employs a range of devices long associated with the mode of satire. Some of these (for example, burlesque and blaming while ostensibly praising) are used in isolation, while others are extended into scenes of disclosure. *The Road Through the Wall* contains Jackson's best specimens of caricature, the satiric device of accentuating through repetition or exaggeration of a specific flaw, as in this description of Mrs. Desmond:

> She was ungenerous because her family had been poor before she married Mr. Desmond, she was unsympathetic because no one had ever required any sensitivity of her, she was gracious because her mother before her had been gracious and because her daughter Caroline must in her turn learn to be womanly and ladylike. Mrs. Desmond was neither intelligent nor unintelligent, because thinking and all its allied attributes were completely outside her schedule for life; her values did not include mind, and nothing she intended ever required more than money [84].

Mrs. Desmond has been shrunken satirically into a one-dimensional, unreflective automaton, a creature of habit, without the humanizing qualities of sympathy and generosity, without the need for "mind" and the bothersome complications that thinking would involve (Test 265; Dentith 2–38). Jackson's characterization of Miss Fielding provides a fuller version of the way she sketches Mrs. Desmond. Miss Fielding, the narrator reports,

> For more years than she could remember ... had been following herself along a well-defined path, around the circle of hours that make a day.... Sometimes it seemed, even, that Miss Fielding's long convalescence from birth would culminate in sufficient strength for her to die without effort.... [After she died], the Pepper Street house would snap back to its original purpose as a dwelling for the living [134–35].

Miss Fielding's hollow, comatose life is a caricature of the life of a normal, emotionally and socially interactive human being. The metaphor of convalescence implies that all of Miss Fielding's energy has been incorporated into her systematic withdrawal from life, into recovering from the illness of being born, until she has managed to exist without actually living.

Satiric irony qualifies as Jackson's sharpest weapon for laying bare the menace and malice of Pepper Street, and satiric irony in turn permeates the most effective trope in the novel, a trope described by Alvin Kernan as the "mob tendency." Examining the mob scene at the conclusion of Nathanael West's *The Day of the Locust* (1939), Kernan theorizes that mobs in satire characteristically pursue and destroy victims, often in search of "compensation" or "fun" (71–73). Kernan's definition of this pervasive satiric fiction localizes Ronald Paulson's claim that satire resonates with violence of all sorts, violence which represents an outburst of energy, the "chaos of uncontrol" (17–20). Jackson shapes her own version of this fiction into a powerful indictment of the hypocrisy, sadism, and "general inhumanity" (Friedman 64) of Pepper Street's inhabitants, young and old.

The first usage occurs early in the story, when a group of Marilyn Perlman's "friends" surrounds her:

> Helen laughed, "Maybe you have two Christmases," she said. She turned around to the other girls, to Harriet, and said, "Marilyn has *two* Christmases. One of her own and one she gets in on with us."
> "I don't get it," one of the girls said, and the one edging toward the door said, "Come *on*."
> "Marilyn knows what I mean," Helen said.
> It was the feeling of having them all around her that bothered Marilyn ... [23].

Marilyn, a Jew, has been beset by a mob of "friends" intent on harassing her about the fact that Jews have a Christmas tradition separate from that of Christians. The mob does not intend physical violence, but psychological: they want to humiliate, to let Marilyn know that, as a minority, she merely "gets in on" the Christian holiday. Perhaps, in Kernan's view, this mob of girls seeks merely "fun" or "compensation," but the fact that their predatory, encircling pleasure will come at Marilyn's expense denigrates them even as they try to denigrate her. Marilyn's unfortunate partner in victimization by mobs is Tod Donald, singled out for special attention by his family at the dinner table, and by other children in the neighborhood:

> Tod was on his own front lawn. "I ate a whole mince pie once," he said, giggling. According to neighborhood ethics, there was only one person who could lead the attack on Tod on his own land. His sister turned slowly to look at him and then back to the other children. "He never does anything really," she said.
> "You never did it," Helen said. "Your sister says so."
> "I did so," Tod began weakly, but Mary Byrne said, "I don't believe you could eat even one piece of mince pie."

"Even a piece as big as an ant," Hallie Martin said. Having nine-year-old Hallie join in against him was the lowest indignity [42–43].

Like Marilyn, Tod has been encircled, again verbally, by a mob intent on ridiculing and humiliating him, feeding off of his innocent insecurity. When these acts of childish mockery mark Tod as a victim, they simultaneously discredit his cruel tormentors. Even after he commits suicide, Tod continues to be harassed by a mob, this time metaphorically. The Pepper Street neighborhood as a whole becomes the largest group of all arrayed against him, as gossip and rumor abound, all of it assuming Tod's guilt. "[Tod] was always strange" becomes the community-mob's epitaph for him, as it slowly devours Tod's reputation.

While the narrative structures of *Life Among the Savages* and *Raising Demons* are essentially comic and those of *The Road Through the Wall* essentially satiric, Jackson achieves narrative intricacy and thematic complication by mixing these modes. In *Life Among the Savages*, the narrator's underscoring of the flaws in Mrs. Skinner, Jannie's know-it-all teacher (498–502) would qualify as satire, along with the presentation of the anti-intellectual Mrs. Ferrier in *Raising Demons* (543). In both episodes, the narrator maintains a judgmental distance between herself, her family and the outsiders, two women guilty of intellectual pretension and overreaching, flaws which the narrator does not participate in or condone. *The Road Through the Wall*, moreover, contains several comic characters and events, especially those involving the elderly Mrs. Mack and her discussions with her dog (98–101) and the eccentric friendship of Miss Fielding and Mr. Donald, whose "conversations" are revealed as the antidialogues of two individuals "given to talking to themselves" (165). Neither Mrs. Mack and her dog nor Miss Fielding and Mr. Donald appear to have any topics in common, and Miss Fielding and Mr. Donald are both immune to the oversights and indifference of each other, so that their attempted interaction registers as foolish and ultimately harmless when measured against the prejudicial, predatory interactions that are the norm in *The Road Through the Wall*. By mixing comedy and satire, Jackson achieves a more nuanced story line, which allows for fine distinctions between comic and satiric behavior. The typically subtle movement of the narrative from comedy to satire and back again often occurs, as S.T. Joshi has claimed, with a minimum of verbal alteration (20), thereby demonstrating Jackson's mastery of narrative craft, her precise control of character, action, setting, and descriptive detail.

## III

An equally significant narrative interaction, quite apart from these satiric-comic overlaps, occurs when Jackson links the satiric mode we have just considered to the fantastic mode in several of its manifestations. Though fantasy has been subject to many codifications over the past quarter-century, the major definitions currently in play all involve what Kathyrn Hume and Eric Rabkin have called a departure from the conventional, "armchair world" of the "normative" (Hume 8–25; Rabkin 13, 16), whether that departure involves a violation of the "reader's conceptions of natural laws" (Heller 43) or a "direct reversal of ground rules" (Rabkin 14). Virtually all postmodern criticism of fantasy incorporates Tzvetan Todorov's notion of the fantastic as "that hesitation experienced by a person who knows only the laws of nature, confronting an apparently supernatural event" (25), as well as his classification of fantastic themes: "a special causality, pan-determinism; multiplication of the personality; collapse of the limit between subject and object; and lastly, the transformation of time and space" (120). The narrative bridging of the satiric and the fantastic that will form the basis of the following discussion of Jackson's fiction has been made very generally in contemporary scholarship, and more specifically by Eric Rabkin, who proposes that satire is "inherently fantastic," locating several points of intersection between the two modes (18–22).

In "The Renegade" (1948) the fantastic serves as a device for clarifying and gradually intensifying the satiric subtext. The narrative predicament of "The Renegade" is that Mrs. Walpole's presumably gentle dog, Lady, has been accused of killing the neighbors' chickens. That the narrator wishes to challenge the values of the normative can be inferred from the first report Mrs. Walpole gets of Lady's alleged crimes, an "early morning call":

> "Do you have a dog? Brown-and-black hound?"
> ..."Yes...." Mrs. Walpole said shortly, "I own a dog. Why?"
> "He's been killing my chickens." The voice sounded satisfied now; Mrs. Walpole had been cornered [71].

The ambivalence embedded in this question, of whether Mrs. Walpole qualifies as "irritable" and "short," perhaps unduly defensive (she answers the phone "forbiddingly"), or whether the neighbor qualifies as cruelly "satisfied," appears to be resolved by the story's fantastic complications. As soon as the warning about a chicken-killing dog on the loose has been sounded, the rural community considers Lady the culprit, not allowing for the possibility of mistaken identity. Fantastic elaborations occur when the narrator recounts the growing enthusiasm for punishing the offender and the sadistic ingenuity beneath that enthusiasm. At first, simple, fathomable remedies are proposed, such as tying Lady with a "good stout chain," but more exotic suggestions soon prevail, displacing the realistic with the incredible. Mr. White's remedy constitutes an example:

"You get a dead chicken and tie it around the dog's neck, so he can't shake it loose, see?"

..."See, when he can't shake it loose at first he tries to play with it and then it starts to bother him, see, and then he tries to roll it off and it won't come and then he tries to bite it off and it won't come and then when he sees it won't come he thinks he's never gonna get rid of it, see, and then he gets scared...."

"But the dog," Mrs. Walpole said ... "How long do we have to leave it around her neck?"

"Well," Mr. White said with enthusiasm, "I guess you leave it on until it gets ripe enough to fall off by itself. See, the head..." [77].

Mr. Shepherd, finally, advises that thick nails be pounded into Lady's collar and that she be turned loose "where there are chickens" (83). Then, when Lady has been made to chase the chickens, the owner pulls on the rope, and "The spikes cut her head off" (83). That this suggestion has been relayed from Mr. Shepherd to Mrs. Walpole by her own children magnifies its macabre effects. One could object that each of these homespun solutions might be possible and would not, therefore, be fantastic according to Todorov's definition, yet their crescendo arrangement from practical and mundane to bizarre and lethal suggests that Jackson deliberately transgresses the plausible and the mimetic in order to intensify the satiric effort of "The Renegade," to disclose the perverse, blighted imaginations of Mrs. Walpole's neighbors. The gruesome torments seem to delight those who propose them, as though punishing the chicken-killing suspect were a means to another, darker, end.

"Pillar of Salt" (1948) incorporates the fantastic in a manner more compatible with postmodern understanding of the concept yet for narrative purposes similar to those of "The Renegade." New York City, the vacation environment of Brad and Margaret, a New Hampshire couple, is aggressively undercut, satirized in several ways, by descriptive details, images, and events. As she shops, Margaret begins to "picture" New Yorkers:

She had a picture of small children in the city dressed like their parents, following along with a miniature mechanical civilization, toy cash registers in larger and larger sizes that eased them into the real thing, millions of clattering jerking small imitations that prepared them nicely for taking over the large useless toys their parents lived by [242].

The images of children and their noisy toys, a deployment of the widespread satiric trope of the robotic, conflate the mechanical and the spiritual, in the process reducing parents to bad imitations of their children, but without the excuse of childhood to justify their "useless toys." If the exterior of the city is unlovely, the attitudes of its inhabitants are coarse and insensitive, as Margaret discovers when mentioning to

one of her hosts that a leg had washed up on the beach near the host's
home:

> [Margaret and Brad] went back to their host and hostess, talking about
> the leg, and their host apologized, as though he had been guilty of a
> breach of taste in allowing his guests to come [upon] a human leg; their
> hostess said with interest, "There was an arm washed up in Benson-
> hurst..." [247].

Sympathy for the owners of the arm and leg seems absent from the reaction of the host and hostess, but the hostess does manage to develop
"interest" in the "arm [that] washed up in Bensonhurst."

The fantastic enters "Pillar of Salt" in a series of impressions that
internalize for Margaret the decay of New York, and allow her to apprehend the city psychologically. She reaches beyond space and time to
"feel" the entropic dissolution of New York, noticing some unusual developments: "She stopped suddenly when it seemed to her that the win-
dowsill she had just passed had soundlessly crumbled and fallen into fine
sand" (249). Another unnerving experience becomes the counterpoint
to Margaret's perceptions of quiet, material decay:

> A crowd of people formed around her suddenly; they had come off a
> bus and were crossing here, and she had a sudden feeling of being jammed
> in the center and forced out into the street when all of them moved as one
> with the light changing, and she elbowed her way desperately out of the
> crowd and went off to lean against a building and wait [251].

This image of the feverish, chaotic energy of the crowd recalls the satiric
trope of the mob, which seems to encircle and crush its victims. Margaret imagines that she has been "jammed ... and forced" by design, captured and hurried off against her will by something as conspicuous and
animated as the forces of entropy she had perceived in the crumbling
sandstone were inconspicuous and inanimate. "Pillar of Salt" enacts very
effectively the moment of hesitation Todorov equates with the fantastic.
On the one hand, Margaret senses that time and motion have become
frenzied. "It went too fast," she says of an elevator (250), and "they all
go by too fast," of a crowd (251). On the other, she witnesses evidence
of the entropic dissolution of everyday objects, evidence normally very
slow to unfold. All of the above might be explained as panic attacks,
threatening but psychologically plausible, culminating in the paranoia of
the story's final paragraph. But another possibility remains; that Margaret has been able to internalize and apprehend emotionally the dete-
rioration, plasticity, and callousness that constitute the mimetic exterior
of New York, described satirically by the narrator. Her fantastic perception metamorphoses the aggressive crowds of New York into the satiric
trope of the chaotic, engulfing, predatory mob. In effect, the fantastic

elements of "Pillar of Salt" reinforce the satiric-mimetic elements, intensifying and personalizing the entropic meltdown of the city.

One of Jackson's most concise, adept narrative mixtures of the satiric and the fantastic, "The Witch" (1949), again uses this mixture to undercut the normative, but in a more subtle, understated fashion than "Pillar of Salt" did. While a mother and her young son journey on a train, the evidently bored child searches for entertainment even as his mother placates and pacifies him. When the boy complains, "How far do we have to go?" his mother answers with a familiar parental refrain, "Not much longer now" (63). When the boy exclaims that he has seen "a big old ugly old bad old witch outside," his mother answers dismissively, "Fine" (64). As the conversation between the child and the man who enters the compartment shifts to the murder and dismemberment of the man's sister, the mother intervenes, demanding that the stranger leave. After the man exits, she tries to assert the normative: "He was just teasing," the mother said, "Just *teasing*" (67). The narrative implies, however, that a darkly fantastic rendering of these events is available, a hint reinforced by the ending: "Prob'ly he was a witch," recalls the boy. As a possible record of a fantastic intervention, "The Witch" contains several chilling alternatives: that the stranger's account of the murder and dismemberment of his sister was not an *ad absurdum* exercise in teasing a child and mocking his imaginative excesses, but a literal event; that the laughter the stranger shares with the child has one connotation for the boy and a far more ominous one for him. The normative point of view, represented by the mother, cannot allow for the option of the horrific, the terrifyingly fantastic invading the everyday world, an option that her placating rhetoric quickly dismisses. The story's implication that the boy's version of what happened (the stranger really was a witch) might have validity undercuts the narrow, conventional, normative sort of adult thinking that disallows the possibility of witches. The fantastic reading of the story's actions reinforces the child's version of them. Rather than merging to reinforce a perspective as they do in "Pillar of Salt," fantastic and mimetic narratives in "The Witch" remain disjunctive, yet with the same overall effect of satiric disclosure.

## IV

The final illustrations of interactive narrative structures to be considered are taken from the portion of Jackson's fiction most commonly characterized as gothic, "The Bus" (1965) and *The Haunting of Hill House* (1959). Each develops unique narrative variations resulting from fundamental revisions in the normative world. Because "The Bus" and *Hill House* are set in gothic environments, the works contain qualities best

described as parodic, both metaphysically and narratively. William Day
has shown that "Gothic fantasy is ... an anticonventional vision of reality ... a parody of other narratives and conceptions of the world" (4). In
brief, the gothic world may be interpreted as a naturally monstrous universe, one that subverts the "cosmological visions" lying behind both
romance and realism (Day 8). Since Jackson's deployment of these conventions in "The Bus" and *Hill House* and her articulation of an intri-
cately parodic normative environment build on metamorphosis and
regression, the comic and satiric narrative patterns we have been examining undergo substantial modifications, into extraordinary combinations. In particular, the gothic normative sharpens Jackson's irony and
intensifies her vision of a flattened, empty world.

She develops "The Bus" around the gothic trope of a circular voyage, a journey with no ending and no exit, which maroons characters "in
an eternal present, without connections in any direction in time or space"
(Heller 169; Malin 126; Botting 14). As the story opens, the elderly Miss
Harper returns home on a bus from an unspecified location on a dark,
drenching night. Given the range of gothic features apparent throughout the tale, darkness here has a quality both literal and metaphorical.
What the narrator presents as the normative setting in "The Bus" seems
diminished in several ways, by strategies recalling those Jackson used to
describe the blighted urban settings in "Pillar of Salt." When Miss Harper
buys her ticket, "the old man at the other end of the counter [puts] down
his paper and [gives] her a look of hatred" (180). Nor does she fare especially well on the bus itself:

> "Look lady," [the bus driver] was saying, "I'm not an alarm clock."
> "Wake up and get off the bus."
> ..."This is as far as you go. You got a ticket to here. You've arrived" [182].

After Miss Harper exits into a thunderstorm at Ricket's Landing, she
begs a ride with two young, unsympathetic men annoyed by her dishev-
elled condition: "Get in," the young man says, and, "My God, you're
wet" (184). Not only are her escorts vaguely threatening, which she learns
when she threatens to report the bus driver for letting her off at the wrong
stop, they are also dull:

> "I've never heard of Ricket's Landing," Miss Harper said. "I can't imag-
> ine how he came to put me off there."
> "Maybe someone else was supposed to get off there and he thought it
> was you by mistake." This deduction seemed to tax the young man's mind
> to the utmost, because he said, "See, someone else might of been sup-
> posed to get off instead of you" [185].

She eventually arrives at an old house that has been converted into a
bar and grill, populated by "perhaps a dozen young people, resembling

the two who had brought Miss Harper here, all looking oddly alike" (187).

Though the looming menace of Miss Harper's plight cannot be overlooked, her own flaws do not escape the narrator's eye either. When Miss Harper orders her bus ticket, she does so "sharply" (180), and nothing she does early on dispels the initial impression of her as peevish, complaining, a fault-finder very easily agitated. No matter her temperament, Miss Harper soon discovers that she has entered the dark world of the fantastic, a discovery that coincides with her growing belief that the ramshackle bar and grill is actually her childhood home, now badly deteriorated, a home complete with a closet full of her old toys:

> The inside of the closet was all alive; a small doll ran madly from side to side, the animals paraded solemnly down the gangplank of Noah's ark.... The noise was louder and louder, and then Miss Harper realized that they were all looking at her hatefully and moving toward her [191].

When the sentient toys move closer, Miss Harper screams, then suddenly wakes. She has apparently fallen asleep on the bus and has had a nightmare. After she wakes, she is dropped off at an ominously familiar location: "Ricket's Landing" (192).

The dark allegory embedded in the ostensibly real events of "The Bus" contains an explanation of the satiric diminishment of all the main characters, an explanation substantially different from the patterns of reduction at work in Jackson's non-gothic tales. As Joan Wylie Hall has noticed, the bus driver recalls the ferryman to the underworld in classical mythology (67). Following Hall's cue, one might easily conclude that the two men in the truck assume the role of Miss Harper's courtiers/guards, who take her to her destination/prison, a gothic building/nightmare world. The catch-phrase greeting of the "hostess"/warden Belle now assumes telling connotations: "'Hell, you say,' the woman said at last. Her voice was surprisingly soft. 'Hell you say'" (187). Assuming that Jackson expected to describe Miss Harper's journey in "The Bus" as a descent into the nether world with its personalized horrors and circular wanderings, a world whose inhabitants are themselves darkened, the satiric diminution noted earlier takes on a narrative appropriateness, and the fantastic scenarios of the story an ironic function: to clarify rather than to obscure the setting. In the netherworld, these bizarre events might seem realistic and normative indeed. The metaphysical terror of "The Bus" lingers no matter how the reader construes Miss Harper's weaknesses. If she is judged worthy of her destination, then she has denied her past crimes and hidden them from her immediate perception; but she will meet these crimes again in hell, as the scene with the advancing, vigilante-like toys suggests. If, alternatively, we consider her not to be truly damnable, a Kafka-like predicament, an unknowable disconnection between crime and punishment, confronts us.

Comic and satiric narrative strands also occur in Jackson's gothic masterpiece, *The Haunting of Hill House*, with their specific connotations again charged by the novel's parodic normative setting. The opening paragraph clarifies the environment within which the various functions of satire and comedy must be evaluated: "Hill House, not sane, stood by itself against its hills, holding darkness within.... Silence lay steadily against the wood and stone of Hill House, and whatever walked there, walked alone" (3). Within this metaphysically distorted place, two major species of comic and satiric expression can be located, the first of which is caricature, familiar from its appearance in *Road Through the Wall* in Jackson's treatments of Mrs. Desmond and Miss Fielding. Caricature appears in two complementary forms, first the obsessive Mrs. Dudley, whose robotic, mechanical repetitiveness sounds like a dull refrain throughout the novel, in such ritualistic forms as "In the night.... In the dark" (45), or "I set dinner on the sideboard at six o'clock" (48). If Mrs. Dudley is laconic, her opposite number, Mrs. Montague, plays the compulsive babbler, rude, intrusive, intent on dominating any conversation she enters. Jackson carefully sets Mrs. Montague's boasts that she can freely access the spirit world against her obliviousness of the aggressive supernatural phenomena that terrify the other guests. Clearly, folly, pretentiousness, and other defects are disclosed in the behavior of these two characters, defects which could be, arguably, either satiric or comic. I would argue that the caricatures are comic when measured against the ominous, mocking universe of Hill House, whose darkness turns ridiculous actions that might seem satiric in a realistic, nongothic setting into comic, silly, relief-giving distractions from the overbearing intensity of the menace about to engulf Eleanor. Such caricatures should be read as farce, a movement away from menace and toward harmless folly.

Another species of undercutting in Hill House, different in technique and intention, likewise attempts to confront the darkness by speaking a parodic version of its own language (Test 121–25; Nichols 53). This dialogue with Hill House itself can be attributed primarily to Theodora, with occasional choric accomplishment from Luke. Theodora replies to Eleanor's fear that "[Mrs. Dudley] probably watches every move we make, anyway; it's probably part of what she agreed to" (48) with an impertinent question:

> "Agreed to with whom, I wonder? Count Dracula."
> ..."I think he spends all his week ends here; I swear I saw bats in the woodwork downstairs" [48].

After one of the manifestations of preternatural cold in the house, Eleanor jokes that she had considered writing to her sister to explain what a "perfectly *splendid*" time she was having. Theodora proposes some amendments: "You really must plan to bring the whole family next summer...." "We sleep under blankets every night...." "The air is so bracing, particularly in the upstairs hall..." (152). What Theodora does in these passages and frequently throughout *Hill House* functions as a strategy of satiric attack, replete with such conventional mechanisms as irony, burlesque, and sarcasm. Yet it is a strategy apart from what Jackson typically employs, and adapted to the gothic normative space. Theodora attempts to fend off Hill House somewhat paradoxically, by seeming to accept its operating premises (those of the gothic universe, themselves reversed), and then reversing them, diminishing Hill House's own nature and identity by *ad absurdum* overapplication and misapplication. She does so in an attempt to achieve distance and control in what amount to systematic gestures of contempt and defiance, "teasing" the house with its own devices by speaking its "language." However, when she echoes the gothic language of Hill House in a parodic, deflating way, Theodora achieves another satiric effect, that of a curse, a form of invective associated with satire's possible origins as a component of primitive tribal ritual (Elliott 286–92). On one level, then, her attack burlesques and exaggerates gothic storytelling conventions and ground rules, and on another, she denounces and aims invective at Hill House, cursing it in an idiom the house will surely recognize.

## V

As we have seen, the predominant narrative structures in Shirley Jackson's work are the comic, satiric, fantastic, and gothic, while her most intricate stories typically derive from combinations of these modes. S.T. Joshi has argued for the unity of the Jackson canon, a unity so well orchestrated that "distinctions about genre and classification become arbitrary and meaningless" (13). In contrast, this essay argues that a modal analysis allows for, at the least, a more detailed awareness of her narrative tendencies and habits and the variations she plays upon recurring structures, as well as a specific familiarity with her craft and control as a maker of fiction. It seems apparent that Jackson's four favored narrative patterns draw upon distinct yet overlapping rhetorical devices and tactics. *Life Among the Savages* and *Raising Demons* have been identified as the most fully developed comic statements, with several distinguishing features: a flawed but redemptive normative setting consisting of the magnification of the daily activities of family life; the snowballing effect of minor problems; frantic, slapstick physical movement, often resulting in collisions, literal and figurative; identity-confusions, jumbled language, and miscellaneous mix-ups; a first-person narrator eager to confess and exemplify her own fallibility. If *Life Among the Savages* and *Raising Demons* amount to domestic comedies of manners for Shirley Jackson, *The Road Through the Wall* reads as a satire of manners. Like her comedies, Jackson's social satire presupposes a flawed setting, but her satiric tactics (principally invective, irony, caricature, and the fiction of the mob) expose an environment blighted by selfishness, hypocrisy, aggressive viciousness, and insidious betrayal. A distant third-person narrator reveals these defects both directly and by insinuation, making no apologies for the failures uncovered, and in fact portraying them as menacing, ugly, and corrosive. While the mood and tenor of Jackson's comedies connote reconciliation, closure, and bonding, the mood and tenor of her satires connote agony, alienation, and anti-closure.

For the most part, her fantastic tales may be explained by the criteria of Todorov and other postmodern theorists: conditions of hesitation between natural and supernatural causality, reversals of ground rules, transformations of time and space. Jackson's gothic narratives represent the extension of these same axioms and procedures into a setting where darkness is normative. Her comic, satiric, fantastic, and gothic structures are sufficiently distinct to qualify as separate and independent. However, this essay has proposed that if critical assessment were to rest simply at the point of definition, Joshi's objections to "arbitrary and meaningless" placement into categories might be valid: the nomenclature could become self-absorbed and limiting. Narrative categorization should, instead, serve as a precondition for appreciating some of Shirley Jackson's most sophisticated, subtly crafted fictions, those in which comic, satiric, fantastic and gothic elements are made to interact, to define, qualify, complicate, intensify, and resolve one another; to engineer reversals and double-reversals and posit complex ironies; and ultimately to shape a unique, authentic signature.

## Works Cited

Botting, Fred. *Gothic*. London and New York: Routledge, 1996.

Cleveland, Carol. "Shirley Jackson." In *And Then There Were Nine ... More Women of Mystery*. Ed. Jane S. Bakerman. Bowling Green, Ohio: Popular Press, 1985, 199–219.

Day, William Patrick. *In the Circles of Fear and Desire: A Study of Gothic Fantasy*. Chicago and London: University of Chicago Press, 1985.

Dentith, Simon. *Parody*. London and New York: Routledge, 2000.

Elliott, Robert C. *The Power of Satire: Magic, Ritual, Art*. Princeton: Princeton University Press, 1960.

Friedman, Lenemaja. *Shirley Jackson*. Boston: Twayne, 1975.

Griffin, Dustin. *Satire: A Critical Reintroduction*. Lexington: University Press of Kentucky, 1994.

Gurewitch, Morton. *Comedy: The Irrational Vision*. Ithaca and London: Cornell University Press, 1975.

Hall, Joan Wylie. *Shirley Jackson: A Study of the Short Fiction*. New York: Twayne, 1993.

Heller, Terry. *The Delights of Terror: An Aesthetics of the Tale of Terror*. Urbana and Chicago: University of Illinois Press, 1987.

Hume, Kathyrn. *Fantasy and Mimesis*. New York and London: Methuen, 1984.

Jackson, Shirley. "The Bus." In *Come Along With Me*. Ed. Stanley Edgar Hyman. New York: The Viking Press, 1968, 180–92.

_____. *The Haunting of Hill House*. 1959. New York: Penguin, 1984.

_____. *Life Among the Savages*. 1953. In *The Magic of Shirley Jackson*. Ed. Stanley Edgar Hyman. New York: Farrar, Straus, and Giroux, 1966, 383–530.

_____. "Pillar of Salt." *The Lottery, or The Adventures of James Harris*. New York: Farrar, Straus, and Company, 1949, 235–53.

_____. *Raising Demons*. 1957. In *The Magic of Shirley Jackson*, 533–753.

_____. "The Renegade." In *The Lottery*, 69–83.

_____. *The Road Through the Wall*. 1948. New York: Popular Library, 1976.

_____. "The Witch." In *The Lottery*, 63–67.

Joshi, S.T. *The Modern Weird Tale*. Jefferson, N.C.: McFarland, 2001.

Kernan, Alvin B. *The Plot of Satire*. New Haven and London: Yale University Press, 1965.

Lecroy, Anne. "The Different Humor of Shirley Jackson." *Studies in American Humor* 4.1–2 (1985): 62–73.

Malin, Irving. *New American Gothic*. Carbondale: Southern Illinois University Press, 1962.

Nichols, James W. *Insinuation: The Tactics of English Satire*. The Hague and Paris: Mouton, 1971.

Paulson, Ronald. *The Fictions of Satire*. Baltimore: The Johns Hopkins University Press, 1967.

Rabkin, Eric S. *The Fantastic in Literature*. Princeton: Princeton University Press, 1976.

Rubinstein, Roberta. "House Mothers and Haunted Daughters: Shirley Jackson and Female Gothic." *Tulsa Studies in Women's Literature* 15.2 (1996): 309–31.

Sullivan, Jack. "Shirley Jackson." In *Supernatural Fiction Writers: Fantasy and Horror*. New York: Scribner's, 1985, 1031–36.

Todorov, Tzvetan. *The Fantastic: A Structural Approach to a Literary Genre*. Trans. Richard Howard. Cleveland: Case Western Reserve University Press, 1973.

Test, George A. *Satire: Spirit and Art*. Tampa: University of South Florida Press, 1991.

Walker, Nancy A. *A Very Serious Thing: Women's Humor and American Culture*. Minneapolis: University of Minnesota Press, 1988.

# 3

# Multiple Personality and the Postmodern Subject: Theorizing Agency

## Marta Caminero-Santangelo

In the midst of the 1950s recasting of femininity, the image of the madwoman took a startling new form in American popular culture: the female multiple personality. Between 1954 and 1957 this disorder was the subject of fiction, film, and a nonfiction case study; in all of them the "patient" was a woman.[1] The sudden interest in the topic was all the more remarkable because professional diagnoses of multiple personality had gone markedly out of fashion at some time in the early twentieth century (Wilkes 331). How, then, are we to understand the resurgence of this particular form of madness and its hold on the popular imagination?

Decidedly, attention to all forms of mental illness was a hallmark of postwar American culture; never before had the disordered mind been to such a degree a topic for popular consumption. The country seemed to turn to a science of individual psychology at just the point when the international situation had become particularly bewildering and frightening; furthermore, psychological explanations for tragedies such as the Holocaust often gave those tragedies a manageable aspect. We have seen how the explosion of popular interest in matters psychological was used to particular effect in the social rearrangement of gender roles after the war. As veterans rushed to seek stability in an idealized image of domesticity, women's wartime occupation of traditionally male jobs needed to be suppressed in the service of male employment and a stable, secure, already nostalgic vision of family life.

Postwar representations of female multiple personality seem to have participated at some level in the reconfiguration of women's roles through the depiction of contradictory selves that could not coexist in a healthy, "normal" woman. For example, Glenna Matthews describes a feature in the April 1945 issue of the *Ladies' Home Journal* that told the story of a woman who "had had a promising career on the concert stage, but the tension of trying to fill multiple roles had induced a nervous breakdown" (Matthews 208). The image of divided or multiple woman, who could be several things at once, was used to suggest a potential threat to the precarious sense of social order, and to the traditional gender relations that provided a domestic haven from the atrocities of the war. Thus, a reviewer of *Lizzie,* the 1957 MGM movie based on *The Bird's Nest,* Shirley Jackson's novel of multiple personality, quipped, *"Lizzie* will probably be pretty confusing to the old-fashioned kind of moviegoer who thinks that when a girl isn't single, it's because she's married" (*Lizzie* 109). Another reviewer disparaged the film version of *The Three Faces of Eve* by objecting: "We never know from one moment to the next just what sort of girl [Eve] is going to be. It develops that when she isn't a drab housewife, she is a low-life girl who ... sneers at her husband, neglects her child, and takes up with any male who will give her a big hello. Her husband, an innocent in psychiatric matters, can't figure out why she is mousy one minute and wanton the next, and presently he says the hell with her and gets a divorce" ("Kiss" 134). A third review was accompanied by a cartoon depicting a naked man being torn in three different directions by women tugging at his arms and legs; the caption reads, "I Never Knew a Woman Like You." The focus in all cases was on the complications that multiplicity in a woman presented for normative gender relations; the figure of multiple personality, in the hands of the media, intimated a vague threat to the sexual contract that was the cornerstone of 1950s domestic life.

If such representations betokened a lingering anxiety that women might not ultimately be satisfied with the reduction in their "roles," that anxiety was easily calmed by the suggestion that woman in her *traditional* role was already many things at once. In September 1957, when the multiple personality fad was in full swing, Bell Telephone used it as a trope in an advertisement. A picture of the same woman, duplicated five times and dressed differently in each, appears over the caption "This Is Your Wife." The copy reads: "This is the pretty girl you married. She's the family chef. And the nurse. And the chauffeur and maid. And when she's all dressed up for an evening out—doesn't she look just wonderful!"

The multiple roles so feared in popular representation for their potential threat to domesticity had been, literally, domesticated. Even when
personalities like the startling Eve Black (in *The Three Faces of Eve)* could
not be made to fit the "good wife" image, they were nevertheless
described and judged in terms of feminine stereotypes ("mousy," "wanton," and so on). A male gaze simply assigned a cliché of femininity to
each manifestation, establishing a comforting range of labels by which
this strange phenomenon of the psyche could be understood.

In this respect, multiple personality as experienced by women is not
significantly different from other forms of female "madness," such as
hysteria a century ago or anorexia nervosa today, which enact a protest
against the socially constructed category of femininity even while they
reside fully within that category. James Glass, a political theorist who has
interviewed women clinically diagnosed with multiple personality disorder, observes that "in none of the accounts offered [in his study] ... did
I see that the phenomenon of [multiple personality] was a creative or playful or regenerative experience.... Multiplicity of identity becomes for
these women an ongoing torment, a horror that..., totally incapacitates
them" (xvi). Multiple personality, in other words, reduces women to
even greater powerlessness. Whatever the threat to dominant gender ideology posed by a figure of multiple feminine selves, that figure is easily
reappropriated in the service of the production of gender, as will be seen.

Yet there is still another issue complicating any discussion of multiple personality *as representation,* and that is its close affinity with conceptions of the postmodern subject. Certainly it is difficult to view the
phenomenon of multiple personality from a postmodern perspective
without considering its relation to the postmodern subject. At least one
discussion of the latter has used the figure of multiple personality as a
metaphor (Dunning 137), and many of the adjectives used to describe
current conceptions of subjectivity make equal sense in a discussion of
multiple personality: "fragmented," "multiple," "shifting," "decentered."
Glass finds the parallels so disturbing that he uses the clinical category
of multiple personality disorder to debunk conceptions of a liberatory
"multiplicity." He suggests that "the most powerful evidence against the
postmodernist concept of self comes not from theory but from the words
and lives of individuals actually experiencing the terrible psychological
dislocation of 'multiplicity,' women with the psychiatric diagnosis of multiple personality disorder.... Postmodern philosophers such as Baudrillard
and Lyotard ... create an aesthetic that celebrates a certain limitlessness....
But for a real person the psychological reality of being multiple, of actually living it out, is an entirely different issue" (xii, xviii–xix). Glass's
account suggests that the only way multiplicity can be experienced in
"real people" is through multiple personality—implying a fundamental

lack of distinction between the postmodern subject and the victim of multiple personality disorder (a point we will return to). Some feminist critics, sharing Glass's unease with current theories of subjectivity and their implications for the concept of subject-as-agent, have also felt it necessary to jettison the notion of the postmodern subject. Nancy Hartsock writes, "Somehow it seems highly suspicious that it is at the precise moment when so many groups have been engaged in ... redefinitions of the marginalized Others that suspicions emerge about the nature of the 'subject....' Why is it that just at the moment when so many of us who have been silenced begin to demand the right ... to act as subjects rather than objects of history, that just then the concept of subjecthood becomes problematic?" (163). On the other side of the debate, critics such as Ruth Leys and Jacqueline Rose seek an alternative "to the argument that feminism needs access to an integrated subjectivity more than its demise" (Rose 15, quoted in Leys 167); the unified subject is a fiction, and a nostalgic wish that things were different will not make them so.

Given the figural similarity thus noted between multiple personality and the postmodern subject, it should not be surprising that Leys, who wishes to rescue that subject for feminism, should focus on representations of multiple personality. She sets up her own thesis by looking to Rose for a way to conceptualize the nonintegrated, postmodern (female) subject as potentially subversive *because* she is not integrated:

> For Rose, the psychic as an "area of difficulty" is important for feminism because it involves a concept of the subject as structured by unconscious fantasies that always exceed the rigid gender positions that are defined as the norm for women and men.... What distinguishes psychoanalysis from sociological accounts of gender..., Rose writes, "is that whereas for the latter, the internalization of norms is assumed roughly to work, the basic premise and indeed starting-point of psychoanalysis is that it does not...." For Rose, the necessary "failure" of identity—the inability of the patriarchal "law" fully to determine human actions and beliefs—is also virtually a condition of possibility for a feminist politics as she understands it [Leys 167–68, quoting Rose 90].

Multiple personality constitutes an even more vigorous and visible "failure" of identity, and thus (according to Rose's logic) would presumably even further elude "patriarchal 'law.'" As we shall see, Leys's argument is that multiple personality can resist or challenge gender ideology by undermining any notion of an original self. Leys turns to a landmark text in multiple personality, Morton Prince's *The Dissociation of a Personality* (1905), in an attempt to move beyond a "theory of the trauma, understood as an external historical event that befalls the already-constituted female subject" (168). Such a theory, she claims, is part of "a discourse which in effect denies the female subject all possibility of

agency" (204 n. 3). Leys is taking issue with prominent factual representations of multiple personality such as Prince's—and, 50 years later,
that of Drs. Corbett Thigpen and Hervey Cleckley, authors of *The Three
Faces of Eve*—which relied on an assumption that some originary trauma
inflicted on the subject caused the initial fragmentation of personalities.
Both of these accounts assume an original integrated subject who had
existed before the trauma; interestingly, in both accounts the doctors
proceed by trying to identify which personality comes closest to the original self and then by enabling that personality to have dominance over
the others. Leys argues that the theory of trauma is problematic because
it posits the female as a passive non-agent, to whom things happen from
the outside; she challenges Morton Prince's (humanist) notion of an
original, integrated self by suggesting that the personalities manifested
by his patient Miss Beauchamp were actually products of a particular
mimetic identification produced by hypnosis: "The hypnotized person
is ... given over body and soul to the hypnotist's suggestions such that
she is the other" (174). That is, the hypnotized subject identifies with
the doctor and, particularly under strong suggestion from him, can view
herself as a "she" rather than an "I"; hence the effects of multiple personality. This model, serving as a paradigm for how all subjectivity is
formed (i.e., by identification and imitation), is potentially subversive
according to Leys because "the mimetic paradigm expressly holds that
no 'real' self exists prior to mimesis, [whereas] the concept of the self as
a multiple of component traits or dispositions lends itself to the common-
sense, essentialist idea that there exists a 'real' or 'normal' self that can
be identified and recuperated" (191). Leys's argument emphasizes the
ideologically loaded nature of any concept of a normal self, which can
lend itself to notions of natural gender traits that must be recovered. (For
example, the normal self who is to be rescued by the male doctors is
inevitably the appropriately feminine one, as we shall see.) The mimetic
model, in contrast, is potentially able to disrupt gender, since it suggests
that gender is always a social construct assumed by imitation. By identifying with a male doctor, a female personality is traversing gender
boundaries in a manner that cannot be viewed as trespass, since there is
no natural female self to begin with.

Nevertheless, there is a fundamental problem for feminism with
Leys's formulation. Certainly her mimesis argument moves beyond concepts of a natural feminine self and allows multiple personality to intimate gender disruption; but in the model Leys holds up as paradigmatic,
that disruption comes about through a female patient's imitation of her
male doctor and extreme acquiescence to his suggestions. Consequently,
although Leys argues against a theory of trauma partly on the basis of
its construction of the feminine as without agency, it is hard to see how

her model of mimesis-suggestion restores agency, for the female subject is reduced to a product of a (male) doctor's suggestions. Furthermore, how is any agency possible without a sense of subjectivity—without, that is, being able to identify oneself as an "I" rather than a "she?" How can a woman's view of herself as absolutely "other," and her identification with a male doctor as the only legitimate subject, be viewed as a figure for transgression, much less transformation of the gender system? Does it not rather duplicate—or imitate—the doctor's view of the woman as an object for study rather than a subject? As Teresa de Lauretis notes, "The discourse of the sciences of man constructs the object as female and the female as object. That ... is its rhetoric of violence" (45). The purpose of this argument is not to reject Leys's hypothesis that hypnosis may actually bring about, or at least exacerbate, the phenomenon of multiple personality; it is, rather, to take issue with her postulation of the mimesis-suggestion model of multiple personality as a means to theorize *more* agency for women. Her countermodel holds far more serious problems than a trauma model because it claims subversive potential while continuing to imply a lack of agency.

In response to such a model, we might offer de Lauretis's formulation of the possibilities for agency in the postmodern (female) subject. If gendered subjects are constructed by discourse and representation, they can nevertheless participate in the (de)construction of gender through the "ongoing effort to create new spaces of discourse, to rewrite cultural narratives." These counternarratives constitute "a view from 'elsewhere,'" de Lauretis observes, although such a view is "not [by way of] ... a movement from one space to another beyond it, or outside: say, from the space of a representation ... to the space outside the representation, the space outside discourse." For if we are constructed within and by discourse and representation, we cannot simply move outside them and somehow start anew. The "elsewhere," the space for our transformative representative practices, is to be found within hegemonic discourses themselves. In other words, any counternarrative must strategically begin with the space opened by existing discourse and must work to reveal the fundamental assumptions and givens that are simultaneously revealed and obscured by such discourse. As discussed earlier, de Lauretis calls this "the space not represented yet implied (unseen)" in dominant discourses (25–26).

The novel that marks a starting point for the post–World War II fascination with multiple personality, *The Bird's Nest* by Shirley Jackson, can be seen as just this kind of counternarrative. Jackson had thoroughly researched her subject, and had made herself particularly familiar with Morton Prince's once famous study, *The Dissociation of a Personality,* from which her novel drew much of its material (Oppenheimer 161–62).

Through her reimagining of Prince's account, Jackson makes central to her text the "elsewhere" of his narrative: the violence his rhetoric inflicts on his subject, Christine Beauchamp, in the service of the (re)production of gender. For as Leys has pointed out, "Prince's writings ... join[ed] the increasingly abrasive turn-of-the-century debate over the 'crisis' of masculinity associated with the New Woman's appropriation of male roles and the breakdown of the traditional separation between male and female spheres" (188), in part by presenting the various personalities of Miss Beauchamp as "a virtual typology of early twentieth-century concepts of the feminine" (182). But Jackson's model of multiple personality also persuasively suggests the lack of real agency in such a phenomenon, as I will show later in this chapter, for though multiple personality can be understood as a demand for the recognition of subjectivity, it ultimately demonstrates the absolute powerlessness of one who cannot completely claim the "I" for herself.

If Prince's text was reacting to "the breakdown of traditional separation between male and female spheres" associated with the emergence of the New Woman in the early twentieth century, Jackson's novel was in many ways responding to the postwar reinscription of those spheres. Multiple personality—a figure of femininity out of control—had the potential to disrupt this rigid ideal. We have seen the anxiety it seems to have caused the reviewers of books and movies on the phenomenon. Certainly it disrupts the complacency of Jackson's Dr. Wright, who, in a parody of Morton Prince, scrambles to defend his precarious worldview by shoring up each portion of the disintegrated personality into a distinct, and wholly separate, image of woman—an activity, as we shall see, that dramatizes what de Lauretis calls the violence of rhetoric. Wright declares of the patient who first walks into his office that "I wasn't much inclined to her at first.... 'Colorless' was a word [that] came to my mind when I looked at her" (176). This is the "first" Elizabeth Richmond, who has been—as the doctor also admiringly notes—"well brought up and taught that a lady seats herself quietly" (178). She is, in other words, a Victorian woman—a "lady," but without sexuality by virtue of that construction, and therefore wholly without interest for the doctor. Notably, Wright (who seems to fancy himself a Victorian gentleman) remains blind to the fundamental conflict suggested by his own, actually quite contemporary representations of gender. Postwar representations that positioned woman in a private domestic sphere—on which both male veterans' fantasies of a safe domestic haven and male participation in the public economic sphere depended—were characterized by a lack of sexuality, paradoxically rendering this ideal potentially uninteresting to the very men who envisioned themselves running home to it.[1]

But if Elizabeth (or R1) bores the doctor sexually, Beth (R2) brings out his manliness by being the figure of the maiden in distress; it is Beth, Dr. Wright tells his imagined audience, "who, although weak and almost helpless, was at least possessed of a kind of winsomeness, and engaging in her very helplessness" (275). It is in the cause of saving Beth that the doctor imagines himself a Prince Charming in a fairy tale: "I saw myself ... as setting free a captive princess" (195). Into this chivalric fantasy intrudes Betsy (R3); the doctor now notes, "I found myself ... much in the manner of a knight ... who, in the course of bringing his true princess home, has no longer any fear, but only a great weariness, when confronted in sight of the castle towers by a fresh dragon to slay" (198). The appearance of a new personality is presented not as a medical complication but as an unwelcome interruption in the resolution of a romance. Furthermore, Wright's chivalric discourse distracts from, but never completely occludes, a discourse of aggressive male sexuality that everywhere colors his representations of psychiatric treatment: "I may liken [Elizabeth Richmond's] state and its cure to ... a stoppage in a water main.... [T]he only way in which I might accomplish [its] removal was by going myself ... down the pipe.... [The metaphor] does, I fear, portray most vividly my own diagnosis of Miss R.'s difficulty and my own problem in relieving it. Let us assume, then, that the good Doctor Wright is steeling himself to creep manfully down a sewer pipe" (186). Miss Richmond's problem, then, must be "relieved" through a manful creeping down her pipe; all she really needs is a good screw, and the doctor is presumably just the one to provide it.

In Wright's catalogue of feminine types, Betsy is the dragon to Beth's princess; more often Betsy is described by the doctor as demonic, the feminine Hyde to Beth's Jekyll: "She was not, I saw, at all handsome, and as I watched her in horror, the smile upon her soft lips coarsened, and became sensual and gross, ... and she laughed, evilly and roughly, throwing her head back and shouting ... a devil's mask.... What I saw that afternoon was the dreadful grinning face of a fiend, and heaven help me, I have seen it a thousand times since" (192). Wright's image of Betsy as a she-demon possessed of a horrible, evil sensuality is difficult to sustain, however, when held up against the narrative of her escape to New York, in which she appears to be little more than a lost child searching for a mother who has been dead for years.

But to stamp Betsy as a creature of no sexuality is as gross a simplification as to accuse her of wantonness. The hints Jackson provides regarding Betsy's sexuality suggest instead that it is highly contradictory. For example, her memories of her mother's lover, Robin, are tormented; identifying closely with her mother, she courts Robin's sexual attentions at the same time that she fears him, in a manner that suggests a previous rape. In one flashback during which she mistakes a stranger for

Robin, something she does repeatedly during her runaway trip to New York, she manifests both attitudes at once in a dizzying manner suggestive of a personality split within Betsy herself: "'I won't let you, not ever any more,' Betsy said to Robin, 'and neither will my mother....' And she could hear him after her, down the hail and down the stairs, praying not to stumble, not Robin again, it wasn't fair no one could do that again, praying to move quickly enough, to be safely out of it and away before he could touch her, to be safely out of it; 'Robin,' she said, 'Robin darling, call me Lisbeth, Lisbeth'" (259). Yet "Lisbeth," Betsy's mother's nickname, is not another personality; it is an aspect of Betsy herself, that part of her which wishes to be her mother. This counternarrative, exposing the contradictions, the fragmentation, within a single "self," suggests a subjectivity that indeed escapes Dr. Wright's efforts to fix and hold it.

In contrast, Elizabeth Richmond's multiple personalities seem to play into the doctor's hands. Presented with the opportunity to label each separate personality, he can suppress disturbing contradictions in the service of a categorical worldview: Betsy becomes "the hateful, the enemy" (198) and "our villain" (204). Elizabeth's Aunt Morgen, Dr. Wright's competitor for control over his patient, also uses such rhetoric in an attempt to gain authority over the phenomenon of multiple personality, comparing her niece's ailment to her own "Jekyll-and-brandy personality" (327), and then immediately distancing herself from Elizabeth through a rhetoric of morality: "[The] cruel and vicious manner [of her niece] ... would automatically set a distinction between the reasonable, regular alterings of a sensible person—Morgen—and the unreasonable, erratic alterings of a non-sensible person—Elizabeth" (328). Unreason is thus linked to evil—a remnant of the concept of moral insanity—and, by implication, reason to moral rectitude.

Although notions of moral madness presumably had been succeeded by more scientific explanations in the late nineteenth and early twentieth centuries (witness Freud's vehement claims to the "science" of psychoanalysis), the rhetoric of morality lingered on, even in discourses that, claiming objectivity, seemed to distance themselves from moral judgments. A wartime study of multiple personality provided a list of characteristics in which the various personalities of a case might differ from one another, including "propriety or good behavior," which was the distinguishing factor (the study reminded readers) in "Jekyll-Hyde differences between the personalities" (Taylor and Martin 289). The rhetoric of moral dichotomy could be used to particular effect in the postwar construction of femininity; for if the Russians were our enemy abroad, our enemy at home was the woman who was not a willing participant in a chivalric fairy tale (soldier returns home, rescues princess, marries her, and sets up house). In *The Three Faces of Eve,* a "true" story of a multiple personality case published three years after Jackson's novel, moral rhetoric, used as a strategy for managing undesirable aspects of woman, seems to govern the entire narrative. The pseudonyms by which the first two personalities are designated in the account, Eve White and Eve Black, are blatantly suggestive of a Jekyll-and-Hyde division of "Eve," the first and paradigmatic woman. Indeed, the authors go on at some length about Stevenson's novel, explicitly feminizing his construction, and in the process betraying their own anxieties about the potential disruption of the domestic haven suggested by multiple personality: "The two famous names [Jekyll and Hyde] in conjunction serve as a rough equivalent for such popular expressions as 'she's a street angel but a home devil'" (Thigpen and Cleckley 42).

In the writers' brush strokes, Eve White, a housewife, is the "figure of propriety" and (therefore?) a "colorless" woman with a "monotonous voice" (9). Eve Black, in contrast, is a trampy seductress, a "creature of ... passion and erotic potentiality and inclination"; the "average man," we are told, "might have found it difficult to avoid the fundamental reactions conveyed in the vernacular by such phrases as *this girl is really stacked, there's something about her that let's* [sic] *you feel she could be a mighty hot dish*" (167). Certainly the authors attempt to mask the effect of their own sexual impulses on their presumably objective account: an "average" man might think such things about Eve Black, but the good doctors stay at least one step removed by reporting on *his* reaction to her. Nevertheless, their hypothetical reconstructions of a scene between Eve Black and Ralph White, the husband of Eve White, leave little room for doubt about their own implication in 1950s gender ideology: "As they sat talking, Eve Black crossed her legs. It is very reasonable to believe that Ralph found what had seemed wantonly flirtatious when directed toward another could be delectable and rich with thrilling promise when directed toward himself.... Some men, after being bitterly disillusioned or icily rejected by what they regard as the sacredly good manifestation of femininity, have been known to fling themselves wildly into the arms of despised harlots" (166–67). The male dilemma could not be made more explicit; the "sacredly good" woman is in fact *too* good; lacking any sexuality, she is boring. (Remarkably, Eve White is the only one of the three personalities who does *not* consider herself a virgin, acknowledging her marriage to Ralph; her representation by the doctors as without sexuality thus suggests yet again the conflict inherent in the 1950s construction of the feminine position.) Her counterpart, the wanton Eve, may provide "thrilling promise" in the short term, but her very wantonness makes her ultimately a threat to domesticity—for she does not direct her sexual charms solely to their proper recipient, her husband, but freely disperses them. It is for this reason that she must be "despised," whatever momentary relief she may offer.

Into the stalemate between two equally unsatisfactory Eves steps "Jane," an answer to the male fantasy produced as though on demand. She is, on the one hand, "far more mature, more vivid, more boldly capable, and *more interesting* than Eve White.... Beside this genuinely impressive newcomer, Eve White appeared colorless and limited" (119; emphasis added)—as if she had not before! Unlike Eve White, Jane is perceived as a sexual being; yet, she contains her sexuality in appropriate ways rather than distributing it "wantonly" like Eve Black: "Everything about Eve Black seemed designed specifically to attract ... attention. Though many polite eyes were likely to note with appreciation Jane's progress along any sidewalk, even a fool would automatically restrain his impulse to whistle. There was about her no flaunting whatsoever of erotic charm, but dull indeed would be the man who would not on second glance surmise that here was an authentic potentiality for what is naturally sensuous" (126). The doctors, disingenuously tentative in their claim that "there was some choice open to the psychiatrist as to which personality he should try to reinforce" (123), predictably choose Jane; their motivation for doing so is made apparent in their observations that "her mind ... suggested the *tabula rasa* of John Locke, the empty sheet upon which experience is to write but which now is blank and without content" (125). As the real "Eve," Chris Costner Sizemore, would observe later in her own account, "Jane" stood for "Jane Doe," meaning "brand new, blank"; and though this suggested a "pallid and colorless anonymous" to Sizemore (274), in search of her *own* identity, it certainly did not to her doctors. To them Jane was, for all practical purposes, waiting to be written on, and Thigpen and Cleckley wrote upon her the text of their own male fantasies, thus revealing the degree to which their scientific "choice" was conditioned by sexual considerations.

In Jackson's novel, the rhetoric of moral dichotomy that imbues Dr. Wright's psychiatric choices is undermined precisely as the product of his own gendered position. Her somewhat caricatured portrayal of the doctor can be understood, in this context, as an attempt to write from "the space not represented yet implied" in psychiatric discourse. Jackson provides strong cues for reading the moral rhetoric that continually creeps into Wright's account. Such rhetoric betrays not simply Wright's acceptance of particular norms of gender but also his personal investedness in those norms. His moral condemnation of some of Elizabeth Richmond's selves is, for example, clearly as much a dire response to challenges to his own (masculine) authority as it is an ideologically loaded ideal of proper feminine submissiveness. Since Wright acknowledges the difficulty he experiences as a "man of science" in being "impartial, and sensible, and invulnerable" (273), it is difficult to accept at face value his characterization of Betsy as a manifestation of evil, wanton femininity without taking into account his anger at her lack of submission to his will. He recounts with indignation the fact that Betsy demonstrates "an air of mockery" (196) towards him, "felt and showed [him] no respect" (200), and, most grievous, "called him a damned old fool!" (200). Wright's backhanded admissions serve as a warning that we should not accept his reductive clichéd characterizations of his patient(s) as objective. Jackson, however, does not allow us to regard Wright's morality-play classifications merely as a benign reflection of the ideological contexts in which he finds himself. As we shall see, his emphasis on his own creative powers betrays psychiatry's complicity in reproducing that ideology, and in producing subjects who would be appropriately interpolated in it.

Psychiatric discourse typically obscured (and still obscures) its own position within ideology, including gender ideology—and therefore its own interest in the reproduction of particular forms of subjectivity—with a rhetoric of scientific neutrality. De Lauretis (citing the work of Wini Breines and Linda Gordon) notes the operation of such rhetoric in "gender-neutral methodological perspectives on incest." She explains:

> In spite of the agreement among statistical studies that, in cases of incest as well as child sexual abuse, 92% of the victims are females and 97% of the assailants are males, "predictably enough, until very recently the clinical literature ignored this feature of incest, implying that, for example, mother-son incest was as prevalent as father-daughter incest...." Such studies ... obscure the actual history of violence against women.... Put another way, even as those studies purport to remain innocent of the ideology or of the rhetoric of violence, they cannot avoid and indeed purposefully engage in the violence of rhetoric [de Lauretis 34, quoting Breines and Gordon 523].

We can use de Lauretis's pertinent discussion as a means to understand how the figure of multiple personality constructed by psychiatric discourse deflects attention from the gendered content of particular forms of violence.

For example, the language in which Drs. Thigpen and Cleckley construct their narrative in *The Three Faces of Eve* suggests unimpeachable neutrality while repeatedly obscuring the violence Ralph White inflicts on his wife, "Eve." They write, "Though ordinarily a kind and agreeable man, [Ralph] eventually became impatient and at last angry with [Eve].... As Ralph remembered the scene, Eve had seized him by the arm in an effort to make him stay home with her. In freeing himself, he inadvertently pushed her in such a way that she interpreted his act as a slap or a blow. He did not realize this at the time" (29). Eve's subsequent miscarriage on that same night is presented as a coincidence, only tangentially related to Ralph's misinterpreted struggle for freedom. The

doctors' empathy with Ralph is palpable: "The husband's role in this situation was undeniably difficult.... It is doubtful if any ordinary man could
have successfully solved the problems that confronted him.... He regret-
ted having struck her lightly in the ensuing quarrel. But who could be
sure of controlling himself under such circumstances?" (84–86).
Although they take great pains to assure their readers that their view is
balanced ("It is difficult to reconstruct the incident in detail through two
differing accounts" [29]), their own representation of Eve's malady as
one that would place a husband in an "undeniably" bad situation subtly locates the fault in the bewilderingly multiplied woman, not her beleaguered husband. Ralph is, after all, only doing what the authors
themselves are doing: attempting to control an excessive profusion of
femininity. The doctors' narrative thus testifies to the violence of postwar psychiatric rhetoric which, in masking gender violence through the
guise of scientific neutrality, also served to legitimate its perpetuation.

The violence "implied (but unseen)" in these psychiatric discourses
is the space in which Jackson builds her characterization of Dr. Wright,
who takes a blatantly obvious, and specifically gendered, pleasure in his
power over his female patient, whom he describes as "a vessel emptied."
He asserts, *"Our* responsibility [i.e., his and Aunt Morgen's] is, clearly,
to people this vacant landscape—fill this empty vessel, I think I said
before—and, with our own deep emotional reserves, enable the child to
rebuild.... She will owe to us her opinions, her discriminations, her
reflections; we are able, as few others have ever been, to recreate, entire,
a human being, in the most proper and reasonable mold" (374).
Although Wright is here conspiring with Aunt Morgen over the "rebuild-
ing" of Elizabeth, the vocabulary he uses is his alone, and is clearly conditioned by his masculine position; he views Elizabeth as the biological
"empty vessel" of womanhood, waiting to be filled by life-giving male
seed and then "peopled" with babies. Psychiatric authority becomes, in
Wright's hands, a quite literal authorship: he longs to write, to create his
feminine heroine from the materials of his own desire.

Wright's self-conscious insistence on the creation of his narrative is
almost inevitably connected to his position as a sexual pursuer. His
extended metaphor likening his treatment of Elizabeth to a manful creeping down her pipe, for example, is interjected with parenthetical statements such as "if my reader will forgive such an ignoble comparison"
and "gracious heaven, how I have caught myself in my own analogy!"
which repeatedly call attention to the status of his narrative as a particularly literary writing (186); and his fantasy about rescuing the distressed
and helpless Beth is, as we have seen, delivered in the language of chivalric romance and fairy tale. He is quite explicit about the connections
between psychiatry and authorship, observing that "a good writer is

much the same as a good doctor," and admitting his propensity for "fan-cying myself Author" (176). The capitalized "Author" suggests, of course, that Wright is God as well as Adam: he is a God who wishes to create the essential Eve for *himself.* His authorship, in other words, is driven by a particularly masculine desire. Authority, Jackson will not let us forget, is inevitably conditioned by gender relations.

At the same time, since Wright wishes to create his feminine ideal, he must deny his patient the powers of authorship he allows himself. In this way his rhetoric "constructs the object as female and the female as object" (de Lauretis 45); hence its violence. When Betsy rejects the numerical designation with which the doctor has fixed her, declaring, "I certainly don't choose to be called R3[;] ... [y]ou can call me Rosalita, or Charmian, or Lilith, if you like," Wright inwardly mocks "the thought of this grotesque creature naming herself like a princess in a fairy romance" (202–3). In general, the doctor does not respond well to chal-lenges to his narrative, attempting to compensate through compulsive assertions regarding his position as an author. His report to Aunt Mor-gen on the condition of her niece is marked by a defensive reaction to his uncomfortable sense of loss of control:

> As I spoke—and I spoke well, having so thoroughly rehearsed myself, and having my notes besides—Miss Jones listened attentively, with every appearance of great fascination; she interrupted me once.... [D]uring her interruption I was strongly afraid of losing the thread of my own narrative, and its perfect balance, and had at last to cut her off in order that I might continue. Again, she asked and insisted on a more detailed and simpler description of the dissociated personality, as described by Doctor Prince, and again I must break off and give it to her. We were wasting time, I thought, since I knew the subject perfectly and she need not know any more than she did [305–6].

Wright's anxiety over the loss of narrative control, as well as his focus on narrative form, suggests his precarious hold on the *content* of his nar-rative; Elizabeth's various selves present the specter of that which might not be containable by the doctor's efforts. Periodically the specter is loosed. When Wright discovers that the personality he believed to be the sweet and malleable Beth is actually Betsy *imitating* Beth—that is, rep-resenting her, and thus exerting control over her own narrative—he beats a retreat: "I was badly frightened and unwilling to jeopardize my own health" (218). And once again his loss of control over his subject mat-ter is immediately suppressed through a renewed attention to narrative form, as his focus shifts to his explanatory letter to Morgen, a piece of prose in which he takes great pride: "I wrote ... very well (indeed, I have saved the letter, and it is before me now)."

But the doctor's attention to form in the face of unmanageable content is only a stopgap measure; ultimately he must regain control over his material through an authorship characterized by violence. Wright's desire to inflict such violence on his patient when she does not conform to his narrative is barely disguised. The language he uses to refer to his professional care of Elizabeth—"her treatment at my hands" (265)—suggests not therapy but brutality; a few pages later he confesses his "sympathy for whoever had gotten a hand around [Bess's] throat" (267). Indeed, the very form of his treatment is brutality, figured in quite graphic physical images. Engaged with Morgen in a literal tug-of-war over Elizabeth's body, he expresses his desire to "rip her in half" (356); and he describes his own psychiatric goals through yet another self-consciously literary metaphor: "I saw myself, if the analogy be not too extreme, much like a Frankenstein with all the materials for a monster ready at hand, and when I slept, it was with dreams of myself patching and tacking together, trying most hideously to chip away the evil from Betsy and leave what little was good, while the other three stood by mockingly, waiting their turns" (276). Once again Wright's emphasis on authority (here through literary allusion) occurs amidst—and as a reaction to—extreme anxiety regarding his ability to manage his subject matter; he fears that his patient is a monster who will escape his control. Notably, even in this image of the creation of a monster, Wright is more a Pygmalion than a Frankenstein, fantasizing an object of desire sculpted from his own hands. His efforts to regain control over his unwieldy creation thus take the additional form of an image of chiseling and chipping, which cannot fail to suggest violence when applied to what is after all not stone but flesh and blood.

If the doctor can contemplate selectively preserving some aspects of each personality while doing away with others, then it should be no surprise that he also contemplates the extermination of entire personalities, as he warns Bess in a moment of anger: "Consider that it is only through my misguided sufferance that you continue to exist at all.... [D]o you think that you may with impunity bring your pert words to bear against a power like [mine]? ... [Y]ou are at best, young lady, only a slight, only a poor and partial creature, and for all your fine words, you will not stay long; ... I promise you, here and now, that you as a person will, with the knowledge of you I have, cease, absolutely and finally and without possibility of petition, cease I tell you, unalterably cease to exist!" (316). The godlike power of creation that Dr. Wright assumes is also a power of destruction, justified by his psychiatric determination that, since each personality is (to quote Prince along with Wright) "a part only of a normal whole self" (quoted in Jackson 199), that self is not a real person with the right to exist but "only a poor and partial creature" which Wright is within his moral bounds to extinguish at will. The psychological "ripping" Wright wishes to inflict on his patient is meant to preserve his preferred personality, the charming and dependent Beth, at the expense of the other three. "My present hope," he tells us, "was to strengthen Beth, by whatever means, and bring her slowly to a complete open realization of the whole personality" (281). (Wright, of course, does not acknowledge the contradiction in his desire to make Beth, who by his own determination is only a part of the whole, dominant over the entire person.) In response to the dangerous specter of feminine multiplicity, in other words, Wright ultimately wishes, whatever his theoretical claims to the contrary, not to reintegrate the personalities into a single (but necessarily shifting and contradictory) self, but to sever them more violently, salvaging one and doing away with the others. Wright's strategy thus indicates how the figure of multiple personality can be easily reappropriated by, and made to function in the service of, the ideology of gender—whatever its initial challenges to that ideology. Under the guise of psychiatric therapy, Wright takes an active hand in the re-creation of a model of femininity that will stand for the natural, normative state (Beth, he tries to convince us, is "Miss R ... as she was meant to be" [186]); what his own metaphors reveal is that the hand of ideological production is also a hand of violence, wielded against women.

On one level, of course, Wright is merely continuing a tradition of the denial of full "personhood" to women based on certain (male) criteria of normalcy; the general outlines of his ideological assumptions and legitimating rhetoric were already at hand in Prince's text. Although Prince (as well as Thigpen and Cleckley half a century later) had a certain stake, for reasons of maintaining his medical reputation, in proving the existence of separate personalities in his patient and therefore the authenticity of his case, he was also ultimately committed to denying the subjectivity of some of those personalities for reasons both professional (he needed to assert that he had "cured" his patient) and—as we shall see—ideological. Prince's oft-quoted explanation of multiple personality—"each secondary personality is a part only of a normal whole self" (3)—suggests that he believed any one personality was as real (or unreal) as another. But his practice throughout much of his 570-page record corresponds to a quite different, and overtly stated, assumption: that *one* of the personalities was the "real, original or normal self, the self that was born and which [the patient] was intended by nature to be" (1) and that it was Prince's job to discover which personality this was and to extinguish all the others. Arguments based on what "nature intended" thus justified what Prince boldly admitted amounted to murder of those personalities that were not the "real" self (conflated uncritically with a "normal" self): "Plainly, if B IV were the real self, she must be kept and the others annihilated. Poor Miss Beauchamp ... must no longer be allowed to live.... In my thoughts the annihilation of Miss Beauchamp seemed in no way different from saying that she must be satisfied with death.... [I]t seemed like a crime we were committing. It was a psychical murder" (245, 248). Prince's self-described task was "to determine which personality was comportable with abnormality and which with normality, and so find the real self" (241). What was not "normal" presumably could not be "real."

Predictably enough, the criteria on which Prince based determinations of normalcy were shaped largely by gender ideology. For example, during the course of Prince's narrative, B IV temporarily becomes a candidate for the "real self" because she dispenses with a traditionally "feminine" emotionality in favor of cool-headed rationality: she "explained her point of view so logically, that the hypothesis that she was the real and original self gained greatly in favor" (245). Unlike B I, B IV "had no shattered ideals, no intensity of sentiment, no discouragement from overwhelming obstacles, but [was] content with the conditions as she found them" (249). Emotion and sentiment thus mark B I as sick and therefore unreal, in comparison to the cool logic of B IV. (No consideration is ever given to whether the obstacles in Miss Beauchamp's life do indeed call for discouragement as an appropriate or understandable response.) Buried behind this evaluation is a larger indictment of the status of women in general; if, as the wisdom of the day had it, women were indeed emotional and men rational, then by Prince's criteria women must be seen as less deserving of a claim to real personhood than men.

But Prince's evaluations also reveal the double bind of madness as a technology of gender that labels women mad simultaneously for their difference from a male model and for their deviations from their feminine position. For B IV is also potentially "real" because she is "so natural and simple" (245). Sally, "mistress of herself" from the moment she is "truly born into this world" (95–96), is "rebellious" and "[fights] to counteract [Prince's] influence" (138); Prince arguably retaliates by judging her from the very first as not a real person. Increasingly, Prince notices that B IV, too, "yielded to no one, [and] demanded to be mistress of herself" (412), as she fiercely pits her own will against Prince's. Not surprisingly, then, B IV turns out not to be the "Real Miss Beauchamp" in Prince's estimation after all. The Real Miss Beauchamp is a modified version of B II, who is absolutely malleable in Prince's hands and lets his will reign supreme even over her own: "B II begged pathetically ... that I would help her, protect her from herself, from every one" (434). Thus those personalities who attempt to assert their own wills and control their own lives are, seemingly for that very reason, declared not "real" people and therefore without the right to self-determination.

Prince arguably was responding to the threat of the New Woman with a humanist discourse of a real, natural, and original self that would serve rigidly to recontain gender by excluding certain types of womanhood from his construction of a real and natural self. (Leys makes essentially this argument.) Jackson's reimagining of Prince's narrative brings its violence to the foreground. When placed in the mouth of Dr. Wright, appeals to the assumption of an integrated, original, noncontradictory subject (through, for example, assertions about what Elizabeth Richmond was "meant to be") ring remarkably false, juxtaposed as they are with his blatant Pygmalion fantasies. In Jackson's hands, psychiatry's appeals to a humanist subject are a discourse violently wielded—a hammer and chisel hacking away at troubling contradiction—against the threat of a potentially uncontrollable feminine self.

It is possible to read the symptoms of multiple personality as a signpost for this sort of rhetorical violence.[3] For those symptoms offer a compelling (one might even say an exaggerated) demand for recognition of subjectivity, precisely when the denial of subjectivity by another has constituted a violent act of silencing. The rebellious personality Sally in Prince's account provides one such counternarrative by composing an "autobiography" about her existence from childhood as a separate personality. The text of her autobiography is preceded on the page by this odd bracketed introduction:

> Sally's Story
> The autobiography begins in a somewhat flowery, childish style with a few brief memories of infancy, while she was in her cradle. When I refused to accept the accuracy of her memory she went on as follows: [371].

Sally's memories blatantly contradict Prince's theory that the fragmentation of self was effected by an incident of much more recent occurrence. Her narrative, that is to say, challenges the accuracy of his. In consequence, Prince must struggle to neutralize the potentially damaging effects of Sally's counternarrative with a counter-counternarrative; he frames her text with this discrediting introduction, concludes it with hypotheses about why Sally "thinks" she remembers events from childhood (396–7), and interjects a footnote pointing out an "error" (390) in her account at just the point when she is explicitly challenging his narrative of personality disintegration. Remarkably, Prince later writes of Sally's "unaccountable anxiety to recover possession of the manuscript of her autobiography" (468), but seems oblivious to her desire to regain possession of her story, though that desire is surely what is intimated by her urgency about recovering her manuscript from Prince's hands. Prince is, in fact, betraying a Wright-like anxiety over narrative form at the very moment when his story is beginning to escape his control. He wishes to posit an exact beginning, middle, and end to Christine Beauchamp's personality disintegration, and can do so only through a violent suppression of her own experience. In the end, that suppression includes the "murder" of Sally, who is allowed by Prince to play no part in the final, ostensibly integrated personality. Prince, that is to say, refuses to recognize Sally's claim to subjectivity, even while, contradictorily, he insists upon it: Sally exists as a separate person—though not a "real" one.

Thigpen and Cleckley enact a similar violent silencing of "Eve." Like Prince, these doctors contain the ways in which she contests their authoritative account of her disorder by imposing rigid narrative form on her story, this time in the shape of a happy ending. In her subsequently published autobiography, Chris Costner Sizemore (the real "Eve") details a long history of attempts, in her coauthor's words, to "tell *her* story, the way *she* lived it and felt it, not the way someone else saw her live it and assumed she felt it" (342–43). Sizemore reveals that this story had for years been forcibly silenced (through both legal means and psychological coercion) by Drs. Thigpen and Cleckley, who had wished to give "the world ... the impression that I had recovered from my dissociative problem—multiple personality" (author's note x). The doctors were aware that Sizemore had experienced subsequent personalities; but, despite her wishes, they had not "included the material, because a book cannot be written with a 'lady or the tiger' conclusion, it had to have a resolved ending" (371).

In Shirley Jackson's account the figure of multiple personality suggests a potential defense against just the sort of discourse that would deny subjectivity—although, as we shall see, that potential proves to be a false one. The Elizabeth we meet at the beginning of Jackson's novel is an "anonymous" person. If her subjectivity is not actively denied by others, it is also not recognized: "The letters signed 'per er' and the endless listings of exhibits vouched for by E. Richmond were the outstanding traces of her presence.... She was not even interesting enough to distinguish with a nickname; where the living ... kept a precarious hold on individuality and identity, Elizabeth remained nameless" (151–52). Elizabeth is not confirmed as a subject by another, and we may usefully recall here R.D. Laing's contention in *The Divided Self* that "the sense of identity requires the existence of another by whom one is known" (139).

But there is one other who recognizes Elizabeth, writing her letters: "watch out for me lizzie watch out for me and dont do anything bad ... dont think i wont know lizzie because i do—dirty thoughts lizzie dirty lizzie" (iii). This other is Betsy, one of the personalities of Elizabeth Richmond and therefore a part of Elizabeth's self; and despite the nasty tone of her letter, it is a confirmation of subjectivity, for it both acknowledges that Elizabeth's thoughts are known by another and demands a reciprocal recognition of an alternative subjectivity—Betsy's—from Elizabeth ("watch out for me").

Elizabeth's obvious fondness for Betsy's letters, regardless of their abusive tone, is clearly motivated by her sense that someone is confirming her existence as a subject: "Someone had written her lots of letters, she thought fondly, lots of letters; here were five. She kept them all in the red valentine box and every afternoon now, when she came home from work, she put the new one in and counted them over. The very feel of them was important, as though at last someone had found her out, someone close and dear, someone who wanted to watch her all the time; someone who writes letters to me, Elizabeth thought, touching the papers gently" (164–65). Elizabeth treats Betsy's epistles as love letters; indeed, in spite of their contempt, they are love letters of a sort, expressing the primary importance of Elizabeth's existence for some other person. Nevertheless, the substitution of the self for an absent, confirming other is ultimately not a viable solution; if multiple personality is a protest against subjectivity denied, it also, to use Susan Bordo's terms, works "as if in collusion with the cultural conditions that produced" it ("Anorexia Nervosa" 105). For the multiple personality completely misrecognizes the self as an other—a distinction crucial to subjectivity—and thus negates the essential precondition of effective agency.

In Prince's classic text, the personalities of Miss Beauchamp manifest an inability to speak (that is, an inability to engage in the symbolic order) at just the moment when Prince is most insistent on the existence of separate persons in his patient. In a discussion devoted to proving the coexisting consciousness of Sally Beauchamp, Prince describes "contests of wills" between two personalities, which "Sally usually won," with the result that "Miss Beauchamp's will would be paralyzed.... [O]ften, after vain effort to speak, [Miss Beauchamp] has given it up, remarking, 'Well, it doesn't matter....' This was nothing more nor less than *aboulia*. Arising in the manner described, it was of importance in that it showed the existence of a secondary consciousness, concomitant or coexisting with the habitual consciousness. For two wills to contend against each other they must exist" (122–23). The intent of Prince's discussion, ironic though it may seem, is to assert Sally's existence as a separate will—to use Leys's words, to "guarantee the status of the subject as a subject" (195)—although what Leys never recognizes is that this is the vital precedent to then denying her subjectivity on the grounds that she is not real. Yet Prince's narrative actually gets ahead of him, offering the disturbing suggestion that, in spite of his insistence here to the contrary, the phenomenon of multiple personality does not magnify the potential for agency (through the coexistence of several "wills") but actually undermines agency—perhaps most drastically the agency of speech. Prince does not define "aboulia" for his lay readers, merely pointing out its "importance" in proving Sally's existence. Jackson, by contrast, makes a point of highlighting the negative, rather than the positive, nature of aboulia. She places its definition, provided by Dr. Wright, in a footnote that calls attention to itself through its separation from the rest of the text: "*aboulia;* a state which I can describe for the layman who reads and runs as an inhibition of will, preventing a desired action; Miss R. showed this largely in speech, almost as though she were *prevented* from uttering a syllable" (176). Far from being a magnification of will, as Prince seems to suggest through his depiction of a "contest of wills," aboulia— a commonly reported effect of multiple personality—is an inhibition of will, depriving the subject of any agency while (in such manifestations) presenting the illusion of a contest.

In *The Bird's Nest,* multiple personality may provide Elizabeth with a comforting sense of recognition by "others," but ultimately her inability to recognize herself as such threatens to destroy Elizabeth Richmond's subjectivity—a threat played out in terms of her ability to use language. Betsy, who has been carrying a dictionary with her during her New York escapade "in case she needed help in talking or writing or spelling" (220), suddenly discovers that "the big dictionary she had brought with her ... was lying just inside the suitcase, its binding torn off, its pages pulled out and crumpled, its millions of good, practical, helpful words hopelessly destroyed" (249). Already, Betsy's extreme tentativeness with regard to her use of words (she carries a dictionary with her) indicates that her place as a separate subject in the symbolic order is highly problematic. Yet another personality within the self provides no better access to language but rather symbolically destroys what access there is. (Bess has torn apart the dictionary.) Finally, in a scene that cannot fail to remind postmodern readers of the Lacanian "mirror stage," Betsy participates in what may be regarded as an exit from language, which is also an exit from subjectivity: "Suddenly, madly, she took up the book, and rising and turning, threw it as hard as she could at the mirror. 'There,' she said out loud, through the crash, 'that'll show you I'm still worse than you are, whoever you are!'" (249). The Lacanian mirror stage is marked by *"an identification"* (Lacan 735) that prefigures "the alienating function of the *I,* the aggressivity it releases in any relation to the other" (737). In other words, seeing her image in the mirror begins the process by which the subject will understand herself as separate (alienated) from all others. But Betsy's aggressivity toward an other is directed toward *her own* image in the mirror—an image with which she utterly fails to identify.

Once again, this scene has its corollary in Prince's narrative, which receives an astute commentary from Leys: "The person with whom I identify is immediately converted into my rival who is seen to occupy my place.... [T]he spectacular as such is linked to the assertion of difference, of essential otherness, indeed of *violent rivalry* with that other who is, as the scene makes clear, a version of the same" (180). But while the image in the mirror is certainly "a version of the same," what is crucial in both Prince's account and Jackson's re-vision is that the personality who looks in the mirror acts as though this identity did not exist. When Betsy is engaged in "violent rivalry" with an other who occupies her place in the mirror, she in no way understands the rival as an aspect of herself. We need no more vivid example of the fundamental lack of identification among Elizabeth Richmond's separate personalities than Bess's attempt to choke Betsy (262), an indication that the disorder has begun to function in collusion with psychiatric violence. Furthermore, in the process of so totally misrecognizing herself in the mirror scene, Betsy retaliates with renewed destruction of the dictionary (249), even though it provides her key to the use of language. Betsy might block Elizabeth from speech, but Bess blocks Betsy from speech, and Bess herself finds that a note written by Beth "turned into meaningless markings when she brought it close enough to read" (261). Multiple personality, Jackson's story suggests, signals the disintegration of the speaking subject.

The problematic nature of multiple personality in terms of agency is also suggested by the trope of naming in *The Bird's Nest*. As we have seen, the failure of others to recognize Elizabeth's subjectivity at the opening of the novel is indicated by her namelessness. Presumably the determined claiming of distinct names by the various personalities might then indicate a renewed "hold on individuality and identity" (152). But naming is as much an attempt to control another as it is a recognition of that other. Dr. Wright suppresses the radical instability suggested by Elizabeth Richmond's multiple personalities by shoring up each personality into a separate feminine type with her own name. His original attempt to categorize the personalities through a numerical system is resisted, as previously noted, by Betsy, who offers her own system of categorization, based on a nursery rhyme: "Elizabeth, Lizzy, Betsy and Bess/All went together to see a bird's nest;/They found a nest with five eggs in it;/They each took one and left four in it" (Friedman 95).[4] The rhyme, however, suggests not how names keep things separate, but how names provide the linguistic illusion of discrete, clearly defined categories that always threaten to break down. For not only do all the names refer to the same person, but also all the names are really the same name.

Betsy, seeming to sense the power of naming, attempts to turn the tables on the doctor in her typical resistant manner. Just as he manifests his authority by naming the personalities in order to exert control over them, so Betsy struggles against his names (resisting his numerical system by suggesting, as alternatives, what Wright derisively refers to as the names of "a princess in a fairy romance") and attempts to reclaim authorship through naming. Thus she tags labels on the doctor—"question-asker" (207), "well-wisher" (208), "eye-closer" (209)—which strung together, construct their own mini-narrative about him. Her most prominent exercise in naming as narrative control, however, is her dubbing of Dr. Wright as "Doctor Wrong." The name becomes part an ongoing battle of wills with the doctor. In a highly comical scene Betsy insists that he call himself by the name she has given him:

> "Then tell me who you are," said Betsy. "I am Doctor Wright."
> "Indeed you are not," said Betsy, laughing.
> I took a deep breath. "I am Doctor Wrong," I said. "Who?"
> "Doctor Wrong," I said.
> "Who?" I could hear her laughing.
> *Doctor Wrong*" [213].

By forcing the doctor to claim as his own the name that *she* has given *him,* Betsy effectively reverses their positions (if only momentarily), "authorizing" herself, as it were, in a counternarrative to his own Jekyll-and-Hyde constructions of her as a fiend, and forcing him to acknowledge his moral culpability (he is "wrong") in his efforts to control her. (As usual, this point is entirely missed by Wright.)

But Betsy's own exercises in naming are not a straightforward self-authorizing; they also can be viewed as a too easy adoption of Wright's strategy of naming in an effort to control the named. Assuming the power of naming, Betsy both echoes Wright's vision of a dichotomous moral universe (Wright/Wrong) and, more generally, uses naming as an attempt to fix and stabilize her own world—an attempt that can hardly be seen as different in kind from Wright's efforts to label each personality with a feminine cliché. Thus, at just the moment when Betsy's narrative seems to be challenging Wright's, it is also an imitation of his authorizing strategies. (Leys's discussion points toward just such a vexed relation between imitation and autonomy for Betsy's prototype, the "Sally" of Prince's case.)

Notably, Wright's strategies of naming are not effective means of agency for his patient. Betsy chants her name repeatedly during her escape to New York, as though the name will secure her identity: "'I am Betsy Richmond,' she said over and over quietly to herself. 'I was even born in New York. And my mother's name is Elizabeth Richmond, Elizabeth Jones before she was married.... My name is Betsy Richmond, and I was born in New York. My mother loves me more than anything. My mother's name is Elizabeth Richmond, and my name is Betsy and my mother always called me Betsy and I was named after my mother. Betsy Richmond,' she whispered softly into the unhearing movement of the bus, 'Betsy Richmond'" (226). Betsy's chant of names, like Sally's "autobiography," is a claim to subjectivity; her "me" grants her the illusion of a stable sense of self, and this is essential during her first solo journey. But she is, simultaneously, suppressing what apparently are some very troubling aspects of her narrative; like Wright-as-author, Betsy imposes a rigid narrative form (the formulaic chant) on her materials in an effort to control them. Betsy's surprise that "two people who ... had the same name liked different things" (228), or her bewilderment at the multitude of listings for "RICHMOND, ELIZABETH" in the phone book (254), betrays a fragile sense of self preserved only by a naive faith in a one-to-one correspondence between signifier and signified (all "Elizabeths" will refer the same person) which is immediately confused by the customary uses of some names as forms of others: are Elizabeth and Betsy the same name, or different ones? Although she disclaims the name Elizabeth Richmond when it refers to the first of the four personalities—"I *hate* her name" (202)—she notes with pleasure elsewhere the similarity of the two names: "My mother's name is Elizabeth Richmond, and my name is Betsy and my mother always called me Betsy and I was named after my mother" (226).

Betsy discovers that names will not do what she wants them to; they continually slide from her control and suggest not the stability but the fluidity of her own identity: "If I had a husband then my mother could marry him and we could all hide together and be happy. My name is Betsy Richmond. My mother's name is Elizabeth Richmond, Elizabeth Jones before I was married. Call me Lisbeth like you do my mother, because Betsy is my darling Robin" (236). The tentative difference provided by the names Betsy and Elizabeth breaks down, and along with it Betsy's sense of her existence as a separate subject; the personal pronouns "I" and "my" now become loosed from exclusive reference to Betsy, the speaker; and float variously between herself and her mother. With her precarious identity thus destabilized, Betsy now views the whole world, or at least everyone she meets in New York, as extensions of herself, and the dramatic triangle involving Robin, her mother, and Betsy is replayed again and again in her mind as she interacts with people on the street.

To be a speaking subject requires a linguistic acceptance of one's own difference from others: "When the child learns to say 'I am' and to distinguish this from 'you are' or 'he is,' this is equivalent to admitting that it has taken up its allotted place in the Symbolic Order and given up the claim to imaginary identity with all other possible positions. The speaking subject that says 'I am' is in fact saying 'I am he (she) who has

lost something'—and the loss suffered is the loss of the imaginary identity with the mother and with the world" (Moi, 99). Having lost her
mother, Betsy seems to enact something like a regression to the presymbolic (i.e., imaginary) period in which she identified with her mother and
with the world. And lest we suppose that this particular conception of
fluid and shifting identity is in fact a means of resisting rigid gender
boundaries and thus subversive, we might turn again to Moi. Using
Lacan to argue against theories that posit a presymbolic realm of merged
identities as a subversive site, Moi forcefully suggests that no truly subversive position can be reached "through a straightforward *rejection* of
the symbolic order, since such a total failure to enter into human relations would, in Lacanian terms, make us psychotic.... There is no *other
space* from which we can speak: if we are able to speak at all it will have
to be within the framework of symbolic language" (170). In losing her
sense of separate subjectivity, Betsy loses her linguistic ability, as suggested by her pronoun confusions. Without the power to speak, she can
have no true agency; Betsy's New York escapade is portrayed not as a
subversive act but as a ludicrous comedy of misidentification. Multiple
personality is simply the same problem in a somewhat different form:
what should be an "I" is instead rendered as "she," or occasionally as
"we." Betsy's inability to identify herself results in an impasse of agency:
there are a multitude of actions that she cannot claim as her own (and
which thus paralyze her with fear).

In contrast, the reintegrated Elizabeth Richmond at the novel's conclusion relishes her awareness of agency: "She looked down at her
clothes, and remembered with an odd kind of tenderness that her own
hands had torn this blouse when she was angry in New York, and ironed
this skirt in a deep rush of love toward herself; she had scratched her
own face" (364). No longer relying on an illusory other to grant recognition of her subjectivity, Elizabeth now takes joy in recollecting the simplest acts, not because the acts in themselves are pleasant—some, indeed,
have been willful strikes at the self—but because they are evidences of
agency, of her own ability to act in anger or love or violence. Her claim
to agency is accompanied by a firm occupation of the "I." When Aunt
Morgen asks, "Who put the mud in the refrigerator?" she can respond,
"1 did" (360). When she cuts her hair without "permission" (362), a
symbolic act of independence from the doctor and the aunt who have
attempted to mold her in their image (an act that is therefore a marker
of a break from mimesis), she quite deliberately rejects the stylist's choice
of pronouns: "Well, how do we like ourselves *now?*"—for the first-person singular: "So, that's what I'm going to look like" (362). The moment
of reintegration is a moment full of potential: "She came out of the doctor's office laughing, feeling her head cool and aware for the first time of

this day as separate from all other days; she walked lingeringly toward the corner where she would catch her bus, thinking, I am all alone and I have no name; I have cut my hair, I'm the gingerbread man, and wanting to prolong this time of perfect freedom" (365).[5] Elizabeth, once again, has "no name"; but in the light of the doctor's constraining moral labels, and even of Betsy's attempts to fix identity through names, this condition can be seen as freeing. We must remember that Dr. Wright's compulsion to fasten a name on each personality has gone hand in hand with his desire to tag each one with a simple descriptive phrase in an attempt to control the threatening multiplicity that was Elizabeth Richmond.

Yet Elizabeth Richmond's reintegration need not stand for a valorizing of the integrated humanist subject, any more than her self-division need be read as a valorizing of madness. The text offers the possibility of a postmodern subject that can be *distinguished* from the mad subject. It is impossible to look at the Elizabeth Richmond of the novel's conclusion without remembering the cleavages in the self that once yawned into chasms. Furthermore, Jackson has provided enough other examples of the divided self (the doctor's frequent and unexplained mysterious illnesses; the contradictions and confusion within a single personality, Betsy) to warn readers against simply viewing the "final product" as a comforting model of wholeness in which all contradiction has been reconciled. Even the doctor's and Aunt Morgen's sinister attempts to rename the now nameless Elizabeth "Morgen Victoria" or "Victoria Morgen" after themselves (380)—thus suggesting their continued, authorizing efforts to mold her in their own images—are unintentionally ironic. Morgen and Wright have absolutely opposed tastes, as Wright's vigorous criticism of Morgen's house and her unfeminine person indicates, and the yoking of their names together thus constitutes a sort of oxymoron, implying contradiction and potential cleavage within itself.

But named Elizabeth must be. Naming is, after all, a linguistic act, an engagement within the symbolic order; it also suggests the ultimately limited nature of our subjectivity. While theories of the subversive potential of madness subscribe to what Susan Bordo calls "a postmodern ideal of narrative 'heteroglossia' [which] ... celebrate[s] a 'feminine' ability to identify with and enter into the perspectives of others, ... [that ideal] obscures the located, limited, inescapably partial, and *always* personally invested nature of human 'story making.'" Against what she calls the "dream of being *everywhere*," Bordo offers "the body [as] a metaphor for our locatedness in space and time" (Bordo, "Feminism" 143–45). But the *name* may serve just as well as such a metaphor. Jackson's early vision of a postmodern subject, in contrast to the ideal of everywhereness, fully recognizes partiality and limitation. Elizabeth's moment of complete freedom in namelessness must ultimately be replaced with the moment at which, personally invested (as Bordo would say) in her own story-making, she must name herself (308). Only by being a subject within the symbolic order can Elizabeth wield any agency whatsoever; Jackson's vision suggests that to locate subversive potential in the postmodern subject, we must separate that subject from figurings of it as "mad."

Furthermore, we will not find the subversive potential of the postmodern subject simply in its multiplicity. Terry Eagleton flatly rejects the notion that "the dismantling of the unified subject [is] a revolutionary gesture in itself; ... bourgeois individualism thrives on such a fetish" (191). If adjectives such as "multiple" and "shifting" characterize certain practices having to do with the continual making and remaking of the self, then they are perfectly in keeping with a consumer society that relies on such self-redefinition (through cars, clothes, cosmetics, and so on). There is nothing subversive in the multiplicity of feminine roles (cook, chauffeur, maid) suggested in the Bell Telephone advertisement described at the beginning of this chapter. It is the capacity of multiple "positions" to coexist simultaneously in a way precluded (and therefore repeatedly elided or obscured) by dominant ideology that offers a theoretical site for the disruption of dominant discourses. The postmodern subject challenges such discourses by having (to use Jackson's words) "too much detail" (372) for any one discourse adequately to fix and contain; or, to recall Ruth Leys's discussion of Jacqueline Rose, the subject "always exceed[s] the rigid ... positions" (even if these are also multiple or changing positions) into which a given discourse would insert it (Leys 167). And the potentially transformative power of the postmodern subject lies in the resulting possibility of creating counternarratives that will contest the dominant discourse in which she finds herself. Sally's autobiography, the force of which is never quite suppressed by Prince's efforts to reappropriate it; Elizabeth's naming of herself, which can never equal her doctor's and aunt's attempts to name her; Chris Costner Sizemore's desire to correct the record of her story: all are examples of counternarratives that resist at the micropolitical level the dominant discourses of gender and the violence engendered by them.[6]

## Notes

1. Despite the fact that popular representations of the disorder in the 1950s, as well as the most prominent of those that would follow (the famous "Sybil" case), invariably depicted the divided self as a woman, and that the diagnosis has consistently been handed out to women far more frequently than to men, the landmark feminist works reviewing the intersections of madness and gender (see works by Chesler, Showaler, and Ussher) have failed so much as to mention multiple personality. They

have thus unintentionally demonstrated a persistent reliance on categories of discussion defined by men. Arguably the two most prominent male figures in the historical development of discourse on madness—Freud and R.D. Laing—focused on hysteria and schizophrenia, respectively; these are, in turn, the forms of "madness" that are most often attended to in revisionist feminist analyses.

2. See Friedan 174 for a discussion of how the predominant feminine image for returning veterans was the (asexual) mother, Halberstram 280 for a discussion of the infuriated public reaction to *Kinsey's Sexual Behaviour in the Human Female.*

3. It is also, of course, quite possibly a sign of literal violence. As Kathleen Wilkes points out, "a repressed, puritanical childhood, often including neglect and physical abuse, seems a pattern common to many cases of multiple personality" (332 n. 2). It seems to me, however, that the "neglect" to which Wilkes points as a cause might be as crucial as physical abuse to an understanding of the counternarrative offered by the symptoms of multiple personality.

4. In Jackson's version of the rhyme, the second name, Lizzy, becomes Beth.

5. Judy Oppenheimer argues, in contrast, that "the reintegration into 'sanity' somehow feels like a loss—of potential, of possibility of self," whereas "the madness itself is a far from miserable state; ... [Elizabeth experiences] a heady rush of delight, exultation, a pure sense of power in its sway" (164). Thus, Oppenheimer shares in the valorization of madness as resistance so common to contemporary feminist criticism.

6. I paraphrase de Lauretis (see 9, 33).

## Works Cited

Bordo, Susan. "Anorexia Nervosa: Psychopathology as the Crystallization of Culture." In *Feminism and Foucault: Reflections on Resistance,* ed. Irene Diamond and Lee Quinby. Boston: Northeastern University Press, 1988.

Chesler, Phyllis. *Women and Madness.* Garden City, N.Y.: Doubleday, 1972.

de Lauretis, Teresa. *Technologies of Gender.* Bloomington: Indiana University Press, 1987.

Dunning, William V. "Post-Modernism and the Construct of the Divisible Self." *British Journal of Aesthethics* 33.2 (April 1993): 132–141.

Eagleton, Terry. Literary Theory: An Introduction. Minneapolis: University of Minnesota Press, 1983.

Friedan, Betty. *The Feminine Mystique.* New York: Dell, 1963.

Glass, James M. *Shattered Selves: Multiple Personalities in a Postmodern World.* Ithaca: Cornell University Press, 1993.

Halberstram, David. *The Fifties.* New York: Villard Books, 1993.

Hartsock, Nancy. "Foucault on Power: A Theory for Women?" In *Feminism/Postmodernism.* Ed. Linda J. Nicholson. New York: Routledge, 1990.

Laing, R.D. *The Divided Self* (1959). Baltimore: Penguin Books, 1973.

Leys, Ruth. "The Real Miss Beauchamp: Gender and the Subject of Imitation." In *Feminists Theorize the Political,* Eds. Judith Butler and Joan W. Scott. New York: Routledge, 1992.

Matthews, Glenna. *"Just a Housewife": The Rise and Fall of Domesticity in America.* New York: Oxford University Press, 1987.

Moi, Toril. *Sexual/Textual Politics: Feminist Literary Theory.* New York: Routledge, 1985.

Oppenheimer, Judy. *Private Demons: The Life of Shirley Jackson.* New York: G.P. Putnam's Sons, 1988.

Prince, Morton. *The Dissociation of a Personality* (1905). New York: Johnson Reprint Corporation, 1968.

Showalter, Elaine. *The Female Malady: Women, Madness and English Culture, 1830–1980.* New York: Penguin, 1985.

Sizemore, Chris Costner, and Elen Sain Pittillo. *I'm Eve*. Garden City, N.Y.: Dou-
    bleday, 1977.
Taylor, W.S., and Mabel F. Martin. "Multiple Personality." *Journal of Abnormal and
    Social Psychology* 39 (1944): 281–300.
Thigpen, Corbett H., and Hervey M. Cleckey. *Three Faces of Eve*. New York: Popu-
    lar Library, 1957.
Ussher, Jane. *Women's Madness: Misogyny or Mental Illness?* Amherst: University of
    Massachusetts Press, 1992.
Wilkes, Kathleen. "Multiple Personality and Personal Identity." *British Journal for the
    Philosophy of Science* 32.4 (December 1981): 331–48.

# 4

# New World Miniatures: Shirley Jackson's *The Sundial* and Postwar American Society

## RICH PASCAL

*[The American home] must be a home built and loved upon new world, and not the old world, ideas and principles.*
—A.J. Downing, *The Architecture of Country Houses* (1850)

"We are in a pocket of time," claims a character in Shirley Jackson's 1958 novel *The Sundial*, "a tiny segment of time suddenly pinpointed by a celestial eye" (45). It is a preposterously oracular utterance delivered by a dithery and slightly deranged figure, yet it hints at an aspect of Jackson's undervalued text that has hitherto escaped the notice of even those few commentators who have directed their attention towards it.[1] *The Sundial*, which focuses upon a handful of people who wait together at a country estate in expectation of a prophesied new world to be born from the destruction of the old, aspires to *be* that celestial eye, pinpointing sociocultural features of its own postwar "pocket of time," calling attention to their origins in the nineteenth and early twentieth centuries, and locating them within the even older historical context of one of America's foundation myths. Like most of Jackson's fictions, it is a narrative that adheres tenuously to basic conventions of naturalistic realism, deploying contrariwise just enough traces of uncanniness to caution against

*This essay originally appeared in* Journal of American and Comparative Cultures *233 (fall 2000): 99–111 and is reproduced by permission of Blackwell Publishing Ltd.*

complete skepticism about the intrusion of the paranormal into the domain of the ordinary. Unlike most, however, it openly essays to comment upon contemporary social issues and delusions and to pronounce upon their implications for the nation.

In this sense the novel is, to borrow Sacvan Bercovitch's famous phrase, Shirley Jackson's American jeremiad, and in one obvious way, it announces itself as such: the "celestial eye" is also a stentorian voice from the heavens that speaks its displeasure with what it has descried.[2] The narrative voice, though generally more satirically speculative than authoritative, can be similarly condemnatory and portentous with regard to contemporary social arrangements. The text's critique, however, is established primarily through its presentation of specific features of American social history in the postwar period: (1) the accelerated relocation of the middle-class segments of the population from urban centers to smaller, neotraditional communities; (2) anxieties about challenges to the dominant patriarchal ideologies of domesticity and gender; (3) the disruptive effects of self-seeking individualism within the nuclear family; and most broadly; (4) the imminent prospect of a society fissured by the triumph of childish solipsism as a national ideal. As is consonant with one of the predominant social obsessions of the initial phase of the postnuclear era, the prospect of widespread annihilation, possibly to be followed by utopian renewal, precipitates all of the action in *The Sundial* and dominates the minds of the characters. Yet even though its shadow is all but palpable throughout, the bomb is never mentioned, a decisive indication that atomic anxiety is not the fundamental source of the apocalyptic mentality that pervades the characters' thoughts. That obsession is traced, rather, to two venerable American traditions that predate the postwar period: the socially sanctioned impulse to retreat to "American miniatures," or small, exclusive enclaves of communal, familial, and individual refuge from the claims of the larger social universe; and the nation's perennial fascination with the promise of some vague but fervently dreamt of communal fulfillment implicit in its originating image of itself as a New World. The former, as the text in various ways implies, began to gain hold in the nineteenth century and has accelerated in the 1950s; and the latter, it suggests, is a construct that derives from Elizabethan imperial aspirations that supplanted a still older, and less holistic, European notion of "world." Miniaturist projects are linked with (even as they are dissociated from) utopian New World imaginings in that they represent, ostensibly, attainable scaled down versions of what was originally a dream of global magnitude and comprehensiveness. And their failure in the postwar era to deliver even the diminished alternative site of worldly fulfillment that they had come to signify, tantalizingly, has issued into a widespread receptivity to apocalyptic fantasies of a world cleansed by horrible destruction into originative, precultural freshness.

## Suburbanization and the American Miniature

Set in a small town that is figured as an anachronistic relic of a largely bygone America, and concerned with the struggles of a rich family and its hangers-on over an inheritance of redoubtable proportions, *The Sundial* must have seemed far removed from the lives and concerns of the postwar middle-class readers who presumably composed its intended and actual audiences. In these and some other respects its trappings brazenly replicate those of the early English Gothic tradition as exemplified by the novels of Walpole, Reeve, and Radcliffe. In constructing feudal pasts cleansed of any threat of social disorder, those fictions signaled a desire to retreat into a tidily controllable new *old* world—modern ideological assumptions comfortingly in hand. Their antique facades were, in this sense, as pointedly ungenuine as Walpole's own lovingly fabricated miniature "castle" in the suburbs, Strawberry Hill. Jackson's narrative ransacks these older texts in order to stage an updated version of the discursive camouflage act that defined gothicism as a modern mode from the very outset. Its fancifully incorporated borrowings are less a summons to imaginative escapism—although they certainly inveigle the reader with that option—than indicators of the modern middle-class impulse to retreat to communities and domestic sites that simulate a past expunged of uncertainty.

More specifically, they function as subtle reminders of the early correlation between the development of the gothic mode and the emergence of the suburban movement in that proto–America, England. In this regard, of course, it is particularly significant that the mansion on the estate in *The Sundial* is likened to Walpole's actual castle—which was, of course, his actual *replicated* castle—rather than to his more famous fictional one, *Otranto* (188–89). The effect of this and other gothic analogs in the novel is to bring to the foreground, by way of exaggeration and parody, a similar though historically more recent and local obsession with fictitious pastness. For the text construes as a native near equivalent to the romanticized feudalism of English gothic fiction the idealized image of the American small town, in which class relations are entirely static and the possession of house and land constitutes an ineluctably secure hedge against social and financial disruption. Americans, as is well known, like to imagine themselves as constituting a large and mighty nation. Yet conversely, many also like to imagine the site of the "true" America as being rural and parochial. But though the image of the small country town basking in somnolent pastoral stability is the

basic model for the nationally venerated small social unit, the social actuality in modern times has been somewhat different. For more than a century, though most spectacularly after the Second World War, the major
demographic shift in the United States has been the migration from the
cities to outlying semirural residential areas. The phenomenon is of
course widely referred to as "suburbanization," a term which, in stressing such communities' subordinate relationship with cities, has tended
to obscure one of its most fundamental aspects. Just as Strawberry Hill
was a make-believe medieval estate, modern suburbs are make-believe
small towns of a bygone era—even when, as has often been the case, the
"suburb" is an old town that has in effect been subsumed within the
commuting range of a relatively nearby urban unit.

In a percipient study of the suburban movement published in the
same year that the *The Sundial* appeared, Robert C. Wood argued that
the middle-class flight to both planned suburbs and pre-existing towns
had been a retreat to more or less fabricated versions of a mythic small
community he astutely termed "the American miniature" (53). Wood
employed that term because he wished it to encapsulate the small town
paradigm that underlies and haunts diverse varieties of suburban community, and to suggest as well that the fundamental reason for its power
over the national imagination is that it is taken to signify the essence of
the American social structure. As we'll see, when applied to Jackson's
novel it can be refined so as to comprehend progressively even smaller
communities—the home, the family, and ultimately that polity of one,
the self. Each of these, the text suggests, is also a miniature world, and
frustrations encountered in one such sphere may inspire emigration to
another that is smaller and more controllable. But the most important
point to take into account initially in thinking about *The Sundial* in this
context is that the town that is sketched lightly therein does not represent in any simple sense the surviving remnant of an older American way
of life that it is taken to be, by its inhabitants as well as by visitors. It is
situated only nine miles away from the nearest city, a negligible distance
in the automotive age. And while the time frame for the narrative is the
contemporary period, the text compels awareness that the process of
"suburbanizing" the area had been initiated well before the story's opening by the very family that sought in it the enclave of pastoral timeless-
ness signified by the timepiece of preindustrial devising that gives the
novel its title. The estate that seems so entrenched within the traditional
configuration of the old-fashioned town was built in the relatively recent
past by an exurbanite migrant, referred to throughout the text as "the
first Mr. Halloran." This figure, the deceased father of two of the adult
characters inhabiting the estate in the 1950s, brought his family to the
town early in the century, during the period in which, according to social

historians, the first significant wave of middle-class migrations to suburban areas occurred.[3]

Mr. Halloran was apparently so rich that his construction of an elaborate private estate in rural surroundings might seem to bear little resemblance to the middle-class suburban flights of the book's time, rather establishing him as an imitator of nineteenth century American plutocrats like Cornelius Vanderbilt, with his famously gaudy mansion on the pastoral cliffs of the Hudson. But the point is that the conspicuous consumption of the Vanderbilts and their ilk actually operated as a source of inspiration for much of the rest of the populace. As Susman and Griffin have noted, the ideal of suburban life that began to take hold in America late in the last century, initially "a fantasy fulfilled only for the wealthy ... continued to be a dream, however, for less well-to-do Americans" (21). Thus a Mr. Halloran, once his fortune had been secured, would have assumed the status of a culture hero who had enacted on a particularly grand scale the exurbanizing project that in more modest forms had become by the 1950s an available alternative even for those of fairly ordinary means. It is and has always been inherently a dream of individual materialistic achievement, but of worldly success in the service of social idealism—of funding fully, that is, a private domain of the self that is also patriotic display.

It follows then that what he attempted in the building of the mansion is only partially indicated by his choice of an old fashioned town for its setting; it was also, and perhaps primarily, the estate itself that was to be his American miniature. He was, we are told,

> a man who, in the astonishment of finding himself suddenly extremely wealthy, could think of nothing better to do with his money than set up his own world. His belief about the house ... was that it should contain everything. The other world, the one the Hallorans were leaving behind, was to be plundered ruthlessly for objects of beauty to go in and around Mr. Halloran's house; infinite were the delights to be prepared for its inhabitants [11].

The retreat from the city to the suburbanized town thus involved yet a further withdrawal, into a domestic site immured against an outside world regarded as deflatingly or threateningly other. Mr. Halloran was not an immigrant seeking affiliation within the pre-established community, but a colonizer, carving out a personal empire within a space that has been transformed, through the power of brute wealth, into virgin land. And this, the novel implies, has been modern America's twist on the traditional valorization of the small community: to a large degree, relocation to a suburban site has signified disaffiliation, virtual secession, from larger social units, including even the local community itself which has become, in the words of Kenneth T. Jackson, "a mass of small, private islands"

(280). The initial stage of the middle-class withdrawal into domestic spaces that are discrete to the point of isolation dates back to the latter half of the nineteenth century. It was during that period, Jackson also notes, that the home "came to represent the individual himself," and "the new ideal was no longer to be part of a close community, but to have a self-contained unit, a private wonderland walled off from the rest of the world" (52, 58). That this ideal was intrinsically a social one—not only, that is, in the obvious sense that even superficially "personal" ideals must to some degree be socially instilled, but in that it was regarded as a communally salutary and even patriotic aspiration—is a distinctive irony of American social history. As Dolores Hayden has commented, "the dream house is a uniquely American form because for the first time in history, a civilization has created a utopian ideal based on the house rather than the city or the nation" (18).

For Mr. Halloran's descendants and their cohabitants, the estate he built in his own image continues to wall out much of the world he wished to abandon. To none, however, is it an entirely personal realm, as is evident from the tendency of several to fashion for themselves pretend spaces, personal miniatures, in which solipsistic control is absolute. Mrs. Halloran, for example, the founder's daughter-in-law and successor as tyrannical ruler of the estate (with implications that we will examine shortly), is inclined to fantasize about "a little, small house" of her own, deep in the woods:

> I will sit in the one chair or I will lie on the soft rug by the fire, and no one will talk to me, and no one will hear me; there will be only one of everything—one cup, one plate, one spoon, one knife. Deep in the forest I am living in my little house and no one can ever find me [113].

The dominant features here are singularity, rusticity, and diminutiveness: it is another, more extreme version of a miniature world, particularly revealing in that it is the fantasy of someone who has attained control over a far grander actual home than the one she loves to imagine. Another character, Aunt Fanny, has actually constructed within the larger house her ideal miniature site, a carefully restored semblance of the apartment in which she passed her childhood. This area she refers to as her "doll house," a formulation that encompasses, both metaphorically and metonymically, all of the miniature worlds under scrutiny in the novel.

Those connections are established most emphatically by the prominence accorded an actual dollhouse possessed by the ten-year-old granddaughter of Mrs. Halloran and great-niece of Aunt Fanny. Fancy, who has been lavishly indulged by well off relations, regards her exquisitely equipped dollhouse as a toy version of the Halloran household to which she is the heiress apparent. "When my grandmother dies," she says, "I am going to smash my doll house. I won't need it any more" (22), suggesting less that the things of childhood will be discarded in pursuit of an adult relationship to the world than that the "real" house will be a scaled-up version of the toy, the fantasy model. Only the toy is literally "miniature," but the estate is analogously a fabrication of the larger "world left behind," rendered safely insular and amenable to the unrestricted play of the proprietary ego. The defining aspect of the miniaturist project, in other words, is not diminutiveness as such, but totalizing sham of the kind that Walpole pioneered with the home at Strawberry Hill to which he once referred as his "toy castle."[4] And the simulation, the toy-like aspect, must be openly evident to at least some degree, for it is the signal that nothing excessive, nothing disturbing to fantasy, will be permitted.

## The Challenge to Patriarchy

On the basis of what has been argued thus far, it would appear that the novel envisions a postwar social world that is essentially an expanded version of the middle-class suburban culture that began to emerge in the previous century. This is certainly the impression conveyed by its presentation of the ethos informing the contemporary miniaturist project in the respects hitherto considered. There is, however, one seeming discontinuity between the social climate of the period in which the first Mr. Halloran lived and that experienced by his midcentury heirs: gender relations are no longer securely in alignment with a patriarchal model. Matriarchy is now threatening to subvert or even invert the traditional (im)balance of power between the sexes, with implications for familial and social structures that are profoundly disquieting—so much so that it is because of the challenge to patriarchy that apocalypse comes to seem imminent, and perhaps even desirable.

To understand why this is imagined to be so, it is necessary to observe first of all that the impression of discontinuity is deceptive in that, as the text indicates, patriarchal ideology had for a long time contained within itself the basis for that challenge. Conventionally, since the early nineteenth century, the private domestic sphere ("home") and the public arena of production and exchange ("world") had been regarded as gendered spaces, female and male respectively (Cott 64–74). By the first Mr. Halloran's era, however, the home was "woman's sphere" only in a formal sense. The estate was from its inception his brain child and ego-projection; his wife, who had no say in the decision to relocate from their urban home, lived in it for only three months and then sickened and died. The point is that the female domain, to which had been ascribed at least a modicum of social power in the first half of the nineteenth century, was later separated and distinguished from the larger world only to be regarded as an inseparable and undistinguished aspect of the male ego. The first Mrs. Halloran, then, was only another of the objects of beauty plundered from the world left behind. That she contracted a fatal affliction in a dwelling far warmer than the family's "bleak and uncomfortable" (175) city apartment signifies clearly that her illness was a form of the malaise suffered by many affluent married women during the era that was the focus of Charlotte Perkins Gilman's famous story "The Yellow Wallpaper" (1892).

By midcentury the estate has become a living space dominated by the presence of females, approximating what "home" in the nineteenth century and "suburbia" in the mid-twentieth were often held to be.[5] The important difference, however, is that in the contemporary era the women really are threatening preeminence, the still dominant patriarchal social norm notwithstanding. It is at the story's opening that the inversion of the traditionally gendered power structure has come to pass decisively. The "second" Mrs. Halloran, wife of the original Mr. Halloran's son, has assumed control of the estate because her son Lionel, the rightful heir, has recently died in shady circumstances in which she herself may well have literally had a hand—he either fell or was pushed down a flight of stairs. Her husband, the owner, is still alive, but only feebly and ineffectually, and the only other male resident at the estate is her kept lover, Essex. The rest, who include, in addition to Aunt Fanny, the widow of the deceased Lionel, her ten-year-old daughter Fancy, and Fancy's tutor, Miss Ogilvie, are all female. As the story progresses, newcomers, mostly women, arrive to stay indefinitely, making the preponderance of females even more pronounced. The one male addition is a fortune hunter who has been picked up by Aunt Fanny to serve as the slightly ridiculous object of her school girlish romantic fantasies. (Strikingly, the only two active men in the household are regarded as commodities purchased for the delight of female inhabitants.)

The accession of the imperious daughter-in-law to full command indicates most decisively that a female-oriented regime has been installed, and, as the ruler of the estate is apparently the most powerful figure in the adjacent town, it is a development that signals at least the possibility of a radical transformation of the gender hierarchy in American communal life more generally. But although the new order is clearly gynecocracy of a sort, it is no less a tyranny than was the system it has supplanted. The second Mrs. Halloran's given name, "Orianna," indicates that she is constructed as a monarch-mother, a matriarch, as it incorporates the name of the wife of the founder, Anna, and it was also one of the literary sobriquets of Queen Elizabeth I.[6] Correspondingly, Mrs. Halloran's primary desire is to rule the household, not to share power with its denizens, much less love and serve them as a conventional mother theoretically would. The inhabitants are considered by her to be quite dispensable, untidy presences within her commandingly personal premises. On the day of Lionel's funeral she announces to the others that the recent "change"—her own son's sudden death, that is!—"has been both refreshing and agreeable," and has convinced her of the necessity of a "housecleaning," by which innocuous-sounding term borrowed from the reassuring rhetoric of domesticity she means the summary dismissal of most of them (17).

The figure of Mrs. Halloran therefore does not signal a brave new world of nurturing femaleness or gender equality, but rather conjures up that most fearsome specter of postwar social mythology, the domineering mother. The period is now remembered one in which most American women were severely oppressed in many ways. They were, of course, but what is sometimes factored out of our latter day impression is that many contemporary commentaries saw the society as being deeply threatened by insidious maternal power. In *Modern Woman: The Lost Sex*, a particularly influential 1947 work by two psychiatrists, it was soberly alleged that via motherhood, "women are the principal transmitting media of the disordered emotions that today are so widely spread throughout the world and are reflected in the statistics of social disorder." (This certainly wasn't true of all mothers, the "study" went on to stress—only "40 to 50 percent" of them!) And "just what have these women done to their sons? They have stripped them of their male powers—that is, they have castrated them" (Lundberg and Farnham 23, 305, 319). Philip Wylie's *Generation of Vipers*, another pervasive influence in the postwar period, asserted that "when the mothers built up their pyramid of perquisite and required reverence in order to get at the checkbook ... they donned the breeches of Uncle Sam," in the course of a tantrum-like jeremiad that climaxes in a histrionic unveiling: "I give you mom. I give you the destroying mother" (200, 203). *The Sundial*, wryly responsive to the discursive climate of its era, gave it a mom who has allegedly destroyed her own son in order to get at his checkbook and don his breeches. The intent is clearly to satirize the era's paranoia over what Wylie mirthlessly dubbed "Momism." Yet traces of that widespread anxiety of the 1950s are discernible in the narrative; Mrs. Halloran and what she represents, it is stressed, will not be easy to live with.[7]

In any case, hers is a matriarchy that has not yet sealed its position securely. The degree to which her newly established dominance constitutes a turbulent incursion upon the patriarchal social order is signaled by the events leading up to Aunt Fanny's initial premonition of an apocalyptic transformation in the near future. On the morning following Lionel Halloran's funeral, when she goes for a walk with Fancy in the garden, the grounds of the estate and everything upon them still reflect in her mind the domineering personality of her father, the first Mr. Halloran. Images of containment, orderliness, and control abound, pompously signifying the enslavement of all that is spontaneous, mysterious, or natural. The water that runs through fountains and pools, for example, though it clothes in sensuous transparency the curvaceous body of a marble nymph, eventually becomes "twisted and trapped and forced down, pushed underground to run secretly" (30). The grounds feature a number of such pieces of ersatz classical statuary—fauns, nymphs, and satyrs that hint at disturbing, socially disapproved modes of sexuality but which, frozen in marble and relegated to a discourse of the ornamental, celebrate bourgeois money's triumph over desire's powerful mischief. In the "present" of the narrative, however, it seems that Mr. Halloran's posthumous imposition of order may be coming undone. The hedges have grown "almost wild," darkening the pathways, and Aunt Fanny remarks that her father would not have tolerated such disrepair (24). Eventually she loses her way and experiences a state of delirium in which surroundings familiar since childhood turn invasive. Lost in a mist evidently more mental than actual, she stumbles and clutches "the long marble thigh" of a tall male figure that stands "soberly on his pedestal," and as her hysteria heightens, she finds herself dodging "a marble embrace" and turns away from "a marble mouth reaching for her throat" (28). With her emotional stability imperiled, she then experiences a restorative frigidity provoked by the reassuring fearfulness of her father's voice calling her name, and subsequently, "with nothing but ice to clothe her," discipline of a sort is restored to Aunt Fanny's mind (31).

The Freudian implications of this spell of panic-stricken passion in the garden are readily apparent. The impingement of transgressive eroticism into the strictly ruled domain of the father, with as its object the very figure of the patriarch (or at least a close approximation), has initiated the return in frighteningly grotesque forms of what has long been repressed; and only the complete refiguring of the father as a deified ethereal voice safely de-eroticizes him and endows him with the power to subdue the demon of sexual desire. But the episode also invites a sociopolitical reading: Aunt Fanny's passion in the garden has been provoked by a radical disturbance within the public order of the estate. That her sexual anxieties have not simmered to the surface until the day after Lionel's funeral, which is to say only once there is no longer a male heir apparent, is telling. Even more so, however, is the gist of the prophecy: in its foretelling of widespread destruction, the voice reclaims the family, the house, and in effect the future, in the name of patriarchy.

When the sky is fair again the children will be safe; the father comes to his children who will be saved. Tell them in the house that they will be saved. Do not let them leave the house; say to them: Do not fear, the father will guard the children. Go into your father's house and say these things" [32].

The others in the household, their awareness of the neurotically troubled soul of the messenger notwithstanding, find themselves tacitly accepting the apocalyptic portent of the prophecy because Aunt Fanny's proclamation of it in the drawing room is spectacularly reinforced by the brief appearance of a "small brightly-banded snake" that is instantly regarded as an emissary of the first Mr. Halloran. That this evidently harmless animal which departs quickly upon being discovered elicits a cowed response from all present is an indication of patriarchy's resilience in the face of the female challenge to its dominance. Egregiously phallic to the point of silliness, the snake represents, so to speak, mystified male power demystified—power which the text both respects for the efficacy with which it commands awe from otherwise sensible (or at least secular-minded) people, and which is also mocked for its incongruous pretensions, in its pretty diminutiveness, to huge importance and venerability.

On one level the target of Jackson's satire is nothing less than the patriarchal basis of the dominant religious tradition of the Western world. The awe-inspiring voice in the garden is clearly a reworking of the Yahweh of Genesis, and the imagery, diction, and apocalyptic portent of the voice's prophecies conjure up the fulminating poetry of the Book of Revelation. But in the America of the mid–twentieth century, the text implies, religion is not a powerful social influence. Its diminished prestige is hinted at with the appearance of some members of a doomsday cult that calls itself the "True Believers," who truly believe that although the end of the world is imminent, a select few will be saved and taken to Saturn in flying saucers.[8] Yet although traditional religious forms no longer provide spiritual sustenance, other than in degenerate versions to handfuls of credulous crackpots, their commanding deity, the all-powerful father, lingers ghostlike within contemporary society's superficially secular myths and values. That the ideology of domesticity is as haunted by father-worship even in the 1950s as it was in the first Mr. Halloran's time is slyly indicated by the phrasing of one of Aunt Fanny's interpretative assertions concerning the thrust of the revelations. "Wrong is wrong and right is right and Father knows best" (111), she says, revealing with those final three words that like many of her compatriots she must often have watched—devotedly, so to speak—the highly acclaimed television domestic melodrama of that name that starred Robert Young as the benign patriarch of an archetypally perfect middle-class American family.[9]

## Nuclear Monsters

The reference to that popular program calls attention to another of *The Sundial*'s disturbing concerns. While it is a text that registers, in its treatment of one woman's unwomanly aspiration to supremacy, postwar society's nervousness about the subversion of the traditional gender hierarchy, its own anxiety is more pronounced with regard to perceived rifts in the structure of the family. From its earliest paragraphs the novel signals that relations between the various family members are coldly Machiavellian at best, and in some cases even gleefully vindictive. Upon returning from her husband's funeral the "young" Mrs. Halloran says to her daughter, "Fancy dear, would you like to see Granny drop dead on the doorstep?"; and Fancy blithely replies, "Yes, mother," and a moment later asks "Shall I push her? ... Like she pushed my daddy?" (3). It is a scandalous, even heretical opening for a narrative of the time. The 1950s, as Lynn Spigel has observed, "was a decade that invested an enormous amount of cultural capital in the ability to form a family and live out a set of highly structured gender and generational roles" (2). The period's veneration of family life was evident not only in numerous popular printed and screened narratives, but in such diverse cultural phenomena as newly coined phrases that highlighted the centricity of the family ("family-size carton," "family room," "family car") and the 1958 American National Exhibition in Moscow which displayed to the enemy as proof of the superiority of its social system a model American home that highlighted the private life of the family (see Marling 278; May 17–18; Susman and Griffin 22).

And "family" almost invariably designated the nuclear unit: parents and one or more children inhabiting the same household. In this regard it may seem odd that in the contemporary period the Halloran estate houses various blood relations as well as diverse visitors, but no complete nuclear group. It is soon made clear, however, that the nuclear model was from the start the fundamental Halloran paradigm, for the extended household headed by Mrs. Halloran has accrued from three successive nuclear units, the most recent of which has only just been rendered incomplete. In its presentation of the problematic ethos informing contemporary family life, *The Sundial* yet again links a venerated mid–twentieth century social ideal back to a nineteenth century origin, and suggests that it contained within itself from the start the seeds of its own undoing. Recent scholarship has demonstrated persuasively that, contrary to a still widely held belief, the nuclear family was not a development of the postindustrial era; nonetheless, the nineteenth century marked a decline in the importance of extended networks of kinship relations, as well as an erosion of the practical preconditions for actively maintaining them. The nuclear unit came then to be regarded not merely as the fundamental building block of the larger society that the "family values" rhetoric of some twentieth century politicians alludes to, but also, and contrariwise, as a sort of countersociety.[10] It is quietly significant therefore that no grandparents for the first generation of Halloran children are mentioned, and that the uncle and cousins to whom Lionel refers at one point have been only distant relations. Clearly the Halloran family in those years was turning inward, isolating itself from its kinship network even as it walled out the larger society.

By the contemporary period, some long-term effects of years and years of rigidly imposed familial exclusiveness, effects that are ironically corrosive of nuclear integrity, are becoming apparent. Aggressive individualism and solipsistic defensiveness belie the weak pantomime of warmth and togetherness enacted in the Halloran household. The nuclear ideal has bred and nurtured social misfits like the first generation siblings, or else rapacious, self-aggrandizing monsters like Mrs. Halloran and her granddaughter. Neither Aunt Fanny nor her brother seems ever to have been capable of dealing with the outside world effectively. Aunt Fanny, in particular, seems trapped within the nuclear paradigm. She has developed the habit of periodically repairing to an area of the house in which she has laboriously replicated the domestic environment of her early childhood, there to pass the time perusing an old family photo album.

> "Some day I will be with my mother," Aunt Fanny would think, turning the pages, "I am with her in this book, no one can separate us *here*. Some day we will all be together again" [177].

Staticity and isolation thus define the true family. It is not a communal group that grows and diversifies over time, or that radiates outward beyond the immediate household, but one that resembles a photograph, a spatiotemporal moment from the past frozen into an image that is noncontiguous and miniature.

Similarly, Mrs. Halloran's monstrous ways are promoted by the nuclear ideal. There is, as suggested by the earlier discussion of 1950s "momism," an ironic aptness about the daughter-in-law's reference to her as an "unmotherly monster" (20); in that era it was often alleged that the essence of motherhood was to depart monstrously from the essence of motherhood. But the text also implies that the nuclear family itself nurtures such tyrannical power mongering, by inculcating in family members a cult of reverence for the head of the household so intensively that envious aspirations to royal prerogative must inevitably be implanted in the souls of some. The absolute sovereignty over her domestic domain that Mrs. Halloran desires obsessively is signified by the crown that she insists, ridiculously, on bestowing upon herself. Yet the self-absorption of even such an imperious ego as hers is also, within a claustrophobically familial context, a necessary *defensive* stance. In her dream of a miniature home of her own, she casts herself as a sympathetic refiguring of the witch in the story of Hansel and Gretel who justifiably resists the vandalism of the two children who want to eat her house. The children bear strong resemblances to Essex and a 17-year-old woman named Gloria (a later arrival at the estate); but they are also imagined as her own offspring, and she, having trapped them in the cupboards, sits in insular serenity in front of her home, "hearing them call pitifully to her from inside" (115).

Those children possessed of such importunate chewing egos instantiate yet another sort of family monster hungry for imperious selfhood that harrowed postwar America's fantasies of idyllic domesticity: the figure of the bad child. Families, it seemed to some contemporary observers, might be conceding to children an imbalance of power that constituted a threat to the ideal of harmonious family life. William H. Chafe has noted that in popular images "this 'new' family was run by children. Filiality had taken the place of both patriarchy and matriarchy" (123). Numerous situation comedies in the electronic and print media focused upon rebellious and mischievous offspring, and if in most such narratives the self-willed and anarchic behavior of the young was regarded indulgently and as a source of reassuring comedy, in many an undertone of anxiety is also discernible. Shirley Jackson's own highly successful semi-autobiographical chronicles of sunny family life, published in popular magazines, and subsequently in best-selling book collections with the insinuating titles *Life Among the Savages* and *Raising Demons*, are prime examples. It is telling also that the now familiar (if slightly dated) phrase "juvenile delinquency" entered common usage in this era. The most unnerving aspect of that term was that it frequently connoted subversion from within the social stronghold of middle-class domesticity; the juvenile delinquents that postwar America worried about were less often alienated youths from underprivileged backgrounds than kids from "nice" families, as is indicated by the popularity of such narratives as William Marsh's novel *The Bad Seed* and Nicholas Ray's film *Rebel Without a Cause*.[11]

The opening of *The Sundial*, as we have seen, confronts the reader with a ten-year-old from a nice family who imagines herself capable of murdering her grandmother and is chillingly blithe about admitting to that capacity. The threat that she represents, not merely to Mrs. Halloran but to the idea of the sanctity of the family, is suggested by a lengthy, superficially digressive discussion of the town's "enshrined murderess," who had killed her parents and two younger brothers not long before the original Halloran family moved to the estate. The incident is overtly based on the famous case of Lizzie Borden of Fall River, Massachusetts, who was accused of the brutal murders of her father and stepmother in 1892. That Borden was 32 years old when the killings occurred is not mentioned in the famous jingle that appeared in the public domain not long after the grotesque event ("Lizzie Borden took an axe/And gave her mother forty whacks/And when she saw what she had done/She gave her father forty-one"), possibly because to imagine them as the work of an adult might have diluted the titillating sense of sacrilege evoked by the thought of a child, especially a daughter, deviating thus spectacularly from the loving dependency that was her allotted role within the family structure (Spiering 5). Borden's fictitious counterpart in *The Sundial*, in any case, represents a similar recasting of the historical record into a myth about generational subversion from within the family, for "Harriet Stuart" was only "a young-looking fifteen" when the act occurred—and she killed her siblings as well as her parents (78).

## Insular Egotism: The Ultimate Miniature

Harriet Stuart's latter-day alter ego eventually does murder her grandmother—or so it appears—and in precisely the same way as the latter is believed to have killed her son. In this as in other respects there is a significant congruency between the two characters. In Fancy, Mrs. Halloran sees her own future, or rather, a means of commodifying it; "Fancy is mine, too, now," she says on the day of the funeral, adding, "some day everything I have will belong to Fancy, and I think to keep Fancy with me" (20). Fancy, for her part, regards herself as, in a sense, the "future" Mrs. Halloran. On that same day she says, "When my grandmother dies, no one can stop the house and everything from being mine" (21), and similar comments are voiced by her on several subsequent occasions. What links the two most closely, and makes Mrs. Halloran seem at times rather childish and Fancy uncannily adult, is not merely the possessive impulse that they have in common, for all of the other characters display at least some degree of avarice. These two, however, are held out as revealingly extreme in that their possessiveness seems not so much materialistic as egoistic at base. It is Fancy who is most taken with the idea of the crown that Mrs. Halloran insists—childishly—upon wearing. At an enormous garden party given by her grandmother for the townspeople on the eve of the day of apocalypse, Fancy asks, "When can I have your crown?," to which Mrs. Halloran replies, after turning slowly to look at her, "When I am dead" (221, 222). They appear to understand one another perfectly: the world can have but one queen, one omnipotent ego. And it is not long afterwards that the body of Mrs. Halloran is found by the others at the foot of the staircase—whereupon Fancy's coldly opportunistic response is to exclaim "My crown!" and bolt down the stairs to claim it (238).

Fancy's climactic attempt to usurp the position of regal supremacy originally claimed by her grandmother carries to a logical extreme the miniaturist tendency that has been a dominant concern throughout the text and, as argued earlier, a recurrent force in American social history in the modern era. Beyond the small community, beyond the family, and beyond the household, and underlying the appeal of all of these as alternative social worlds, there is the most secure and self-gratifying miniature of all: the narcissistic make-believe realm created by "fancy," the childish imagination that desires no restrictions upon its power to play. In *The Sundial* the specter of the inward-looking ego actively condensing and refashioning experience into a fantasy module that offers a controllable alternative to the larger world recurs often, and it is construed as being inherently childish. What is at stake in the struggle between Mrs. Halloran and Fancy is in this respect essentially the same as the house for which the former's dream siblings and dream witch compete: pure candy, a confectionary otherness to be pleasurably ingested by the maw of self.

And childish imperialism of this sort isn't some perverse inclination restricted to the strange individuals who have clustered together within the walls of the Halloran estate. The world beyond those walls, Gloria tells Fancy, "isn't real," and her elaboration seems less the independent assessment of a bright 17-year-old than an authorially ventriloquized commentary influenced by such contemporary social commentators as William H. Whyte and David Reisman[12]:

> "It's real inside here, *we're* real, but what is outside is like it's made of cardboard, or plastic, or something. *Nothing* out there is real. Everything is made out of something else, and everything is made to look like something else, and it all comes apart in your hands. The people aren't real, they're nothing but endless copies of each other, all looking just alike, like paper dolls, and they live in houses full of artificial things and eat imitation food—"
> "My doll house," Fancy said, amused [185–186].

Intuitively, Fancy comprehends the gist here: the conformist, commercially and politically engineered postwar society is an endlessly mimetic fantasy, a vast public dollhouse. As such, it is to be evaded if at all possible—but in favor of what? "I wouldn't like being a doll in a doll house," Gloria goes on to say, a sentiment that sums up the defensive rationale for withdrawing into one's own fantasy constructs, which are at least more personalized, and enable a degree of agency for the self. When the external social world is a substanceless sham—when "the only real people left any more are the shadows on the television screens" (186)—the miniature domain of the insular self, further populated (if at all) only by a severely restricted group of others, may offer some measures of autonomy, security, and—to the extent that the concept retains any credible referential significance—reality. Such, at least, is Gloria's hope, rather forlornly expressed.

## New World Miniatures

And such, in the view of the novel, is the state of the American nation at midcentury. As a narrative in which various notions of a world are repeatedly summoned, and in which much of the action gravitates toward the prospect of exiting from one world and beginning afresh in another, *The Sundial* ends teasingly, on the eve of what may or may not be the beginning of the apocalyptic transformation. Neither climactic nor resoundingly the opposite, its bleary denouement is the perfect unsatisfying termination of a text that has delighted in dangling before the reader a variety of miniature worlds in which the self may aspire to rest secure and reign supreme. As these are shown to be substanceless and more or less overtly solipsistic, it is not surprising that the anticipated new world is progressively revealed to be only the sum of various characters' subjective projections upon the prospect of it—a sum that does not add up to a cohesive or coherent whole. For Aunt Fanny, it will be a fresh new Eden, with no moral prohibitions or inhibitions; for Mrs. Halloran it will be much the same as the present, a small social universe that she will rule autocratically and puritanically; and Gloria has several visions, all of which she conjures up while gazing absorbedly into a mirror. Ironically it is left to the one actual child in the group to call attention to the narcissism and delusiveness of the futurist fantasies of the others. Fancy, who despite her regal yearnings hasn't yet felt sufficiently disappointed by the ego-abashing ways of the larger world to wish to see it obliterated, points out to Gloria that as the supposed new world will be inhabited by the same old unhappy people who have failed to appreciate the present one, an Eden that will suit all is unlikely. It will inevitably incorporate, she stresses, the very frustrations, frictions, and disappointments that inspired it: "you all want the whole world to be changed so *you* will be different," she says, "but I don't suppose people get changed any by just a new world. And anyway, that world isn't any more real than this one" (165).

Fancy may understand her hard words in this instance to be directed at the "you all" who inhabit the Halloran estate, but the text's encouragement to the reader to understand a wider reference has been set in place by a series of earlier invocations of the key phrase "new world."

Thus construed, her criticism of her housemates becomes *The Sundial*'s address to its American reading audience, one of several indications that the millenarian expectations and miniaturist projects that entrance the characters in this narrative are endemic to the national character. Hinted at here is that strange irony of American social history mentioned earlier: the socially sanctioned belief in the prospect of a "world" that is radically "new" has, particularly in the postindustrial era, encouraged middle-class Americans to think small and to look inward. The once globally scaled master narrative of the nation has degenerated into a confused mélange of airbrushed old constructions of society, home, and self.

That America's originating desire for a new world remains influential even in the 1950s is made clear by the text's ironic presentation of Mrs. Halloran as a latter-day incarnation of Elizabeth I. Elizabeth was not only the most powerful queen in the history of Britain, and thus, as suggested above, a comically apt model for Mrs. Halloran's pretensions to matriarchal might; she was also the monarch who presided over England's initial entry into the Americas. This the text reminds us of in an early incident wherein Mrs. Halloran ("Orianna") stands before the sundial in the garden and "caressingly" touches part of the inscription on it: the word "world" (46–47). The scene draws its significance from its mimicry of yet another Elizabethan referent, the late seventeenth century "Armada Portrait," in which the queen of the nation that was poised for dominance in the wake of its defeat of the Spanish fleet is depicted as fingering lightly a globe of the earth placed prominently just to her right. Like her namesake, Jackson's Orianna too wills to exert possessive sovereignty over a miniature model of a world that is to be recast, made new, in homage to her.

But be that new world the Halloran estate, her dream house in the woods, or the future as transformed by apocalypse, residual traces of the world beyond imagining, the world of contingent actuality, will perpetually intrude, defying the efforts of even the most imperious self to exclude, replace, or colonize it. Fancy is right: there is a "this" world that will always be the measure of all fantasized new ones in that they will all, upon being tested, be forced to come to terms with it. Early on in the narrative the reader's attention is directed to a quizzical inscription on the sundial, taken from Chaucer's "Knight's Tale":

> Intruding purposefully upon the entire scene, an inevitable focus, was the sundial, set badly off center and reading WHAT IS THIS WORLD? [13].

"An inevitable focus ... set badly off center": the oxymoron subtly insinuates the futile effort of the individual to superimpose an egocentric pattern upon actuality in all its intrusive *ec*centricity and asymmetry. "What

"The Armada Portrait" of Elizabeth I by George Gower, 1588. ©His Grace the Duke of Bedford and the Trustees of the Bedford Estates. Reproduced with the kind permission of the Duke of Bedford and the Trustees of the Bedford Estates.

is this world?" is in this sense a rhetorical question: the only possible answer, one that defeats all notions of global dominance on even a minia-ture scale, is "This world is what." But that non-answer gestures at the possibility of a lived response, albeit one that modern society has largely lost sight of. Slightly farther along, the quotation in bold face is aug-mented by the lines that follow in the original Chaucer text:

> "What is this world?" Essex said quietly, "What asketh man to have?
> Now with his love, now in his colde grave, Allone, with-outen any compa-
> nye." [14].[13]

In the context of *The Sundial* the somber wisdom of these words from another cultural milieu is made to seem both anachronistic and pointed—the first, because they suggest that in Chaucer's time, but no longer in the present, it was possible to conceive of the self in "this world" as desirous beyond all else of ego-transcending social intercourse, of love

and "companye"; and the second, because they foreshadow contemporary society's valorization of miniature worlds of subjectivity and link
them with the chill solipsism of the one truly exclusive miniature world
of selfhood, the grave. "I dislike it," Mrs. Halloran says of the Chaucer
passage (14), and her response is clearly not an aesthetic judgment. She
has taken the point—which is also the text's point, as refracted through
the Chaucerian fragment—and, with the childlike imperiousness that is
as characteristic of Shirley Jackson's America as it is of Mrs. Halloran
herself, chosen to reject it.

## Notes

1. The only extended study is John G. Parks's "Waiting for the End: Shirley Jackson's *The Sundial*," *Critique* XIX, no.3 (1978): 74–88. More general commentaries
on Jackson's work or aspects of it that devote some attention to *The Sundial* include
Lenemaja Friedman, *Shirley Jackson* (Boston: Twayne/G.K. Hall, 1975); James Egan,
"Shirley Jackson's Domestic and Fantastic Parables," *Studies in Weird Fiction* 6 (1989):
15–24; S.T. Joshi, "Shirley Jackson: Domestic Horror," *Studies in Weird Fiction* 14
(1992): 9–28; and Roberta Rubenstein, "House Mothers and Haunted Daughters:
Shirley Jackson and Female Gothic," *Tulsa Studies in Women's Literature*, vol. 15, no.
2 (fall 1996): 309–331.

2. The allusion is of course to Sacvan Bercovitch's famous phrase. Readers who
are familiar with *The American Jeremiad* may object that *The Sundial*, in the reading
presented in this study, does not conform to Bercovitch's conception of the "American Jeremiad" as a discourse that "simultaneously [laments] a declension and [cel-
ebrates] a national dream" (180); as will be seen, virtually nothing American is
celebrated in Jackson's text, though much is lamented. Nonetheless, it seems to me
legitimate and useful to invoke Bercovitch's term given that it contains within it an
oppositional subcategory, that of the American "anti-jeremiad," or a discourse that
involves "the denunciation of all ideals, sacred and secular, on the grounds that America is a lie" (191).

3. The text does not specify the precise year or decade when the Hallorans relo-
cated; but the story is clearly set in the 1950s (several references to television confirm
this), and as one of the Halloran siblings, Aunt Fanny, is said to be 48 years old at
the start of the narrative, it is apparent that the family moved to the estate in the first
or second decade of the century.
The earliest stirrings of suburbanization in the United States date back to the nineteenth century, when improved methods of public transport first created the possibility of rapid and efficient daily travel between urban centers and outlying districts.
Suburban relocation was nonetheless almost exclusively a prerogative for the very well
off at that time, and as Margaret Marsh has observed, the critical elements of the ideological impetus for such a move did not coalesce until late in the century, well after
the actual technology facilitating it was in place. Only then, it appears, did the notion
that it was in the best interests of the family to locate the home outside the city in a
"country" environment become circulated sufficiently enough to initiate a small trend
(15–16). Not until the decade following the First World War did suburbanization
become a "demographic process of magnitude for the first time," however (Donaldson 35); by 1930, the suburban population of American cities was 45 percent as large
as the central-city population (Palen 50). And as is well known, it was in the period
after World War II that the movement, curtailed for awhile by the Depression and
World War II, accelerated so enormously as, in the words of one historian, to "rip

apart and remake the texture of social life in America." In the 1950s, suburbs grew six times faster than cities; and by the end of the decade, one out of four Americans lived in them (Chafe 117; Diggins 181–3).

An abbreviated summary of the suburban movement such as this one cannot adequately register the nuances and permutations that scholarly researchers call attention to, or gesture more than briefly towards those aspects of it that are often debated; as Donaldson points out, homogenizing generalizations tend invariably to break down under scrutiny, because there are "suburbs and suburbs" (51). For our purposes here, however, such problems of definition are tangential, for *The Sundial* is less concerned to represent or comment upon the actual natures of various suburban social structures than to explore the mythic formulation that almost invariably shimmers within what Palen has called the "marvelous vague agreement" that the term "suburb" is self-defining: the image of a reconstituted small town as the ideal (8). Wood is one of numerous commentators to take note of the recurrence of the small town paradigm in suburban social planning and the ideology informing it. (See, for other examples, Fischer and Jackson 280–304; Rowe 120; and Baldassore, 47.)

4. Quoted in Lewis, xi.

5. Scott Donaldson, writing in 1969, noted that "the observation about matriarchy in the suburbs has been made so often that it threatens to become axiomatic" (122). (See also Dobriner 18; Kenneth Jackson 243; and Palen 163.)

6. For the significance of "Orianna" in Elizabethan literature, see Drabble 719. *The Sundial* incorporates a number of corroborating references to Elizabethan England—Mrs. Willow's older daughter is named "Arabella," for example, and Elizabeth had a courtier named "Essex"—in order to ensure, perhaps, that the "Orianna" allusion does not go unremarked.

7. James Egan suggests that the character represents "a monstrous parody of the nurturing mother" (20). The contention here, however, is that something more complex is insinuated: Jackson's figure both reflects and parodies the widely prevalent social nightmare of the domineering mother, which itself inadvertently parodied the era's venerated image of saintly motherhood by way of grotesque inversion. On the pervasive influence of *Modern Woman: The Lost Sex* and *a Generation of Vipers*, see Marsh 185; Palen 84; and Strickland and Ambrose 536–7.

8. It was probably a widely publicized such cult of the early '50s that gave Jackson the idea for the flying saucer "believers." See the 1956 study *When Prophecy Fails* by Festinger, et al.

9. For an excellent discussion of the patriarchal ideology informing *Father Knows Best,* and the implications of the program's enormous popularity, see Leibman, especially 87–89; 120–26. In the light of the earlier discussion of the significance of the miniaturist ideal in suburban ideology, it is useful to relay also Lynn Spigel's observation that the family home in *Father Knows Best* was represented "as if it were a public spectacle, a monument commemorating the values of the ideal American town" (131).

10. On the increased significance of the nuclear family in the postindustrial era, especially its function as an oppositional miniature society, see Davis 16 and Demos 5, 31.

11. *The Bad Seed,* which quickly metamorphosed into equally successful stage and screen versions, featured an innocent seeming eight-year-old murderess who may well have been, along with Lizzie Borden (see below), Jackson's inspiration for the character of Fancy. Its sociological significance as an indication of the postwar period's anxiety about child-rearing and juvenile delinquency, and its importance as a precedent for later and more extreme "child as monster" films, is discussed insightfully by Kathy Merlock Jackson 112–14; 137–54, and by Strickland and Ambrose 561–66.

12. Gloria's brief diatribe is still more reminiscent of John Keats's *The Crack in the Picture Window* (1956), a best-selling attack on suburban conformity. (With regard

to that text, it may be of some significance that the Halloran mansion contains a picture window that shatters [112].) My reason for alluding to Riesman's *The Lonely Crowd* (1950) and Whyte's *The Organization Man* (1954) is that these are now the most well remembered social critiques of middle-class life of a period in which such "state of the nation" commentaries proliferated and were popular. Wylie's *A Generation of Vipers*, mentioned earlier, also falls into this category.

13. These are lines 2777–79 in the Robinson version of the tale in his edition of Chaucer's works (Chaucer, 44).

## Works Cited

Baldassare, Mark. *Trouble in Paradise: The Suburban Transformation in America*. New York: Columbia University Press, 1986.

Bercovitch, Sacvan. *The American Jeremiad*. Madison: University of Wisconsin Press, 1978.

Chafe, William. *The Unfinished Journey: America Since World War II*. New York: Oxford University Press, 1986.

Chaucer, Geoffrey. *The Works of Geoffrey Chaucer*. Ed. F.N. Robinson. 2nd ed. Boston: Houghton, 1957.

Cott, Nancy F. *The Bonds of Womanhood: "Woman's Sphere" in New England, 1780–1835*. New Haven: Yale University Press, 1977.

Davis, David Brion. "The American Family and Boundaries in Historical Perspective." *The American Family: Dying or Developing?* Eds. David Reiss and Howard A. Hoffman. New York: Plenum Press, 1979, 13–41.

Demos, John. *Past, Present, and Personal: The Family and the Life Course in American History*. New York: Oxford University Press, 1986.

Diggins, John Patrick. *The Proud Decades: America in War and Peace, 1941–1960*. New York: Norton, 1988.

Dobriner, William M. *Class in Suburbia*. New Jersey: Prentice-Hall, 1963.

Donaldson, Scott. *The Suburban Myth*. New York: Columbia University Press, 1969.

Drabble, Margaret, ed. *The Oxford Companion to English Literature*. 5th Edition. Oxford: Oxford University Press, 1985.

Egan, James. "Sanctuary: Shirley Jackson's Domestic and Fantastic Parables." *Studies in Weird Fiction* no. 6 (fall 1989): 15–24.

Festinger, Leon, Henry W. Riecken and Stanley Schachter. *When Prophecy Fails*. Minneapolis: University of Minnesota P, 1956.

Fothergill, Brian. *The Strawberry Hill Set: Horace Walpole and his Circle*. London: Faber and Faber, 1983.

Hayden, Dolores. *Redesigning the American Dream: The Future of Housing, Work, and Family Life*. New York: Norton, 1986.

Jackson, Kathy Merlock. *Images of Children in American Film: A Sociocultural Analysis*. Metuchen: The Scarecrow Press, 1986.

Jackson, Kenneth T. *Crabgrass Frontier: The Suburbanization of the United States*. New York: Oxford University Press, 1985.

Jackson, Shirley. *The Sundial*. New York: Farrar, Straus, and Cudahy, 1958.

Lewis, W.S. Introduction to *The Castle of Otranto: A Gothic Story*, by Horace Walpole. London: Oxford University Press, 1964.

Leibman, Nina C. *Living Room Lectures: The Fifties Family in Film and Television*. Austin: University of Texas Press, 1995.

Lundberg, Ferdinand, and Marynia F. Farnham. *Modern Woman: The Lost Sex*. New York: Harper, 1947.

Marling, Karal Ann. *As Seen on TV: The Visual Culture of Everyday Life in the 1950's*. Cambridge: Harvard University Press, 1994.

Marsh, Margaret. *Suburban Lives.* New Brunswick: Rutgers University Press, 1990.
May, Elaine Tyler. *Homeward Bound.* New York: Basic Books, 1988.
Palen, J. John. *The Suburbs.* New York: McGraw-Hill, 1995.
Rowe, Peter G. *Making a Middle Landscape.* Cambridge: MIT Press, 1991.
Spiering, Frank. *Lizzie.* New York: Random House, 1985.
Spigel, Lynn. *Make Room for TV: Television and the Family Ideal in Postwar America.* Chicago: University of Chicago Press, 1992.
Strickland, Charles E., and Andrew M. Ambrose. "The Changing Worlds of Children, 1945–1963." *American Childhood: A Research Guide and Historical Handbook.* Eds. Joseph M. Hawes and N. Ray Hines. Westport: Greenwood Press, 1985, 533–585.
Strong, Roy. *The Cult of Elizabeth: Elizabethan Portraiture and Pageantry.* n.p. [London?]: Thames and Hudson, 1977.
Susman, Warren, and Edward Griffin. "Did Success Spoil the United States?: Dual Representations in Postwar America." In *Recasting America: Culture and Politics in the Age of the Cold War.* Eds. Lary May. Chicago: University of Chicago Press, 1989, 19–37.
Walpole, Horace. *The Castle of Otranto: A Gothic Story.* (1764). Oxford: Oxford University Press, 1996.
Wood, Robert C. *Suburbia: Its People and Their Politics.* Boston: Houghton-Mifflin, 1958.
Wylie, Philip. *A Generation of Vipers.* New York: Rinehart, 1942.

# 5

# "The People of the Village Have Always Hated Us": Shirley Jackson's New England Gothic

BERNICE M. MURPHY

Published in 1948, Shirley Jackson's short story "The Lottery" famously caused such a stir upon its appearance in *The New Yorker* that the author soon became the unwitting recipient of hundreds of (mainly hostile) letters from disgruntled readers who objected to the tale's brutal climax and air of studied ambiguity. As Jackson later noted in her witty essay "Biography of a Story," many of the letters she received that summer were from people who "wanted to know where these lotteries were held and whether they could go there and watch" (*Come Along with Me*; hereafter referred to as C) (213)—the line between reality and fiction apparently proving a difficult border to negotiate for such correspondents. There were also letters from readers who had already decided where the ritual had taken place—and New England seemed to be the most popular choice. Jackson quoted from some of these letters in her essay:

[Texas] Could it be that in New England or in equally enlightened regions, mass sadism is still part and parcel of the ordinary citizen's life?
[New York] Is there some timeless community existing in New England where human sacrifices are made for the fertility of the crops? [C 213].

As Faye Ringel has noted in her study of New England's gothic literature, "though Jackson never indicates where 'The Lottery' takes place,

104

presumably the names of the characters, their willingness to follow old customs even when they no longer understand why, and their ability to slaughter innocent scapegoats and then return to daily life as though nothing had happened, made readers assume a New England setting.... For today's readers, New England is a logical setting for Gothic Medievalism, a place where anything *could* happen, because unthinkable, supernatural things once *did* happen there" (Ringel 201, 204). This essay will briefly discuss Shirley Jackson's conflicted and overwhelmingly negative portrayals of rural New England in an attempt to reach some sort of understanding of her feelings towards the region that provided her with the perfect setting for her unique brand of gothic fiction.

It must be noted that Jackson was by no means the first and certainly not the last gothic writer to find inspiration in the dark possibilities presented by New England's bloody past and suggestive landscape. Nathaniel Hawthorne, and more recently H.P. Lovecraft and Stephen King, have all used New England as the fruitful setting for their own most famous novels and short stories. Whilst an essay comparing Jackson's evocations of the region with those of other gothic and horror notables would undoubtedly prove interesting, the goal of this essay is rather to look at the way that Jackson's own feelings of being an outsider within a small, isolated New England community influenced her fiction. For significantly, unlike Lovecraft (who was from Providence, Rhode Island), King (from Maine), or Hawthorne (who was born in Salem, Massachusetts), Jackson was not a New England native.

Born in the prosperous San Francisco suburb of Burlingame, Jackson lived in California until she was 14 when her parents moved to Rochester, New York. Jackson attended university there briefly, and then later enrolled in Syracuse, where she met her future husband—the academic and literary critic Stanley Edgar Hyman. Shortly after graduation, the young couple married and moved to Chelsea, New York. It is interesting to note that Jackson's debut novel, *The Road Through the Wall* (1948) is her only full-length fiction set in her childhood state. It is also the only Jackson novel in which both the location (a suburb of Cabrillo, 30 miles from San Francisco) and the date (the summer of 1936) are specifically mentioned. This degree of exactness is highly unusual for Jackson: as Joan Wylie Hall has observed, "in none of her later books is Jackson as explicit about the time and geographical location as she is here" (Hall 263). This exactness is probably at least partially due to the fact that *Road* is Jackson's most obviously autobiographical novel: Pepper Street, the sheltered middle-class enclave in which almost all the text's action take place, is clearly modeled on her childhood residence of Burlingame. The rest of Jackson's novels and many of her short stories would be set in a never explicitly situated, generally slightly vague version of rural New England.

Jackson and her family moved to the region in 1945 when Hyman was offered a job at the all-female Liberal Arts college of Bennington, located amidst the mountains of southwestern Vermont. The promise of a larger house for their rapidly growing brood encouraged the couple to make the move from New York to the somewhat quieter pastures of New England, though it also seems likely that the move would have provided a welcome relief to the increasingly anxious Jackson. The many stories she wrote about women for whom the chaos, noise and sheer activity of New York becomes simply too much to bear ("Nightmare," "The Tooth," "Pillar of Salt") seem to suggest that she was herself finding the city somewhat overwhelming.

Although most of the academics employed at Bennington found accommodation on or near the campus, the Hymans decided to venture into civilian territory instead and settled in the blue collar mill town of North Bennington—"one of the oldest and most historic towns in Vermont" (Westbrook 236). Apart from a period when the family resided in Westport, Connecticut (1949–51), Jackson lived in North Bennington from 1945 until her death in the summer of 1965.

Jackson would always be an outsider in New England. As is common in small, insular communities the world over, newcomers can remain categorized as such even many decades after their arrival. Not only had the family moved from New York City, but they were also part of the sometimes-resented academic community that had sprung up around the recently built college—which meant, as Perry Westbrook has put it, that she and her husband "were outsiders on two counts." He then adds (a trifle melodramatically perhaps), "among primitive tribes and in secluded rural settings like some New England towns, outsiders tend to arouse gratuitous suspicion and hate" (Westbrook 232). Whatever Jackson's own personal experiences of New England (and biographer Judy Oppenheimer does go into certain incidents in some detail), there can be no denying the fact that her fiction time and time again depicts clashes between unwitting newcomers or outsiders and insular, laconic locals as her protagonists repeatedly and generally naively violate longstanding codes of behavior and etiquette.

Of course, Jackson's fiction has always focused on women who for one reason or another find themselves perennial outsiders: as Lynette Carpenter has succinctly put it, "The typical Jackson protagonist is a social misfit, a young woman not beautiful enough, charming enough, or articulate enough to get along with other people" (Carpenter 145)— to which Carpenter might also have added, given the tendency of Jackson's heroines to blur the line between fantasy and reality: not quite *sane* enough to fit in either.

Of chief interest here is the relationship that her inevitably damaged protagonists have with the small-town communities in which they so frequently find themselves. To begin, let us examine the way in which this issue is treated in Jackson's two volumes of family chronicles, *Life Among the Savages* (1953) and *Raising Demons* (1957).

Like two other popular texts in the postwar domestic comedy subgenre, Jean Kerr's *Please Don't Eat the Daisies* (1957) and Betty McDonald's *The Egg and I* (1945), *Savages* begins as the narrator and her family are transplanted from the city to an unfamiliar rural environment. This move from a familiar urban locale to deepest New England would also provide a starting point for several of Jackson's more obviously literary texts. After all, *Hill House* opens with Eleanor's fateful drive from the city to the remoteness of rural Hillsdale, while stories such as "The Flower Garden," "The Renegade," "Home" and "The Summer People" also depict naive city dwellers struggling to adjust to life in the unwelcoming countryside.

*Savages* opens as the narrator describes how she and her family acquired their new home (a characteristic Jackson preoccupation, of course). Within days of arriving, she relates, the family have been maneuvered by the canny locals into purchasing a large old house, despite the fact that the narrator has a instinctive dislike for the place upon first viewing it. Interestingly, Jackson's first response is to flee (*Savages* 17) and her reaction is described in terms quite similar to those that she would later employ when Eleanor Vance gets her first, horrified glimpse of Hill House—"I should have turned back at the gate, Eleanor thought..." (*HH* 35). Yet just as Eleanor overrules her own (accurate) initial response and enters the building, so too does the narrator of *Savages* radically reconsider her initial impressions. After all, it seems that the Fielding place (as the house is known by the locals) is the last available place in town; moreover, the elderly lease holder presumes without even discussing the matter that the family are going to move in and then offers them the place at a ridiculously cheap rent. So, despite the narrator's initial misgivings, when the family returns a few weeks later, they find that the house has been transformed: "literally scraped clean; down to the wood in the walls, straightened up, painted and repaired." Seeing the house on this occasion, the narrator voices a completely different opinion: "It's beautiful"—a remark that anticipates Eleanor's similar *about-face* in *Hill House* and her remarks that "I don't think we could leave now even if we wanted to"(*HH* 75). It is also significant that the family's new home has rooms that seem to choose where furniture should go, and instinctively prefers old things to those brought from the city:

> All these things, the ones that had been in the house before, and other things which had been in similarly old houses and knew their ways, fell naturally into good positions in the rooms, as though snatching the best places before the city furniture could crowd in [*Life Among the Savages* 21].

We have already the sense of an inevitable caving in to the demands of antiquity and of the countryside as the old (i.e. *local*) furniture instinctively crowds out the newer, *city* possessions—a subtle, but telling example of the rural/urban divide that appears so often in Jackson's more obviously sinister fictions.

It's a conflict also present in the opening pages of Jackson's follow up to *Savages, Raising Demons*. Again, the text opens with the process of moving house. This time, we are wryly told, the clutter that litters the narrator's home has become too much to bear and so again without ever having made an active decision, she and her family are subtly maneuvered by the local community into a new home, a process that creates in the narrator "an extraordinary sense of inevitability" (*RD* 12). Like so many of Jackson's more obviously fictional heroines, the narrator realizes that her fate is subject to powerful forces beyond her control: "I have not now the slightest understanding of the events which got us out of one big white house which we rented and into another, bigger white house which we own" (*RD* 7). The narrator soon discovers the real reason why the local community was so eager to see them move. It transpires that a member of the old local family who had originally owned the Fielding house has returned to town and decided to reclaim her ancestral property in a particularly pushy manner. When this descendant arrives to inspect the property, she displays a sense of entitlement that shocks the narrator: "I thought someone had told you," she said, "I was a Fielding before I was married ... we are coming home again" [*RD* 10].

In *Savages* and *Demons*, the network of gossip that fuels small town discourse is treated in fairly comedic fashion: for example, although the local people are encouraging a move of house for their own reasons, they help the narrator's family find a new home very quickly because they know exactly what they're looking for. The family's situation, as the narrator discovers on a trip into town, is common local knowledge: "I was to learn later that the grocer not only knew our housing problems, but the ages and names of our children, the meat we had served for dinner the night before, and my husband's income" [*RD* 10]. Obviously played for laughs here, the same reservoir of local knowledge can, with just a slight change of emphasis, become downright disturbing. The following section of this essay will discuss the manner in which Jackson depicted New England and its natives in her novels and short stories.

Jackson's debut novel *Road* is set in California, not New England; that is not to say, however, that it does not have much in common with later novels. Like *Sundial* and *Castle* and to an extent, *Hill House*, *Road* focuses on an enclosed, isolated, chronically self-absorbed community. It's just that in this case, the community consists of snobbish suburbanites living on the outskirts of San Francisco rather than latter-day aristocrats living in a large house that looms over a small New England village. The setting, a large cast of mostly unlikable characters, and the skewed, inward looking worldview explored here mean that *Road* has much in common with *Sundial* in particular—including the fact that they are the two Jackson novels contemporary reviewers had the greatest reservations about.

That's certainly not the case in *Hangsaman* (1951), Jackson's fascinating, much overlooked second novel. Although the setting of the novel is not stated, the all-girl liberal arts college that troubled teenager Natalie Waite attends is obviously modeled upon Bennington. It's also worth noting that the climactic scenes in which Natalie struggles to regain her sanity take place partly in the woods just outside of town—as would so often happen in the American gothic (and of course, the gothic in general), the forest is seen as a locale where the laws of conventional reality can be easily breached and where, as a result, the unwary traveler is all too vulnerable to demons both real and imagined. Although in Jackson's stories her disturbed heroines usually lose control of their sense of reason in the city (cf. "A Day in the Jungle," "The Tooth," "Pillar of Salt" and Elizabeth Richmond's delusional flight to New York in *The Bird's Nest*), there is however another Jackson story in which a young girl is lost (though this time in a physical rather than psychological fashion) in woods modeled upon those that surround Bennington.

In "The Missing Girl" (*Just an Ordinary Day*, 1996) Martha Alexander, a colorless teenager attending summer camp, vanishes. She has made so little impact that no one can even remember her proper name, or, soon, whether she was even there at all. The story may have been suggested by a real-life disappearance from Bennington in 1946. Paula Welden, a student at the college, went for a hike in the forests nearby and never came back. Her body was never found, and no cause for her disappearance was ever firmly established. The fact that this was merely the latest in a succession of such disappearances locally led to the area being dubbed the "Bennington Triangle" and caused speculation that a serial killer may have been on the loose.[1] As a resident of the area during this period, Jackson would have been all too aware that the wilderness of rural Vermont could be a threatening, dangerous place, particularly for young women. Natalie Waite, who eventually emerges from the woods, apparently having bested her imaginary friend "Tony"—and come to some sort of peace—is one of the lucky ones.

In Jackson's similarly themed (but structurally and tonally very different) follow-up to *Hangsaman*, *The Bird's Nest* (1954), geographical setting is of no particular importance, although, as previously noted, Elizabeth's journey to New York midway through the novel marks the onset of her most disturbed phase, one in which her original personality is completely dominated by her three demanding alter egos, Beth, Betsy and Bess. While New England doesn't feature prominently in Jackson's first three novels, the region had already provided the setting (either explicitly stated or strongly implied) for many of the most important stories in her first collection, *The Lottery and Other Stories, or The Adventures of James Harris* (1949).

In "The Renegade," "Flower Garden," and "Men with Their Big Shoes," we find explored, in a rather less benign fashion than would later be employed in the family chronicles, the relationship between newcomers and locals in small, insular, and often deeply prejudiced New England communities. In what is probably the best of these stories, "The Renegade," the news that the family dog has been seen killing chickens provides the catalyst for a sudden, devastating crisis of confidence in Mrs. Walpole, a naive newcomer to rural life. Watching her pragmatic neighbor adeptly make doughnuts, she comes to a bleak realization:

> They were still city folk and would probably always be city folk, people who were not able to fend for themselves against the limited world of earth and food and weather that the country folk took so much for granted [*L* 55].

Mrs. Walpole, like so many of Jackson's insecure city folk, is humbled by her neighbor's "safety, her confidence in a way of life and a security that had no traffic with chicken-killing, no city fears" (*L* 56). Her feelings of profound inadequacy and anxiety increase during a strained visit to the local grocery store (as we shall see, the shopping trip is very often the time when the clash between country and city folk becomes most obvious). As in the family chronicles, everyone knows what is going on in the protagonist's life, and everyone has his or her own ruthlessly pragmatic suggestions about how to prevent the dog from killing again. Mrs. Walpole desperate optimism is soon quashed: "Isn't there any way to cure the dog?" Mrs. Walpole asked. "Sure," the man said. "Shoot him" [L56].

Her feelings of claustrophobia and entrapment are heightened when the dog comes home, obviously blood-spattered, and her children, with "hard hands and sunburned faces," follow soon afterwards, full of excited, gruesome ideas about how to curb their pet's appetite. Torn between resentment at "the murderous brutality" the countryside has brought out in the dog she so obviously identifies with, and horrified dismay at the fact that her own children are mouthing the cruel, ruthlessly unsentimental opinions of the locals, Mrs. Walpole "closed her eyes, suddenly feeling the harsh hands pulling her down, the sharp points closing in on her throat" (*L* 58).

"The Flower Garden" is another tale of a vulnerable newcomer falling afoul of the entrenched opinions of rural New Englanders. The setting—rural Vermont—is stated in the opening paragraph. The story begins as old and young Mrs. Winning—capable matriarch and her dutiful daughter-in-law—"who have grown a great deal alike," carry out domestic chores in their large, old farmhouse. Jackson quickly establishes a sense of ruthless, unsentimental continuity: there are two Mrs. Winnings (and Jackson's protagonist, the younger of the two, has resigned herself to the fact that her mother-in-law will only relinquish her authority over the household when she becomes hopelessly infirm), two Howards, and a baby playing with toys that have been played with by members of the family for generations. "Young" Mrs. Winning knows that she is only the latest in a long succession of wives to inhabit the house of the "oldest family in town." Working silently alongside her mother-in-law, she imagines for a moment that

> they must resemble some stylized block print for a New England wall paper; mother, daughter and granddaughter, with perhaps Plymouth Rock or Concord bridge in the background [L 77].

Unusually for Jackson, the story is told from the perspective of the younger Mrs. Winning, a local, an insider—rather than that of an outsider—although the fate of a newcomer is the central concern. Mrs. Winning's feelings of confinement are sublimated into her long-held yearning for a home that will truly be her own (a common desire of Jackson's heroines: one most cruelly fulfilled in *Hill House*)—specifically the pretty little cottage next door. When a Mrs. McLean, a young widow with a small son, moves in, Mrs. Winning is at first delighted and approving: "'She *has* done it right; this is the way it should look after all' ... exactly as Mrs. Winning might have done if she were eleven years younger"(*L* 88). She sees Mrs. McLean as a younger version of herself, as she might be without a husband and the baggage of his old New England family tying her down. Although a friendship soon develops between the two women, it quickly flounders when Mrs. McLean—open, naive, friendly— violates the unspoken protocol of her new community by befriending the black man she has hired to work as her gardener.

Mrs. Winning is unable—and unwilling—to withstand the pressure put upon her to condemn her onetime friend (the key test of loyalty, which she fails, naturally takes place in the local grocery store), and soon becomes as close-minded and unfriendly towards the unfortunate newcomer as the rest of their small community. The story ends as Mrs. Winning again shuns her friend—her only chance to break free of the bonds of local opinion and continuity—and fully accepts her place in the family hierarchy: "Mrs. Winning swung round without speaking, and started, with great dignity, back up the hill towards the old house" (*L* 100).

Yet another naive city newcomer is defeated by stubborn New

England logic in "Men with Their Big Shoes." It is Mrs. Hart's first summer in the country: she is newly married, heavily pregnant, and ill-prepared to defend herself against the not-so-subtle manipulations of the local woman she hires as household help. Mrs. Anderson is said to have an air of "belligerent authority," and, like Mrs. Walpole's competent neighbor, has "knowledge of canning and burnt sugar gravy and setting yeast rolls out to rise" (*L* 187). "All elbows and red face," Mrs. Anderson is simply among the earliest of a long line of unsatisfactory local servants in Jackson's fiction, in what will become a common descriptive pattern, we are told that she "never quite got anything clean." As we shall see, a persistent association with dirt is one of the most telling things about Jackson's portrayal of rural New England.

As her name suggests, Mrs. Hart is vulnerable and soft, unable to impose any sort of authority within her own home. She soon becomes completely dependent on her ill-natured employee. It's the kind of unacknowledged, unequal power struggle between an older and a younger woman that, as Joan Wylie Hall has noted in her study of Jackson's short fiction, appears on several occasions in *The Lottery*. The unhappily married Mrs. Anderson does her best to sow the seeds of marital discord between her young employer and her husband. While on a trip to the local store, Mrs. Hart is horrified to find that her alleged marriage problems are common knowledge and feels "a quick fear touching her, her kind neighbors watching her beneath their friendliness, looking out quickly from behind closed curtains" (*L* 192). It's the sort of powerful paranoia that would eventually find its fullest expression in *We Have Always Lived in the Castle* (1962).

Eventually maneuvered, against all her better instincts, into inviting the pragmatically manipulative Mrs. Anderson into moving in with her after the baby is born, Mrs. Hart has by the story's end been roundly defeated by her Yankee nemesis. Her final thoughts have much in common with those of the similarly constrained Mrs. Walpole: "Mrs. Hart realized with a sudden, unalterable conviction that she was lost" (*L* 194). Like the rest of Jackson's naive newcomers, she never had a chance. The story is a slightly more malign version of "Tootie in Peonage" (*Come Along with Me*), a light-hearted though fairly condescending tale of a New York family's efforts to adjust to the ignorance, filth, and incompetence of their New Hampshire maid.

The most famous Jackson tale to have a (presumably) New England setting is "The Lottery"—a tale that, like *Castle*, does for small town New England what *Deliverance* did for backwoods Georgia. However, the doomed outsider in "The Lottery," the unfortunate Tessie Hutchinson, was once one of their own, and is singled out by ballot for her singularly unpleasant death by stoning. Although Jackson did remark that she imagined the story as taking part in her own town—i.e. Benning-ton—much of the tale's power lies in the fact that, were one unfamiliar with the author and the origins of the tale, one could imagine it taking place in virtually any isolated rural community. Mob violence, supersti-tion, and complicity are not limited to specific geographical locations. Given the portrayal of New England and its environs in her writing, however, it does seem obvious that Jackson was firmly of the belief that the conditions likely to inspire such a ritual were rather more plausible there than in many other places. While in New York, Jackson's heroines are generally threatened either by their own vulnerable mental state ("The Tooth," "Pillar of Salt") or by unseen, anonymous forces beyond their own control ("Nightmare"); significantly, the threat in her rural loca-tions comes more typically from one's neighbors than from one's self.

Perhaps the best illustration of this trend is in "The Summer Peo-ple." The premise is simple: the Allisons, "sanitary city people" on the verge of old age, have for the past 17 years spent their summers in a pic-turesque but isolated country cottage. With no pressing commitments back in the city, they decide to stay a month longer than usual—despite the fact that as the local grocer laconically (and ominously) observes, "Nobody ever stayed at the lake past labor day before" (C 67). Yet again, a trip to the grocery store is a means for Jackson to dramatize the gulf that exists between incomers and "natives." The Allisons are torn between irritation at the slower pace of life in the countryside—expressed by the length of time it takes the grocer to tie a parcel—and a professed admiration for these very qualities: "It was horrible to think into what old New England Yankee stock had degenerated. 'It's generations of inbreeding. That and the bad land'" (C 68), Mr. Alison declares—sen-timents that could have come straight from Lovecraft's "The Dunwich Horror." A moment later, however, they assure themselves that the locals are nevertheless "so solid, and so reasonable, and so honest"—with the unspoken assumption perhaps that scrupulous honesty is in itself the hallmark of a less sophisticated civilization than they are used to.

Their feelings of comfortable familiarity soon erode. The Allisons discover that the kerosene to light their lamps and fuel their stove can't be delivered (the local who distributes it claims that he hasn't ordered enough). The mail comes late, and with "an unusual number of dirty fingerprints on the envelope" (C 77). Most ominously of all, their pre-viously cooperative, pleasant neighbors prove themselves unwilling to help, and the old couple realizes just how dependent they are upon the good will of the local population. As though following the logical pro-gression of a horror movie, the Allisons next find that their car (and only means of escape) no longer starts and that the phone has gone dead. The story ends as the old couple huddle together in their cottage, waiting to see what terrible fate (if any) will befall them. The dichotomy between rural and city people has never been as starkly nor as atmospherically expressed in Jackson's work.

The Sundial (1956) is the first Jackson *novel* in which the relationship between her protagonists and the inhabitants of the neighboring village is of great significance. There is a strong undercurrent of class tension and mutual resentment in all three of Jackson's later novels (as there was in her first), an undercurrent as strong as that found in any classic eighteenth century gothic text. The country house is in its own way as potent a symbol of power and wealth as any castle; they are the "power houses of a ruling class," as Richard Davenport Hines characterizes the nineteenth century British variety (Hines 61). The country mansion is where the squire or lord traditionally resided, a figure whose wealth was based upon the rent and labor of his tenants. The house in such cases functioned as both headquarters and showcase: an intimidating symbol of power whose very solidity gave an illusion of permanence, and a visible reminder of the wealth and taste of its occupier. The psychological and social importance of such a building is given a unique resonance when transported to the colonial landscape of America, which is partly why the feature of the antebellum plantation house recurs with such frequency in the southern gothic. However, it is worth bearing in mind that Jackson's habitual New England landscape—rarely explicitly located, but always implied—is the place where the British colonies in America were first established. Jackson's gothic mansions, are clearly intended to represent modern-day versions of the traditional gothic castle; generic clichés reconfigured for a new age, and created with a strong awareness of (and willingness to adapt) the generic codes that lend them such resonance in the first place.

It is interesting to note, therefore, that Jackson's final novels all feature a mansion built by Victorian exemplars of American free enterprise, the new aristocracy in American life; and that her protagonists are all removed from the inhabitants and the locality in which they live—a removal symbolized by the actual physical barriers between them and the outside world.[2] We are told in *Sundial* that "the Halloran land was distinguished from the rest of the world by a stone wall, so that all inside the wall was Halloran and all outside was not" (*S* 11). Hill House is separated from the village of Hillsdale by a heavy iron gate, while the Blackwood mansion in *Castle* has been fenced off from the surrounding area. Such physical barriers—like the eponymous wall in *Road*—symbolize the self-absorption and snobbery of the residents within.

The Halloran clan view themselves as the aristocracy of their own little village: indeed they do have a self-appointed queen (Orianna), an heiress (Fancy), loyal servants (Essex, Miss Ogilvie), and understandably resentful subjects (the villagers). They arrange jobs for ungrateful locals, pay the schoolteacher, and graciously make a point of trading in the village, but their largesse does have its limits:

> At one point, however, the first Mr. Halloran had made an unbreakable law: the servants in the big house came, without exception, from the city. Villagers, Mr. Halloran maintained, belonged to the village, and not within the walls of the big house [*S* 68].

It's a rule enforced even at the climactic garden party, which takes place entirely outside. At this party we find that the first Mr. Halloran's suspicion of villagers is perhaps due to the fact that part of his estate is built on land stolen from their grandfathers, a discovery greatly at odds with Aunt Fanny's typically rose-tinted remembrances:

> When he first spoke of building the big house, he spoke at once of you villagers. "We must take care of them always," he said, "They will look to us for guidance and security" [*S* 162].

The entire scene is riddled with irony: Aunt Fanny makes this pronouncement to a group of villagers that includes the postmaster, whose grandfather's farm was flooded so that the Hallorans could have a lake (complete with vicious swans). Nor does the alleged Halloran benevolence towards their neighbors stretch to warning any of them about the (alleged) impending apocalypse: no villager is offered shelter in the big house despite its vast size, and so the Hallorans happily preside over the garden party despite their firm belief that all of their guests will be dead in less than a day. It's a contradiction that prompts the sociopathic but perceptive Fancy to ask her grandmother,

> "Why do you bother to give them all that good food and stuff to drink?" "One last indulgence. Now we can remember them as being happy and carefree" [*S* 168].

Tellingly, the only big-house resident to voice any reservations about their abandonment of the villagers is Miss Ogilvie, the downtrodden governess, who, carried away by alcohol and the bacchanalian cavorting of the early hours, wails, "Please let them come with us" (*S* 174). Of course, no one pays her any attention: like Cassandra, her cries go unheeded. The feudal nature of the relationship between the Hallorans and the local village is reinforced by the fact that Orianna insists upon wearing her specially commissioned crown during the party (fittingly, that same crown will be snatched from her warm corpse less than a day later by the gleeful Fancy). As Jackson's most satirical novel, the condescension and snobbery displayed by the Hallorans are all further indications that they should be amongst those *least* deserving of a special place in the "New World." Unlike the clash between naive city dwellers and canny locals in so many of Jackson's short stories, the relationship between the Hallorans (not newcomers by any means, but certainly separated from natives by wealth, arrogance and class) and their "subjects" is mostly played for laughs—that is, until we come across a scene that, as Jack Sullivan has noted, "seems to have sneaked into the novel from one of Jackson's darker short stories" (Sullivan 228).

Julia Willow, reluctantly drafted in by her mother to join the "chosen people," decides to flee to the city before the appointed date with destiny. Her escape attempt is foiled by a terrifying taxi driver who announces, "I live in the village, of course" (*S* 116) and begins to tell her during the journey that he once decapitated a litter of puppies with his pocket knife and poured kerosene on kittens. His declaration in other circumstances might have seemed laughably extreme—but in this instance, Julia is a vulnerable young woman trapped in a car with a very menacing man (during a heavy fog as well, just to add to the occasion). Again, a local is associated with lack of cleanliness: "he touched her on the back with his great dirty hand" (*S* 118). When she finally manages to get out of the cab—ignoring the cabby's unconvincing protests that he was only kidding—Julia finds that she has no choice but to shamefacedly trudge back to the house. The tensions between rich and poor, and upper and lower classes, and the fear of what will happen when unspoken rules of protocol are violated infuse this scene as they do so many of Jackson's stories.

A large, gothic house set in a small New England village also provides the setting for Jackson's most famous novel, *The Haunting of Hill House*. Hillsdale, the village one must pass through in order to reach the malign Hill House, is from the very beginning of the novel portrayed in a negative light—as though the malevolence of the house has somehow contaminated the very land and people that surround it. Dr. Montague warns (accurately) in his letter giving Eleanor Vance directions, "The people there are rude to strangers and openly hostile to anyone inquiring about Hill House" (*HH* 16). In characteristic Jackson fashion, when Eleanor does reach Hillsdale, she finds that it is "a tangled, disorderly, mess of dirty houses and crooked streets," with an "unattractive diner" and "broken kerb" (*HH* 24). Two "elaborately silent" young boys lounge against a fence (making the already jittery Eleanor feel even more ill at ease). Out of some kind of desperate pride or bravado, Eleanor enters the local diner (a scene very close to one that takes place in the opening pages of *Castle*) and forces herself to interact with the sullen occupants despite the "grey counter and smeared glass bowl." It is, as one might expect at this stage, a less than salubrious establishment:

> Perhaps Eleanor's coffee was poisoned; it certainly looked it. Determined to plumb the village of Hillsdale to its lowest depths, Eleanor said to the girl, "I'll have one of those doughnuts too, please" [*HH* 24].

When Eleanor, out of genuine curiosity and a game attempt to start a conversation, asks if there are any city folks in the hills, renovating old houses for themselves, the sole local customer can barely conceal his disdain: "People *leave* this town," he said. "They don't *come* here" (*HH* 25). Given the events that constitute the rest of the novel, the local's scorn is understandable; after all, the most prominent local monstrosity was constructed by a wealthy newcomer who "built his house to suit his mind," with horrific consequences. "They go away, the lucky ones," the surly waitress finally declares—a truth that Eleanor will finally learn the hard way (*HH* 26).

The most prominent representatives of Yankee hospitality in the novel are of course Mr. and Mrs. Dudley—the caretaker and housekeeper of Hill House. Mr. Dudley, "dark and threatening as the padlock" of his fiercely defended gate (*HH* 28), at first refuses to let Eleanor enter the grounds and forces her to uncharacteristically assert herself. Mrs. Dudley, an essentially comic character due to her dour demeanor and constant repetition of ominous warnings, is a true match for her husband, and probably the least welcoming housekeeper since Mrs. Danvers in *Rebecca* (whom she may well parody—both enter rooms without making a sound). Jackson describes her in by now familiar fashion:

> Her apron was clean, her hair was neat, and yet she gave off an indefinable air of dirtiness, quite in keeping with her husband, and the suspicious sullenness of her face was a match for the malicious petulance of his [*HH* 36].

Eleanor does ask herself for a moment if her first, entirely negative impressions are sound, and have not perhaps been unduly influenced by her environment: "If I hadn't seen Hill House, would I be so unfair to these people?"—to which we must answer yes; given that she is a protagonist in a Shirley Jackson novel, she is unlikely to have formed positive impressions of the staff.

While first Theo and Eleanor, and then the Doctor and Luke as well, mock Mrs. Dudley behind her back and scoff at her ominous pronouncements (such as "I leave before dark" [*HH* 39]) their amusement means that they fail to take seriously the fact that she and her husband are the only people who truly understand what the house is capable of. Having cared for the house for as long as anyone can remember, they understand that bravado and wit are no defense against a place of concentrated ill will:

> Eleanor sensed, with a quick turn of apprehension, that flippant or critical talk about the house bothered Mrs. Dudley in some manner; maybe she thinks it can hear us, Eleanor thought ... [*HH* 43].

Conflict between the cloistered inhabitants of the big house and the villagers over whom that house looms is—we must not forget—at the heart of the reputed cause of the titular haunting. When Dr. Montague outlines the house's history we discover that Hugh Crain's eldest daughter hired her servants in the village (the first Mr. Halloran would no doubt have disapproved). There were, we are told, initially no hostile feelings between the residents of Hill House and the village; in fact, it was considered quite an honor to work there. That all changed when the old woman died while the village girl hired to be her companion was rumored to be neglecting her duties.

It is a tale that obviously parallels Eleanor's life—11 dreary years spent caring for her invalided, querulous mother and unresolved feelings of guilt make her the perfect subject for Hill House's attentions. We are told that the young companion insisted that the house has been left to her, and so a bitter, lengthy legal battle erupted between her and Hugh Crain's younger daughter. It was then that the first suggestions of a haunting occurred: the companion complained of numerous small thefts and claimed that someone was creeping about the house at night. Though she won the case, she was mercilessly hounded by the younger sister and "went in terror" due to the sounds and disturbances she experienced at night. Perhaps the younger sister was making trouble, or perhaps the long dead Hugh Crain had been angered by the thought of a local girl inheriting the house built for his daughters. Worst of all for the companion was the fact that once she became mistress of Hill House, the entire village turned against her; she had usurped her natural position and was no longer one of their own. As Montague explains,

> They did not believe that she would murder her friend, you see, but they were delighted to believe that she was dishonest, certainly because they were capable of dishonesty themselves when the opportunity arose. Well, gossip is always a bad enemy. When the poor creature killed herself.... "Killed herself?" Eleanor, shocked into speech, half rose. "She *had* to kill herself?" [my italics] [*HH* 80].

This marks the onset of Eleanor's ultimately fatal identification with the young, significantly unnamed companion. While Theo feels sorry for the young Misses Crain, cooped up for their entire childhood in a dark, isolated house, Eleanor's sympathies, tellingly, already lie elsewhere:

> "You keep thinking of the little children," Eleanor said to Theodora, "but I can't forget that lonely little companion, walking around these rooms, wondering who else was in the house" [*HH* 103].

Eleanor's past, her inability to change her servile personality (such as when she has to be stopped from doing the dishes after dinner), her deep-seated neuroticism, all lead her to fall deeper and deeper into this dangerous affinity. Her instinctive abhorrence of the library, the place where the companion hanged herself, signposts the inevitable conclusion. Consider Eleanor's words on first hearing the companion's story. "She *had* to kill herself"—as though there were no other choice. It is significant phrasing, for as the house encourages Eleanor to reenact the old tragedy, she is finally, fatally, unable to resist. Just like her predecessor, she ultimately finds herself, in a poignant rejoinder to the Hillsdale waitress's dour observation, unable to leave, and therefore one of the *unlucky* ones—a fate shared by so many of Jackson's other visitors to New England.

The class tensions that represent an intriguing (and largely overlooked) facet of *Hill House* arise, much more obviously, in Jackson's final (and finest) novel, *We Have Always Lived in the Castle* (1962). While in *Sundial*, the Halloran clan's condescension towards the local population is treated satirically, and (as in *Road*) their ill-treatment of the working classes is an indication of the snobbishness and self-absorption of Jackson's generally unpleasant protagonists, *Castle*, fascinating for many reasons, essays a remarkably jaundiced portrait of the New England villagers who live alongside Merricat and Constance Blackwood. Here, in fact, the mutual loathing that exists between the Blackwoods and the rest of the world (as represented by their neighbors) supplies the very backbone of the story.

*Castle* is really a novel-length version of a macabre little anecdote first recounted in *Sundial*. Halfway through that novel, Jackson intersperses an account of the Hallorans' shopping trip to the local village with the details of the region's most famous murder case—a case obviously based upon that of Lizzie Borden, nineteenth century New England's most infamous alleged murderess. The village next to the Halloran house has one real tourist attraction, we are told: the house where 15-year-old Harriet Stuart (an obvious Borden surrogate, just like Merricat) bludgeoned her entire family to death with a hammer—but was nevertheless acquitted at the trial (as was Constance) because no one could believe such a young girl could commit such an act. The murders are now a point of some pride, locally: "Fall River, Massachusetts, was nothing to the villagers near Mr. Halloran's proposed big house: Harriet Stuart was their enshrined murderess" (*S* 64).

As if the briefly mentioned Stuart case were a rehearsal, *Castle* becomes Jackson's broad fictionalization of the Borden case or more accurately, its aftermath, when Borden and her sister returned to the town in which their father and stepmother were so brutally murdered and remained there (in Borden's case) for the rest of their lives.

Communal hostility permeates *Castle* from the very outset. The masterful account of Merricat's final shopping expedition, which constitutes the first chapter, has strong echoes of the many other fraught shopping expeditions in Jackson's work. What makes this scene different, however, is the overt nature of the hostility Merricat encounters during her walk through the village and the sheer intensity of the hatred she in turn feels towards the villagers. Like Hillsdale, the unnamed village in *Castle* is described as "grey," "ugly" and "resentful." "The people of the village have always hated us," remarks Merricat during these opening pages, confirming that the hostility between the two camps was present even before the murders took place: at another point she declares that she can "tell a local car by the quick ugly glance from the driver" (*W* 403). The entire scene is laid out like the moment in a Western film where a feared and hated outlaw strides warily through the main street of a one-horse town: that is certainly how it seems to Merricat, who can feel eyes watching her the entire time. The atmosphere is weighed down with suspicion and, above all, mutual resentment. The chapter gradually reveals the extent of Merricat's mental disturbance and the depths of the loathing that the rest of the village seem to feel toward her family. Even the short trip to the grocery store is a terrifying ordeal for Merricat, who is frightened of the local children and their mothers: "I was afraid of them. I was afraid they might touch me and the mothers would come at me like a flock of taloned hawks; that was always the picture I had in my mind—birds descending, striking, gashing with razor claws" (*W* 408). There is a horrified reaction in the store when Merricat blithely asks for sugar and a leg of lamb (both key components of the Blackwood family's fatal last supper six years previously), and we get the sense that Merricat enjoys provoking this kind of reaction. From the very beginning of the novel, there is the sense that she and the rest of the Blackwoods have long thought themselves superior to the people of the village, who, according to Merricat, "disliked the fact that we always had plenty of money to pay for whatever we wanted" (*W* 404). Despite Constance's admonition that it is wrong to hate the villagers because "It only weakens you," Merricat wonders "why it had been worth creating them in the first place" (*W* 406)—as though they are some sort of irritating inferior life form instead of human beings. In the village café, a local man taunts her until she must leave:

> It was Jim Donell and I knew at once that today I had bad luck. Some of the people in the village had real faces that I knew and could hate individually; Jim Donell and his wife were among these, because they were deliberate instead of just hating dully from habit like the others [*W* 409].

Despite such provocation, Merricat resists the urge to retaliate; family pride and a kind of fierce, savage dignity (instilled in her by Constance) are still important to her. The sisters are like the Hallorans, politely hosting a garden party on what they believe to be the eve of the apocalypse, or the Allisons in "The Summer People"—all trying to maintain a kind of ritualistic pretence of gentility and politeness despite the circumstances.

The depth of Merricat's loathing for the villagers she encounters, and of the extent of her madness, is made clear in her graphic fantasies of murder and violence. As she makes her way down the main street, she wishes "they were all dead and I was walking on their bodies" and, even more gruesomely, "thought of them rotting away and curling in pain and crying out loud; I wanted them doubled up and crying on the ground in front of me"(*W* 407). Merricat's bluntly worded desire to see her (perceived) enemies doubled up in agony—which we initially perceive as a means of expressing the fear and hatred she feels as a result of their hostility—is given fresh significance when we accept that she has disposed of her family in just such a fashion:

> Their tongues will burn, I thought, as though they had eaten fire. Their tongues will burn when the words come out, and in their bellies they will feel a torment hotter than a thousand fires [*W* 413].

It is unclear just how long the Blackwoods have lived in the community. Merricat does tell us that her mother was born there, in the so-called Rochester house, once "the loveliest in town," and we do learn that their "father brought home the first piano ever seen in the village" (*W* 401). It seems that the family have therefore for some time been part of the fading local gentility, whose decline is symbolized by the slowly decaying remains of their homes in the center of the village:

> Perhaps the fine houses had been captured—perhaps as punishment for the Rochesters and the Blackwoods and their secret bad hearts—and were help prisoner in the village; perhaps their slow rot was a sign of the ugliness of the villagers [*W* 404].

It seems likely that the resentment between the villagers and the Blackwoods really started when John Blackwood, the family patriarch, fenced off the property because his new wife disliked the sight of anyone walking past her house—"before, everyone used the path as a short cut from the village to the library"—and so the fence inconvenienced almost everyone (*W* 415). Their mother seems to have been motivated by sheer snobbery: she is said to have declared that "the highway's built for common people, and my front door is private" (*W* 415). This sense of social superiority has been passed onto her daughters, and in particular the deranged Merricat, who divides the world into them and us, rich and poor, dirty and clean:

> Up and down the driveway went the good people, the clean and rich ones dressed in satin and lace, who came rightfully to visit, and back and

forth along the path, sneaking and weaving and sidestepping servilely, went the people of the village [*W* 415].

In the aftermath of the murders and Constance's trial, the process of withdrawal begun during their parents' lifetime is merely exaggerated, so that the Blackwoods, although technically locals, have become feared and hated outsiders due to their snobbishness, isolationism and murderous tendencies.

Initially, we are unsure whether Merricat's hatred of the village is justified or is rather a product of her obviously damaged mind. However, it is her paranoid worldview and not the rather more optimistic, conventional hopes of her sister Constance that is vindicated in the novel's violent conclusion. Tellingly, their cozily domesticated way of life comes to an end when their villainous cousin Charles arrives on their doorstep and insinuates himself into their lives. The fact that he quickly acquaints himself with the locals is an ominous sign: as a Blackwood male, and one who is untainted by involvement in the murder of the previous Blackwood patriarch, it seems that he will be readily accepted into the community. All he has to do is impose his authority on the Blackwood women and persuade the rather naive Constance to marry him. Merricat's spot of (semiaccidental) arson soon disrupts his plans, but when the villagers arrive to put out the fire, years of resentment and hatred spill over into an orgy of destructive violence. The climax of *Castle* is therefore the malevolent flipside of *Sundial*'s patronising garden party: instead of watching their manners while in the presence of their supposed social superiors, these villagers are staging an impromptu revolt.

As in "The Lottery," stones are employed by this vengeful mob as well. Once the fire has been extinguished, the fire chief, Jim Donnell, sets down his hard hat and hurls a rock through the window of the drawing room while the sisters watch from their hiding place. After a moment's pause, everyone else joins in, and the beautiful house is systematically vandalized:

> Above it all, most horrible, was the laughter. I saw one of the Dresden figurines thrown and break against the porch rail, and the other fell over unbroken and rolled along the grass. I heard Constance's harp go over with a musical cry, and a sound, which I knew was a chair being smashed against the wall [*W* 494].

Apart from its clear links to "The Lottery," this scene also strongly resembles the moment in so many classic black and white horror movies when the local peasants gather their torches and pitchforks and storm the hated castle in order to kill the "monstrous" creature within. Perhaps this is part of the reason why Jackson chooses to make the house/castle analogy so obvious, both in the title and when Merricat remarks of the blackened ruins: "Our house was a castle, turreted and open to the sky" (*W* 507). The interesting thing about such scenes in the classic horror film is that the audience, despite the usually despicable crimes of the monster involved, usually ends up feeling a strong pang of sympathy for it anyway—consider Frankenstein's monster in the James Whale–directed classic *Frankenstein*: the most poignant monster of all.[3] In a similar manner, even though the reader knows that Merricat has murdered six people and that Constance has shielded her from any punishment, our sympathy, like Jackson's, is very much with the persecuted, not the mob, whose actions only cease when Uncle Julian's (natural) death is discovered.

Though some of the villagers do come to regret their actions, and attempt to atone for them by leaving baskets of food in the blackened ruins, these gestures are inspired more by fear than remorse. For the sisters have become the witchlike, shadowy figures they were always believed to be, and the villagers fear some sort of preternatural vengeance. It's a more than fitting end for Jackson's final completed novel: after all, what better place for a pair of modern-day witches than rural New England?

So, ultimately, what are we to make of Shirley Jackson's depictions of New England and New Englanders? It is probably safe to say that she would never have been offered a job with the Vermont state tourist board: her New England does not (even in the family chronicles) strike one as a particularly welcoming place. At best, as in the family chronicles and a few of the more light-hearted short stories, it is depicted as a place that must be gradually adjusted to, with a way of life very different from that of the city. At worst, the region is portrayed as a place in which optimistic newcomers encounter fear, terror and intimidation—often when they have violated some unspoken but binding rule of conduct (such as befriending a black gardener, or staying on past Labor Day). What is particularly interesting is that although Jackson's newcomers frequently end up isolated and persecuted, they do generally bring this punishment, brutal and disproportionate it may be, upon themselves. Of course, it may be nigh on impossible, as Jackson suggests, to avoid violating some such unspoken rule, but that's their own problem.

The same principle applies to those who may actually be locals themselves, but who would certainly not consider themselves part of the local population, and who belong to the wealthy upper class: the Blackwoods, the Crains and the Hallorans. They are outsiders by choice, but are tolerated, unless, like the Blackwood sisters, they break a law too big to be ignored (such as mass murder). Having inspired much resentment even before Constance is acquitted of murder, the Blackwoods have lost the safety that their class and wealth (as well as place of birth) would otherwise have afforded them. All that is needed is the right spark (literally in this case) to ignite the flames of violence and destruction.

As we have seen, Jackson's portrayal of the typical New England community is at best condescending and at worst quite offensive. The locals her protagonists encounter are at various times insular, glowering, resentful, inbred, threatening, violent, prejudiced and supercilious. Of course at times (in the family chronicles) they are portrayed in a rather more positive light, and one must also remember that (as with Merricat's journey into the village and the Hallorans' garden party) her depiction of local color is also a way of highlighting the snobbishness or skewed worldview of her protagonists.

However, Jackson's use of certain adjectives time and time again while describing the region is telling. As I have shown, the villages (and frequently, the villagers) that appear in Jackson's work are usually described as being somehow unclean—dirty, grey, grimy—in contrast to her "sanitary" city folk. At its most heightened, Merricat's hatred of the villagers seems to come from a deep-seated fear of contamination, as though the dirt and greyness of the village will infect her: while this is obviously also a symptom of her psychotic mindset, one wonders if it is an exaggerated version of some of the feelings that Jackson herself had towards New England. The frequency with which the same descriptive terms reoccur would seem to suggest this possibility.

While "The Lottery" may be Jackson's most famously negative portrayal of New England village life, there is, as I have shown, an increasingly unpleasant depiction of the region in her work over a longer period of time, an unpleasantness that climaxes with the paranoid fantasies of *Castle*. Merricat's hatred of the villagers, so graphically expressed, is of course a reflection of her madness, but there is perhaps the feeling that in her invective Jackson is expressing (in greatly exaggerated form) some of the feelings she herself was harboring towards her neighbors. Certainly, Jackson's biography suggests that relations between her and the townspeople of Bennington deteriorated over the years. It is not such a stretch to imagine that these events influenced her writing. It is also notable that when local people do feature in Jackson's work, they usually appear as servants, or in a subordinate role of some kind—as virtual subjects, as maids, tradesmen, grocers, or schoolteachers paid by the inhabitants of the big house. Very few of her locals become full-fledged characters in their own right. They tend to exist as foils for Jackson's real concern: her outsiders. Jackson's working classes have as their most prominent form of local activity the angry mob.

A topic like this demands that we ask the following question: How would Jackson's writing have differed if she had remained in California? Or New York? Or if she and her husband has decided to move to Georgia, or Texas, instead of backwoods Vermont? It's impossible to be certain, but almost all of what would become Jackson's most characteristic themes are present in *Road* (written shortly after the move to Vermont but set in California). This would seem to suggest that her unique authorial voice and keen interest in the darker side of human nature, the effect of one's living environment, and insular, self-absorbed communities were already present before she moved to New England. But as early as the mid-to-late 1940s, when the stories that constituted *The Lottery* were written and compiled, the influence that New England was having upon Jackson's work was becoming apparent, with many of the stories included in the collection obviously reflecting to some extent her mixed feelings towards her new home.

In New England's unique environment—and in her own sometimes-difficult adjustment to that environment—Shirley Jackson discovered the perfect geographical corollary to her own fictional concerns. We find in many of the short stories and in her final novels an irresistible, unmistakable connection between writer and place. We can never know what kind of novels Jackson might have written had she settled elsewhere. Her gothic inclinations were already obvious early in her career, while one could say, with some justification, that "The Lottery," *Sundial, Hill House* and *Castle* could be set in any isolated rural community in America. The point is that they weren't: though rarely explicitly identified in her work, New England's landscape and inhabitants have left an indelible impression upon Jackson's writing. Without this imprint, Jackson's often funny, sometimes charming, and frequently menacing fictional universe would not be nearly as compelling.

## Notes

1. Between 1945 and 1950, seven people disappeared in the woods around Bennington. There was no evidence to suggest murder, and only one of those who had vanished was ever found dead, although this was in a spot previously covered by search parties, which suggests that the body was placed there after the alarm was raised. Those who vanished seemed to have no connection or resemblance to one another: they included a 75-year-old man who failed to return from a deer hunt (1945), an eight-year-old boy who vanished from his father's truck (1950) and, two weeks later, an experienced female hiker. There were further disappearances in November and December of 1950.The disappearance of Paula Welden in December 1946 was the case most widely reported in the press, and her father made a series of anxious radio broadcasts requesting information. Given the fact that the Bennington student body at the time was only about 300, and that her husband was on the faculty during this time, it seems likely that Jackson would have been more than familiar with the case: indeed, the stories "Louisa Please Come Home" and "The Missing Girl" seem to be obvious fictionalizations of the case. For more information, consult "The Mad Murderer of the Long Trail" from *Into Thin Air: People Who Disappear* by Paul Begg (1979; Sphere; London, 1981 ed.); *They Never Came Back*, by Allen Churchill; and *The New York Times*, 4–24 December 1946.

2. For more on this topic, see Pascal, "New American Miniatures," Journal of American and Comparative Cultures 233 (fall 2000): 99–111.

3. Much the same image is employed by Sylvia Plath in the poem "Daddy"—
"There's a stake in your fat black heart/And the villagers never liked you./They are
dancing and stamping on you./They always knew it was you." For a humorous modern version of such a scene, see Tim Burton's 1987 film *Edward Scissorhands* in which
the pastel-clothed residents of a suburban neighborhood end up storming their local
castle in order to oust the eponymous outsider.

## *Works Cited*

Carpenter, Lynette. "Domestic Comedy, Black Comedy, and Real Life: Shirley Jack-
son, a Woman Writer." *In Faith of a Woman Writer.* Eds. Alice Kessler-Harris and
William Mc Brien. New York: Greenwood Press, 1988.
Hall, Joan Wylie. *Shirley Jackson: The Short Fiction.* New York: Twayne Publishers,
1993.
Hines, Richard Davenport. *Gothic: 400 Years of Excess, Horror, Evil and Ruin.* Lon-
don: Fourth Estate, 1998.
Jackson, Shirley. *The Bird's Nest.* 1954; London: Michael Joseph, 1954.
_____. *Come Along with Me.* 1966; New York: Penguin, 1996.
_____. *Hangsaman.* London: Victor Gollancz, 1951.
_____. *The Haunting of Hill House.* 1959; New York: Penguin, 1987.
_____. *Just an Ordinary Day.* New York: Bantam, 1996.
_____. *Life Among the Savages.* 1953; London: Michael Joseph, 1954.
_____. *The Lottery and Other Stories, or The Adventures of James Harris.* 1949. *The
Masterpieces of Shirley Jackson.* London: Raven, 1996.
_____. *Raising Demons.* London: Michael Joseph, 1957.
_____. *The Road Through the Wall.* 1948; New York: Farrar Straus, 1975.
_____. *The Sundial.* 1958; New York, Ace Books, n.d.
_____. *We Have Always Lived in the Castle.* 1962. *The Masterpieces of Shirley Jackson.*
London: Robinson, 1996.
Oppenheimer, Judy. *Private Demons: The Life of Shirley Jackson.* New York: G.P. Put-
nam's Sons, 1988.
Ringel, Faye. *New England Gothic Literature: History and Folklore of the Supernatural
from the Seventeenth Through Twentieth Centuries.* New York: E. Mellen Press, 1991.
Sullivan, Jack, ed. "Shirley Jackson." *In the Penguin Encyclopaedia of Horror and the
Supernatural.* New York: Viking, 1986.
Westbrook, Perry D. *The New England Town in Fact and Fiction.* Lonon: Associated
University Press, 1982.

# 6

# House Mothers and Haunted Daughters: Shirley Jackson and the Female Gothic

ROBERTA RUBENSTEIN

Although for many readers, Shirley Jackson is indelibly linked with her chilling and universally anthologized short story "The Lottery," her *oeuvre* (six novels, with a seventh left unfinished at her death, and over a hundred short stories) deserves wider recognition for its emotionally resonant literary representations of the psychology of family relationships. This essay explores the ways in which Jackson's fiction demonstrates her increasingly masterful, and also increasingly gothic, representations of the primitive and powerful emotional bonds that constitute the ambivalent attachment between mothers and daughters in particular.[1] This discussion is situated within several contexts: Shirley Jackson's life, feminist and object-relations psychology,[2] and the conventions of gothic narrative—specifically the pattern of characteristics identified as female gothic.

These contexts intersect in several pairs of strongly marked elements that occur in tension throughout Jackson's *oeuvre*; these pairs can be identified as *inside/outside, mother/self, home/lost,* and *"eat or be eaten."* "Inside/outside" signifies the fluid emotional boundaries that occur as an infant progressively distinguishes itself from her or his environment during the formation of identity.[3] The tensions between "mother/self"

*This essay first appeared in* Tulsa Studies in Women's Literature *15 (1996): 309–31, and is reproduced here with the permission of* Tulsa Studies in Women's Literature *©1996.*

and between "home/lost" connote a young child's ambivalent desires and
fears: both to remain merged with the mother (who becomes emotionally identified with "home") and to separate from her, with the attendant danger of being "lost."[4] "Eat or be eaten" suggests the literal and
figurative correspondences between consuming and being consumed or
incorporated.[5] Psychoanalytically, a female's anxieties about food and
body image suggest that her body is (or once was) a battleground in the
struggle for autonomy in the face of what she may experience as her
mother's consuming criticism, possessiveness, or withholding of love.
Moreover, food involves a transition across boundaries as it is transformed from "outside" to "inside" the self by the act of consumption;
less literally, incorporation may signal a predatory "consume or be consumed" relationship, as indeed exists between several mother-daughter
pairs in Jackson's fiction.

The author's biography confirms that issues in her personal life res-
onate with these narratively expressed motifs in her fiction. Though of
course biography cannot (and should not) be used uncritically to explain
literary texts, it is nonetheless instructive to acknowledge some of the
sources of Jackson's narrative preoccupations within their psychological
and social contexts. According to the author's remarks about and correspondence with her mother as well as other evidence supplied by her
biographer, tensions between daughter and mother originated early in
the author's life and were not resolved by the time of her premature death
of a heart attack at the age of 46. As Judy Oppenheimer determines in
her account of Jackson's life, Geraldine Jackson's attitude toward her
daughter was a deeply disconfirming one from the very beginning: Shirley
"was not the daughter her mother wanted; that much was clear from the
start."[6] Throughout her life, Shirley was distressed by her mother's profound insensitivity to her actual personality, combined with persistent
attempts to control her unconventionality. By contrast, Shirley's father
seems to have been a figure on the margins of her life who corroborated
his wife's conventional expectations for their daughter.

For much of her life, Jackson was significantly overweight, even
obese, a fact that her mother never accepted and tried repeatedly to alter
through disparaging remarks and disapproving actions: "Years after
Shirley had left home, married, and given birth to her own children, her
mother still sent her corsets in the mail, trying foolishly but persistently
to rein in the overgrown creature she had somehow, unbelievably produced" (Oppenheimer 14).[7] Indicative of Geraldine Jackson's preoccupation with her daughter's size and physical appearance, her letters to
Shirley were punctuated with such comments as "Glad you're dieting."
"Excess weight is hard on the heart." "You should get down to normal
weight. Try non-fat milk" (Oppenheimer 161). Soon after the publication

of Jackson's last novel, *We Have Always Lived in the Castle*, her mother responded to the publicity picture of the by-then obese Shirley by writing, "Why oh why do you allow the magazines to print such awful pictures of you? ... I have been so sad all morning about what you have allowed yourself to look like" (Oppenheimer 245–46).

Jackson's relationships with her own four children, particularly her two daughters, duplicated some of the ambivalence she experienced in her relationship with her mother. A deeply committed and involved mother, she was also "emotional and erratic.... Her moods and her anxieties colored the children's days; her demands, both surface and subterranean, often confused and upset them. No one could be more loving; no one could be meaner" (Oppenheimer 199). She saw her children not only "as individuals, but ... as mirrors ... reflecting her various parts. With time, this would be refined into only two rays—Joanne and Sally, her daughters" (Oppenheimer 163). As Shirley did with her own mother, her first daughter, Joanne, felt "from a very young age, that 'I was not the daughter she wanted.... I was too conventional'" (Oppenheimer 201). Jackson's second daughter, Sarah (Sally), was much more like Shirley herself: volatile, impetuous, unconventional. As a young child, Sarah's "wildness, her arguments, her maverick ways ... were the very things that made Shirley identify so strongly with her" (Oppenheimer 200).

Virtually all of Jackson's longer narratives and a significant number of her short stories demonstrate a preoccupation with family relationships, if not also with problematic mother-daughter relationships, ambiguous houses, and eating or incorporation. Her family chronicles, *Life Among the Savages* (1953) and *Raising Demons* (1956), are wryly comic explorations of her experiences as a mother of four lively children; yet their droll tone is belied by the title words, underscoring the "savage" and "demonic" elements that laced Jackson's vision of family. While in the domestic comedies the doting if unorthodox mother regards her children, albeit genially, as savages and demons, in a number of her short stories and in most of her longer fiction, Jackson represents her own far darker relational anxieties from not only a maternal but a filial perspective.

As Joan Wylie Hall observes of Jackson's *oeuvre* of over 110 stories, the short fiction frequently focuses on "imperiled females" and "divided" or "anxious" women[8]: "Whether her mood was comic or serious, Jackson often wrote of ordinary characters—typically women in their twenties and thirties—who become enmeshed in extraordinary situations that either free them or, more often, trap them."[9] In the longer narratives, the central female characters, typically at the pivotal age between childhood and womanhood, are particularly anxious and ambivalent about their relationships with their mothers. In the first two novels, the mother is invasively present in the daughter's life; in each of the four succeeding novels, the mother is dead but no less powerfully present. In fact, the mother's absence becomes a haunting presence that bears directly on the daughter's difficult struggle to achieve selfhood as well as to express her unacknowledged rage or her sense of precariousness in the world.

Jackson's choice of the gothic genre—for her last three novels in particular—is especially appropriate, given the psychological issues that dominated her own life. Gothic narratives pivot upon anxieties about selfhood and entrapment, represented through bizarre or exaggerated events that may or may not be explained as manifestations of the (typically) female central character's troubled imagination.[10] More specifically, Jackson's later narratives contain distinct elements of the type of gothic narrative that has been termed "female gothic."[11] Claire Kahane identifies the characteristics of traditional gothic narratives, including "an imprisoning structure" within which the protagonist, "typically a young woman whose mother has died, is compelled to seek out the center of a mystery, while vague and usually sexual threats to her person from some powerful male figure hover on the periphery of her consciousness" (334). Kahane notes that critical approaches to gothic narratives characteristically emphasize an underlying oedipal or incestuous struggle between a powerless daughter and an erotically powerful father or other male figure (335). She proposes, instead, that the central feature of female gothic is not an oedipal conflict but, implicitly, a preoedipal one,[12] embodied in the daughter's search for or fear of "the spectral presence of a dead-undead mother, archaic and all-encompassing, a ghost signifying the problematics of femininity which the heroine must confront" (336). Thus, in these narratives authored by women and focusing on female protagonists, traditional elements of the gothic genre are elaborated in particular ways, notably through the central character's troubled identification with her good/bad/dead/mad mother, whom she ambivalently seeks to kill or merge with; and her imprisonment in a house that, mirroring her disturbed imaginings, expresses her ambivalent experience of entrapment and longing for protection.

Events that pivot on an unstable, threatening, or anxious relationship between mother and daughter, as well as concerns about food and nurturance or body image, are present from the beginning of Jackson's fiction and become increasingly central in succeeding short stories and longer narratives. In the interest of focus, this essay will briefly mention aspects of several stories and early novels that either anticipate or exhibit these central preoccupations and will then concentrate on the later novels, which most vividly represent within gothic narrative frameworks the psychological oppositions suggested above.

In an early story, "I Know Who I Love" (1946), a daughter attempts to come to terms with the emptiness of her life and her feelings about her parents, who had demanded too much filial compliance. Catherine's widowed mother, who lives with her until her death, responds to her dutiful nurturance with contemptuous disregard, expressing her feelings with comments such as "You always were an ungrateful, spoiled child."[13] Catherine replies, "You eat, don't you? ... Something must make me take care of you and feed you."[14]

Another of Jackson's early stories and her early novels focus not on the mother-daughter relationship but on a woman's progressive estrangement from herself and her domestic surroundings. In "The Beautiful Stranger" (1946), a young woman initially believes that her husband has been replaced by an imposter, a "beautiful stranger." Ultimately, when she returns after a shopping trip in town, she cannot even recognize her own home. The estranged environment and self assume a different expression in Jackson's first novel, *The Road Through the Wall* (1948): an apparently benign suburban neighborhood is exposed as a hypocritical—indeed, terrifying—place in which two children die, shockingly, by murder and suicide. Harriet Merriam, one of two adolescent girls who figure among the novel's many characters, is overweight while her best friend is skinny; observing herself as others see her, Harriet acknowledges "a gross, a revolting series of huge mountains, a fat fat fat girl."[15] Natalie Waite, the emotionally unstable adolescent protagonist of Jackson's second novel, *Hangsaman* (1951), also inhabits an estranged environment. She hears secret voices, in particular the voice of a police detective who interrogates her about a murder committed in her house. Natalie also struggles with anxieties about her parents and her body image. Her mother induces powerful guilt in her for the family sacrifices made in order for her to attend college, while her bombastic father also exerts a consuming role in her emotional life. A writer himself, he alternately praises and disparages her written efforts, even sharply critiquing her letters home from college.[16]

During her first year away from home, Natalie's apprehensions increase: she begins to eat more and becomes preoccupied with her weight (her surname, Waite, is a homonym of "weight"), and at the same time she fears the annihilation of her self, thinking about "when [she] would be dead."[17] In her loneliness and self-doubt, she fantasizes a secret female companion named Tony, who may be understood as her braver, more self-sufficient alter ego. At one point late in the novel, Natalie's emotional disorientation is externalized as she becomes literally lost. Wandering in confusion in a forest near the college, she briefly considers suicide and wishes that her mother would "come to take [her] home" (276). Eventually she masters her fears, asserting to herself—in words that sound rather hollow, given the anxieties that shape her story—that she is "now alone and grown up, and powerful, and not at all afraid" (*Hangsaman*, 280).

Jackson represents filial anxiety, ambivalence, and anger, as well as the consuming aspect of maternal power, with greater psychological and narrative complexity in her middle novels, *The Bird's Nest* (1954) and *The Sundial* (1958). In *The Bird's Nest*, Elizabeth Richmond's mother has been dead for four years before the narrative commences. Twenty-three-year-old Elizabeth—who shares her mother's name and is thus implicitly identified with her—lives with her mother's sister, the jealous and tyrannical Aunt Morgen, who regards her deceased sister as a "brutal, unprincipled, drunken, vice-ridden beast."[18] Veiled references in the narrative suggest that Elizabeth's mother was herself a victim of an abusive lover who may also have abused Elizabeth as a child. Other details imply that Elizabeth contributed directly to her mother's death through a physical attack precipitated by anger at maternal neglect, the circumstances of which she cannot remember. As a manifestation of both the estranged environment and the emotional disarray that ultimately fragment Elizabeth's inner life, the museum where she works begins to collapse on its foundations: "It is not proven that Elizabeth's personal equilibrium was set off balance by the slant of the office floor, nor could it be proven that it was Elizabeth who pushed the building off its foundations, but it is undeniable that they began to slip at about the same time" (150). In her fictional representation of what is currently termed multiple personality disorder,[19] Jackson persuasively portrays the disintegration of Elizabeth's personality into four distinct and partial "selves," which act out either excessive concern with good behavior or the guilt and rage she feels toward her unavailable mother—feelings that the previously undissociated Elizabeth has repressed.

The unresolved question that occupies the subtext of *The Bird's Nest* is whether Elizabeth in fact killed her mother or only imagined it, either as the wish to annihilate her or the fear that she might have done so. Jackson splits the daughter's feelings towards the mother not only psychologically—the four fragmentary personas into which Elizabeth disintegrates—but narratively: between Elizabeth, whose unresolved grief and longing for her absent mother, as well as her unacknowledged guilt concerning her contributory role in her mother's death, precipitate her personality fragmentation, and Aunt Morgen, who "enjoyed every minute of [her sister's death]" (311)—that is, who celebrated the death that Elizabeth could not. Ultimately, through the intervention of a pointedly named psychiatrist, Dr. Victor Wright, Elizabeth achieves reintegration into a single self, but that recovery is not without cost. At the novel's conclusion, the "nuclear family" is ironically reconstituted with the tyrannical Aunt Morgen as mother, the equivocal Dr. Wright as father, and

Elizabeth—divested of the name she shared with her mother and renamed "Morgen Victoria" by the new "parents" who have assumed possession of her—as the reintegrated but psychologically diminished, compliant daughter.

As expressed in this narrative, Jackson's solution to the problem of personal integration within the social realm illuminates the predatory element she identified within family relationships. In a view that invites comparison with the law of the jungle—"eat or be eaten"—Dr. Wright of *The Bird's Nest* dryly concludes that "each life ... asks the devouring of other lives for its own continuance; the radical aspect of ritual sacrifice ... its great step ahead, was in organization; *sharing* the victim was so eminently practical" (378, emphasis in original). In Jackson's final novels, not only sacrifice but incorporation and consumption become both literal and figurative as the expression of connection—or, more accurately, disconnection—between mothers and daughters.

In *The Sundial,* the female gothic sensibility is elaborated through a daughter's ambivalent relation to both (dead) parents. The visionary Fanny Halloran believes she has received a revelation of the end of the world from her deceased father's spirit. All but one of the other occupants of the Halloran country estate enter into Fanny's fantasy, longing for a benevolent being who will lead them into the promised land suggested by her apocalyptic vision; collectively, they reinforce her conviction of the world's imminent annihilation. The exception is Fanny's sister-in-law Orianna, a Halloran by marriage only, whom the others regard distrustfully as a predatory mother who pushed her own son down a flight of stairs to his death. Orianna (Mrs. Halloran) functions in the story as Fanny's dark double; seizing power over the credulous lodgers who await the apocalypse, she establishes herself as the house mother or queen, even fashioning a crown to signify her authority.

*The Sundial* is the first of Jackson's novels to represent the precariousness of female selfhood through the image of a house that becomes the daughter's fortress against a threatening and hostile world outside its boundaries. (Several of Jackson's short stories also feature distinctly Gothic houses, including those described in "The Visit" [1950] and "The Little House" [1962].) Psychologically, the house embodies the legacy of the all-powerful parents lodged within an insecurely developed self. In Fanny Halloran, the ego's precarious but heavily defended boundary between what exists "inside" and "outside" the self is expressed through her father's message of incipient danger from the external world: the Halloran estate is "distinguished from the rest of the world by a stone wall ... so that all inside the wall was Halloran, all outside was not."[20] Additionally, the regressive dimension of Fanny's orientation to the world is signaled by her apartment in the attic of the house, a retreat that she maintains as a virtual shrine to her childhood and to her since-deceased parents.

Like Natalie Waite of *Hangsaman,* Fanny Halloran briefly becomes literally what she is psychologically: a lost child who longs for reunion with her mother. Though it is her father whose spiritual presence fuels her apocalyptic fantasies, it is her mother whose image she invokes when she is in distress. Wandering in a maze on the estate grounds, she recalls that, as a child, "I used to come along this path pretending I was lost and could never go home again" *(The Sundial* 88). Reaching the center of the maze and discovering that she is indeed lost, she thinks, "mother, mother" (89) before she finds her way out of the maze and experiences her first "revelation." The image of the mother is thus split between the "good mother" for whom the daughter longs—protective and idealized, but absent—and the "bad mother"—the predatory and tyrannical Mrs. Halloran.[21] In order for Fanny and the other occupants of the house to enact their collective fantasy of apocalypse and the regressive desire for escape from the world, they must annihilate the woman who usurps the maternal role—Fanny's nemesis, Orianna Halloran. Though the world does not come to an end by the conclusion of *The Sundial,* the "bad mother" does: in an event that reproduces her own earlier murderous act against her son, Mrs. Halloran is apparently pushed down a flight of stairs to her death by one of her followers. One observer unrepentantly remarks, "Live by the sword, die by the sword" (187).

The tensions between inside/outside, mother/self, and home/lost persist not only through her early stories and novels but throughout her *oeuvre.* Two late stories elaborate on the psychological estrangement of mother and daughter and the impossibility of the daughter's returning home. In "Louisa, Please Come Home" (1960), 19-year-old Louisa ran away from home two years earlier, changing her name and relishing her freedom from her family. Once a year her mother makes an emotional plea for her return in a radio message. Louisa finally decides, "Maybe I did want to go home. Maybe all that time I had been secretly waiting for a chance to get back" *(Come Along with Me* 165). When she ultimately returns, no one in her family recognizes her. They all believe she is an imposter—in fact, one less convincing than others who have shown up to claim the reward for her return. Louisa acknowledges that "maybe once my mother had looked in my face and seen there nothing of Louisa, but only the long careful concentration I had put into being Lois Taylor, there was never any chance of my looking like Louisa again" (168). The story ends ironically with the mother who has failed to acknowledge her true daughter imploring once again on the radio: "Louisa ... please come home.... Your mother and father love you and will never forget you" (169–70).

In "The Bus" (1965), the narrator reveals early in the story—ostensibly referring to the poor bus service that the elderly traveler, Miss Harper, deplores—that "getting away from home was bad enough ... but getting home always seemed very close to impossible" *(Come Along with Me* 180). Miss Harper is let off the bus in the rain and darkness, only to discover that the driver has, as she phrases it, "put me off ... at the wrong stop and I can't seem to find my way home" (187). Lost, wet, and bedraggled, she gets a ride to a roadhouse converted from an old mansion that oddly reminds her of her childhood home. When she opens the closet in the bedroom where she expects to sleep, the toys frighten her by coming alive. In a plea that implicitly reverberates throughout much of Jackson's fiction, she screams, "Mommy, Mommy" (191). Awaking from her nightmare, she finds herself still on the bus. As the earlier sequence of events uncannily repeats itself, the driver proceeds to let Miss Harper off at the place she has just dreamed about, declaring as she exits, "This is as far as you go" (192).

The bus driver's darkly resonant comment suggests the coherence within Jackson's shorter and longer gothic fiction, sustained through images of "home" (an emotional space) and houses (which often function as the material manifestation of that space) that typically captivate their female occupants or seekers in both appealing and threatening senses. As Jackson identified the ambivalent tension in her work, in an unsent letter written late in her career, "I have always loved to use fear, to take it and comprehend it and make it work.... I delight in what I fear" (Oppenheimer 233–34).

In Jackson's two final novels, the gothic pleasure-in-fear that she acknowledged as a driving force in her fiction blends with preoedipal preoccupations to dramatize explicitly not only the ambivalence of the mother-daughter relationship but its figurative expression in consuming houses or other representations of incorporation. In the 1959 novel *The Haunting of Hill House* (a paradigmatic female gothic text, according to Kahane), the mother is dead and the daughter is confined within a house that functions figuratively as the externalized maternal body, simultaneously seductive and threatening. The daughter, Eleanor Vance, is drawn to Hill House as a participant in the study of occult phenomena. As Kahane observes,

> from the very beginning the house itself is presented as ... a maternal antagonist ... [that singles] out Eleanor as its destined inhabitant.... Jackson dislocates [readers] in typical Gothic fashion by locating [us] in Eleanor's point of view, confusing outside and inside, reality and illusion, so that [we] cannot clearly discern the acts of the house—the supernatural—from Eleanor's own disordered acts—the natural. But whether the agency of the house is inside Eleanor's mind or outside it, in either location it clearly functions as a powerful maternal imago [341].

While Kahane valuably highlights the female gothic elements of the narrative, I want to complicate her reading by suggesting that the confusion between inside and outside that structures this novel (and also *We Have Always Lived in the Castle*) is additionally represented through food as literal and symbolic substance. In both narratives, food signals both desire and fear: both the longing for sustenance and the predatory "consume or be consumed" relationship between mother and daughter. Moreover, in these final novels, tensions between opposing elements introduced in the earlier narratives—inside/outside, mother/self, and home/lost—overlap and converge to achieve their fullest representation. For Eleanor Vance of *The Haunting of Hill House*, the mother's death precipitates the daughter's existential homelessness and her literally annihilating experience of being lost: the loss of the self.

Early in the narrative, Eleanor stops at a country restaurant for lunch en route to Hill House for the first time; there she observes a young child who refuses her milk because it is not served in the familiar "cup of stars"[22] from which she is accustomed to drink at home. Eleanor appropriates the image of the child's magical milk cup with its suggestive sense of the mother's absent and idealized nourishment. The very fact that Eleanor never possessed such a cup but makes it hers in imagination, referring to it several times, betrays her distance from and longing for maternal nurturance. However, when Eleanor mentions her recently deceased invalid mother, the association with nourishment is negative. As she explains to Theodora, the other young woman of the group who becomes her confidante, "In my mother's house the kitchen was dark and narrow, and nothing you cooked there ever had any taste or color" (111). The cook who provides food for the guests at Hill House, Mrs. Dudley, prepares delectable dishes, yet is the antithesis of a nurturing figure, utterly mechanical in her insistence on a rigid and undeviating schedule of meals.[23]

Even before the "hauntings" begin, Eleanor is seductively drawn into the house while feeling as if she is being consumed by it, "like a small creature swallowed whole by a monster" (42). When the first manifestation occurs—terrifyingly loud pounding on her door in the night—Eleanor believes it is her dead mother knocking (127). Later she admits her guilt about the circumstances of her mother's death: "She knocked on the wall and called me ... and I never woke up" (212). For Theodora, the manifestation of knocking suggested someone trying "to get in and eat us" (133); in Eleanor's words, "The sense was that it wanted to consume us, take us into itself, make us a part of the house" (139). As Eleanor is progressively incorporated—and infantilized—by the malign powers of Hill House, she feels as if she is quite literally being consumed: "I am disappearing inch by inch into this house, I am going apart a little bit at a time" (201–02). The walls of Hill House exude messages intended specifically for Eleanor: "HELP ELEANOR COME HOME" (146). Later the newly arrived Mrs. Montague attempts to communicate with spirits through her "planchette" (Ouija board), which repeatedly produces the words "mother," "child," "lost," and "home" (192–93).

The meaning of "home" is deeply ironic, and Hill House is indeed both an enticing and a devouring mother[24]: Eleanor, acknowledging its powerful attraction, *chooses* to "relinquish my possession of this self of mine, abdicate, give over willingly what I never wanted at all; whatever it wants of me it can have" (204). Ultimately, the haunted Eleanor is destroyed by her own ambivalent submission to maternal domination.[25] Of all of Jackson's protagonists, she is most literally consumed by the entrapping and embracing house that overpowers her even as she submits almost joyfully to it. Her assertion, "I am home, I am home..." (232), paired with her conviction that she cannot leave Hill House because "I haven't any [other] home to return to" (239), vividly exemplifies the convergence of desire and fear in the oppositions inside/outside, mother/self, and home/lost. By the novel's end, Eleanor is dead, having crashed her car into a tree just outside the house in a gesture that may be understood as a suicidal sacrifice to the embracing and consuming mother/house.[26]

In each of Jackson's final novels, the daughter struggles with the powerful presence of her mother's absence, along with her ambivalent wish and fear, expressed as "eat or be eaten": either she is the source of her mother's annihilation or her mother is the source of hers. The association between literal and psychological incorporation that originates in the (female) preoedipal attachment and is narratively represented in Jackson's own transformations of female gothic culminate in the author's final completed novel[27] through the further elaboration of the several opposing motifs traced thus far.

The question of death or murder that typically lingers at the edge of awareness in gothic narratives depends in *We Have Always Lived in the Castle* not on whether one occurred—several did—or even why, but on what follows from the perpetrator's efforts to contain her guilt. Six years before the narrative present, when Mary Katherine (Merricat) Blackwood was 12, she had laced the sugar bowl with arsenic, an action that resulted in the deaths of both of her parents as well as her brother and her aunt. The villagers presumed (and still presume) that the actual murderer was her older sister Constance. Although a trial in the town had ultimately acquitted Constance, both Blackwood sisters are still ostracized by the villagers. The two young women continue to reside in the Blackwood family mansion with their father's brother, Uncle Julian, the only other survivor of the mass murder, who is paralyzed, delusional, and dependent on Constance's ministrations as chief cook and home-maker. As a result of her reputation in the village as a murderer, Constance is literally housebound; periodically, Merricat goes to the village, as if running a gauntlet, on essential household errands, including the purchase of groceries. The trio of surviving occupants of the Blackwood family thus functions as an ironic nuclear family: an incapacitated and dependent male figure, a housebound maternal figure who soothes anxieties and provides literal and figurative nurture, and a child who lives in a fantasy world sustained by magical thinking.

The brilliance of Jackson's narrative arises from her success at presenting the story from Merricat Blackwood's skewed perspective as the guiltless murderer who neither accepts responsibility nor feels remorse for her extreme action in the past. Jackson simultaneously represents the daughter's inner division and externalizes her ambivalent emotional relationship to the mother by splitting her into two separate characters: the saintly Constance and the "wicked" Merricat. Although on the literal level their relationship functions convincingly as a reciprocally affectionate sibling bond, psychologically it mirrors an idealized mother-daughter attachment, fantasized from the younger female's (Merricat's) perspective. The appropriately named Constance, six years older, is good enough to have accepted responsibility for the monstrous crime Merricat committed against their family. Thus while the "daughter" is narratively split into separate "good" and "bad" parts (Constance and Merricat), within Merricat herself the internalized "mother" is also split: between the "bad" parent whom she killed and the "good" mother whose place is assumed by her saintly older sister. If one understands Constance psychologically not only as the idealized maternal figure for whom the daughter longs but also as a projection of the idealized "good" aspect within the daughter herself, then the "wicked" aspect (the murderous, angry Merricat) is threatened by the loss of both her "good" mother and her "good" self.[28] Each time the possibility arises that Constance might leave the claustrophobic world of Blackwood House—might go "out-side"—Merricat feels emotionally imperiled or "chilled."[29]

The question of evil that pervades most gothic narratives, and Jackson's later narratives, is ambiguously refracted in *We Have Always Lived in the Castle*: Is Merricat Blackwood the source or the victim of the malice she feels around her? Locating evil in the external world rather than within herself, Merricat constructs a protective fantasy world defined by arbitrary magical talismans, taboos, and rituals that she feels compelled to observe. The reader, privy to Merricat's thoughts and feelings as the sole narrative voice but also to her blurring of inside and outside, can never ascertain whether her skewed vision of the world is the cause or the result of her murderous deed six years before. However, through her exaggerated childish vision, we can discern the intensity of her (and Jackson's) psychological preoccupations.

In female gothic narratives, houses and mansions function figuratively as maternal spaces: "the maternal blackness to which every Gothic heroine is fatefully drawn [which encompasses] the mysteries of identity and the temptation to lose it by merging with a mother imago who threatens all boundaries between self and other" (Kahane, 340). The few times that Merricat refers directly to her deceased mother early in the novel establish her filial ambivalence. The sight of the house where her mother was born fills her with anxiety: "I could not bear to think of our mother being born there" (7). Her uneasiness is a screen for anxiety concerning her own literal birthplace—the "maternal blackness" of her mother's body.

On the evening of the fateful dinner at which Merricat's parents, brother, and aunt died by poison, Merricat had been "sent to bed without her supper" (48) for reasons not explained, although Constance reveals years later to one of the infrequent guests at Blackwood House that her younger sister was a "wicked, disobedient child" (49). Constance had frequently carried a tray of food up the back stairs for Merricat when she was barred from the family meal in the dining room. The affectionate attachment between the sisters is mutual. Since childhood, Merricat has idealized Constance as a young child idealizes not a sibling but the emotionally primitive, fantasized "good" mother with whom she is partially merged: "When I was small I thought Constance was a fairy princess.... She was the most precious person in my world, always" (28). Constance is explicitly identified with nurturance, not only emotionally but literally. As Merricat phrases it, "food of any kind was precious to Constance, and she always touched foodstuffs with quiet respect" (29). She enjoys reading cookbooks, preserves vegetables, and prepares meals for her reconfigured family as she had done before her parents' deaths. Though Merricat "bring[s] home food," she is "not allowed" to prepare it (29); through magical thinking and ritual, she sets rules (as if imposed by someone other than herself), dictating restrictions on her actions as a way to order her world.

The most powerful magical metaphor—and object-relations issue—governing Merricat's vision of the world is her attempt to maintain and control the unstable boundary between "inside" and "outside" in order to defend her conviction that destructive evil exists apart from, not within, herself. The Blackwood mansion is her fortress, and she repeatedly attempts to secure its boundaries. Thus, although Merricat leaves the house and fenced-in grounds on occasional errands, the mere suggestion that Constance might "after all this time of refusing and denying ... go outside" (39–40) produces great anxiety and dread ("chill") in Merricat, provoking her attempts to control her surrogate mother's actions through symbolic magic. In one particularly resonant instance, when two curious women from the village are having tea with the sisters, she deliberately smashes her mother's best milk pitcher, leaving the pieces "on the floor so Constance would see them" (39) and bringing another pitcher of milk to the drawing room.

The more serious assault on Merricat's defensive castle is a "demon-ghost" (127): an opportunistic cousin, Charles Blackwood, whose greatest threat is not his interest in the Blackwood money (which he believes is hidden in the house) but the prospect that he will take Constance away. Despite Merricat's efforts to secure the boundary between inside and outside, Charles penetrates the barrier and enters the house. Persevering as if in male sexual penetration of female space, he is "the first one who had ever gotten inside and Constance had let him in" (82). Merricat's "wall of safety ... crack[s]" (83), and the "inside" becomes even less secure when Constance entrusts Charles with a key to the gates. Charles threatens not only to usurp but also to reproduce the original Blackwood family by assuming the role of the patriarchal father,[30] appropriating Constance as the submissive wife and mother, and punitively controlling the "child's" behavior—a configuration that threatens Merricat because it dangerously mimics the emotional reality of her childhood.

Because Charles radically threatens the defensive but precarious order of her world, Merricat wishes his death in a variety of ways, including magical incorporation, with her mother-surrogate's collaboration. As she suggests to Constance, "I was thinking that you might make a gingerbread man, and I could name him Charles and eat him" (109). Alternatively, identifying Charles with her father, Merricat believes that she can destroy the interloper by magically controlling objects that belonged to John Blackwood. Nonetheless, Constance, under Charles's influence, begins to dream of a more traditional life and to question their prolonged isolation from the world. While she regards as merely "silly" Merricat's increasingly desperate actions to protect her from Charles's presence, Charles demands that Merricat's unacceptable behavior be punished. She responds, "Punish me? You mean send me to bed without my dinner?" (137).

The anticipated punishment prescribed by the "disobedient child" herself—withholding of food—suggests a crucial link to Merricat's earlier life, as she unconsciously reproduces the structure of her earlier experience of punitive rejection by her family.[31] The withholding of food as a form of punishment may reflect emotional dynamics in Jackson's own family life, from both maternal and filial perspectives. As Oppenheimer writes, Jackson's daughter Sally "could drive Shirley around the bend faster than any other kid in the house—and once went an entire year without seeing the end of a meal because she was sent to her room long before dessert every single night" (135). In the novel, Merricat retreats to a decaying summer house located on the Blackwood property, where she constructs a conversation from her childhood as a soothing magical antidote to the threat represented by Charles's malign presence "inside" her world. Her deceased parents are revised as adoring, even worshipful, rather than rejecting:

> "Mary Katherine, we love you."
> "You must never be punished. Lucy, you are to see to it that our most loved daughter Mary Katherine is never punished."
> "Mary Katherine would never allow herself to do anything wrong; there is never any need to punish her."
> "I have heard, Lucy, of disobedient children being sent to their beds without dinner as a punishment. That must not be permitted with our Mary Katherine." "I quite agree, my dear. Mary Katherine must never be punished. *Must never be sent to bed without her dinner.* Mary Katherine will never allow herself to do anything inviting punishment."
> "Our beloved, our dearest Mary Katherine must be guarded and cherished. Thomas, give your sister your dinner; *she would like more to eat*" [139, emphasis added].

This fantasized conversation is critical to an understanding of Merricat's inner world, for it emphasizes the emotional resonances between love (or its withholding) and food.

Although Merricat's banishment from the family table was apparently initiated by her father with her mother's acquiescence, it is specifically maternal affection whose withdrawal Merricat seeks to reverse through her consuming attachment to her older sister. Constance, untouched by the poison since she never uses sugar (the association between sugar and poison is not without irony), is the one person who, through unconditional love, can neutralize the inner deprivation that shapes Merricat's relation to the world. No wonder Merricat feels compelled to do all within her power to restore the security of her "castle" and to expel the man who threatens its idealized maternal order.

Prohibited by her own codes from handling food, Merricat chooses another form of consumption: fire. Brushing Charles's still-smoldering pipe into a wastebasket filled with newspapers, she intends for the fire to remain magically "inside" her father's room, "belonging entirely to Charles" (148). However, in endeavoring to destroy the father-rival alone, Merricat inevitably facilitates consumption of part of the mother as well (the protective space of the house). Local firefighters attempt to extinguish the fire that spreads through the Blackwood mansion, while vindictive villagers urge them to let it burn. In a chilling detail reminiscent of Jackson's classic story "The Lottery," the fire chief, having fulfilled his professional duty, removes the hat bearing his official insignia and tosses a rock at the house, unleashing a public stoning by the vengeful onlookers.

Following the stoning of the house, Merricat conveys her beloved Constance to her secret lair on the estate grounds. Together with her mother-surrogate in that safe shelter "on the moon"—her term for an idealized magical sanctuary—Merricat admits to Constance that she would like to

> "put death in all [the villager's] food and watch them die."
> ..."The way you did before?" Constance asked.
> It had never been spoken of between us, not once in six years. "Yes," I said after a minute, "the way I did before" [161].

After Merricat verbalizes her culpability for the murders six years earlier, she expresses a poignant fantasy that the irrevocable events she has precipitated might be undone; this is the closest she ever comes to remorse for her prior actions:

> Perhaps the fire had destroyed everything and we would go back tomorrow and find that the past six years had been burned and they were waiting for us, sitting around the dining-room table waiting for Constance to bring them their dinner.... Perhaps the fire might be persuaded to reverse itself and abandon our house and destroy the village instead.... Perhaps the village was really a great game board, with the squares neatly marked out, and I had been moved past the square which read "Fire; return to Start," and was now on the last few squares, with only one move to go to reach home [164].

Though the Blackwood mansion, now bereft of its roof, becomes "a castle, turreted and open to the sky" (177), the maternal presence still reigns silently: Lucy Blackwood's face "[looked] down on us graciously" from her portrait "while her drawing room lay destroyed around her" (174). As if to propitiate the dead mother whose house/space has been seriously compromised, Constance places beneath her portrait a Dresden figurine that has escaped destruction; the sisters close the door to their mother's favorite room, figuratively entombing her image and the world over which she had presided, and "never [open] it afterwards" (176). Constance, undeterred by the demolished household, calmly reestablishes order and resumes her nurturant role, salvaging the most important room in the house, the kitchen, which has been ransacked by spiteful pillagers, in order to prepare meals for Merricat and herself amid the shards.

The self-abnegating Constance also blames herself for the destruction, the indirect result of her temptation to accept Charles Blackwood's vision of her. Assuring Merricat that "somehow it was all my fault" (174), she once again absolves Merricat of guilt and responsibility for her destructive actions. One might ask, at this or other points in the narrative, how are we to understand what motivates Constance? If Merricat embodies the principles of infantile impulsive anger and selfish action, Constance is her complementary double, representing a selfless, idealized maternal love whose virtue is its own reward. In a sense, the two young women are "two halves of the same person"—in fact, two aspects of Shirley Jackson herself, as well as representations of her two daughters and of her ambivalent relationships with them (Oppenheimer 233).[32]

The house fire that Merricat initiates, like the murders she had perpetrated before, radically transforms her world. However, rather than being expelled from the magical maternal space as she had been as a child, Merricat succeeds in permanently ejecting the patriarchs, Charles Blackwood (who leaves) and Uncle Julian (who dies in the fire), while consolidating her merger with her "good mother," Constance. Absolved of guilt and forgiven for her "wicked" actions both past and present by the mother surrogate who loves her unconditionally, she succeeds in sustaining her regressive fantasy, incorporating Constance into her emotionally primitive magical world. She is confident enough of the durability of that world to observe of the repentant villagers outside her castle, "Poor strangers.... They have so much to be afraid of" (214). Speaking as the good daughter gratifyingly merged with her good mother, Merricat declares in the narrative's final line, "Oh, Constance ... we are so happy" (214).

Merricat's ironic comment about strangers who have much to fear is illuminated by an observation Jackson made concerning the emotional reality that fed her characters' psychology. In an unsent letter, she commented,

> We are afraid of being someone else and doing the things someone else wants us to do and of being taken and used by someone else, some other guilt-ridden conscience that lives on and on in our minds, something we build ourselves and never recognize, but this is fear, not a named sin. Then it is fear itself, *fear of self* that I am writing about ... fear and guilt and their destruction of identity [ellipsis in Oppenheimer 233; emphasis added].[33]

Although Jackson was referring specifically to the Blackwood sisters of *We Have Always Lived in the Castle,* her comments clarify the link between her other mother-haunted narratives and central issues within her own life. Much of her fiction derives its power from the emotional truth and energy of her lifelong defensive struggle against a consuming mother (not simply Geraldine Jackson but the universally fantasized internal image of "mother"), which may in turn have led to her troubled relationships with her own two daughters and to her excessive consumption of food and drink. Additionally and poignantly, for an author who made emotionally resonant houses the central image of her later fiction, Jackson was virtually consumed by her own house: she developed agoraphobia several years before her death. During an especially difficult period, "she was unable to leave the house ... unable, for much of the time, even to leave her bedroom" (Oppenheimer 247).

Jackson's narratives refract and transform some of her own idiosyncratic emotional history; at the same time, they illuminate a darker aspect of the ambivalent mother-daughter relationship in general, amplified through the devices of female gothic narrative structure. In several of Jackson's stories and virtually all of her novels, a woman's troubled relation to her mother (whether alive or dead) or to a house or to "home" produces anxieties about the world that coincide with a central element in female gothic narratives, "fear of self."[34] One source of that emotional predicament is the tension between desire and fear that originates as the (female) infant negotiates the unstable boundaries between inside and outside, "goodness" and "badness," *self* and *(m)other*[35] during the process of establishing selfhood; its residues persist within and influence the self into adulthood and (for women) motherhood.

Thus the fusion of the ideas of mother and home—the "mother house ... housemother" *(The Haunting of Hill House,* 211) that looms so large in Jackson's later fiction—may be understood as the materialized specter or structure of anxiety that haunts and even paralyzes the daughter as she struggles with her confusion concerning "inside" and "outside." That dilemma is expressed through her ambivalent desires: on the one hand, to leave home to become an autonomous self and, on the other, to remain an unindividuated child within its protective—but also consuming—enclosure. Indeed, in Jackson's fiction, the daughter's conflict is embodied as both the temptation and the torment of her wish/fear to return "home" and to her mother and of not knowing whether she is lost or saved when she finds herself either stranded far from home or "inside the house, with the door shut behind" *(We Have Always Lived in the Castle,* 142).

## Notes

1. As Adrienne Rich has phrased it, "Few women growing up in patriarchal society can feel mothered enough; the power of our mothers, whatever their love for us and their struggles on our behalf, is too restricted. And it is the mother through whom patriarchy early teaches the small female her proper expectations," in *Of Woman Born: Motherhood as Experience and Institution* (New York: Bantam, 1977), 246. Several critics have specifically highlighted Jackson's protofeminist impulses by focusing on her representations of female characters who are oppressed within patriarchy. Lynette Carpenter considers the impact of patriarchy not only on Jackson's female characters but on her own situation as a woman writer, in "Domestic Comedy, Black Comedy, and Real Life: Shirley Jackson, A Woman Writer," in *Faith of a (Woman) Writer,* ed. Alice Kessler-Harris and William McBrien (New York and Westport, Connecticut:

Greenwood Press, 1988), 143–48. See also feminist readings of individual novels: Carpenter, "The Establishment and Preservation of Female Power in Shirley Jackson's *We Have Always Lived in the Castle*," Frontiers VIII, no. 1 (1984): 31–38; Tricia Lootens, "'Whose Hand Was I Holding?' Familial and Sexual Politics in Shirley Jackson's *The Haunting of Hill House*," in *Haunting the House of Fiction: Feminist Perspectives on Ghost Stories by American Women*, ed. Carpenter and Wendy K. Kolmar (Knoxville: University of Tennessee Press, 1991), 166–92; and Judie Newman, "Shirley Jackson and the Reproduction of Mothering: *The Haunting of Hill House*," in *American Horror Fiction: From Brockden Brown to Stephen King* (New York: St. Martin's Press, 1990), 120–34.

Besides the 1988 biography of Shirley Jackson by Judy Oppenheimer, the only book-length studies of her work are Lenemaja Friedman's *Shirley Jackson* (Boston: Twayne/G.K. Hall, 1975) and Joan Wylie Hall's *Shirley Jackson: A Study of the Short Fiction* (New York: Twayne, 1993). Most scholarly essays on Jackson's work focus on individual stories—especially "The Lottery"—or novels. Those most pertinent to my own approach (in addition to those listed above) include Stuart C. Woodruff's "The Real Horror Elsewhere: Shirley Jackson's Last Novel," *Southwest Review 52*, no. 2 (1967): 152–62; Steven K. Hoffman's "Individuation and Character Development in the Fiction of Shirley Jackson," *Hartford Studies in Literature* 8, no. 3 (1976): 190–208; John G. Parks's "The Possibility of Evil: A Key to Shirley Jackson's Fiction," *Studies in Short Fiction* 15, no. 3 (1978): 320–23; Parks's "Waiting for the End: Shirley Jackson's *The Sundial*," *Critique* 29, no. 3 (1978): 74–88; Parks's "Chambers of Yearning: Shirley Jackson's Use of the Gothic," *Twentieth Century Literature* 30, no. 1 (1984): 15–29; and James Egan's "Sanctuary: Shirley Jackson's Domestic and Fantastic Parables," *Studies in Weird Fiction* 6, no. 1 (1989): 15–24.

Several collections of essays on detective and horror fiction contain discussions of one or two of Jackson's novels: Mary Kittredge's "The Other Side of Magic: A Few Remarks About Shirley Jackson," in *Discovering Modern Horror Fiction 1*, ed. Darrell Schweitzer (Mercer Island, Washington: Starmont, 1985), 3–12; Jack Sullivan's "Shirley Jackson," in *Supernatural Fiction Writers: Fantasy and Horror*, ed. E. F. Bleiler (New York: Scribners, 1985), 103–136; and Carol Cleveland's "Shirley Jackson," in *Then There Were Nine: More Women of Mystery*, ed. Jane S. Bakerman (Bowling Green, Ohio: Popular Press, 1985), 199–219.

2. In contrast to classical Freudian psychoanalytic theory, which focuses primarily on instinctual drives, object-relations psychology focuses primarily on the individual's relationships with others in his or her external world; see Jay R. Greenberg and Stephen A. Mitchell, *Object Relations in Psychoanalytic Theory* (Cambridge: Harvard University Press, 1983), 20. However, within this broad context, a number of different, even incompatible, perspectives exist in place of a unitary theory. As Greenberg and Mitchell define this group of approaches within the larger context of psychoanalytic theory, the term "object relations" "designates theories, or aspects of theories, concerned with exploring the relationship between real, external people and internal images and residues of relations with them, and the significance of these residues for psychic functioning" (12).

Nancy Chodorow was among the first feminist scholars to use object-relations theory to revise Freud's position concerning early mother-infant relations by focusing on significant differences between female and male experiences. See *The Reproduction of Mothering: Psychoanalysis and the Sociology of Gender* (Berkeley: University of California Press, 1978).

3. Psychoanalytically, the determination of what constitutes "inside" and "outside" is problematic. As Roy Schafer phrases the problem, "how is one to understand the inside or outside location of an object? Inside of what? Outside of what? It can only be inside or outside the subjective self ... [which] comprises a variety of changing, more or less organized and overlapping selves ... the self-as-agent (the 'I'), the self-

as-object (the 'me'), and the self-as-place (for which no pronoun is specific). These selves are not synonymous or necessarily congruent," in *Aspects of Internalization* (New York: International Universities Press, Inc., 1968), 79–80.

4. In an object-relations context, "merging with another person is essentially a primary-process phenomenon. It condenses representations of the total subjective self and the object. In the subject's experience, it is as if there were only one person, not two" (Schafer 151–52). Moreover, "a person's early relation to her or his mother leads to a preoccupation with issues of primary intimacy and merging. On one psychological level, all people who have experienced primary love and primary identification have some aspect of self that wants to recreate these experiences." However, "fear of fusion may overwhelm the attraction to it, and fear of loss of a love object may make the experience of love too risky" (Chodorow 78–79).

5. Incorporation refers to the idea in object-relations psychology that "one has taken a part or all of another person (or creature or thing) into one's self corporeally, and, further, that this taking in is the basis of certain novel, disturbing, and/or gratifying sensations, impulses, feelings, and actions of one's own and of correlated changes in one's experience of the environment.... Incorporation may be said to indicate a de-emphasis of the boundaries between the inner and outer worlds" (Schafer 20–21). Additionally, "the wish to incorporate an object [or person] is usually the wish to eat it in a sucking or biting fashion" (Schafer 121).

6. Judy Oppenheimer, *Private Demons: The Life of Shirley Jackson* (New York: Fawcett Columbine, 1988), 11. Subsequent references will be cited parenthetically in the text.

7. According to Susie Orbach, who first theorized the sources of eating disorders from a feminist perspective in the 1970s, female obesity and overeating may be understood as "a symbolic rejection of the limitations of women's role, an adaptation that many women use in the burdensome attempt to pursue their individual lives within the proscriptions of their social function." Furthermore, "women are prepared for this life of inequality by other women who themselves suffer its limitations—their mothers. The feminist perspective reveals that compulsive eating is ... an expression of the complex relationships between mothers and daughters," in *Fat Is a Feminist Issue* (New York: Paddington Press, 1978), 26.

More recently, Susan Bordo has illuminated the relationship between consumption and consumer capitalism as regulator of desire. In that context, "the obese and anorectic are ... disturbing partly because they embody resistance to cultural norms.... In the case of the obese, in particular, what is perceived as their defiant rebellion against normalization appears to be a source of the hostility they inspire," in "Reading the Slender Body," in *Unbearable Weight: Feminism, Western Culture, and the Body* (Berkeley: University of California Press, 1993), 203.

8. Joan Wylie Hall, *Shirley Jackson: A Study of the Short Fiction*, xiv, 25, 27.

9. Hall, xii.

10. See Eve Kosofsky Sedgwick's valuable discussion of the structure and conventions of gothic narratives in *The Coherence of Gothic Conventions* (New York and London: Methuen, 1986).

11. See Ellen Moers, *Literary Women* (Garden City, New York: Doubleday, 1976), 90–110, and Claire Kahane, "The Gothic Mirror," in *The (M)other Tongue: Essays in Feminist Psychoanalytic Interpretation,* ed. Shirley Nelson Garner, Kahane, and Madelon Sprengnether (Ithaca: Cornell University Press, 1985), 334–51, esp. 334. Subsequent references will be cited parenthetically in the text.

12. "Preoedipal" refers to the early developmental period before gender identity is established by a child at about the age of three. As Chodorow describes this phase, "The content of a girl's attachment to her mother differs from a boy's precisely in that it is not at this time oedipal (sexualized, focused on possession, which means focused on someone clearly different and opposite). The preoedipal attachment of

daughter to mother continues to be concerned with early mother-infant relational issues. it sustains the mother-infant exclusivity and the intensity, ambivalence, and boundary confusion of the child still preoccupied with issues of dependence and individuation" (Chodorow 97).

13. Years after Jackson published this story, during the last year of her life, her mother wrote in a letter, "You were always a wilful child" (Oppenheimer 14).

14. Jackson, "I Know Who I Love," in *Come Along with Me*, ed. Stanley Edgar Hyman (New York: The Viking Press, 1968), 51. Subsequent references to stories in this collection will be cited parenthetically in the text.

15. Jackson, *The Road Through the Wall* (New York: Farrar, Straus and Co., 1948), 264.

16. Fathers, both living and dead, figure in several of Jackson's later novels as well. My intent here is not to disregard their presence but to emphasize the central tension within the mother-daughter relationship.

17. Jackson, *Hangsaman* (New York: Farrar, Straus and Young, 1951), 130. Subsequent references will be cited parenthetically in the text.

18. Jackson, *The Bird's Nest*, in *The Magic of Shirley Jackson*, ed. Hyman (New York: Farrar, Straus and Giroux, 1966), 307. Subsequent references will be cited parenthetically in the text.

19. Interestingly, *The Bird's Nest* antedates by three years the publication of the more widely known nonfictional case history, *The Three Faces of Eve*, by Corbett Thigpen and Hervey M. Cleckley (New York: McGraw-Hill, 1957).

20. Jackson, *The Sundial* (New York: Ace Books, 1958), 11. Subsequent references will be cited parenthetically in the text. Sedgwick identifies as a central convention of gothic narratives the focus on spatial topography: "what's inside, what's outside and what separates them" (12). See also note 3 above.

21. Melanie Klein—a central, although controversial, analyst and formulator of object-relations theory—proposed that in the very earliest stage of psychological development, an infant's primitive wishes and fears become split between pleasurable and terrible experiences of the mother (as presumed from the infant's essentially undifferentiated perspective): the "good mother" who provides nurture and the "bad mother" who withholds gratification. As Thomas Ogden outlines Klein's position on this primitive mechanism of emotional division, "Splitting allows the infant, child, or adult to love safely and hate safely by establishing discontinuity between loved and feared aspects of self and object," in *The Matrix of the Mind: Object Relations and the Psychoanalytic Dialogue* (Northvale, New Jersey: Jason Aronson, Inc., 1986), 65. The residue of this primitive split may persist into adult object relations. See also notes 28 and 32 below.

22. Jackson, *The Haunting of Hill House* (New York: Viking Penguin, 1984), 21. Subsequent references will be cited parenthetically in the text.

23. Although this cannot be biographically confirmed, one may speculate that as an infant Shirley Jackson was probably fed, like others of her generation, according to the principles of child-rearing of her mother's generation: on a rigid schedule unrelated to the infant's own desires.

24. Lootens, who has traced the evolution of the novel through several drafts, observes that "Hill House is the original womb/tomb, with all the comforts of home. There are good beds, excellent cooking, companionship; and nothing to do but die in a house that does not want you ... but that does not want to let you go" (176). Kahane describes the house as "protector, lover, and destroyer" (342).

25. Newman also explores the ambivalent mother-daughter bond that structures Eleanor's emotional reality, although she draws somewhat different conclusions from mine. In her view, Eleanor "detests the mother's dominance, resenting the loss of her own youth in the forced assumption of the 'mothering' role.... [She also] feels guilt at not having mothered adequately. Both images are internalized so that Eleanor is haunted by guilt as a mother over the neglected child within herself" (126).

26. Interestingly, shortly before Jackson began to write *The Haunting of Hill House*, she wrote a one-act play for her children's school, "a variation on *Hansel and Gretel*" titled *The Bad Children* (Oppenheimer 222). Defending her unorthodox revision of the fairy tale—it is the children who are wicked, not the witch—she noted in an unpublished lecture that she "resented violently the fact that Hansel and Gretel eat the witch's house and never get punished for it" (Oppenheimer 222). In the play, the children are "horrible" brats (222) who deserve what they get; in *The Haunting of Hill House*, it is instead the house itself that is "horrible." Moreover, rather than the children consuming the house, as in the fairy tale, in the novel the house consumes the childlike Eleanor.

27. Jackson's unfinished and posthumously published novel, *Come Along with Me*, consists of only 30 pages, so one can only speculate on the direction it would have taken if completed. Although lighter in tone than her other novels, it retains several suggestive links to the recurring emotional issues suggested here. The narrative opens with the first-person narrator's comment, "I always believe in eating when I can" (3). Forty-four years old, the speaker has sold her house after her husband's death; having "erased [her] old name" (4), she seeks a new life and a new "place to go" (3) to practice her clairvoyant powers. As she considers names for the new identity she intends to establish, she confesses, "what is really more frightening than being without a name, nothing to call yourself, nothing to say when they ask you who you are?" (9). Eventually, she decides she will be Angela Motorman. She takes a room in a rooming house, repeatedly stressing the room's perfect squareness. The gothic element seems to be directed toward a more comic vein: as Angela explains her vocation, "I dabble in the supernatural. Traffic with spirits. Seances, messages, psychiatric advice, that kind of thing" (12).

28. As Ogden explains Melanie Klein's theoretical perspective on the splitting of the object (mother), "one achieves safety in relation to internal danger by magically placing the danger outside of oneself; one protects oneself against persecutory objects by acquiring a greater army of good objects; one projects an *endangered* aspect of *self* by *magically transforming another person into a repository for* that *aspect of* self, thus *preserving oneself in the form* of another *with whom* one *maintains a* connection of identity *(projective identification)*" (76, emphasis added).

29. Jackson, *We Have Always Lived in the Castle* (New York: Viking Press, 1962), 38–39. Subsequent references will be cited parenthetically in the text.

30. Carpenter focuses on Jackson's "portrayal of the institution of patriarchy and its terrifying power over women" in *We Have Always Lived in the Castle*. In her view, Charles Blackwood "reintroduces the [patriarchal] notions of punishment and competition into a house where they have not been invoked for years" (32, 35).

31. Jean Wyatt notes that feminist object-relations psychology "accounts for women's compulsion to perpetuate the structures of their own oppression: unconscious desire becomes enmeshed with the setting of their earliest experiences of satisfaction (or frustration) in the nuclear family; so desire always moves them (unconsciously) to reconstruct in their adult lives the patterns of their original family life," in *Reconstructing Desire: The Role of the Unconscious in Women's Reading and Writing* (Chapel Hill: University of North Carolina Press, 1990), 9. Chodorow also explores the blurred boundaries between inside and outside and between mother and (female) self.

32. Jackson "quite consciously [split] herself into the two characters, Merricat and Constance, and at the same time [modeled] them directly after her daughters" (Oppenheimer 234).

Unsent letter from Shirley Jackson to Howard Nemerov, circa 1960, quoted in Oppenheimer 233.

33. Jackson's phrase anticipates Moers's observations concerning the relationship between gothic narratives and female anxieties. As Moers phrased it, "Despair is

hardly the exclusive province of any one sex or class in our age, but to give *visual* form to the *fear of self*, to hold anxiety up to the Gothic mirror of the imagination, may well be more common in the writings of women than of men" (107; the first emphasis is Moers's, the second is added).

34. In a somewhat different context, Madelon Sprengnether usefully distinguishes between "mother" as "a fantasy of plenitude" and "(m)other" as a sign for "the otherness contained in the figure of mother" or as "that which cannot be appropriated by the child's or infant's desire and hence signals a condition of division or loss," in "(M)other Eve: Some Revisions of the Fall in Fiction by Contemporary Women Writers," in *Feminism and Psychoanalysis,* ed. Richard Feldstein and Judith Roof (Ithaca and London: Cornell University Press, 1989), 300, n. 5.

# 7

# "Whose Hand Was I Holding?": Familial and Sexual Politics in Shirley Jackson's *The Haunting of Hill House*

## Tricia Lootens

Sometime during the late 1950s, Shirley Jackson set out to write "the kind of novel you really can't read alone in a dark house at night" (1D).[1] *The Haunting of Hill House,* the novel she ultimately produced, is the story of four people who agree to participate in a ghost-hunting expedition reminiscent of those that took place early in this century: Dr. Montague, an academic who has organized the expedition; Luke, the charming if disreputable heir of Hill House; Theodora, a sophisticated beauty; and Eleanor, a lonely, vulnerable woman who has been chosen, like Theodora, for her history of susceptibility to psychic manifestations. They are a congenial group, and, from the beginning, they play at being a family. The premise of the novel is standard ghost story fare, but by the end of the book, it is clear that this is no ordinary haunting. For what devastates Hill House's victims is not a losing struggle with the forces of the next world, but a brutal, intimate exposure of the ineffectuality of their own dreams. Hill House's ghosts come not with the face of the unknown, but with that of each character's most intimate fears.

---

*This essay originally appeared in* Haunting the House of Fiction: Feminist Perspectives on Ghost Stories by American Women, *ed. Lynette Carpenter and Wendy K. Kolmar (Knoxville: University of Tennessee Press, 1991). Reproduction by permission of the University of Tennessee Press.*

Surely one of the most terrifying aspects of Hill House's haunting is its intimacy, which is simultaneously familial and erotic. What happens in Hill House is a process, not merely a "sighting"; a haunting, not merely a ghost. At its source is the house's growing knowledge of its inhabitants' illusions and of their deadly needs. Hill House's ghosts are what Jackson called the "statement and resolution" of its inhabitants' apparently insoluble problems (1D); the haunting is personally designed for the haunted. What Hill House reveals to its guests is a brutal, inexorable vision of the "absolute reality" *(Hill House* 3) of nuclear families that kill where they are supposed to nurture. In this perception, Jackson touches on the terror of her entire culture.

Hill House sets out to separate its guests, and it locates Eleanor as the weak link. Although each of the others has reasons to cherish the illusion of belonging together, Eleanor cannot even pretend to herself that she belongs anywhere else. She is ready to give her life for love, and she fixes her romantic fantasies both on Luke and on Theodora. As it becomes clear that neither is willing or able to reciprocate, the haunting increasingly singles her out. It (and the desperation it reveals in her) separates her from the others even as it seduces her into believing that Hill House, and Hill House alone, wants and needs her. As the original "family" of guests begins to disintegrate, the house is invaded by representatives of spiritualist sentimentality and criminally unimaginative common sense, in the persons of Dr. Montague's overbearing wife and her martinet companion. By the time the others discover that Eleanor is vulnerable to murderous manifestations that she alone perceives, it is too late. She reveals what the reader—and the house—have known all along: she has nowhere else to go. In a ruthless ending, she kills herself rather than leave the only home she knows. She dies in vain, for after her death as before it, "whatever walk[s] in Hill House, walk[s] alone" (1).

By the time she began *Hill House,* Jackson had already explored the establishment (and destruction) of women's coherent sense of self in such works as *Hangsaman* and *The Bird's Nest.* As Lynette Carpenter has noted, inquiry into "causes and consequences of female victimization" runs throughout Jackson's work (32). She had written about human sacrifice, not only in its most brutal, literal sense as in "The Lottery" or perhaps in "The Summer People," but also in connection with seduction and demon lovers, as in "The Visit" and "The Rock." In *Life Among the Savages,* she had written in a far different vein about the vicissitudes of family life. Given all this, what could be more natural than to turn to domesticity, self-sacrifice, and the disintegration of a woman's personality as sources of terror?

It is for this reason that the drafts of *Hill House* in the Library of Congress come as such a surprise. Jackson's early versions of the novel are unmistakable proof that the character of Hill House's haunting was not clear from the beginning. She seems to have set out to write a fairly standard ghost story, not a horror story about the ways in which people, especially women, are destroyed by the nuclear family, sexual repression, and romantic notions of feminine self-sacrifice.[2]

At the very earliest stage of her work on *Hill House,* Jackson seems to have created a series of sketches that briefly explore a possible past for her haunted house, a cast of characters, and above all a vision of the character she first calls Vancey, and later, Theodora Vane. "The book is told in the first person by a woman named Vancey," Jackson writes in a typed paragraph that seems to introduce her first description of the manifestations at Hill House: "She is one of four people hired to spend three months in a house which has acquired a bad reputation because no one will live there. The owners and the renting agents are most anxious to prove that there is nothing wrong with the house, without at the same time involving themselves in any of the wild joy with which newspapers handle any stories about haunted houses" (TS).

Jackson devotes the majority of her sketches on the "woman named Vancey" to character development. We see Vancey on her way to a weekly dinner at her sister's house (1D, TS), being recruited for Hill House (TS), possibly facing the house for the first time (as an unnamed narrator; TS), engaging in fantasies about herself for the entertainment of her fellow guests at the house (1D), facing her first manifestation (1D), and most importantly of all, facing herself and her fantasies in order to tell the reader her story (1D, TS). "Well," she says in one passage of self-introduction,

> My name, as I've said, is Mary Bothwell Stuart Vance, and most people—most people? I have perhaps ten friends—call me Vance, or Vancey; if you could see me you'd know why no one ever thinks twice to call me Mary.... What I am trying to say is that I am one of those curious creatures who is [well!] not lovely. I've spent a number of years facing it and I don't know why it's so hard each time I say it, but there it is—I am content, I think, and I've managed to carve myself a good life, and I don't go around bawling on other people's shoulders, unless I get into that particular drunken state where feeling sorry for yourself is a lovely thing, and even then I usually try to feel sorry for myself for something else—even then, you will say, refusing to face it. Say what you please; I defy you to match my life [TS].

The tone is characteristic. Vancey is the feminine equivalent of the bluff, hearty bachelor narrator of so many classic Victorian ghost stories—with a difference, of course. Invited to Hill House because she appears to be a "sensible young woman" (TS), Vancey is not entirely what she seems. Jackson clearly intends to play not only with outsiders' assumptions of what it means to be a sensible young woman, but with those of Vancey herself.

Vancey may present a front of common sense, but she is also a romantic, lonely woman who feels entrapped by the peaceful, ordered existence symbolized by her weekly visits to her married sister's house. In a half-ironic, half-rueful tone, she informs the reader that she was "made to die for love," and that love "hasn't asked" (TS). Her position is nevertheless far stronger than that of any of the women who will succeed her as Jackson's protagonists. She is her own woman, both intellectually and economically.

In different sketches, Vancey lives on her inheritance (TS) or her salary (1D), but she always survives by her wits. In her dry humor and intellectual independence she is also not unlike Jackson herself. She even dreams of being an author: "I'm going to be a great writer," the young Vancey tells a little suitor, "and I'm never going to get *married*.... If I ever do get married it will be Humphrey Bogart, or somebody like that" (1D).

Such a story is typical of her. At another point, she wryly evokes Shakespearean comedy, tragic love, and her sister's matchmaking, all on the basis of a hardware store sign:

> I turned the corner and thought, "O stay and hear, your true love's coming, that can sing both high and low...." That was because R. Sweeting Hardware store stood on the corner; "Trip no further, pretty sweeting: journey's [sic] end in lovers [sic] meeting...." Poor Pretty Sweeting Hardware; were *his* lovers all untrue?
>
> They did frequently end in lovers [sic] meetings, my visits to my sister.... Carrie wanted me to get married, for some inscrutable reason. Perhaps she found the married state so excruciatingly disagreeable herself that it was the only thing bad enough she could think of to do to me [1D].

Vancey's choice of song is significant: her private jest evokes the comic world of *Twelfth Night,* in which an exiled, sexually ambiguous heroine finds a new home, a lost brother, and true love. Like a "blind motif" in a fairy tale, retained long after it has lost its original context and meaning, Vancey's "R. Sweeting" song will be passed down to the central figure of each draft. By the time it reaches Eleanor in the final draft of *Hill House,* the phrase "journeys end in lovers' meeting" has become a ritual invocation of faith by a woman who does not know its origin; who does not even believe in the value of knowledge; and who is afraid that if she remembers the whole song, she will discover it is "improper." This expression of Vancey's saving grace—her wit and her rich inner life—will become the expression of Eleanor's bankruptcy and the voice of her downfall.

Two more main sketches in the *Hill House* papers seem to have been narrated by Vancey: her account of the first view of Hill House and that of the first manifestations within the house (1D). Both are retained essentially untouched in later versions; but as Jackson's protagonist changes, their significance, like the significance of the R. Sweeting song, is vastly altered. Vancey's successors echo her loneliness, her motherlessness, her hunger for change, and certain aspects of her situation, but none has her independence or her humor—and none has the first-person narrator status, which guarantees that somehow she will survive.

In order to distinguish her from the character later named "Theodora," I will call the protagonist of what seems to be the next series of sketches "Trapped Theodora Vane." She is a weakened version of Vancey, both in descriptive vividness and in personality. Where, for example, Vancey responded to her sister's announcement of a male dinner guest with "Do you think *he'll* want to marry me?" (TS), Trapped Theodora goes out to buy new shoes (TS). In her, emotional vulnerability is matched by economic vulnerability: Trapped Theodora has lost not only Vancey's brashness, but her home and independent means. She may have an apartment, but metaphorically speaking, she has no room of her own (TS).

What Trapped Theodora loses in self-sufficiency, she gains in family ties. Vancey's affection for her sister was limited at best; she may have longed for romantic adventures, but she was openly critical of nuclear families (TS). Theodora's reaction to her baby sister's matchmaking seems to temper exasperation with genuine affection, perhaps even gratitude (TS). She combines longing for a family of her own with lack of a strong sense of self. Where Vancey went to Hill House because she was bored with her ordered life, Trapped Theodora goes because she is bored with herself. Where Vancey was clearly sane, Trapped Theodora may not be. One brief letter in the *Hill House* files, signed "Theodora," is clearly that of a madwoman (TS).

As the novel's protagonist becomes more vulnerable, Hill House's evil becomes more specific. What confronted Vancey at Hill House was arrogance and, above all, humorlessness—the ultimate evil in the eyes of a woman who measures her self-respect and sanity by her ability to laugh. What confronts Trapped Theodora in the house is another negation: "It has never been anyone's *home,* if you know what I mean," she is told. "There seem to be houses like that—one meets them sometimes—which have never known families growing up" (TS). Nothing could make the depth of Hill House's coming transformation clearer. From a house that has "never known families," it is destined to become one that knows entirely too much about the subject.

The haunting itself, which began by threatening Vancey with physical violence, now moves to exploit Trapped Theodora's vulnerability by underscoring her emotional isolation. The Trapped Theodora sketches mark the first appearance of the "cousins" scene in which two women, newly arrived at Hill House, establish a fantasy family connection and lazily plan a picnic—until Jackson shatters the intimate moment with a rush of icy air and the view of spectral footsteps (1D).

As with Vancey's manifestations, this scene remains essentially untouched as the novel develops, but its resonance is radically transformed. Jackson has already created a house for which the innocent pleasure of picnics is anathema; what she has yet to create is a house that entraps its inhabitants with fantasies of domestic bliss even as it forces them to recognize such fantasies as delusions. The "cousins," playful assertion of kinship will come to reveal more and more desperation; their dream of sharing everyday celebrations of domesticity will become increasingly poignant and sinister. By the final draft, Theodora will still be holding out the futile promise of a picnic at Hill House moments before Eleanor smashes into a tree.

With the next draft, which I call the "Erica draft" (TS/C4), Jackson seems to have undertaken her first full sketch of *Hill House*'s plot.[3] There are pages missing from this draft, but it is nevertheless clear that with Erica, Jackson moved the haunting beyond her initial plans and beyond most of the "real" hauntings she had studied.[4] "Experience and Fiction" offers an oblique explanation for her decision to take the haunting's outcome beyond exile into death: "The ghosts were after me" (203). One morning, she says, she came downstairs and found "a sheet of copy paper moved to the center of my desk, set neatly away from the general clutter. On the sheet of paper was written DEAD DEAD in my own handwriting. I am accustomed to making notes for my books, but not in my sleep; I decided that I had better write the book awake, which I got to work and did" (203).

In this draft, Erica Vance, an angry, defensive, and lonely woman with none of Vancey's or Trapped Theodora's wit, is driven to Hill House by "self-disgust and dullness" (1D). She meets a stock romantic hero, Luke; a glamorous rival, Theodora; and a happily married scholar, Dr. Montague. *Hill House*'s basic plot is set: "The story is primarily about Erica, who is going to have to be a good deal more complex than she seems now," Jackson explained in a note to her publisher, adding: "the emphasis upon (yippee) togetherness; the house wants to separate them and drive them away, the people want to stay together in the house; where the others want to stay together because they are afraid to be alone in the house Erica wants to stay with them because she is afraid to be alone anywhere, anytime; her life will be indicated as a pattern of loneliness which she is trying to break" (1D).

Though Jackson seems to implicate Erica as a potential human agent behind the manifestations of haunting in this draft, she has nevertheless begun to transform Hill House into its final form. This draft begins with the sentence that will open the published novel: "No live organism can continue for long to exist sanely under conditions of absolute reality" (TS/C4 1). With the house's transformation in this draft, the transformation of characters seems to be accelerating. Erica goes to Hill House to find herself (TS/C4 26) and we are told that she has had a secret desire for death "for no very clear reason, since she was seventeen years old" (TS/C4 37). Although the draft does not contain a final scene, it seems clear that her secret wish will be fulfilled.

Even after writing the "Erica draft," however, Jackson still seems to have been making "comfortable" assumptions about being able to haul in a standard moaning specter at the crucial moment. "There are going to be some dandy ghosts," she vaguely assured her publisher. "I set up the story of the house so that any of its previous inhabitants might enjoy coming back to haunt it, and—although my own preference is for a veiled lady, moaning—I think it may turn out that different people see different things; see, in fact, just exactly what they are expecting to see" (1D). As it turns out, of course, the final draft has no woman with a veil, and no ghost that is exactly what any character expects to see, unless one counts the absurd monks and nuns obligingly dished up by Mrs. Montague's planchette. There is a reason: between the Erica Vance draft and the one that followed, Jackson seems to have found her "real" ghosts.

When Vancey arrives at Hill House, she knocks on a heavy wooden door (1D); when Erica arrives, she finds a knocker with a lion's head (TS/C4 7); but by the time Jackson walks her final protagonist, Eleanor Vance, up the steps to Hill House, the knocker has become a child's face (TSI 16). Jackson had found the source of Hill House's peculiarly intimate brand of horror: what her final heroine, Eleanor Vance, enters is above all a family home.

Two words are scrawled on the bottom of a page of notes for *Hill House:* "FAMILY, FAMILY" (1D). Given Jackson's story of having written "DEAD DEAD" in her sleep, it is easy to imagine that her notes express a parallel though presumably waking revelation. In any case, there is no question that some time between the "Erica Vance" draft and that which followed, the first "Eleanor" draft (TS1), Jackson reached a decision. The final or "second Eleanor draft" (TS 1/C) that follows only expands the transformation the first "Eleanor" draft has begun. By the time Jackson's haunting of Hill House reaches its culmination, "FAMILY, FAMILY" and "DEAD DEAD" are close to synonymous.

From a sinister shell to be filled up with ghosts and observers (as though a literary moving van had been drawn up to the door), the Hill House of Jackson's final version has become a vicious travesty of a family home, the leering equivalent of James Thurber's personified housefront. In this version, the characters are trapped within a nightmare embodiment of the nuclear family, an insidious Home Sweet Home that will not allow its victims to belong or to be happy, but will not let them go.

On the basis of her readings of both Freud and the psychic researchers, Jackson had come to believe that ghosts provided the "statement and resolution" of their percipients' problems–problems that could not "be solved realistically" because "impossible problems require impossible solutions, after all" (1D). Perhaps in part as a result, she transformed the haunting of Hill House into the "statement and resolution" of the irreconcilable conflict between Jackson's characters' dreams of belonging in "one big happy family" and the reality of the family's failure in their lives. "Hill House is the haunting," Jackson wrote in pencil somewhere among her notes for the novel (1D). With each succeeding draft, the house becomes a more brutal parody of a family home, and its guests more vulnerable to delusions of togetherness.

Designed to satisfy the arrogance of the family's founding father, Hugh Crain, and to "suit his mind" by mirroring its distortion (*Hill House* 105), the house of the final draft has surpassed any human being in its capacity for evil. In the first Eleanor draft, we hear that Hill House's founder must have "disliked the sensible square houses he saw other people building" (TS1 64); by the final version, we are told that he "must have detested other people and their sensible, squared away houses, because he made his house to suit his mind" (107). For all its upright walls and firm floors, Hill House has become a "masterpiece of architectural misdirection," a structure whose proportions deliberately undermine one's "senses of balance and reason" (107). Once begun, the house has eluded human control: "This house, which seemed somehow to have formed itself, flying together into its own powerful pattern under the hands of its builders, fitting itself into its own construction of lines and angles, reared its great head back to the sky without concession to humanity" (35).

In its form, Hill House is now a parental house. Warped to fit the mind of the vicious patriarch, it is furnished with symbols of the destructive power of motherhood. "It's all so motherly," says Luke, who has no mother. "Everything so soft. Everything so padded. Great embracing chairs and sofas which turn out to be hard and unwelcome when you sit down, and reject you at once" (209). For him, it is "a mother house ... a housemother, a headmistress, a housemistress" (211). The "heart of the house" (119) is like the "doorway of a tomb" (118): It is the nursery, decorated by two "grinning heads" whose "separate stares, captured forever in distorted laughter, met and locked at the point of the hall where the vicious cold centered" (120). Gathered comfortably into the heavy, pressing surrounding hills, Hill House is the original womb/tomb, with all the comforts of home. There are good beds, excellent cooking, companionship; and nothing to do but die in a house that does not want you—that "almost" shudders around you and the mess you make by opening doors (92, 97, 115)—but that does not want to let you go. Like the worst kind of family, Hill House "takes care" of its inhabitants in both senses of the phrase.

For Eleanor, the house is associated with both mother and father. On the same page on which Jackson wrote, "FAMILY, FAMILY," she wrote, *"Leaving house = betrayal of mother.* Eleanor does not belong anywhere. Betray mother by being born—taking away part of mother" (1D). If Eleanor has betrayed her mother by being born, there is only one way to assuage her guilt: to be "unborn." The house exudes the smell of the grave, a reminder of her mother, from the library door, the entrance to the tower in which one woman is said to have died already. The library, with its tomblike smell and maternal associations, is only the entryway to its male counterpart, a tower of "gray stone, grotesquely solid, jammed hard against the wooden side of the house, with the insistent veranda holding it there" (112). Built to fit the mind of its founder, who "guarded" his daughter's "virtue" by a combination of threats, obscene pictures, and promises of a heavenly end in "her father's arms" (171), Hill House has become more phallic with each rewriting. In the final draft, as Eleanor joins the haunting on the last night, she asks Hugh Crain's grotesque statue to dance with her—and the house takes her hands. She goes out for a last look at the tower, "held, so tightly in the embrace of the house, in the straining grip of the house" (231) and then walks up the library steps toward seduction and death:

> And here I am, she thought. Here I am inside. It was not cold at all, but deliciously, fondly warm.... Under her feet the stone floor moved caressingly, rubbing itself against the soles of her feet, and all around the soft air touched her, stirring her hair, drifting across her fingers, coming in a light breath across her mouth, and she danced in circles.... She thought, ... I have broken the spell of Hill House and somehow come inside. I am home, I am home, she thought [232].

Eleanor is about to reverse the birth process through which she "betrayed" her mother.

In the last two drafts, as the house becomes an increasingly more powerful parent, the haunting it creates for its guests most frequently takes the form of a child: a child who calls for mercy in the night (162); a child whose "little caressing touch," moving "intimately and softly" on the doorknob, and whose "wheedling to be let in" accompany the house's onslaught against its guests' doors (201); a child who scrawls names and pleas or demands on walls (145–46, 55); and a child whose "voice, singing sweetly and thinly, ... 'Go in and out the windows'" (226), evokes childhood games of connection and entrapment for Eleanor alone. When Eleanor runs down the halls of Hill House, nearly following a ghostly "mother" to her death, she seems to be dreaming that she is already one of Hill House's children, taunting the grownups in residence: "What fools they are," she thinks, "we trick them so easily" (230).

The ghostly manifestations of some of the earlier drafts had already pointed to the longing for family: the "cousins" scene, for example, or the night walk into the ghostly picnic. Others are rewritten in this draft to emphasize family. The writing on Hill House's walls, originally "Help, Eleanor Come Help" (TS3 93) becomes "Help Eleanor Come Home" (146). The manifestation on the second night, which told Vancey to go away (1D), now leads Eleanor to believe her mother is knocking against the wall for help (127). More awake, she consoles herself that the noise "sounds like something children do," and hears "little pattings," "small seeking sounds," the sound of something "fondling" the doorknob, and "little sticky sounds" (131). Mad ghostly children outside the door, human counterparts within: when the manifestation's "thin little giggle" ends, Eleanor and Theodora are clutching each other "like a couple of lost children" (131).

All of these manifestations and descriptions combine to make the Hill House of Jackson's final version a house of delusions of family. Hill House will be glad to give you a hand to hold in the night, someone to be there, a sense of belonging. When it is too late, you will realize that all along you were really alone, clinging to your enemy—or to nothing at all. The house's furnishings have "hands everywhere," Luke says: "Little soft glass hands, curving out to you, beckoning—" (209). So do its ghosts. In a scene that Jackson marks as containing the "key" to the book (1D), Eleanor clutches Theodora's hand as she works up the courage to cry out against the torture of a ghostly child. She suddenly looks up to see Theodora on the other side of the room. She screams, *"Whose hand was I holding?"* (162–163). The horror behind Eleanor's scream is not that she was alone in the dark, but that she believed herself to have someone there.

In these last drafts, Jackson restructures her characters' personal histories to reveal their vulnerability to fantasies of belonging in a family. On a single sheet of paper Jackson wrote, among other things, "Theo divorced? Excitement/Luke—too wise—indolent/doctor foolish/Eleanor IS house/" and then, in large capital letters, "ALL DISTORTED LIKE HOUSE" (1D). Although Theodora's background changes, the plan seems clear: each character will be rewritten to emphasize a weakness Hill House can exploit, a literal kinship with the house. Luke, Theodora, and Eleanor, for example, the three "children" (69, 142) are all in some sense orphaned. Theodora has symbolically rejected all ties by eliminating her patronym (8); she had "thousands of uncles," she says (53) and her family "sent her away to boarding school" (45,53). Luke's only family is his aunt, who doesn't trust him with the family silver (10); and though his confession of suffering from motherlessness may be as banal and self-pitying as it seems to Eleanor, that need not make it any less true (166–67). Eleanor herself has had no home, even nominally, since her mother died (8). Vancey had her house; Trapped Theodora, her "apartment 3B"; Erica, her dim apartment in the city (TS/C4 50, 59–60). Eleanor has an apartment in one early sketch (1D), but by the time Jackson includes her in a full draft, she is defined by her lack of a home. "ELEANOR IS HOMELESS," Jackson scrawled on a page of notes (1D).

Jackson's introductions of her three "orphans," written as she was creating Hill House's family haunting, are worth watching. Luke is a liar and a thief (9); Theodora is "not at all like Eleanor" (8); Eleanor "hates" only her sister now that her mother is dead (7). All these statements seem to be true; but so are their opposites. In fact, Luke plays into Hill House's hands through his honesty; Theodora, through her ties to Eleanor; and Eleanor, through her desperate need for a family to love.

In their isolation as perhaps in the disintegration of the initial easy affection between them, Theodora, Luke, and Eleanor are heirs to Hill House's first children. Jackson had experimented with several versions of Hill House's past, but only in the final draft does she envision the house's history as one of death, betrayal, and homelessness, especially for women. Founder Hugh Crain's first wife is killed on the grounds before she ever reaches the house (75); his second dies of a mysterious fall (76). The third, a consumptive, leaves the country—and leaves her stepdaughters to Hill House until she too dies (76). One sister takes "a girl from the village to live with her" at Hill House as "a kind of companion" (77); when she wills Hill House to the "little companion," the other sister (perhaps aided by the house itself) engages in wild attacks on Hill House's new owner until she hangs herself—reportedly in the library tower (77–81). Only one man is said to have died at Hill House— a guest who made the mistake of attempting to leave after dark and was crushed against a tree (75). As Dr. Montague points out, the family history and the house's nature are intimately connected: "Essentially, the evil is in the house itself, I think. It has enchained and destroyed its people and their lives, it is a place of contained ill will" (82).

In the final version, there are other parallels between the house's past and the histories of its guests. Eleanor may say that she and her sister are nothing like the sisters of Hill House, for example; but her denial only points up the way in which the Hill House sisters' struggles over the house echo the conflict that forced her to reach Hill House by "stealing" a car that was half her own (10–12). When Luke's aunt fears that he will abscond with the family silver, she is continuing a Hill House tradition that began with accusations about stealing the house's china (78). Even the story of the little companion has its bitter echoes, not only because Eleanor had been forced to live as a kind of companion to her invalid mother, but because the younger woman's vulnerability is a mocking reminder that Theodora can never extend the security of family status to her own roommate/companion/lover.

Like the house, the guests come to be defined by the failures of their family ties. Hill House makes deadly use of both Dr. Montague's willingness to play "father" (69, 142) and the fatuous pride he takes in "his" haunted house. Initially an impersonal elderly scholar whose work has been devoted to the "suppression and elimination of superstitious beliefs" (TS), he is described in the final draft as a man who belongs "before a fire in a pleasant little sitting room, with a cat on his knee and a rosy little wife to bring him jellied scones" (60). His wife is no such figure. In the first Eleanor draft, she is a foolish, absurdly girlish woman, but a loving mother to her children (TS); Dr. Montague is portrayed as patient with her foibles. By the final draft, the happy children and the fondness have disappeared: Mrs. Montague makes no pretense of having the slightest respect for her husband, thus exposing his ability to imagine himself happily married as absurd and painful. What is more, she brings another "housemaster" to take over her husband's pretense at being a protector (211).

Mrs. Montague not only assists in effecting her husband's transformation, she plays a crucial, independent role in the creation of the house's familial haunting. If Theodora, Luke, Eleanor, and the doctor represent outsiders in a world of family homes, Mrs. Montague is an insider. Certainly her sentimentality about the needs of "spirits" and her imperviousness to both the needs of the living and to actual manifestations provide needed comic relief. Yet there is a more disturbing side to the counterpoint she provides. When she and the housekeeper, Mrs. Dudley, settle for a cozy chat in the kitchen of Hill House, they do not render the house any less vile. Rather, the house creates a new and sinister context for their prosaic occupation. The dishes "belong on the shelves" (101) in Hill House; and by extension, the same drive for domestic order that moves Mrs. Montague and Mrs. Dudley to handle their dishtowels moves the house to close doors after its guests when they leave the room. Hill House, which almost "shudders" at the noise and confusion of living inhabitants, is the original self-cleaning house, ready to exterminate or expel anyone or anything that makes a mess. In an early draft, when Mrs. Dudley says, "The dishes belong on the shelves," Theodora asks "wickedly, 'And the guests?'" (TS1 60).

Like the characters, the novel's plot essentially remains stable, even as the shift in the nature of the haunting profoundly alters its significance. From the beginning, Jackson seems to have assumed that sexual tension between the two women at Hill House would play a central role. She seems to have left the nature of such tension open as long as possible: as late as one draft of scenes including Eleanor, she was still experimenting with one scene in which the two women openly argue over Luke and another in which Theodora's lesbianism is openly discussed and the attraction between the two women clearly acknowledged (1D). By the final draft, of course, Eleanor is drawn both to Luke and to Theodora, neither of whom can offer her the familial love she so desperately needs.

In the final version, the main sexual tension is clearly not competition over Luke. Luke has been transformed from the stock romantic hero of earlier versions to a more ambiguous figure. Eleanor does experiment with romantic fantasies about him, but these do not take real form until the breach with Theodora is virtually inevitable, and they are short-lived. "The only man I have ever sat and talked to alone," Eleanor thinks, "and I am impatient; he is simply not very interesting" (167). The focus of Eleanor's romantic and sexual longings throughout virtually the whole novel is now Theodora. In the final haunting, the sexual tension between Eleanor and Theodora becomes an inexorable and tortuous battle over the nature of identity and morality. Eleanor's reactions to Theodora crystallize not only her longing for a sister who loves her, and for a lover, but her hopeless attempt to assert a new sexuality and sense of self without questioning the family structure and morality that have governed her life before Hill House.

It is no accident that Jackson's final version presents Theodora in opposition not only to family but to Eleanor herself. Theodora has cast off her surname, we learn from Jackson's introduction—and she is "not at all like Eleanor" (8). As usual, the characterization must be approached with skepticism. In many ways, the Theodora of the final draft is Eleanor's mirror image, an image of the kind of woman Eleanor is afraid even to dream of becoming. Eleanor has tried to forget the terrifying poltergeists who threw stones at her house when she was an adolescent (and who, according to most theories of poltergeist manifestations, may have arisen in response to her own psychological turmoil at the death of her father); Theodora tells the others that after having thrown a brick through a greenhouse window she "thought about it for a long time, remembering the whipping but remembering also the lovely crash, and after thinking about it very seriously I went out and did it again" (73). When the groundskeeper at Hill House is rude to Eleanor, she is shocked by her fleeting impulse to run him down (30). Theodora actually aims the car at him (46). Eleanor is nearly overwhelmed by her daring in having bought slacks, a red sweater, and red sandals. "Mother would be *furious*," she thinks, and hides them in the bottom of her suitcase (41). Theodora wears slacks and bright colors without apparently caring "at all what other people [think] of her" (96).

Theodora's mirroring of Eleanor is fortunate, dangerous, erotic; she is her other self, her potential sister, lover, murderer. The following passage in the *Hill House* papers is crossed out and replaced by the note, "Precede by Nell—Theo talk—I'm going where you do—semi-comic/ Theo against Nell, of course: to each of us—if we are fortunate—is given one other person, the true doppelganger, the other half of the self, and the union here is sometimes star-crossed, sometimes illicit, always deadly; it is the moment of perception when the victim sees his murderer, the brother discovers his sister, beauty destroys [embraces] the beast" (TS3 n.p.).

Jackson's handwritten notes include another more cryptic indication of the complex ways in which Theodora both personifies and negates Eleanor and her family: "Theo *is* Eleanor/"NO ONE TO LOVE ME = NO HOUSE Therefor [sic] Eleanor invisible/THEO SISTER" (1D). The deep connections between the women are too complex to be set out in rational terms; but Jackson's final haunting clearly evokes their power.

When Theodora paints Eleanor's toenails red in a scene added to the final draft, the gesture is both seductive and aggressive. She mockingly validates Eleanor's earlier fantasy of being a "famous courtesan," but she also says, "By the time I'm through with you, you will be a different person; I dislike being with women of no color" (116).

This scene and Hill House's response to it are roughly framed by two others. In the first, in a rare moment of pleasure in her own separate identity, Eleanor finds herself "unexpectedly admiring her own [unpainted] feet" (83). That same evening, Theodora tells Eleanor she is attractive and touches her hand (86). Eleanor, who tells herself she hates to be touched, is suddenly afraid she herself is not "clean": "Her fingernails *were* dirty, and her hand was badly shaped," she thinks, "and people made jokes about love because sometimes it was funny" (86). After the toenail painting and its sequel, the guests discover a ghastly book of precepts for one of the original daughters of Hill House, compiled by the self-proclaimed "author of [her] being and the guardian of [her] virtue" (171)—complete with obscene illustrations, expressions of fanatical morality, and a signature in blood. The juxtaposition of Eleanor's sexual self-hatred and Hugh Crain's teachings has everything to do with what happens between Theodora and Eleanor.

"Your feet are dirty," Theodora says casually, as she paints Eleanor's toenails—and Eleanor panics:

"It's *horrible*," she said to Theodora, "it's *wicked*," wanting to cry. Then, helplessly, she began to laugh at the look on Theodora's face.... "I hate having things done to me.... I don't like to feel helpless.... My mother—It's wicked. I mean—on *my* feet. It makes me feel like I look like a fool" [117].

"You've got wickedness and foolishness somehow mixed up," a startled Theodora tells her (117). In part, of course, she is right. In part, however, she misses the point. Eleanor has been raised in the ideological world of Hugh Crain's precepts; she may surreptitiously buy red clothing, but to glory in her own sexuality, to be a "woman of some color," she would have to be a "different person" indeed. If it is fine for her to do so, what does that say about her entire past? Either such self-indulgence is wicked, or she has been played for a fool.

The message is clear: Eleanor cannot cope with her own sexuality. Henceforth, she will pursue Theodora as an intimate companion, but she will shrink in disgust from her touch. Theodora seems to sense how serious matters are. "You're about as crazy as anyone I ever saw," she says cheerfully at first; and then "gravely," "I have a hunch that you ought to go home" (117). What she cannot know is that Eleanor has no home; and that she, Theodora, has exposed herself as Eleanor's true double, able simultaneously to seduce and annihilate.

The haunting's strategy of separating the guests seems to aim particularly at separating Eleanor and Theodora. By the next day, Eleanor's name has been scrawled on the walls, and the two women have begun to fight. What follows is probably Hill House's most vicious manifestation: a stinking, bloody attack on Theodora's room, with "HELP ELEANOR COME HOME ELEANOR" scrawled on the walls (152–58). Earlier drafts showed blood on Theodora's walls and dressing table alone (TS), and one even shows Mrs. Montague later soaking it out with cold water (TS/C4 211–12). Now the attack is spectral, and it is extremely intimate. The menstrual imagery seems unmistakable here: Hill House echoes and amplifies Eleanor's hatred of "dirty" female bodies, including her own. Theodora's bright clothes are trampled and soaked in blood (155). Even more significantly, she herself is bloodied—literally rendered a scarlet woman—and Eleanor's name, like Hugh Crain's in the obscene book of "moral" instruction, is written on the walls in blood (155, 157–58). Beside herself, Theodora blames Eleanor, whose wild, secret hilarity reveals the extent to which Hill House has indeed fulfilled her hidden desires. "Journeys end in lovers meeting," she says silently to steady herself (154).

In the end, however, Hill House is a treacherous ally even in retaliation. The morality of Eleanor's upbringing is only momentarily vindicated. True, she may now call Theo *"filthy"* (158) and tell herself she has "never felt such uncontrollable loathing" for anyone (157), but she must watch as Theodora, newly scrubbed and cheerily admitting to being a fool, casually appropriates her own cherished and daring red sweater, asserting with equal casualness that she and Eleanor are "practically twins" (158). The haunting has thus moved to cut Eleanor off not only from Theodora but also from her own timid dreams of becoming more colorful. Even Theodora's assertion of kinship seems a form of aggression to Eleanor now, and it is true that she can no longer rely on Theodora's good will. It is no accident that the manifestation that follows is what Jackson called the key scene of the novel: the scene in which Eleanor holds Theodora's hand, only to discover there was no one there.

Is Theodora a kind of demon lover, a human parallel to the ghostly hand that offered Eleanor transitory, delusive comfort? Is she too a victim of Hill House? Or is she both? It is never quite clear whether Jackson implies an intrinsic relationship between the selfishness she seems to attribute to Theodora, Theodora's dangerous function as a double, and Theodora's lesbianism. (The connection between the latter two was much stronger in *Hangsaman*.)[5] What does seem clear is that Theodora betrays Eleanor in part because she betrays her own desires. The evening before Eleanor reaches for Theodora's hand and finds that of Hill House, the four guests talk about fear. "I am always afraid of being alone," Eleanor confesses, but for Theodora, fear comes from "'knowing what we really want....' She pressed her cheek to Eleanor's hand, and Eleanor, hating the touch of her, took her hand away quickly" (159–60). Just as she fought with her lover rather than admitting to her need to go to Hill House (9), Theodora is drawn into fighting with Eleanor rather than admit to the sexual awareness that makes her realize that she is unable to cope with Eleanor's confused longings for intimacy.

Later, when the two women walk into negative light, fighting over Theodora's anger at Eleanor's willingness to listen to Luke's confidences, one of the first manifestations Jackson wrote takes on new irony and poignancy. Originally written as a vicious parody of the famous "adventure" at Versailles, which Jackson believed had united two real British schoolmistresses, Miss Moberly and Miss Jourdain, in bonds of labor and probably of love, the manifestation now reverses its model in function as well as form.[6] In earlier drafts, the haunting shatters the women's intimacy before either can ask a question about Luke (1D). This time, the question Hill House does not allow them to ask is "Do you love me?" (174).

In her own way, Theodora, too, seems to have been seduced by Hill House's delusive promises. Just before Eleanor is sent away, she says, "Oh Nellie, my Nell—be happy; please be happy. Don't *really* forget me.... Oh, Nellie! I thought you weren't going to say good-by to me" (244).

We have seen the destruction of Eleanor's romantic fantasies. "Journeys end in lovers meeting," she thinks, meaning first Luke and then

Theodora; but as they themselves admit, she cannot trust them (213). In the "absolute reality" of Hill House, Eleanor begins to face a second truth she has tried to flee: her self-sacrifice has been inadequate and ultimately pointless. On the one hand, she could never give her family enough: "It was going to happen sooner or later in any case," she says of her mother's death. "But of course no matter when it happened it was going to be my fault" (212). On the other hand, what she did give, she seems to have given for nothing. She hated her mother and hates her sister; and she has no home. "Do you *always* go where you're not wanted?" an exasperated Theodora asks her at one point. "I've never been wanted *anywhere*," Eleanor "placidly" replies (209).

Hill House comes to embody what Claire Kahane calls a "primary Gothic fear" of "nonseparation from the castle as mother": in the secret center of Hill House, "the secret center of the Gothic structure ... boundaries break down, ... life and death become confused, ... images of birth and death proliferate in complex displacements" (Garner 337–38). Eleanor herself increasingly swings between what Kahane calls "the polar oppositions of experience within the symbiotic bond: the illusion of being all or nothing" (338). By the last night, Eleanor *is* the haunting for the other guests who hear her pounding at their doors (228–29).

Hill House's spectral "family," initially a mirror of all the guests' deepest conflicts, now belongs to Eleanor alone, and with secrecy a new dynamic emerges. As the violence of Hill House's most dramatic manifestation reaches its peak, Eleanor can no longer differentiate herself from the haunting. She thinks the noise is in her own head, and she feels as if she is "disappearing inch by inch" into the house. The house begins to rock as it is literally tearing itself into pieces. "We are lost," she thinks, "lost; the house is destroying itself. She heard the laughter over all, coming thin and lunatic, rising in its little crazy tune, and thought, No; it is over for me. It is too much.... I will relinquish my possession of this self of mine, abdicate, give over willingly what I never wanted at all; whatever it wants of me it can have" (204). "I'll come," she says; and the manifestation stops (204). Once more, a woman has sacrificed her own identity to hold her "family" home together. Eleanor's surrender leaves one with an uneasy question: can a woman sacrifice herself if she has never really had, or perhaps even wanted, a self? Does Eleanor know she has a choice? Is her death suicide—or murder?

To sacrifice oneself, after all, Jackson implies, one must have been allowed to develop a "self," and one must have a choice; it is not clear that Eleanor has either. Her death is only the dramatic accomplishment of a domestic murder that began long ago. Even her suicide is not her own: "In the unending, crashing second before the car hurled into the tree she thought clearly, *Why* am I doing this?" (246). What is left at the end of *Hill House* is a vision of failed human bonds, and of the forced sacrifice of a victim too weak, and too drugged by fantasy, to resist.

Perhaps the greatest horror of Jackson's haunting is not that the house seduces Eleanor into literally sacrificing herself for the sake of belonging, but that having done so, it still does not let her belong. Eleanor may imagine herself to be joining the ghostly children who try to enter her room, sing to her, hold her, and ask her for help, but this promised intimacy is as delusive as any other in Hill House. In Kahane's terms, Eleanor has given her life to become "everything" and has become nothing. The house does not want her any more than anyone else does; it wants her dead. After all, whatever walks in Hill House walks alone.

## Notes

1. I believe I can distinguish four main versions in the drafts of *Hill House* at the Library of Congress. For the sake of convenience, I have named them after their protagonists (Vancey, Trapped Theodora, Erica, and Eleanor), assuming that those sketches that are furthest from the final draft were probably written first.

The "Vancey" and "Trapped Theodora" versions are drawn from folders labeled "First Draft" (1D) and "Typescript" (TS). These same folders contain a series of jumbled and, for the most part, unpaginated sketches for what I believe are later drafts, the "Erica" and "Eleanor" versions. They also contain Jackson's introduction and publishing house readers' reactions to an early draft (probably the Erica version); unused sketches for Hill House's history; drawings and floor plans for the house; notes and commentary on Jackson's research into psychic manifestations; and a description of *Hill House*'s composition, which appeared in shortened form in her essay, "Experience and Fiction"; as well as one or two sketches that seem to be unrelated to the novel.

The majority of the "Erica" version appears in the folder labeled "Typescript Carbon 4" (TS/C4). This folder contains pages one through 66 of a draft of the novel's opening. It also contains two short sketches of scenes about a protagonist named "Eleanor." These pages (136–40 and 211–18) appear to be part of a lost draft; the incidents they describe had not yet been integrated into the "Erica" draft.

The final, or "Eleanor," version may be found in two sets of files. One set is marked "Typescript 1," "Typescript 2" and "Typescript 3" (TS1, TS2, TS3); the other, "Typescript Carbon 1," "Typescript Carbon 2," and "Typescript Carbon 3" (TS/C1, TS/C2, TS/C3). "Typescript Carbon 3" also contains unnumbered pages. The set marked "Carbon" is not a copy of the first set, but it does incorporate corrections penciled on that set. Both are numbered, and both drafts are very close to the final form of *Hill House*. Uncorrected page proofs are also in the collection.

2. The personal context from which Jackson wrote about the destructiveness of the nuclear family is suggested by Judy Oppenheimer's biography of Jackson.

3. Erica appears as the protagonist of sketches scattered through the "Typescript" and "First Draft" folders as well. In the most disturbing of these, she suddenly walks into a hospital emergency room "because she genuinely wanted to be in touch, somehow, with another human being to whom some ultimate thing was happening, because she was lonely" (TS). On the same page, Jackson wrote, "Reality is an interminable sentence, but as long as it allows for the slight irregularity of hope it is bearable."

4. In writing *Hill House,* Jackson embarked on "a lot of splendid research reading all the books about ghosts I could get hold of" ("Experience" 202). She seems to

have read and drawn on accounts of some of the most famous hauntings in the English-speaking world, particularly the hauntings at Borley Rectory and Ballechin Castle, which are mentioned by Dr. Montague in the novel (*Hill House* 141) Accounts of these hauntings include: Eric J. Dingwell, Kathleen Goldney and Trevor H. Hall, *The Haunting of Borley Rectory* (London: Gerald Duckworth, 1956); Harry Price, *"The Most Haunted House in England": Ten Years Investigation of Borley Rectory* (London: Longmans, 1940); *The End of Borley Rectory, The Most Haunted House in England* (London: Longmans, 1940); and A. Goodrich-Freer, Colonel Lemesurier Taylor and John, Marquess of Bute, eds., *The Alleged Haunting of B-House* [Ballechin Castle] (London: George Redway, 1899).

While Jackson certainly borrowed manifestations and descriptions for *Hill House* from these and other hauntings, she seems to have come away from her research intrigued by the human relationships and self-revelations that come from the groups of psychic researchers pursuing these ghosts. She writes in some undated notes that in every documented case she has investigated, there is "a reason for the perception of the supernatural; that is, the ghost may or may not have a reason for appearing, but the percipient most certainly has a reason for *seeing* it" (1D).

5. When Jackson first discovered that Jeannette Foster had included *Hangsaman* in her *Sex Variant Women in Literature,* she wrote a letter that vilified the lesbian poet and scholar as "some dirty old lady," asserting her own reading as definitive: "damnit, it [*Hangsaman*] is about what I say it is about" (Oppenheimer 232–33). Although Oppenheimer echoes Jackson's horror at what the biographer terms a misreading, apparently accepting the author's statement as conclusive, she quotes enough of the remainder of Jackson's impressive letter to reveal the writer moving beyond her initial response and engaging in a self-critical exploration of the fear and denial suggested by her own overwhelming response to the association of her characters with a "named sin" (233–34).

6. Jackson made frequent references to the "adventure" of Charlotte Moberly and Eleanor Jourdain, in which apparitions at Versailles helped to create a lifetime union between these two British schoolmistresses. A version of this adventure appears as one of Hill House's most frightening manifestations. An account of the women's experiences is given in Charlotte Moberly, *An Adventure* (London: Macmillan, 1911); and in *An Adventure with Appendix and Maps* (London: Macmillan, 1913).

## Works Cited

Carpenter, Lynette. "The Establishment and Preservation of Female Power in Shirley Jackson's *We Have Always Lived in the Castle.*" *Frontiers* 8 (1984): 32–38.

Garner, Shirley Nelson, Claire Kahane, and Madelon Sprengnether, eds. *The (M)Other Tongue.* Ithaca: Cornell University Press, 1985.

Jackson, Shirley. "Experience and Fiction." In *Come Along with Me: Part of a Novel, Sixteen Stories, and Three Lectures.* Ed. Stanley Edgar Hyman. New York: Viking, 1959.

_____. *The Haunting of Hill House.* New York: Viking, 1959. (Paperback: New York: Popular Library, 1959)

_____. Book File 22: "First Draft," "Typescript," "Typescript 1," "Typescript 2," "Typescript 3," "Typescript Carbon 1," "Typescript Carbon 2," "Typescript Carbon 3," and "Typescript Carbon 4." Shirley Jackson Papers, Library of Congress, Washington, D.C.

Oppenheimer, Judy. *Private Demons: The Life of Shirley Jackson.* New York: Fawcett, 1988.

# 8

# Shirley Jackson and the Reproduction of Mothering: *The Haunting of Hill House*

## JUDIE NEWMAN

One of the most enduring mysteries of horror fiction consists in its exploitation of the attractions of fear. Why, one may ask, should a reader seek out the experience of being terrified, particularly by horror fiction, which adds abhorrence, loathing and physical repulsion to the purer emotions of terror evoked by the supernatural tale? For H.P. Lovecraft[1] the answer lay in the human fear of the unknown. Freud however, developed a different hypothesis, describing the experience of the "uncanny" (*unheimlich*) as that class of the frightening which leads back to what is known of old and long-familiar.[2] Observing that *heimlich* (familiar, homely) is the opposite of *unheimlich,* Freud recognizes the temptation to equate the uncanny with fear of the unknown, yet he noted that *heimlich* also means "concealed," "private," "secret," as the home is an area withdrawn from the eyes of strangers. In Freud's argument, therefore, the experience of the uncanny arises either when primitive animistic beliefs, previously surmounted, seem once more to be confirmed (Shirley Jackson's "The Lottery" is a case in point) or when infantile complexes— formerly repressed, are revived (a theory that brings *The Haunting of Hill House* into sharp focus). For Freud, various forms of ego disturbance involve regression to a period when the ego had not marked itself off

*Judie Newman, "Shirley Jackson and the Reproduction of Mothering: The Haunting of Hill House" first appeared in American Horror Fiction: From Brockden Brown to Stephen King (1990) published by Macmillan; reproduced here with the permission of Palgrave Macmillan.*

sharply from the external world and from other people. In the context of a discussion of ghosts and doubles, Freud cites Otto Rank's description of the double as originally an insurance against the destruction of the ego, an energetic denial of the power of death. (In this sense the "immortal soul" may be considered as the first double of the body.) The idea of doubling as preservation against extinction therefore springs from the unbounded self-love of the child. When this stage of primitive narcissism is surmounted, however, the double reverses its aspect, and, from being an assurance of immortality, becomes the uncanny harbinger of death and a thing of terror. Since Freud considered art as an organized activity of sublimation, providing the reader with pleasures "under wraps," it is tempting to argue that the horror tale actively eliminates and exorcises our fears by allowing them to be relegated to the imaginary realm of fiction.[3] Rosemary Jackson, however, has indicated the case for the fantastic as a potentially subversive reversal of cultural formation, disruptive of conventional distinctions between the real and the unreal.[4] Arguably, although Shirley Jackson builds her horrors on the basis of the *heimlich* and of repressed infantile complexes, in the process she subverts the Freudian paradigm, both of art as sublimation, and in broader psychoanalytic terms. In this connection, new developments in psychoanalytic theory offer fresh insights into Jackson's work. Recent feminist psychoanalytic theorists[5] have set out to revise the Freudian account of psychosexual differences, which bases gender, anatomically, on possession or lack of the phallus. In the Freudian paradigm, the male achieves adulthood by passing through the Oedipus complex, which fear of castration by the father induces him to overcome. Fear facilitates acceptance of the incest prohibition, promoting the formation of the superego, which thereafter polices desire in accordance with adult social norms. In a parallel development, the female discovers the lack of the phallus, sees herself as castrated, recognizes her mother as similarly inferior, and therefore abandons her attachment to the mother to form the oedipal relation with the father, which is the necessary precursor of adult heterosexual relationships—always the Freudian goal. Feminist analysts, however, have shifted the focus from the oedipal to the preoedipal stage, tracing the influence of gender on identity to the dynamics of the mother-infant bond. Nancy Chodorow in *The Reproduction of Mothering* offers a persuasive analysis of early infant development in these terms. Because children first experience the social and cognitive world as continuous with themselves, the mother is not seen as a separate person with separate interests. In this brief period of immunity from individuality, the experience of fusion with the mother, of mother as world, is both seductive and terrifying. Unity is bliss; yet it entails total dependence and loss of self. In contrast the father does not pose the original threat to basic ego integrity, and is perceived from the beginning as separate. Thus, the male fear of women may originate as terror of maternal omnipotence in consequence of the early dependence on the mother, and may be generalized to all women (in images such as the witch, the vampire and the Terrible Mother)[6] since it is tied up with the assertion of gender. Boys define themselves as masculine by difference from, not by relation to, their mothers. Girls, however, in defining themselves as female, experience themselves as resembling their mothers, so that the experience of attachment fuses with the process of identity formation. Girls therefore learn to see themselves as partially continuous with their mothers, whereas boys learn very early about difference and separateness. Male development therefore entails more emphatic individuation, and more defensive firming of experienced ego boundaries, whereas women persist in defining themselves relationally, creating fluid, permeable ego boundaries, and locating their sense of self in the ability to make and maintain affiliations. Female gender identity is therefore threatened by separation, and shaped throughout life by the fluctuations of symbiosis and detachment from the mother. Girls may also fear material omnipotence and struggle to free themselves, idealizing the father as their most available ally. Daughterly individuation may be inhibited by paternal absence and by over-closeness to mothers, who tend to view their daughters as extensions of themselves. Conversely, coldness on the mother's part may prevent the loosening of the emotional bond because of the unappeased nature of the child's love. In maturity women may form close personal relationships with other women to recapture some aspects of the fractured mother-daughter bond. Alternatively they may reproduce the primary attachment, by themselves bearing children, thus initiating the cycle once more, as the exclusive symbiotic relation of the mother's own infancy is re-created. Mothering therefore involves a double identification for women in which they take both parts of the preoedipal relation, as mother and as child. Fictions of development reflect this psychological structure. Recent reformulations of the female Bildungsroman[7] have drawn attention to the frequency with which such fictions end in deaths (Maggie Tulliver, Rachel Vinrace, Edna Pontellier) understandable less as developmental failures than as refusals to accept an adulthood that denies female desires and values. In addition, a persistent, if recessive, narrative concern with the story of mothers and daughters often exists in the background of a dominant romance or courtship plot.

An exploration of *The Haunting of Hill House* in the light of feminist psychoanalytic theory reveals that the source of both the pleasures and the terrors of the text springs from the dynamics of the mother-daughter relation with its attendant motifs of psychic annihilation, reabsorption by the mother, vexed individuation, dissolution of individual ego boundaries, terror of separation and the attempted reproduction of the symbiotic bond through close female friendship.[8] Eleanor Vance, the central protagonist, is mother-dominated. On her father's death the adolescent Eleanor was associated with an outbreak of poltergeist activity, in which her family home was repeatedly showered with stones (the event invites comparison with "The Lottery," in which the victim of the stoning, Tessie Hutchinson, is not only a mother, but a mother who sees her daughter as so much an extension of herself that she attempts to improve her own chances of survival by involving Eva in the fatal draw). Eleanor clearly resented her recently dead mother, whom she nursed for 11 years: "the only person in the world she genuinely hated, now that her mother was dead, was her sister" (9). Initially her excursion to Hill House to participate in Dr. Montague's study of psychic phenomena appears as an opportunity for psychological liberation, the first steps towards autonomy. The trip begins with a small act of assertion against the mother-image. When Eleanor's sister refuses to allow her to use their shared car ("I am sure Mother would have agreed with me, Eleanor" [14], Eleanor reacts by simply stealing it, in the process knocking over an angry old woman who is clearly associated with the "cross old lady" (10) whom she had nursed for so long. Once en route Eleanor is haunted by the refrain "Journeys end in lovers meeting," suggesting (as the *carpe diem* theme of the song confirms) that Eleanor's goal is the realization of heterosexual desires.

Eleanor's fantasies on the journey, however, imply that her primary emotional relation remains with her mother. In imagination she dreams up several homes, based on houses on her route. In the first, "a little dainty old lady took care of me" (19), bringing trays of tea and wine "for my health's sake." The fantasy reveals just how much Eleanor herself wishes to be mothered. In the preceding period, as nurse to a sick mother, Eleanor may be said to have "mothered" her own mother, losing her youth in the process. A second fantasy centers upon a hollow square of poisonous oleanders, which seem to Eleanor to be "guarding something" (20). Since the oleanders enclose only an empty center, Eleanor promptly supplies a mother to occupy it, constructing an enthralling fairy world in which "the queen waits, weeping, for the princess to return" (21). Though she swiftly revises this daydream of mother-daughter reunion, into a more conventional fantasy of courtship by a handsome prince, she remains much preoccupied with images of protected spaces and magic enclosures, of a home in which *she* could be mothered and greeted as a long-lost child. A subsequent incident reinforces this impression. Pausing for lunch, Eleanor observes a little girl who refuses to drink her milk because it is not in the familiar cup, patterned with stars, that she uses at home. Despite material persuasion, the child resists, forcing her mother to yield. The small tableau emphasizes both the child's potential independence and resistance to the mother, and the attractions of the familiar home world, here associated with mother's milk and starry containment. Eleanor empathizes with the little girl's narcissistic desires: "insist on your cup of stars; once they have trapped you into being like everyone else you will never see your cup of stars again" (22). Eleanor's final fantasy home, a cottage hidden behind oleanders, "buried in a garden" (23), is entirely secluded from the world. Taken together, her fantasies suggest her ambivalent individuation and the lure of a magic mother-world. They form a striking contrast to the reality of Hillsdale, a tangled mess of dirty houses and crooked streets. For all its ugliness, however, Eleanor deliberately delays there over coffee. Despite her reiterated refrain, "In delay there lies no plenty," Eleanor is not quite so eager to reach her goal and realize her desires as she thinks. Another scene of enforced delay, negotiating with a surly caretaker at the gates of Hill House, further retards her progress. The emphasis here on locked gates, guards against entry, a tortuous access road, and the general difficulty in locating the house reinforces the impression of its desirability as *heimlich*, secret, a home kept away from the eyes of others. Entry to this protected enclave provokes, however, a response that underlines the consonance of the familiar and the uncanny: childish terror. Afraid that she will cry "like a child sobbing and wailing" (34), tiptoeing around apprehensively, Eleanor feels like "a small creature swallowed whole by a monster' which 'feels my tiny little movements inside" (38). The intrauterine fantasy immediately associates Hill House with an engulfing mother. Eleanor's fellow guest, Theo, reacts in opposite terms, characterizing the two women as Babes in the Woods (abandoned by parents) and comparing the experience to the first day at boarding school or camp. The vulnerable continuity between fear of engulfment and fear of separation is indicated in the women's response to the threat. Reminiscing about their childhoods, they eagerly associate themselves through fancied family resemblances, until Theo announces that theirs is an indissoluble relationship: "Would you let them separate us now? Now that we've found out we're cousins?" (49). Yet on the arrival of the remaining guests, Luke and Dr. Montague, Theo's assertion of female strength through attachment is swiftly replaced as the four establish their identities, in playfully exaggerated form, through separation and differentiation: "You are Theodora because *I* am Eleanor"; "I have no beard so *he* must be Dr. Montague" (53–4). Fantasy selves are then elaborated. Luke introduces himself as a bullfighter; Eleanor poses as an artist's model, living an "abandoned" life while moving from garret to garret; Theo describes herself as a lord's daughter, masquerading as an ordinary mortal in the clothes of her maid, in order to escape a parental plot of forced marriage. Interestingly, though both women characterize themselves as homeless, Eleanor converts homelessness into an image of abandonment, Theo into active escape from an oppressive parent by asserting a different identity. For Eleanor, however, identity remains elusive. In envisaging herself as an artist's model she acquiesces in a self-image created by a controlling other.

Introductions over, the foursome make a preliminary exploration of Hill House that confirms its character as an ambivalent maternal enclave. Comfortable, its menu excellent, the house has "a reputation for insistent hospitality" (59), and is distinguished by inwardness and enclosure. Labyrinthine in layout, its concentric circles of rooms, some entirely internal and windowless, make access to the outside world problematic. Doors close automatically on its occupants, who are further confused by its architectural peculiarities. In Hill House every apparent right angle is a fraction off, all these tiny aberrations of measurement adding up to a large overall distortion, which upsets the inhabitants' sense of balance. An encircling verandah obscures awareness of the distortion. While this structure mirrors the conventional twisted line of gothic (in plot as in architecture), baffling the reader's sense of direction and threatening to lead at any point out of one world and into another, it also emphasizes an internalized entrapment that threatens reason and balance. Luke is in no doubt as to the house's identity: "It's all so motherly. Everything so soft. Everything so padded. Great embracing chairs and sofas which turn out to be hard and unwelcoming when you sit down, and reject you at once—" (174). The ambivalent suggestions here of maternal comfort and maternal rejection invite comparison with *The Sundial,* in which the labyrinthine connection between mother as security and mother as trap is made literal in a physical maze, to which only Aunt Fanny knows the key. The pattern of the maze is built upon her mother's name, Anna, so that by turning right, left, left, right, then left, right, right, left, the center is reached. As long as the mother's name is remembered, Fanny is secure in "the maze I grew up in," despite the activities of the matriarch, Orianna, the murderess of her own child.[9]

Paradoxically, the doctor's history reveals that Hill House is actually notable for an absence of mothers. The first Mrs. Craine died in a carriage accident in the drive, the second in a fall, the third in Europe of consumption. Since Hugh Craine's two daughters were therefore brought up without a mother, the house is simultaneously associated with mothering and with motherlessness. Later the older of the two daughters took possession of the house, dying there amidst accusations that her young companion had neglected her. The latter, persecuted by the younger sister's attempts to regain the house, eventually hanged herself. The history of the house therefore provides a psychic configuration

not unlike Eleanor's own, which also involves a dead mother, two war-
ring sisters, and a neglected old lady. Eleanor later accuses herself: "It
was my fault my mother died. She knocked on the wall and called me
and called me and I never woke up" (177). On learning the history of
the house, however, Eleanor empathizes with the unmothered girls and
the companion. Eleanor has been both mother and child. On the one
hand she detests the mother's dominance, resenting the loss of her own
youth in the forced assumption of the mothering role. On the other, she
feels guilt at not having mothered adequately. Both images are internalized so that Eleanor is haunted by guilt as a mother over the neglected
child within herself.

As a result two rooms in Hill House are of special significance to
her—the library and the nursery, the one associated with the mother, the
other with the unmothered child. Eleanor is quite incapable of entering
the library: "'I can't go in there....' She backed away, overwhelmed with
the cold air of mould and earth which rushed at her. 'My mother—'"
(88). Eleanor's mother had forced her to read love stories aloud to her
each afternoon, hence the library's sepulchral associations. The library
is also the point of access to the tower, where the companion hanged
herself. Theo jokes, "I suppose she had some sentimental attachment to
the tower; what a nice word 'attachment' is in that context" (88). If
attachments can be linked with annihilation and willful surrender of the
self, their absence can be equally damaging. The nursery of the unmothered girls is marked by a cold spot at its entrance "like the doorway of a
tomb" (101). On its wall is painted a frieze of animals which appear as
if trapped or dying. Ironically Dr. Montague describes this area of cold
nurturance as "the heart of the house" (101).

The stage is now set for the first appearance of the "ghost," which
occurs at the heart of Jackson's novel, almost exactly at its center.
Eleanor's internalization of both the "unmothered child" and the "neglected mother" images is reflected in the double mother- child nature of
the haunting. Awakening, Eleanor at first thinks that her mother is calling and knocking on the wall. In fact a tremendous pounding noise,
beginning close to the nursery door, accompanied by a wave of cold, has
disturbed her. The violence of the phenomenon suggests a force strong
enough to threaten the boundaries of the ego; amidst deafening crashes
it very nearly smashes in the door. Nevertheless, Eleanor's first reaction
is relief that it is *not* her mother, but "only a noise" (108). Indeed, she
sees it as "like something children do, not mothers knocking against the
wall for help" (108). The ghost now undergoes a metamorphosis, its
vehement demands yielding to an insidious seductive appeal. The doorknob is "fondled," amidst "little pattings," "small seeking sounds," "little sticky sounds" (111). The relentless emphasis on smallness and the

affectionate pattings suggest a child. Eleanor and Theo, huddled together in fear, have also been reduced to "a couple of lost children" (111). Importantly, the haunting is limited to the women. (The men, outside chasing a mysterious dog, hear nothing.) Alarmed, Dr. Montague draws the conclusion that "the intention is, somehow, to separate us" (114). Eleanor, however, argues that "it wanted to consume us, take us into itself, make us a part of the house" (117). The threat, which the men perceive in terms of separation, is understood by both women in terms of fusion and engulfment. In the light of this identification of the haunting with the reassertion of the ambivalent mother-daughter bond, it is unsurprising that Eleanor awakens next day with a renewed feeling of happiness, a fresh appetite and the urge to sing and dance. When Dr. Montague argues for the reality of the haunting, given the presence of independent witnesses, Eleanor cheerfully suggest the possibility that "all three of you are in my imagination" (118). The doctor's warning that this way madness lies—a state that would welcome Hill House in a "sisterly embrace" (118)—points to an incipient narcissism in Eleanor that would make self and world conterminous once more, assimilating all to the subjective imagination.

Initially Eleanor responds to the threat of ego dissolution by a strategic attachment to Theo, quickly forming a close friendship in which more than one reader has detected lesbian content (as the film version also implied). A similar uncertainty besets the reader of *Hangsaman*: Is Natalie's mysterious friend Tony real, imaginary, supernatural, a double or a lesbian lover? Since Natalie is always terrified of being alone with *her* mother, the attachment may be read as the result of the projection of the symbiotic bond onto an alter ego. Similarly Eleanor fosters autonomy by division, creating in Theo a double as insurance against the destruction of her own self, and as simultaneous confirmation of relational identity. Several incidents in the novel make sense only in these terms. On her first evening at Hill House, Eleanor revels in her own individuality, contemplating her feet in new red shoes: "What a complete and separate thing I am ... individually an I, possessed of attributes belonging only to me" (72). In contrast she regards her hands as ugly and dirty, misshapen by years of laundering her mother's soiled linen. Theo, telling Eleanor teasingly that she disliked "women of no color" (99), paints Eleanor's toenails red in celebration of her emergent independence. Unlike the highly individuated Theo, Eleanor is drab, mousy, with a tendency to merge into her surroundings. Theo's subsequent casual comment that Eleanor's feet are dirty provokes a violent emotional reaction, for Eleanor cannot cope with the clash between color and grime, between individuation and association with the mother. The sight of her feet now fills her with an immediate sense of helpless dependence:

"I don't like to feel helpless. My mother—" (99). In what follows, Eleanor fluctuates ambivalently between an antagonistic and an associative relation to Theo.

When a second apparent manifestation occurs (the message "HELP ELEANOR COME HOME" chalked in the hall), Eleanor both revels and recoils. On the one hand the message expresses her own desire for home. On the other, she is anxious at being identified by name. *Her* identity is targeted; she has been "singled out" (124) and separated from the group. Indeed, the message also effectively divides Eleanor and Theo, sparking a quarrel when each accuses the other of writing it. Eleanor's outburst reveals both her own suppressed need for attention, and her projection of the childish identity onto Theo: "You think *I* like the idea that I'm the center of attention? *I'm* not the spoiled baby after all" (124). Separate identity is thus both desired and rejected.

When the message is reinscribed on Theo's walls, and her clothes smeared with a substance which may be paint or blood, Theo immediately accuses Eleanor, who views the "bloody chamber" with smiling satisfaction, admitting that it reminds her of Theo applying red polish (131). The reader puzzles as to whether the hauntings are supernatural or caused by Eleanor, thus drawing attention to the central question of the novel— the degree of Eleanor's independent agency. Eleanor's apparent hostility is double-edged. Scrubbing the color off Theo, she feels uncontrollable loathing for her polluted alter ego, who is "filthy with the stuff," "beastly and soiled and dirty" (132). Watching her, Eleanor thinks, "I would like to batter her with rocks" (133). The conjunction of the two images of enforced laundering and of stoning indicates Eleanor's hostility to the mother, and to the mother within herself. The destruction of Theo's clothes, however, suggests an attempt to destroy an independent identity (the reader recalls Theo's previous fantasy of disguise), rendering Theo colorless and bringing the women into close association. Theo now has to share Eleanor's clothes and bedroom. As she comments, "We're going to be practically twins" (133). The entire sequence culminates in an admission from Eleanor of her own fear of disintegration. Contemplating Theo, dressed in Eleanor's sweater and therefore presenting an alternative self-image in which narcissism and self-hate are almost equally involved, Eleanor expresses her desire to return to a state of primal unity:

> There's only one of me, and it's all I've got. I hate seeing myself dissolve and slip and separate so that I'm living in one half, my mind, and I see the other half of me helpless ... and I could stand any of it if I could only surrender [134].

Forming a close relation with Theo, constituting Theo as "other half," are strategies that culminate disastrously in the replication rather than the repudiation of the symbiotic bond, and a desire to surrender autonomy altogether.

In consequence, the subsequent "haunting" is quite different in character, and limited to Eleanor. In the night Eleanor appears to hear a voice in Theo's empty room: "It is a child," "I won't let anyone hurt a child" (136). While the voice babbles, Eleanor tries but fails to speak; only when it pauses is she able to cry out. It thus appears to emanate from her. Indeed, Eleanor recognizes its screams from her own nightmares. Throughout the scene Eleanor has been holding Theo's hand for reassurance, clutching it so hard that she can feel the "fine bones" (137) of the fingers. On coming to consciousness (it has all been a dream) she discovers Theo sitting apart in her own bed, and shrieks, "Whose hand was I holding?" (137). The juxtaposition of a skeletal dead hand, first as reassurance then as terror, with a child's voice screaming is consonant with Eleanor's deepening neurosis. Although she adopts a mothering role ("I won't let anyone hurt a child") the penalty is to be associated with a form of security that is also a horror, with the mother as death to the self.

In desperation Eleanor makes a last attempt to establish identity outside the mother-daughter bond. But when she solicits a confidence from Luke, in a bid for a special token of affection, his response horrifies her: "'I never had a mother.' The shock was enormous. Is *that* all he thinks of me" (139). Luke's subsequent comment, that he had always wanted a mother to make him grow up, prompts Eleanor's acid reply, "Why don't you grow up by yourself?" (140), indicating her impatience with a courtship model that provides no escape from the dynamics of the original relationship. That night, when Theo teases Eleanor about Luke, the women are the victims of another haunting while they are following a path through the grounds. Ostensibly squabbling over Luke, they are described in terms that suggest the persistence of a more primary bond. Each is "achingly aware of the other" (145) as they skirt around an "open question." The language suggests that they are trembling on the brink, *not* of an open quarrel, but of mutual seduction: "walking side by side in the most extreme intimacy of expectation; their feinting and hesitation done with, they could only wait passively for resolution. Each knew, almost within a breath, what the other was thinking" (146).

As they draw closer, arm in arm again, the path unrolls before them through a suddenly "colorless" (147) landscape, in an "annihilation of whiteness." Ahead there appears a ghostly tableau of a family picnic, in a garden full of rich color, "thickly green" grass (148), red, orange and yellow flowers, beneath a bright blue sky. Theo's immediate response is to run ahead, screaming, "Don't look back," placing colorlessness behind her, along with the risk of annihilation in a symbiotic relationship. Eleanor, however, her development definitively arrested, collapses, feeling "time, as she had always known time, stop" (149). The haunting foreshadows the outcome of their relationship. When Eleanor announces her intention of accompanying Theo to her home, Theo rejects her once and for all, impatient with what she perceives as a schoolgirl crush, "as though I were the games mistress" (177). As Eleanor's identity founders, Theo's is secured: her clothes are now restored to their original condition.

The image of the two women trampling the "happy family" vignette under foot also foregrounds the insufficiencies of the oedipal model, a point which is generalized by Luke's discovery of a book, composed by Hugh Crain for his daughter. Ostensibly a series of moral lessons, with illustrations of Heaven, Hell, the seven deadly sins, the book purports to guide the child in the paths of righteousness, threatening her with various terrible fates, and offering the reward of reunion in her father's arms in Heaven "joined together hereafter in unending bliss" (143). The erotic content of the offer is fully revealed in the obscenity of Craine's accompanying illustration to "Lust." The pretence of guiding the child's moral development is actually an excuse to indulge in sensation, transgressing in the guise of moral admonition. Jackson thus explodes both the Freudian view of the father as former of the superego, and of art as an activity of sublimation, replacing instinctual gratifications. Here, far from being the basis of psychic ascension, the oedipal model is an alibi for male self-indulgence, and a legitimation of patriarchal tyranny. Importantly, Crain has cut up several other books to form his own, so that his individual text draws upon all the resources available in the cultural formation of the female subject.

The arrival of Dr. Montague's wife, a conventional spiritualist, measures the distance between fashionable psychic explanations and more radical theories of the psyche. The parodic Mrs. Montague is primarily notable for the bookishness of her images of psychic phenomena, most of which are drawn from obvious sources.[10]

Thus, receiving a spirit message via planchette from a mysterious nun, she promptly conjures up a monk and extrapolates to a heterosexual courtship model, broken vows and the nun walled up alive. Although a long correspondence in *The Times* in 1939 failed to establish evidence of any such immurement, nuns remain the most common of reported apparitions,[11] their popularity possibly the result of the recognition that the repression of female desires is a source of psychic disturbance (as in *Villette*). The planchette also produces the words "Elena," "Mother," "Child," "Lost," "Home," endlessly repeated. As a result of botched introductions Mrs. Montague takes Theo for Eleanor, and passes the message to the former. The suggestion lingers that Eleanor's bid for independent identity has failed, and that she is locked into psychic repetition.

It is therefore appropriate that the next haunting repeats the features of the others (Theo remarks on the ghost's exhausted repertoire [166]. Noisy knockings are followed by a "caressing touch" (168), "feeling intimately and softly," "fondling" and "wheedling" at the door, and by a babbling both inside and outside Eleanor's head. For Eleanor, the distinction between self and world is collapsing: "I am disappearing inch by inch into this house, I am going apart a little bit at a time" (168). As Eleanor resists dissolution, so the house shakes and threatens to fall, until she surrenders: "I will relinquish my possession of this self of mine, abdicate.... 'I'll come,' she said" (170). Instantly all is quiet, and the chapter ends with Theo's joke, "Come along, baby. Theo will wash your face for you and make you all neat for breakfast" (171). Eleanor has thus given up all hope of mature individuation, welcoming the role of child.

From this point on, only Eleanor is haunted, by ghostly footsteps and a welcoming embrace (178), and by a child's voice at the empty center of the parlor singing, "Go in and out the windows" (189)—a singing-game which replaces the earlier refrain. In surrendering to the child within, Eleanor finally becomes herself the haunter, assuming the attenuated identity of the ghost. Rising by night, she thinks "Mother," and when a voice replies "Come along" (190) she runs to the nursery to find the cold spot gone, darts in and out of the encircling verandah, and continues the childish game by pounding on the others' doors. Around her the house is "protected and warm" (193), its layout entirely familiar. Ego dissolution has become primal bliss. Hearing Luke's voice, she recognizes that of all those present she would least like *him* to catch her, and flees from male pursuit into the library, now "deliciously fondly warm" (193), its rotten spiral staircase perceived not as a danger but as a means of escape. Though in fact Eleanor is caught in a spiral of fatal repetition, moving towards complete annihilation, she is exultant: "I have broken the spell of Hill House and somehow come inside. I am home" (194). Eleanor has transferred her "crush" to the house, described by Luke as "a mother house, a housemother, a headmistress, a housemistress" (176), and now becomes entirely conterminous with her chosen world, alive to sounds and movements in all its many rooms. Unsurprisingly, when Dr. Montague excludes her from his experiment, Eleanor finds separation unthinkable and accelerates her car into a tree in the driveway. Her last thoughts reveal a fatal connection between female self-assertion and annihilation: "I am really doing it, I am doing this all by myself, now, at last; this is me, I am really really really doing it by myself" (205). In the second before collision her last lucid thought is "*Why* am I doing this?"

Feminist psychoanalytics offers an answer that is oddly confirmed in the conclusion. The novel closes with a repetition, almost without alteration, of its own original paragraph, as the cycle of creation closes only to begin once more.

If, by repressing desire, human beings condemn themselves to repeat it, the appeal of Jackson's work to both male and female readers is secure. Just as each individual haunting derives its horrors from the fear of regression to infantile complexes, specifically of fusion with the mother, so the general features of Jackson's fiction are comprehensible in terms of the reproduction of mothering. The anticipation of revisionist psychoanalytics in the reformulation of the sources of horror may also be traced in *The Bird's Nest*, which attributes Elizabeth Richmond's breakdown to her motherlessness; in the murdered child of *The Road Through the Wall*; in the murderous and eventually murdered mother of *The Sundial*, and in Jackson's own fascination with the Lizzie Borden case, which looms behind the acquitted murderess, Harriet Stuart, of *The Sundial* and the unconvicted Merricat (*We Have Always Lived in the Castle*), who poisons the rest of her family in order to establish the symbiotic bond with her sister. It would be impertinent, not to say impossible, to speculate on the influence of Jackson's own experience of mothering on her fiction. She was herself a devoted mother of four children, as her two humorous chronicles of family life reveal. Interestingly, the titles of these celebrations of maternal experience, *Raising Demons* and *Life Among the Savages*, immediately suggest works of horror fiction.

## Notes

1. H.P. Lovecraft, *Supernatural Horror in Literature* (New York: Dover, 1973).

2. "The Uncanny," in *The Standard Edition of the Complete Psychological Works of Sigmund Freud*, ed. James Strachey, vol. xvii (London: Hogarth Press, 1955).

3. See Peter Penzoldt, *The Supernatural in Fiction* (London: Peter Nevill, 1952).

4. Rosemary Jackson, *Fantasy: The Literature of Subversion* (London: Methuen, 1981).

5. See Nancy Chodorow, *The Reproduction of Mothering* (Berkeley, Calif.: University of California Press, 1978); Carol Gilligan, *In a Different Voice: Psychological Theory and Women's Development* (Cambridge, Mass.: Harvard University Press, 1982); and Jean Baker Miller, *Towards a New Psychology of Women* (London: Allen Lane, 1978).

6. A motif traced, in Jungian terms, in Jackson's work by Steven K. Hoffman, in "Individuation and Character Development in the Fiction of Shirley Jackson," *Hartford Studies in Literature*, 8 (1976), 190–208.

7. Elizabeth Abel, Marianne Hirsch and Elizabeth Langland (eds.), *The Voyage In: Fictions of Female Development* (Hanover, N.H.: University Press of New England, 1983).

8. Page references in parentheses relate to Shirley Jackson, *The Haunting of Hill House* (London: Michael Joseph, 1960).

9. Shirley Jackson, *The Sundial* (New York: Penguin, 1986), 109.

10. Mrs. Montague's discoveries recall the worst excesses of the ghost hunter, at Borley Rectory in Essex. See Harry Price, *The Most Haunted House in England: Ten Years Investigation of Borley Rectory* (London: Longmans, Green, 1940) and *The End of Borley Rectory* (London: George G. Harrap, 1946). Jackson refers to Borley in the text (p. 101). Though an examination of Jackson's sources would run to another essay, it is worth noting that almost all the psychic phenomena are drawn from the above work, including a haunted Blue Room, a cold spot, the girl in the tower, the nun and monk, immurement, the digging-up of an old well (proposed by Mrs. Montague), messages on walls and from a planchette, nightly crashings and patterings at doors, and investigation by a team of psychic researchers. Jackson described her book as originating in an account of nineteenth century psychic researchers, almost certainly those of Ballechin House, also referred to in the text (p. 8). See A. Goodrich Freer and John, Marquess of Bute, *The Alleged Haunting of Ballechin House* (London: George Redway, 1899).

11. See Peter Underwood, *Dictionary of the Occult and Supernatural* (London: George C. Harrap, 1978), 147.

# 9

# Shirley Jackson: Domestic Horror

## S.T. JOSHI

Shirley Jackson (1916–1965) and Ramsey Campbell are the two leading writers of weird fiction since Lovecraft. This assertion does not merely bypass other writers who, at least in their own minds, aspire to that title—in particular the best-selling quartet of Stephen King, Peter Straub, Clive Barker, and Anne Rice—but makes the problematical claim that Jackson is a weird writer at all. It is true that only one of her novels is avowedly supernatural—the masterful *Haunting of Hill House* (1959)—others are weird only slightly or not at all; it is also true that perhaps at most 15 or 20 of her hundred-odd short stories can be said to belong either to the weird tale or to the mystery story or to science fiction. Certainly there is nothing supernatural about "The Lottery" (1948), whose impact rests on the very *possibility* of its occurrence. But Jackson can be placed within the realm of weird fiction not only for the nebulous reason that the whole of her work has a pervasive atmosphere of the odd about it, but, more importantly, because her entire work is unified to such a degree that distinctions about genre and classification become arbitrary and meaningless. Like Arthur Machen, Shirley Jackson developed a view of the world that informed all her writing, whether supernatural or not; but that world view is more akin to the cheerless and nihilistic misanthropy of Bierce than to Machen's harried antimaterialism. It is because Shirley Jackson so keenly detected horror in the everyday

*From* The Modern Weird Tale ©*2001 S.T. Joshi, used by permission of McFarland & Company, Inc., Publishers, Box 611, Jefferson, NC 28640. www.mcfarlandpub.com.*

world, and wrote of it with rapier-sharp prose, that she ranks as a twentieth century Bierce.

Jackson began her career writing short stories—the first one, "Janice," dating to 1938, when she was attending Syracuse University. In late 1941 she published a sketch, "My Life with R.H. Macy," in the *New Republic,* and from 1943 onward she appeared regularly in *The New Yorker, Mademoiselle, Harper's, Woman's Home Companion, Good Housekeeping, Collier's, Ladies' Home Journal, Woman's Day,* and other general fiction or women's magazines. "The Lottery," of course, catapulted her to fame and notoriety, setting off a furor after its appearance in the *New Yorker* for June 26, 1948; Jackson wittily recounts the story's reception in a lecture, "Biography of a Story" (1960; *C*). Shortly thereafter her first novel, *The Road Through the Wall* (1948), appeared. The celebrity of "The Lottery" caused Jackson's publishers to push for a collection of her stories, and it emerged in early 1949. This heterogeneous volume shows signs of hasty assemblage: the stories are for the most part notable, but their rather disconcerting variety does not produce a unified effect, especially as two of the stories—"My Life with R.H. Macy" and "Charles" (1948)—are plainly, if peculiarly, autobiographical.

This strain of quasi-autobiography became much more pronounced from the late 1940s onward, as Jackson began to write a whole series of stories about her family, most centering around her four children. First published in women's magazines, these stories or sketches were collected in two of her most popular books, *Life Among the Savages* (1953) and *Raising Demons* (1957). The former was actually a bestseller for a short time, and it continues to be reprinted.

It is remarkable that Jackson never subsequently made an effort to collect her nondomestic short fiction. Not merely did *The Lottery* fail to include all the fiction she had published up to that time (it also included nine stories that appear to have been previously unpublished), but there are some 20 stories written subsequent to *The Lottery* that were not reprinted in the posthumous collection, *Come Along with Me* (1968), edited by her husband Stanley Edgar Hyman. About a dozen of her later family stories also remain uncollected. Some of these stories are not only among her most famous and most frequently anthologized—including "One Ordinary Day, with Peanuts" (1955), first published in *Fantasy and Science Fiction*—but among her best. Some of them have now been gathered in a rather heterogeneous collection, *Just an Ordinary Day* (1997).

The course of Jackson's novelistic career (she wrote six novels, not including *Come Along with Me,* left unfinished at her death) reveals both a growing mastery of the novel form and an increasing dosage of the weird, culminating with *The Haunting of Hill House. The Road Through the Wall* is an entirely mainstream satire on suburban life, but is too episodic to be effective as a whole; it reads like a series of short stories stitched together in no especial order. *Hangsaman* (1951) has more unity and a fine atmosphere of the strange—probably the result of Jackson's employment of stream-of-consciousness, which produces a weirdly hallucinatory effect—but in the end is also a non-weird Bildungsroman. *The Bird's Nest* (1954) approaches the weird in its study of a woman with multiple personalities—a phenomenon explicitly compared by the woman's psychiatrist to demonic possession (*B* 198–99)—but, aside from being very clumsy in its execution, involves nothing genuinely supernatural or weird. Indeed, the very analogy of split personality to demonic possession renders the concept wholly natural, since it is now something entirely encompassed within the bounds of natural science (or, at least, it is so presented by Jackson, whose character is cured in the end by psychoanalysis). *The Sundial* (1958) is wholly unclassifiable: although there are some powerful dream—or hallucination—sequences, this tale of a twisted family convinced that the rest of the world is soon going to end borders on the weird through the author's bland suggestion that perhaps the family members, far from being insane, may actually be right. It is one of the most vicious satires ever written. *The Haunting of Hill House,* of course, is explicitly supernatural and was so conceived by Jackson, although we will find that its true emphasis may lie elsewhere. It is certainly her most polished and integrated novel. *We Have Always Lived in the Castle* (1962) seems to be regarded as a weird tale by many (perhaps because it was initially marketed as such by her publishers, who wished to capitalize on the success of *Hill House*); but if it is weird, it is in a highly peculiar and perhaps backhanded way, for all that it is a gripping work. *Come Along with Me* promised to be supernatural, but I do not know enough about its genesis or purpose to say whether it would actually have turned out to be so.

Jackson's world view does not extend into the realm of metaphysics: it is not possible to deduce from her work any coherent conception of the nature of the universe. She is wholly and avowedly concerned with human relationships, and it is from their complexities that both horror and the supernatural emerge in her work. Both early and late in her career Jackson was affirming that, at least for her, the supernatural is a metaphor for human beings' relation to each other and to society. Consider a remark in 1948:

> I have had for many years a consuming interest in magic and the supernatural. I think this is because I find there so convenient a shorthand statement of the possibilities of human adjustment to what seems to be at best an inhuman world ... everything I write [involves] the sense which I feel, of a human and not very rational order struggling inadequately to keep in check forces of great destruction, which may be the devil and may be intellectual enlightenment [Oppenheimer 125].

In 1962 she wrote in a lecture,

> Just remember that primarily, in the story and out of it, you are living in
> a world of people. A story must have characters in it; work with concrete
> rather than abstract nouns, and always dress your ideas immediately. Sup-
> pose you want to write a story about what you might vaguely think of as
> "magic." You will be hopelessly lost, wandering around formlessly in
> notions of magic and incantations; you will never make any forward
> progress at all until you turn your ideas, "magic," into a person, someone
> who wants to do or make or change or act in some way. Once you have
> your first character you will of course need another to put into opposition,
> a person in some sense "anti-magic"; when both are working at their sepa-
> rate intentions, dragging in other characters as needed, you are well into
> your story. [C 153–54].

It is appropriate, then, that a proper starting point for the study of Jackson's fiction from a weird perspective may not be her actual weird work
but those tales for which she gained an entirely different following: her
family chronicles collected in *Life Among the Savages* and *Raising Demons*.

## Domestic Fiction

The strain of autobiography that is so dominant throughout Jackson's work can be traced to her very earliest writing. Her first profes-
sionally published story, "My Life with R.H. Macy" (L), appears to be
a lightly fictionalized account of a job she had as a saleswoman at Macy's
department store. The stories she wrote about her family date no earlier
than 1948, several years after she began her literary career; but they continued at a fairly constant pace to the end of her life. Jackson admitted
to her parents that many of these stories were potboilers:

> They are written simply for money and the reason they sound so bad is
> that those magazines won't buy good ones, but deliberately seek out bad
> stuff because they say their audiences want it. I simply figure that at a
> thousand bucks a story, I can't afford to try to change the state of popular
> fiction today.... I won't write love stories and junk about gay young mar-
> ried couples, and they won't take ordinary children stories, and this sort of
> thing is a compromise between their notions and mine ... and is unusual
> enough so that I am the only person I know of who is doing it [Oppen-
> heimer 145].

This dismissal of her domestic fiction may be somewhat disingenuous:
to be sure, they brought in needed income ($1,000 per story came in
very handy in supporting four children, as Hyman, a university professor, never made much money of his own from his literary criticism), but
the zest, vigor, and wit with which they are written testify to their importance to Jackson. Even if many of these tales are written with the sort of

coy, innocuous, and resolutely cheerful tone expected in contributions to women's magazines in the 1950s, they nevertheless contain certain disturbing undercurrents that may subvert their surface hilarity.

James Egan, in a thoughtful essay that attempts to reconcile Jackson's domestic fiction and her weird work, sees a twofold division of her work, as "either the expression of an idyllic domestic vision or the inversion of that vision into the fantastic and Gothic" (Egan 15). While assessment seems fundamentally correct, it may require a little more shading. Especially when we examine the chronology of Jackson's short fiction, we will find that the domestic stories themselves undergo a gradual modification—brought on, perhaps, by her marital problems or simply by the fact that her children grew up and no longer exhibited that affinity to "magic" (see Oppenheimer 209) which Jackson thought the very young reveal—so that the later domestic fiction now and then displays a brooding irony and even misanthropy that bring it surprisingly close in tone to her other work.

*Life Among the Savages* and *Raising Demons* were both stitched together from a number of stories originally published in magazines. Jackson's skill in this process of editing and rewriting the tales into a unified whole cannot be overemphasized, especially in the former work. It is true that both books remain somewhat episodic, but Jackson has weaved the tales together in such a way that they flow naturally one into the other; some of the stories have been so extensively revised as to be nearly unrecognizable from their originals. Although Jackson appears to pay lip service to the conventions of middle-class life in the 1950s, the vibrancy of her writing, the flawlessly exact capturing of her children's idiosyncrasies, and above all her complete lack of sentimentality make these stories pungent and vivid even today. Their sociological implications will not be examined here, but much interesting work might be done on gauging how exactly these tales do or do not reflect the stereotypes of their class and time.

What is interesting is the degree of their veracity; that is, the extent to which they are unvarnished or faithful transcriptions of actual events in Jackson's life and in the life of her family. It is, of course, naive to imagine that any autobiographical writing simply relates events as they occurred; and Jackson's remark that these stories allowed her to see her children "through a flattering veil of fiction" (Oppenheimer 119) may be all we need to infer that her domestic fiction, no less than her other work, is in some sense a creation of the imagination. Egan's reference to this work as "idyllic" is correct insofar as Jackson systematically attempts to present what may in reality have been highly traumatic events as the sources of harmless jests—her son being struck by a car, for instance, an event in which he suffered a concussion and some broken bones.

The importance of this domestic fiction—as regards her other work, at any rate—rests in its manipulation of very basic familial or personal scenarios that would be utilized in her weird work in perverted and twisted ways: things like riding a bus, employing a maid, taking children shopping, going on vacation, putting up guests, and, in general, adhering—or seeming to adhere—to the "proper conduct" expected of her as a middle-class housewife. It is interesting that her function as a writer is almost never mentioned in these works, or if it is, it is to poke fun at it as an anomaly for a wife with four children. "The Third Baby's the Easiest" captures the idea perfectly, as Jackson registers with a desk clerk at the hospital:

> "Age?" she asked. "Sex? Occupation?"
> "Writer," I said.
> "Housewife," she said.
> "Writer," I said.
> "I'll just put down housewife," she said [LS 426].

An earlier sketch, "Fame" (1948), amusingly tells of a gossip columnist who phones Jackson and is interested in everything about her except the fact that her first novel is soon to be issued by a major New York publisher.

It is important to note, however, that this body of domestic fiction really does undergo some significant changes over the years; it is in no sense a monolithic block of determined cheer. Some cracks begin to appear as early as "Lucky to Get Away" (1953), in which Jackson emphatically betrays a weariness with the unending round of housework required of her as a mother, especially as her husband contributes nothing to the household chores:

> I got to feeling that I could not bear the sight of the colored cereal bowls for one more morning, could not empty one more ashtray, could not brush one more head or bake one more potato or let out one more dog or pick up one more jacket. I snarled at the bright faces regarding me at the breakfast table and I was strongly tempted to kick the legs out from under the chair on which my older son was teetering backward [LS 583].

The humor in this passage is, surely, a little sardonic.

Three other pieces show that Jackson's relationship with her husband might not have been one of unending bliss. One of the many curious things about these stories is the infrequency with which her husband even appears: they are all about herself and her children, and when her husband does make an appearance it is almost always as a clumsy buffoon ("The Life Romantic," "The Box"). In "Queen of the May," in which Hyman has been invited to judge a beauty contest, the tone becomes a little more sinister: the jealousy Jackson felt toward her husband (a known philanderer) is much in evidence:

"Daddy is going to see a lot of girls," Sally told Barry. She turned to me. "Daddy likes to look at girls, doesn't he?"

There was a deep, enduring silence, until at last my husband's eye fell on Jannie. "And what did you learn in school today?" he asked with wild enthusiasm [*RD* 661–62].

Still odder and still more bitter is "One Last Chance," in which her husband announces somewhat sheepishly that an old flame of his will be dropping by (in fact she cancels her plans and never arrives), tactlessly and unintentionally suggesting that this woman is much prettier and a better cook than his wife. I have no idea whether this was an actual incident in Jackson's life; but it is interesting to note that her vindictiveness here becomes directed even at her children:

I gathered up ten clean sheets and six pillowcases and went first into Barry's room, where I removed six Teddy bears ... a green rabbit, two hidden lollipops and a wooden train from the bed and stripped and made it. Then I took up my armload of linen and went into Sally's room, sighed and removed from her bed a stack of coloring books, a disintegrated box of crayons, two dolls and an Oz book. I stacked the stuff on the floor where she would be sure to fall over it and quickly stripped and made the bed.

Most telling is the article "On Being a Faculty Wife," which scathingly lays bare Jackson's resentment at the ostracism and condescension she suffered from the academic community of Bennington College, where the young girls all revere her husband but take scant notice of her. Incredibly, the following bit of venom was omitted when the piece, first appearing in *Mademoiselle,* was reprinted in *Raising Demons*:

She [a student] turned to me and asked casually, "How long have you been married?"

"Sixteen years."

"Sixteen *years?* Gosh, he doesn't look that old. Where did you meet him?"

"In college."

"You went to college too? How many years?"

"Four."

"Gosh. How come you just ended up doing housework and stuff? Couldn't you get a job?"

"I have a job. I cook and sew and clean and shop and make beds and drive people places and B ..."

"No, I meant a *job.* Like ... you know, doing something. Because wouldn't it give you something to talk about at home? Because after all he's a very cultured man, you know."

Note here Jackson's curious response to the query "Couldn't you get a job?" Although by now an author of some stature, she does not reply, "I am a writer," but "I cook and sew and clean...." No doubt the point is to emphasize that housework is indeed a job of some consequence, but, as with nearly all the domestic stories, Jackson suppresses or conceals a major facet of her life—her writing.

Some of the later, uncollected domestic fiction comes off sounding a little tired: Jackson must have realized that her material was running dry, especially as her children were growing up into the less superficially "cute" stage of young adulthood. Indeed, a late piece, "Karen's Complaint" (1959), is quite poignant in depicting Jackson's sense of loneliness and aimlessness as her youngest child begins to go to school and she faces the prospect of an empty house for the first time in nearly two decades. However haphazardly her household appeared to be run, she took evident pride in providing a loving home for her husband and children. It is exactly this sense of togetherness and warmth that is obtrusively lacking in her other fiction. Where the reality of her own family lay, no one but she herself could have answered: perhaps all the carefree and well-adjusted children in her domestic fiction were themselves imaginary—her greatest fantasy.

## Domestic into Weird

The transformation of some incidents found in the domestic fiction into something very different and much more disturbing can occasionally occur with scarcely an alteration save that of context. I am reminded of Plautus' remark in the prologue to *Amphitryo:*

> Are you disappointed
> To find it's a *tragedy?* Well, I can easily change it.
> ...I can easily make it a comedy,
> And never alter a line [Plautus 230].

The textbook example of this is the story "Charles." Here the transition has occurred in the reverse direction, as the story was first published in a magazine and gathered in *The Lottery* before being reprinted in *Life Among the Savages.* In its earlier two contexts the story is subtly menacing and rather grim: her son Laurie (mentioned by name in all three versions), attending kindergarten, tells of a strange boy, Charles, who is by turns extremely unruly and even evil ("Today Charles hit the teacher.... He kicked the teacher's friend" [*L* 71–72]) and excessively well-behaved. Later, when Jackson meets Laurie's teacher, she finds out that there is no Charles in the class. I shall return to the implications of this story later, but here I wish to note what a remarkably different atmosphere this story has when it is buried in the genial confines of *Life Among the Savages:* there the whole tale comes off as simply another prank by her cute but headstrong son, whereas in the former instances one has the strong sensation that her son may well have serious problems of adjustment.

Another means for effecting the transition from domestic to weird, or vice versa, is omission. A very peculiar tale, "The House," was reprinted in *Life Among the Savages*—but not all of it. The latter portion was excised, no doubt because it is precisely here that the tale veers off into suggestions of the supernatural. At the outset it is difficult to ascertain whether, in its magazine appearance, this story is genuinely autobiographical, since Jackson never refers to her husband or children by name. In any case, the story concerns her family moving into an old, somewhat ramshackle, and faintly sinister house in New England (the precise location is never specified in the original appearance). The narrative of fixing up the house for habitation and moving in is told with mild humor—certainly not with the overt hilarity of pieces like "Look, Ma, We're Moving!" (1952) or "Worldly Goods"—but with an undercurrent of the strange. The house seems almost animate:

> There was a door to an attic that preferred to stay latched, and would latch itself no matter who was inside; another door hung by custom slightly ajar, although it would close good-humoredly for a time when some special reason required it. We had five attics, we discovered, built into one another; one of them kept bats, and we shut that one up; another one, light and cheerful in spite of a small window, liked to be a place of traffic and became a place to store things temporarily.
>
> An old clothesline hung across the basement, and after the line I put in the back yard had fallen down for the third time, I resigned myself and hung a new line in the basement, and clothes dried there quickly and freshly.... One bedroom chose the children. It was large and light and showed height marks on one wall, and seemed to mind not at all when crayon marks appeared on the wallpaper and paint got spilled on the floor.

The house controls its inhabitants, not the inhabitants the house. It is on its sufferance that they are there at all. All this may be only mildly disturbing; but then an old lady comes to pay a visit:

> "It's a lovely old house," I said.
>
> "Do you think so?" She turned quickly to look at me. "Do you really think it's a lovely old house?"
>
> "We're very happy here."
>
> "I'm glad." She folded her hands and smiled again. "It's always been such a good house," she said.
>
> "The old doctor always used to say it was a good house."
>
> "The old doctor?"
>
> "Doctor Ogilvie."
>
> "Doctor Ogilvie?"
>
> "I see they kept the pillars, after all," she said, nodding. "We always thought they gave the house character."

"There was a hornets' nest in one," I said weakly. Doctor Ogilvie had built the house in 1816!

The first passage I quoted above was included in *Life Among the Savages,* but again context robs it of any undertones of the weird; and that reprint breaks off the tale shortly thereafter. If anything, this story could be a model of Jackson's ability to transform the events of her own life into weird fiction.

Jackson's work returns time and again to certain fundamental domestic themes, sometimes in an autobiographical manner, sometimes in a mainstream manner, and sometimes in a weird manner. I again emphasize that these distinctions are arbitrary and nebulous; it takes only a small touch to push a story from one of these groups to another, and some stories remain resolutely averse to clear categorization.

Consider, for example, the number of stories by Jackson involving the hiring of a maid. There are at least four such tales, and they all play startling variations of tone and mood upon this one theme. Chronologically the first is "Tootie in Peonage" (1942; *C*), one of Jackson's earliest stories. It tells of a young woman, Tootie Maple, whom the narrator hires to help with the housework. It is an amusing tale of how Tootie has too many other pressing things to do—painting her toenails, finishing the latest issue of *True Confessions*—to get down to her actual duties; but the real object of satire is the housewife who hired her, who lacks the strength of will either to order Tootie to do her work or to fire her. The next maid story, "Family Magician" (1949), is a rather odd and benign weird tale about a maid, Mallie, who appears to fulfill her household responsibilities through magic. The tale is not of much note save in being Jackson's first avowedly supernatural work. Then comes "Monday Morning," incorporated in *Life Among the Savages* and similar in tone to "Tootie in Peonage." In this explicitly autobiographical story we read of the maid Phoebe, who shows up more than an hour late. It is all very amusing:

"Where's Phoebe?" she [Jannie] said.
"She didn't come today," Laurie said. "Mommy's *terrible* mad. Mommy's probably going to kill her."
"Laurie," I said, but they had already started, "Mommy's going to kill Phoebe, Mommy's going to kill Phoebe" [*LS* 438].

Then we come to the extremely nasty "Strangers in Town" (1959). The tale does not focus upon the maid, named Mallie (as in "Family Magician"), but it is clear that this maid too has supernatural powers: she gathers an acorn, a mushroom, and a scrap of grass and makes a stew out of them.

The simple act of riding a bus or train and traveling to a strange location—usually a big city—has generated a number of Jackson's most powerful stories, whether weird or otherwise. We see an innocuous version of this in chapter 4 of *Raising Demons,* in which Jackson relates taking her children to New York; other tales are much more ominous. "The Tooth" (1949; *L*) is a queer and meandering story of a young woman who travels to New York to see a dentist; I confess to being at a loss as to what point this story is trying to make, but the atmosphere of shimmering, dreamlike fantasy that was to become a Jackson trademark finds its first genuine embodiment here. "Pillar of Salt" (1948; *L*) involves a nearly identical scenario, although here a couple from New Hampshire comes to New York for a vacation. The emphasis is, inevitably, on the wife, whose appreciation of the city oscillates between amazement and condescension (looking at a set of miniature milk bottles being sold as toys, she notes archly, "We get our milk from cows" [*L* 177]). Gradually the giganticism, pace, and impersonality of the city overwhelm her, and her plight is keenly encapsulated by her complete inability to cross a busy street even when the light is with her:

> The minute the light changes, she told herself firmly; there's no sense. The light changed before she was ready and in the minute before she collected herself traffic turning the corner overwhelmed her and she shrank back against the curb. She looked longingly at the cigar store on the opposite corner, with her apartment house beyond; she wondered, How do people ever manage to get there, and knew that by wondering, by admitting a doubt, she was lost [*L* 184].

"Journey with a Lady" (1952) has an entirely different atmosphere. Here a young boy is making his first trip alone in a train to visit his grandfather. Unlike Jackson's female protagonists, the boy has no fears of the journey and is in fact irked by the excessive concern his mother exhibits prior to his voyage. Further adding to his irritation, once his journey begins, is the fact that a woman sits in the seat next to him, even though the car is largely empty. To both the conductor and a policeman who enters the car the woman boldly pretends that the boy is her son; he is too speechless with amazement to contradict her. She then admits to the boy that she stole some money and is on the run. At this point the boy's interest begins to grow, and they end up having a very entertaining time. She is picked up at the next station, rather to the boy's regret ("It's a shame the cops had to get her after all" [*J* 263]); but of course no one believes him when he tells his story. This story, first published in *Harper's,* was later reprinted in *Ellery Queen's Mystery Magazine* and can, I suppose, loosely be termed a crime story; but of course its emphasis, as always, is on character—and, perhaps, on both the dangers and the delights that may be encountered when one is away from one's familiar milieu. The "lady" of the title shares with a number of Jackson's female protagonists the ability to shed her old identity and adopt a new one at will, precisely because she is in a place where no one knows her; and in this instance she has also subsumed the boy into her new role.

"The Bus" (1965; *C*) finally takes this topos into the realm of the supernatural. An old woman is dropped off at the wrong stop late at night, eventually catches a ride on a truck to some dismal-looking roadhouse, and, as the atmosphere becomes at once more menacing and more unreal, the old woman imagines herself a child in her room, looks in a closet, and finds her old doll speaking to her: "Go away, old lady, go away, old lady, go away" (*C* 200). At this point the old woman wakes up—it was all a dream and she is still on the bus! Not content with this trite device, Jackson gives it a further predictable twist by having the old woman get off at the same wrong stop as before.

Several other stories speak of the peculiar vulnerability of people on vacation, away from their friends and their familiar environment. "The Summer People" (1949; *C*) is a mordant tale about an elderly couple who decide to stay on in their summer cottage past Labor Day, something they have never done before. The dour countryfolk of the region appear to resent this decision "Nobody ever stayed at the lake past Labor Day before" (*C* 73)—and insidiously conspire against them: the couple cannot get kerosene or ice, the mail suddenly stops, the groceries can't be delivered, and so on. This masterful story is worth considering in several other respects, but the gradual isolation of the couple, as one by one the locals turn against them through sheer inaction, is harrowing. There is, of course, nothing supernatural about this tale, but a work like this makes the strongest possible case for the inclusion of the nonsupernatural horror story as a genuine subset of the weird tale.

"The Lovely House" (1952; retitled "A Visit" in C) introduces the supernatural in the subtlest way. A college girl, Margaret, goes with her friend Carla Rhodes to the latter's palatial home, whose location is never specified. Initially it all seems idyllic:

> Carla stopped before the doorway and stood for a minute, looking first behind her, at the vast reaching gardens and the green lawn going down to the river, and the soft hills beyond, and then at the perfect grace of the house, showing so clearly the long-boned structure within, the curving staircases and the arched doorways and the tall thin lines of steadying beams, all of it resting back against the hills, and up, past rows of windows and the flying lines of the roof, on, to the tower [*C* 98].

The tale develops a powerful atmosphere of weirdness through the deliberately artificial dialogue. It is as if all the characters know they are in a work of fiction. Carla's brother Paul arrives; Margaret spends much time with him. She goes up to the tower and has an enigmatic talk with Carla's grandmother. Throughout the story Mrs. Rhodes is weaving a tapestry of the house. This is the end of the tale:

"You will not leave us before my brother comes again?" Carla asked Margaret. "I have only to put the figures into the foreground," Mrs. Rhodes said, hesitating on her way to the drawing room. "I shall have you exactly if you sit on the lawn near the river."

"We shall be models of stillness," said Carla, laughing. "Margaret, will you come and sit beside me on the lawn?"[*C* 120].

What does this mean? What is the significance of Paul's remark that "'without this house I could not exist'" (*C* 119)? Is this not a pun, meaning that neither he nor the entire family can live *without* (i.e. outside of) the house? And isn't Margaret now being woven into the fabric of the house by way of the tapestry? This exquisite and haunting tale—a fantastically transmogrified version of a visit Dylan Thomas paid to Jackson's home in Westport, Connecticut (Oppenheimer 151–52)—exemplifies the "quiet weird tale" at its pinnacle. And, of course, it embodies a theme that we can already see is a dominant one in Jackson's work and perhaps also her life: the manner in which a house can subsume its occupants.

Some of Jackson's strangest stories—which are perhaps only on the borderland of the weird—seem like satires of middle-class tact and etiquette. A few of the domestic stories may be of some relevance here, as Jackson feels (or claims to feel) embarrassment at the unruly antics of her children in public. In "Shopping Trip" she tries to control her children as they act up in a department store: "I was beginning to be aware of a familiar and dreadful feeling: that of being stared at by hordes of people—salesladies, floorwalkers, mothers, immaculate children, and perhaps truant officers. 'Come on,' I said nervously, and added just in time, 'my dears'" (*LS* 458–59). Some of her nondomestic stories read like exaggerated versions of things of this sort. In "Like Mother Used to Make" (1949; *L*)—founded, apparently, on a genuine incident experienced by one of her friends (Oppenheimer 102)—a man has invited a woman in a neighboring apartment to a dinner he has taken great pains to make. A friend of the woman arrives, thinking it is her apartment, and this unwanted guest makes himself right at home; in fact, so spineless and so afraid of causing (and suffering) embarrassment is the actual owner of the apartment that he simply leaves, pretending that *he* is the guest. A single paragraph etches his character: "David stood up. For a minute he thought he was going to say something that might start, 'Mr. Harris, I'll thank you to...' but what he actually said, finally, with both Marcia and Mr. Harris looking at him, was, 'Guess I better be getting along, Marcia'" (*L* 34). I suppose Jackson can get away with being a misogynist: Marcia has made no effort to disabuse Mr. Harris of the true state of affairs. A very similar story is "Trial by Combat" (1944; *L*). A woman, Emily, finds small items missing from her apartment and discovers that an old woman living in the downstairs apartment, Mrs. Allen, is the culprit. But Mrs. Allen is so seemingly "nice" and harmless that Emily cannot confront her on the matter. Jackson again encapsulates an entire life in a paragraph: "Emily found that she was staring at the picture of Mrs. Allen's husband; such a thoughtful-looking man, she was thinking, they must have had such a pleasant life together, and now she has a room like mine, with only two handkerchiefs of her own in the drawer" (*L* 39).

"The Summer People" might also be worth considering from this perspective, as the elderly couple cannot slough off their exterior of "good behavior" and come to terms with the brutal treatment they are receiving at the hands of the countryfolk. The conclusion finds the two of them cowering in the dark, waiting for the dawn—or for the next piece of viciousness from their once-friendly neighbors.

## Conclusion

What are we to make of Shirley Jackson? Is she a weird writer even in part? That second question is difficult to answer in any definitive way, save to note the obvious supernaturalism in a fairly representative core of her work. If *The Haunting of Hill House* is one of the greatest haunted house novels ever written, if "The Lottery" is among the cruelest non-supernatural horror stories ever written, what do we do with something so nebulous as *The Sundial* or "The Lovely House?" We can, however, see the tightly knit unity of Jackson's work, its constant reworking of the interlocking themes of domesticity and loneliness, love and hate, madness and sanity, society and the individual; and we can see how each of these threads is pursued successively in tales that, from the point of view of genre, might be termed supernatural, nonsupernatural, mainstream, or autobiographical. It is true that Jackson, even in her avowedly supernatural work, presents no coherent metaphysics: her supernatural manifestations fail to suggest any putative reordering of the cosmos. But if she lacks the cosmic perspective of a Lovecraft, a Blackwood, or a Dunsany (or, indeed, of Ramsey Campbell or T.E.D. Klein), if her focus is solely on human characters and human relationships, with even the supernatural phenomena subservient to or symbols for these relationships, then she at least distinguishes herself by the intensity, accuracy, and subtlety of her portrayal of human concerns; as with Bierce, her pitiless and sardonic exposing of human weakness makes her a horrific satirist who does not require the supernatural to arouse fear and horror. Her icy prose, clinical detachment, and utterly refreshing glee at the exhibition of human greed, misery, and evil ought to give her a high rank in general literature; that she chose to devote even a part of her talents to the weird is something for which we ought all to be grateful.

# Works Cited

## Works by Shirley Jackson

*The Bird's Nest.* New York: Farrar, Straus, 1954. Rpt. in *The Magic of Shirley Jackson.* New York: Farrar, Straus and Giroux, 1966, 147–380. [Cited in the text as *B.*]

"The Bus." *Saturday Evening Post* 237, no. 22 (27 March 1965): 62–67. In *C.*

"Charles." *Mademoiselle* 27, no. 3 (July 1948): 87, 114. In *L.* and in *LS.*

*Come Along with Me.* Ed. Stanley Edgar Hyman. New York: Viking, 1968. Rpt. New York: Popular Library, n.d. [Cited in the text as *C.*]

"Fame." *The Writer* 61, no. 8 (August 1948): 265–66.

"Family Magician." *Woman's Home Companion,* September 1949, 23, 92–93, 98, 100. In *J.*

*The Haunting of Hill House.* New York: Viking, 1959. Rpt. New York: Popular Library, 1977. [Cited in the text as *HH.*]

"The House." *Woman's Day* 15, no. 8 (May 1952): 62–63, 115–16, 118–19. In *LS* (in part).

"Janice." *The Threshold* 1, no. 1 (February 1938): 15. In *C.*

"Journey with a Lady." *Harper's* 205, no. 1 (July 1952): 76–81. Rpt. *Ellery Queen's Mystery Magazine* 31, no. 6 (June 1958) (as "This Is the Life"). In *J.*

*Just an Ordinary Day.* Edited by Laurence Jackson Hyman and Sarah Hyman Stewart. New York: Bantam, 1997. [Cited in the text as *J.*]

"Karen's Complaint." *Good Housekeeping* 149, no. 5 (November 1959): 38, 40, 42, 46.

*Life Among the Savages.* New York: Farrar, Straus, 1953. Rpt. in *The Magic of Shirley Jackson.* New York: Farrar, Straus and Giroux, 1966, 383–530. [Cited in the text as *LS.*]

"Like Mother Used to Make." In *L.*

"Look, Ma, We're Moving." *Good Housekeeping* 134, no. 2 (February 1952): 49, 173–75.

"The Lottery." *New Yorker* 24, no. 18 (26 June 1948): 25–28. In *L.*

*The Lottery.* New York: Farrar, Straus, 1949. Rpt. New York: Popular Library, n.d. [Cited in the text as *L.*]

"The Lovely House." In *New World Writing: Second Mentor Selection.* (New York: New American Library of World Literature, 1952, 130–50. In *C* (as "A Visit").

"Lucky to Get Away." *Woman's Day* 16, no. 11 (August 1953): 26, 117–19. In *RD.*

"Monday Morning." *Woman's Home Companion,* November 1951, 21, 57, 60. In *LS.*

"My Life with R. H. Macy." *New Republic* 105, no. 25 (22 December 1941): 862. In *L.*

"On Being a Faculty Wife." *Mademoiselle* 44, no. 2 (December 1956): 116–17, 135–36. In *RD* (in part).

"Pillar of Salt." *Mademoiselle* 27, no. 6 (October 1948): 152–53, 242–50. In *L.*

"Queen of the May." *McCall's* 82, no. 7 (April 1955): 47, 73, 75, 78. In *RD.*

*Raising Demons.* New York: Farrar, Straus, 1957. Rpt. in *The Magic of Shirley Jackson.* New York: Farrar, Straus and Giroux, 1966, 531–753. [Cited in the text as *RD.*]

*The Road Through the Wall.* New York: Farrar, Straus, 1948.

"Shopping Trip." *Woman's Home Companion,* June 1953, 40, 85–87. In *LS.*

"Strangers in Town." *Saturday Evening Post* 231, no. 48 (30 May 1959): 18, 76–77, 79. In *J* (as "The Very Strange House Next Door."

"The Summer People." *Charm* 73, no. 1 (September 1950): 108–9, 193–97. In *C.*

*The Sundial.* New York: Farrar, Straus, 1958. Rpt. New York: Ace, n.d. [Cited in the text as *S.*]

"The Third Baby's the Easiest." *Harper's* 198, no. 5 (May 1949): 58–63. In *LS*.
"The Tooth." *Hudson Review* 1, no. 4 (winter 1949): 503–21. In *L*.
"Tootie in Peonage." 1942. In *C*.
"Tial by Combat." *New Yorker* 20, no. 44 (16 December 1944): 72, 74–76. In *L*.
*We Have Always Lived in the Castle*. New York: Viking, 1962.

## Other Works

Egan, James. "Sanctuary: Shirley Jackson's Domestic and Fantastic Parables." *Studies in Weird Fiction* no. 6 (fall 1989): 15–24.
Oppenheimer, Judy. *Private Demons: The Life of Shirley Jackson*. New York: Putnam's, 1988.
Plautus. *Amphitryo*. In *The Rope and Other Plays*. Trans. E.F. Watling. Harmondsworth: Penguin, 1964.

# 10

# The Establishment and Preservation of Female Power in Shirley Jackson's *We Have Always Lived in the Castle*

## Lynette Carpenter

When Mary Katherine Blackwood, at the age of 12, poisoned her family by putting arsenic in the sugar, she was careful not to endanger her sister Constance, whom she calls "the most precious person in my world, always."[1] Now, six years later, with everyone dead but the invalid and feeble-minded Uncle Julian, Constance has become head of the Blackwood family, which consists of Constance, Mary Katherine (affectionately called Merricat by her sister), Uncle Julian, and Jonas the cat. When the events at the beginning of Mary Katherine's narrative take place, they live in seclusion in the Blackwood house, surrounded by extensive Blackwood property, barricaded against the intrusion of the outside world. They might have continued to live contentedly enough, had their neighbors allowed it. But female self-sufficiency, Jackson suggests, specifically women's forceful establishment of power over their own lives, threatens a society in which men hold primary power and leads inevitably to confrontation.

---

*This essay was originally published in* Frontiers *vol. III, no. 1 (1984): 32–39. Reproduced here with the permission of* Frontiers *and the University of Nebraska Press.*

Jackson's portrayal of the institution of patriarchy and its terrifying power over women predates by more than five years Kate Millett's introduction of the terminology of contemporary feminist criticism in *Sexual Politics*. Her rendering of a modern confrontation between witches and witch hunters anticipates by more than ten years the writings of Andrea Dworkin and Mary Daly on the gynocide of the witch hunt as one patriarchal response to female rebellion.[2] Jackson's last completed novel and a bestseller, *We Have Always Lived in the Castle* is her most radical statement on the causes and consequences of female victimization and alienation, a theme that runs throughout her work. The novel may represent a personal culmination for Jackson, who suffered a nervous breakdown shortly after its publication in 1962; her journal from that period records longings for "freedom and security," "self-control," and "refuge" that echo the novel's central concern with the self-determination of women in a safe environment.[3]

When the book opens, masculine authority has already suffered a decisive defeat at the hands of Mary Katherine Blackwood, its narrator (although the identity of the poisoner is not revealed or confirmed until the climactic scene much later): the poisoning has resulted in a transfer of power from Blackwood men to Blackwood women. The motive for the poisoning is not clear at first, but we are given clues in the characterizations of the victims throughout the narrative. Of the men, the most clearly drawn figure is John Blackwood, father of Merricat and Constance and head of the Blackwood family. A redoubtable patriarch, he was a man of property who, as Uncle Julian relates, "took pride in his table, his family, his position in the world" (47). He gave sparingly and grudgingly of his wealth and viewed all such transactions as financial investments to be taken down in his notebook, where, according to Merricat, "he used to record the names of people who owed him money, and people who ought, he thought, to do favors for him" (77). When he quarreled with his wife the night before their deaths, Uncle Julian assumed the quarrel was about money (32). In short, John Blackwood's power in his family and his community derived not only from his gender but also from his material wealth. Six years after his death, Merricat says of the villagers, "I knew they talked about the money hidden in our house, as though it were great heaps of golden coins" (9).

A financial failure, John's brother Julian was dependent on his brother's charity and subject to his authority. In a society that values masculine authority and the accumulation of private wealth and defines that accumulation as a male responsibility and prerogative, Uncle Julian was twice victimized by expectations he could not fulfill. He is perhaps the Blackwood man who most deserved to survive the assault, yet his continuing denial of Merricat's existence serves as a reminder of her former status in the Blackwood family and of her especial invisibility to the Blackwood men. Both legally and symbolically he must be rendered powerless (in/valid) in order to ensure the empowerment of Constance and Merricat. His invalid state no doubt confirms the general belief that financial failure for men leads to powerlessness, dependency, emasculation. The heir to the Blackwood money and property was ten-year-old Thomas, Constance and Merricat's younger brother, who, according to Uncle Julian, "possessed many of his father's more forceful traits of character" (48). It was no accident that Thomas used the most sugar.

Of Julian's wife very little is said; she may or may not have been an undeserving but unavoidable victim. Constance and Merricat's mother, on the other hand, emerges as the primary keeper of the Blackwood possessions, a woman obsessively tidy and aloof. Her snobbery, inherited by her daughters, later ensures their seclusion: "Our mother disliked the sight of anyone who wanted to walking past our front door, and when our father brought her to live in the Blackwood house, one of the first things he had to do was close off the path and fence in the entire Blackwood property" (26). Like Blackwood wives before her, she added her share of material goods to the Blackwood family wealth. But in one important respect she broke with the tradition of the Blackwood women: she was a bad cook. Although she made her obligatory contribution to the cellar legacy of the Blackwood women—her six jars of apple jelly crowded by "jars of jam made by great-grandmothers, ... and pickles made by great-aunts and vegetables put up by our grandmother" (60)— she left the cooking and gardening to Constance. To the visiting Mrs. Wright's question about Mrs. Blackwood's cooking, Uncle Julian replies with a shudder, "I personally preferred to chance the arsenic" (50). Mrs. Blackwood's indifference to the kitchen and garden not only sets her apart from her daughters but violates the creative tradition of the Blackwood women, whose accumulated preserves Merricat calls "a poem" (54).

Functioning as the family preservers, the Blackwood women, cleaners and dusters of Blackwood property, lavished attention on a different kind of preserves, burying the fruits of their creative labor beneath the accumulated wealth of their dowries and other Blackwood acquisitions. What property they brought to the Blackwood house became Blackwood property, by law or tradition passed from father to son rather than from mother to daughter, as Merricat suggests by her comment on the Rochester house: "Our mother had been born there and by rights it should have belonged to Constance" (4).

While her daughters appear to value objects as artifacts from the domestic history of the Blackwood women (a respect they do not afford masculine possessions), Mrs. Blackwood deviated from her female predecessors and from her daughters in valuing the objects over the food-stuffs, the teacups over the tea itself. This attitude aligns her with the Blackwood men, whose highest regard is reserved for money, a thing of no intrinsic value. Obsessed with the preservation of order in her drawing room, she had not allowed her daughters to enjoy its beauty (33–34), making it a monument to Blackwood physical wealth and spiritual desiccation.

The Blackwood family exploited its women if they were docile and dismissed them if they were not. Mary Katherine, the middle child who was neither a useful daughter nor a male heir, had no appropriate function in the family and was frequently dismissed from its presence for her rebellion against its laws. On the day of the poisoning she had been sent to her room without supper, as Constance reports with a smile: "Merricat was always in disgrace. I used to go up the back stairs with a tray of dinner for her after my father had left the dining room. She was a wicked, disobedient child" (48–49). Constance's reminiscence suggests whom Merricat disobeyed, whose will she opposed. Six years after the fall of the Blackwood patriarch, she is still being dismissed by the surviving male member of her family, Uncle Julian, who insists that she is dead.

Merricat's raging rebellion, culminating in her overthrow of the Blackwood patriarchy, established Constance as the head of the Blackwood family and the sisters' mutual affection as its binding force. At first glance, theirs may appear to be a relationship between opposites—Constance, the domestic, traditional, even unimaginative one, and Merricat, the unrestrained, creative, imaginative one.[4] Yet Merricat's self-imposed rules and her insistence on routine reveal an obsession with order, just as Constance's skill at growing and preparing food reveals her creativity. Although Merricat's rules do not allow her to prepare food, she helps Constance in the kitchen and garden. Merricat's knowledge of poisonous plants, upon which she bases much of her claim to magical power, comes from Constance.

This shared knowledge, passed from sister to sister, is only one manifestation of a deeper bond between the two women, a bond that has ultimately united them against the Blackwood patriarchal power structure. Constance herself had been a victim of that structure; as elder daughter, she was the unpaid, unrecognized family servant. The smile with which she reports her sister's disobedience suggests her sympathy. In revealing deadly secrets to Merricat, Constance empowered her sister to use them and therefore shares responsibility for the deaths that followed. Yet her complicity was more direct, according to the account Uncle Julian gives Mrs. Wright: "It was Constance who saw them dying around her like flies—I do beg your pardon—and never called a doctor until it was too late. She washed the sugar bowl" (52–53). Constance herself purchased the arsenic—"to kill rats," she explains, with another smile for Merricat (52). The general belief that Constance was the poisoner both underscores Merricat's invisibility to a society that has no place for her and points to Constance's actual guilt. She not only protected her sister by destroying evidence; she aided her by waiting to call the doctor. Uncle Julian adds, "She told the police those people deserved to die" (53), a comment suggesting that, whatever her ambivalence later, the docile, constant Constance shared her sister's rage and outrage.

Having vanquished one patriarchy, the women are confronted with another in the form of a village controlled by men, by other fathers. Although Constance has been acquitted of murder, the two women must remain vigilant against the encroachment of hostile villagers. Merricat explains, "The people of the village have always hated us" (6), but the sisters are more vulnerable now that they no longer have the protection of the Blackwood men; the town's hostility has become overt, expressed, active. The original source of that hostility was the Blackwood economic and social self-sufficiency, a self-sufficiency underscored by the Blackwood sisters' survival. Villager Jim Donell complains of "the way they live up in their fine old private estate, with their fences and their private path and their stylish way of living" (19). That this conflict can now be viewed in terms of sexual politics is suggested by Merricat's description of the village power structure: "In this village the men stayed young and did the gossiping and the women aged with grey evil weariness and stood silently waiting for the men to get up and come home" (4). In such a society, the Blackwood wealth might be an affront, but Blackwood wealth in the hands of women is a travesty. Initially, the village women in general are silent, weary noncombatants in the struggle between the male villagers and the Blackwood sisters. When Merricat imagines the village children learning the rhyme with which they taunt her, she thinks not of their mothers but of their fathers, "Jim Donell and Dunham and dirty Harris leading regular drills of their children" (22).

The parallel between a witch hunt and the attempt to purge the village of the Blackwood sisters is suggested first by Merricat's own experiments with magic. When she tells us in the third sentence of her narrative, "I have often thought that with any luck at all I could have been born a werewolf" (1), she expresses a longing for power that is one of her chief characteristics. Her magic words and charms constitute attempts to gain power over a world in which, first as the second girl child in a patriarchal family and then as a grown woman in a patriarchal society, she is essentially powerless. Elizabeth Janeway has written, "The witch role permits the woman to imagine that she can exercise some sort of power, even if it is evil power."[5] With any luck at all, Merricat could have been a "real" witch, but her magic is largely ineffectual. What power she has derives from the knowledge she has gained from Constance about plants and their properties. This knowledge links Constance with the countless women healers of the past who were persecuted and executed as witches.

The familiarity of those women with the curative properties of plants presupposes other deadlier knowledge. In her 1921 classic, *The Witch-Cult in Western Europe,* Margaret Alice Murray asserts, "The society of witches had a very creditable knowledge of the art of poisoning."[6] It is also interesting to note that at least one writer, William Duffy, has argued that the Church persecuted witches as healers for speaking out against sugar at a time when the Church had an economic interest in the prosperity of the new sugar industry—a further link to Constance, on whose habit of refusing sugar Merricat depends to save her life at the time of the poisoning.[7]

Jackson, whose works include *The Witchcraft of Salem Village* (1956), owned an extensive collection on witchcraft and demonology. She would certainly have known the major sources, including the now infamous *Malleus Maleficarum* (1486), or Hammer of Witches, used for over 200 years as a guide to the identification and punishment of witches.[8] Its authors' fear of female power is particularly evident in their attention to the threat of actual or perceived castration. These anxieties about male sexual impotence suggest anxieties about male political impotence as well. The Church fathers were threatened by female indomitability and by the followers attracted by women who lived outside the regime of the Church and the familial social unit it controlled.

Thus, significantly, Merricat and Constance are seen as witches because they choose to live outside the boundaries of patriarchal society, because they choose to live with women rather than with men, and because they have challenged masculine power directly by the poisoning. The invalid Uncle Julian survives as a reminder to the patriarchal village of the two women's choice and of their ability to act on that choice. Their only other male companion, the black cat Jonas, completes the popular image of two witch sisters with their feline consort, the devil in disguise.

If the primary source of the village's hostility is not simply Blackwood self-sufficiency but female self-sufficiency, then the most logical attack would be an undermining of the relationship between the two women. In fact, the beginning of the final assault on the Blackwood women is marked by a visit from Helen Clarke, who, as self-proclaimed friend of Constance, bears a revealing message to her: "It's spring, you're young, you're lovely, you have a right to be happy. Come back into the world" (38). Several unspoken premises lie behind this piece of advice, not the least ludicrous of which is the assumption that the world, or in this case the village, could make Constance happy. Of course, Helen Clarke also assumes that Constance is not happy living with her sister, indeed could not be happy living with a woman when she is young and lovely enough to attract a man. Ultimately, she tempts Constance with the illusion of romantic happiness upon which the continuation of masculine dominance so heavily depends, and Constance is tempted because she forgets or discounts her own past experience. Her choice and Merricat's of celibacy or homosexuality (the latter an option made less explicit here than in other Jackson novels), their replacement of heterosexual romance with sisterhood as their central emotional bond, makes them less vulnerable to sexual coercion by men and keeps their fortunes out of men's hands. Constance's marriage would not only disrupt the relationship between the sisters but would also bring them and their wealth back into the realm of masculine control and restore patrilineal inheritance. That a woman initiates the assault suggests the degree to which village women have come to collude with men in the perpetuation of women's oppression.

Helen Clarke's visit prepares the way for the arrival of Cousin Charles Blackwood, Merricat's archrival, who aspires to be the new Blackwood patriarch, a pretender both to family position and to the family fortune. Appropriately, as Constance tells Merricat, "he looks like Father" (82); his face exposes him to Merricat as "one of the bad ones" (79). Charles is the son of Arthur, the only Blackwood to be more acquisitive and less generous than Constance and Merricat's father. And he immediately begins to acquire things: Father's room, Father's place at the table, Father's gold watch chain, Father's clothes. If, as Merricat tells Constance, "Charles is a ghost" (99), she recognizes immediately whose ghost he is. His presence causes a series of confrontations between the values of the Blackwood women and the values of the Blackwood men. He cannot understand, for example, Constance and Merricat's disregard for gold and money, the legacy of the Blackwood men; what Constance and Merricat value most is the legacy of the Blackwood women—Dresden figurines, dishes brought to the house by generations of Blackwood brides, preserves made lovingly by generations of Blackwood wives. Charles reintroduces the notions of punishment and competition into a house where they have not been invoked for years. He accords Uncle Julian no respect. Having dismissed Uncle Julian as inconsequential, he attempts to enlist the sympathies of the only other male member of the household, Jonas.

The village men, who have always hated Blackwoods, form an alliance with Charles because he embodies their means of destroying the Blackwood women. Following him to the village one day, Merricat watches him sit down on the benches with the men who are her worst tormentors: "If I went into the village shopping again Charles would be one of the men who watched me going past" (118). The men's acceptance of Charles is a recognition that his family name is not as important as his gender. Their friendship signals approval of his plan to restore Blackwood wealth to masculine control.

To Merricat's horror, Charles's campaign begins to succeed, and the relationship between the two sisters changes:

> She [Constance] was increasingly cross with me when I wanted Charles to leave; always before Constance had listened and smiled and only been angry when Jonas and I had been wicked but now she frowned at me often, as though I somehow looked different to her [114].

To masculine eyes, Merricat does look different—not imaginative, independent, and interesting, but eccentric, rebellious, and dangerous. Under Charles's influence, Constance experiences shifts in vision and begins to talk and act strangely:

> "We should have been living like other people. You should...." She stopped and waved her hands helplessly. "You should have boy friends," she said finally, and then began to laugh because she sounded funny even to herself [118–19].

Besieged by Charles, Constance takes on maternal guilt for depriving her sister of a "normal" life, while recognizing that her sister would find, indeed has found, a "normal" life intolerable. For her part, Merricat clearly perceives the source of the threat to their relationship and does not allow herself to be used against her sister, saying, "Constance needed guarding more than ever before and if I became angry and looked aside she might very well be lost" (115).

Merricat's stubborn resistance to Charles leads to a cataclysmic confrontation between the forces of the male power structure and the forces of female self-sufficiency. The scene is richly symbolic. Still seething because of Charles's attempt to assert a fatherly authority over her, Merricat discovers a family heirloom, a saucer from her great-grandmother's dowry, being used as an ashtray in her father's bedroom, now Charles's room. She says, "I brushed the saucer and the pipe off the table into the wastebasket and they fell softly onto the newspapers he had brought into the house" (145). Her act literally sparks a conflagration as two symbols of masculinity, the pipe and the newspaper, begin to burn.

That Merricat herself starts the fire complicates the symbolic reading of this scene as a witch burning. It is the only point in Jackson's novel when the reader is asked to believe that Merricat's perceptions are limited, inadequate. She does not seem to be aware of what she has done. From her perspective, she has disposed of Charles's pipe and newspapers, which in turn have started a fire; they are to blame, not she. The sentence following her description of her actions reads, "I was wondering about my eyes; one of my eyes—the left—saw everything golden and yellow and orange, and the other saw shades of blue and grey and green" (145). Although the reader might suspect that Merricat is intelligent enough to know a fire when she sees one, she does not clarify the passage by identifying what she saw. When Charles and Constance later smell smoke and Constance remembers Charles's pipe, Merricat responds, "Would it start a fire?" (147), suggesting that she is not aware of the situation, unless her true motive is to disrupt Charles's relationship with Constance by blaming him. Yet, although she might wish to destroy Charles's (and her father's) room, she could hardly wish to destroy the house that she and Constance love so dearly, again unless she believes the sacrifice necessary to repudiate the material heritage of the Blackwood men and to exorcise her father's ghost.

The fire brings the villagers and the fire fighters; Jim Donell, the village spokesman and Merricat's greatest enemy next to Charles, is their chief. The firemen put out the fire, despite one woman's exhortations to "let it burn" (152). His duty done, however, Jim Donell carefully removes his fire hat and leads an assault on the house:

> While everyone watched, he took up a rock. In complete silence he turned slowly and then raised his arm and smashed the rock through one of the great tall windows of our mother's drawing room. A wall of laughter rose and grew behind him and then, first the boys on the steps and then the other men and at last the children, they moved like a wave at our house [153–54].

The mob stones the house as an extension of the two women who live in it and strongly identify with it. The scene recalls other stonings, including the ancient practice of stoning witches and the fictional stoning in Jackson's own fable about a sacrifice ritual, "The Lottery." The villagers attempt to destroy the women by destroying the house, focusing their energies on the drawing room and the kitchen, special domains of the Blackwood women; they leave Charles to struggle with the family safe, protector of the monetary legacy of the Blackwood men. Their rage is directed at those objects most precious to Constance and Merricat, the dishes and silverware contributed by Blackwood grandmothers, great-grandmothers, aunts, and great-aunts, and at the foodstuffs that Constance holds sacred. Adding insult to injury, they leave the house a mess when it has only just been tidied, a severe blow to Constance. They verbally abuse and physically threaten the two sisters, who are saved, ironically, by Uncle Julian's death. The crowd leaves not out of respect for the sisters but out of respect for Uncle Julian, whom they perceive to have been the sisters' last surviving victim. Defeated, Charles leaves as well.

The confrontation of the fire scene is necessary to prove to Constance what Merricat has always believed—that heterosexual romance is
a dangerous illusion, that patriarchy is an inherently destructive institution, and that no compromise is possible. Just as Constance has always
felt a responsibility to take care of Merricat, to be a kind of mother to
her, so Merricat has always felt a responsibility to protect Constance
from an outside world her sister has not clearly understood, a world of
hatred and violence. To Merricat, the overthrow of the Blackwood patriarchy six years before had been an act not merely of vengeance but of
self-preservation; banished from the family's presence one too many
times, she was in very real danger of disappearing altogether. Now, with
renewed conviction, Constance and Merricat turn their backs on the outside world, barricading themselves inside the ruined house. There are
no more compromises: they do not answer the voices that call to them;
they do not allow Helen Clarke in for tea. Dishes and silverware have
been broken or bent in the onslaught, sugar has been spilt, but the preserves of the Blackwood women stand undisturbed in the cellar, emblems
of the sisters' survival. Ironically, they also retain possession of the safe,
a bitter reminder to Charles and the villagers that their survival constitutes a victory not only in their own terms but also in those of the village men.

When the offerings of food begin to arrive from the villagers, the
accompanying notes express regret and shame for individual acts of
destruction, but the scene evokes other scenes of ritualistic food offerings
to ancient deities. Fear seems a more likely motive than genuine regret,
especially as tales about the house and its two invisible occupants spread
throughout the village. Women speak in hushed voices on the front lawn
and frighten their children with stories of the sisters' penchant for eating little girls and boys. The sisters' perceived power has grown since
the fire: after all, they are two witches who have survived a burning and
a stoning.

At the same time, the food offerings establish a new relationship
between the Blackwood women and the women of the village, perhaps
recalling that deities can be simultaneously loved and feared. In this
matter, the village women seem able to assert themselves, as the sisters
imagine: "We thought that the men came home from work and the
women had the baskets ready for them to carry over" (204). Constance
handles the food lovingly and speculates on the circumstances of its
preparation:

> Everything's still warm.... She must have baked them right after dinner
> so he could bring them right over. I wonder if she made two pies, one for
> the house. She wrapped everything while it was still warm and told him to
> bring it over [203].

The sisters come to know the village women by their distinctive culinary traits, and the food becomes a means of communication, its careful preparation a sign that the women feel more than fear toward the rebellious Blackwood sisters.

Readers and critics have struggled to explain the effect that *We Have Always Lived in the Castle* has on them. The *Time* reviewer wrote, "The book manages the ironic miracle of convincing the reader that a house inhabited by a lunatic, a poisoner, and a pyromaniac is a world more rich in sympathy, love, and subtlety than the real world outside."[9] Many readers express discomfort at being made to identify with a madwoman, but is Merricat mad? If paranoia depends upon delusion, Merricat is not paranoid because the hostility she perceives in the villagers is real. Like most of Jackson's protagonists, she seems young for her age, but immaturity is not madness.

Perhaps the aspect of Merricat's character that is most difficult to accept, however, is the violence. Early in the book, the violence of Merricat's fantasies is horrifying; while confronting hostile villagers in the grocery store, she says, "I would have liked to come into the grocery some morning and see them all, even the Elberts and the children, lying there crying with the pain and dying" (12). The villagers' hostility, although misdirected if they believe the poisoner to be Constance and not Merricat, might at first seem a justifiable response to a daughter's particularly cruel murder of four members of her family. Readers' sympathy with Merricat remains uneasy, even though they may feel, as Stuart Woodruff has suggested, that "parricide on such a scale is certainly regrettable, but the real horror in Miss Jackson's novel originates elsewhere."[10] Yet the villagers' own violence invalidates once and for all their moral judgment of the sisters and indicates that the poisoning is only one violent action in a world where violence threatens to erupt at any moment, a world familiar to readers of Jackson's fiction. Thus Merricat's belief that she is literally embattled is confirmed, and her rage against the villagers is justified. Within the context of feminist psychology, rage is the most appropriate response to oppression. In Jackson's time as now, it was also the most dangerous, the most likely to be labeled madness and treated by institutionalization. Merricat's rage against her family and the murders that resulted from it are less justifiable on the basis of the scant information her narrative provides; apart from sketchy descriptions of the victims and their treatment of Merricat, the reader has only Constance's word that "those people deserved to die" [53]. Because the danger to Merricat in this case seems to be one of psychological or emotional violence rather than physical violence, many readers feel uncomfortable with her response. Ihab Hassan has written that the novel addresses "the human ambivalences of guilt and atonement, love and hate, health and psychosis."[11] By identifying Charles with Father and with the villagers, Jackson relates physical and psychological violence; both can destroy human beings.

Jackson died in 1965 before the current resurgence of feminism and its accompanying new body of feminist theory, including psychological theory. But she studied psychology in college and often wrote psychological studies of women in her fiction. The typical Jackson protagonist is a social misfit, a young woman not beautiful enough, charming enough, or articulate enough to get along with other people—like Merricat, a woman with no recognized place in society. In the early sixties, Jackson herself fell victim to attacks of severe anxiety and depression. Shortly after publication of *We Have Always Lived in the Castle,* the woman known to neighbors and friends as a tireless family chauffeur, an energetic cook and hostess, an active PTA mother, and a model faculty wife retreated into seclusion and underwent psychiatric treatment.[12] A letter from family friend Howard Nemerov during this period suggests that Jackson's illness was publicly attributed to the strain of success when *Castle* was nominated for a National Book Award. To her parents, Jackson wrote that her illness had been building for eight years.[13]

From the perspective of current feminist criticism, it is difficult to read biographer Lenemaja Friedman's account of Jackson's numerous domestic and literary achievements without wondering how she sustained her sanity as long as she did. Many of her literary predecessors have recorded the special difficulties faced by women who aspire to be great writers. Jackson's own journal from the period of her illness is revealing. She writes of insecurity and anxiety, but also often of her status as a professional writer. Not a journal keeper by nature, she kept it at her psychoanalyst's suggestion, even though she "always hated stream of consciousness" (Dec. 2). Yet she found her journal therapeutic and hoped that it would help her with her fiction, once commenting, "writing is the way out, writing is the way out, writing is the way out" (Dec. 3), and "there is a calm which begins to come" (Dec. 3). She claimed that she wrote surreptitiously, fearful of censure from her husband, the distinguished literary critic Stanley Edgar Hyman: "there is literally no telling him what I am doing. I think he would regard me as a criminal waster of time, and self-indulgent besides" (Dec. 3). A few sentences later, she observes more succinctly, "I feel I am cheating stanley because I should be writing stories for money" (Dec. 3). Still further on, she comments, "this is the most satisfying writing I have ever done" (Dec. 3). The picture of Jackson that emerges from these lines is one of a dedicated writer who is concerned because the writing she now enjoys most is not sufficiently remunerative to fulfill her husband's expectations and to remove the stigma of "criminality" from her act of "self-indulgence."

Whether or not this concern represented a fair assessment of Hyman's views, the anxiety was real to Jackson.

Like her female protagonists before Constance and Merricat, Jackson expressed a strong sense of inferiority, asking, "why am I less, why am I inferior, why am I put down?" (Dec. 18). Although the terminology suggests that some person or persons are acting against her, she often represented her "problem" or "obsession" as "imaginary" (Dec. 2): "it isn't real, it is a huge cloud of looming nothingness triggered off by small events" (Feb. 7). Earlier she wrote, "the troubles I dwell on are closer to fiction than to real life" (Dec. 2), but later in the same entry she reflected on the vital connection between her life and her fiction:

> insecure, uncontrolled, I wrote of neuroses and fear and I think all my books laid end to end would be one long documentation of anxiety. if I am cured and well and oh glorious alive then my books should be different. who wants to write about anxiety from a place of safety? although [sic] I suppose I would never be entirely safe since I cannot completely reconstruct my mind [Dec. 2].

Jackson was implying either that she projected her own unrealistic fears in her fiction as if they were real, or that all of her female protagonists are neurotics whose problems can be cured by reconstructing their own minds. The latter contradicts her own fictional accounts of female victimization, often by men—from the psychological oppression of domineering fathers (portrayed in *Hangsaman* [1951] and *The Sundial* [1958]) to the sexual abuse by a mother's boyfriend that helps to precipitate Elizabeth's multiple personalities in *The Bird's Nest* (1954). And surely none of these portrayals of female oppression is unrealistic, whatever fantastic or fabulistic qualities the narrative itself may demonstrate. The attack on the Blackwood house is the most dramatic example of male violence against women in the Jackson canon since the stoning of Jessie Hutchinson in "The Lottery" (1948).[14] In the earlier story, the victim is female presumably by chance; the implications of *We Have Always Lived in the Castle* are darker, surely more unsettling personally for a woman writer sensitive to oppression, one known to call herself "the only practicing witch in New England."[15]

The journal reiterates a longing for safety and security in the context of personal liberation, and it emphasizes Jackson's desire to be alone: "I look forward every now and then to freedom and security (and I do mean security by myself)" (Dec. 2). She describes "the glorious world of the future" when she will be "alone, safe" (Dec. 3), and her aspirations:

> to be separate, to be alone, to *stand* and *walk* alone, not to be different and weak and helpless and degraded [now that word again; if there has

been a refrain that word is part of it] and shut out. not shut out, shutting out [Dec. 3].

The correction in the last line again suggests a conflict between her own perception that she is being victimized and the belief, perhaps supported by her psychological studies and her psychoanalyst, that her fears are unfounded.[16] Contemporary feminists might well question whether a male psychoanalyst in the early 1960s could have understood the kind of psychological danger Jackson perceived (not only to herself, but to all her female characters) in masculine control over women's lives.

The solution Jackson proposes in *We Have Always Lived in the Castle* is a self-contained community of women, however small—one that shuts out the violence of the surrounding patriarchal society but accepts the support of its women. Jackson must have known that such a fantasy was more permissible in fiction than in reality.

Jackson's mental health improved in the final years of her life. At the time of her fatal heart attack in 1965, she was working on a new book. From the surviving fragment, it appears to be the "happy book" she looked forward to in her journal, but it was not about "husbands and wives" as she had speculated (Dec. 2). In it, a middle-aged woman buries her husband, picks a city at random, and sets off alone to make a new life for herself, with a new name of her own invention.

# Notes

ACKNOWLEDGMENT: I would like to thank Neil Nakadate for teaching *We Have Always Lived in the Castle* in an undergraduate literature course at the University of Texas in 1972 when I was his student assistant.

1. Shirley Jackson, *We Have Always Lived in the Castle* (New York: Viking, 1962), 28. All further references are to this edition of the text.

2. See Kate Millett, *Sexual Politics* (Garden City, N.Y.: Doubleday, 1970); Andrea Dworkin, *Woman Hating* (New York: E.P. Dutton, 1974); and Mary Daly, *Gyn/Ecology: The Metaethics of Radical Feminism* (Boston: Beacon, 1978).

3. All journal quotations are from undated journal pages (in the Library of Congress) headed only by the month and day, by which I will subsequently refer to them. This one is headed "Dec. 2." From internal evidence, I would date the journal to 1963.

4. I am indebted to a student, James Bradbury, for his discussion in a paper of the differences between the two sisters.

5. Elizabeth Janeway, *Man's World, Woman's Place. A Study in Social Mythology* (New York: William Morrow, 1971), p. 129.

6. Margaret Alice Murray, *The Witch-Cult of Western Europe* (1921; rpt. Oxford: Clarendon Press, 1971), 279.

7. William Dufty, *Sugar Blues* (New York: Warner Books, 1975), 31.

8. Henricus Institoris, *Malleus Maleficarum,* trans. and ed. Montague Summers (London: Pushkin, 1948).

9. *Time,* September 21, 1962, p. 94.

10. S.C. Woodruff, "The Real Horror Elsewhere," *Southwest Review* 52 (spring 1967): 152.

11. Ihab Hassan, *New York Herald Tribune Book Review,* September 23, 1962, p. 5.

12. See Lenemaja Friedman's account in *Shirley Jackson* (Boston: Twayne, 1975), pp. 26–43.

13. All manuscripts referred to here are in the Jackson and Hyman collections, Library of Congress. The letter from Nemerov is in the Hyman collection (uncatalogued), dated January 23, 1963; Jackson's letter to her parents (in the Jackson collection) is only dated 1963 (I would place it around April).

14. Although women participate in the stoning, the authority who presides over the lottery is Mr. Summers.

15. Friedman, 33.

16. My colleague Ellen Peel has suggested that these lines may instead record a desire for solitude and the power to enforce it, to shut others out. She read this essay in draft and made a number of helpful suggestions, as did Heather Arden.

# 11

# King of the Castle: Shirley Jackson and Stephen King

DARA DOWNEY AND DARRYL JONES

Stephen King once protested that the cover blurb for *The Shining* "referred to me as 'the master of the modern horror story,' neatly ignoring the likes of Shirley Jackson, Richard Matheson and Ira Levin, none of whom I have yet approached."[1] Jackson, in particular, has operated as an habitual cultural and literary reference point for King throughout his extraordinarily prolific and successful writing career. *Danse Macabre*, his engaging critical memoir from 1982, contains a 30-page analysis of *The Haunting of Hill House*, by far the longest space given to any single work in the book, and uses "The Lottery" as the prime example of his own central theoretical argument about the significance—the cultural provenance and affect—of the entire horror genre:

> The horror film is an invitation to indulge in deviant, antisocial behaviour by proxy—to commit gratuitous acts of violence, indulge our puerile dreams of power, to give into our most craven fears. Perhaps more than anything else, the horror story or horror movie says it's OK to join the mob, to become the total tribal being, to destroy the outsider. It has never been done better or more literally than in Shirley Jackson's short story "The Lottery," where the entire concept of the outsider is symbolic, created by nothing more than a black circle colored on a slip of paper.[2]

*Danse Macabre* closes, rather characteristically for King, with a list of "roughly one hundred books" which "all seem—to me at least—important to the genre we have been discussing."[3] This list contains three books by Shirley Jackson: *The Lottery*, *The Sundial* and (of course) *The Haunting of Hill House*. King further notes that *The Shining*, perhaps his finest novel, "was written with *The Sundial* very much in mind."[4] Certainly, King does Jackson the honor of naming one of *The Shining*'s major characters, the psychic chef Dick Halloran, after *The Sundial*'s dysfunctional, doomwatching family, and particularly its wheelchair-bound patriarch, Richard Halloran.

It is intriguing that King should so consistently display such obvious signs of affinity with Jackson, a writer from whom he is ostensibly so very different. She is subtle and satirical where he is crude and sarcastic: *The Sundial* closes, maddeningly, with a gesture of refusal and conscious irresolution, while King, seemingly unable to leave anything unsaid, acknowledges his own propensity to go for explicitness, "the gag reflex of revulsion," in powerful contradistinction to what he figures as Jackson's "low insinuating voice."[5] "I will try," he writes, "to terrorize the reader. But if I find I cannot terrify him/her, I will try to horrify; and if I find I cannot horrify, I'll go for the gross-out, I'm not proud"; whereas "terror ... the finest emotion" is "used to almost quintessential effect" in *The Haunting*, Robert Wise's celebrated 1963 film version of *The Haunting of Hill House*.[6] King's *Firestarter* is dedicated "In memory of Shirley Jackson, who never needed to raise her voice."[7]

Jackson writes from a subject-position of middle-class domesticity, while King's affiliations are proudly blue-collar and assertively masculine: he writes in a Portakabin on an industrial estate, to the accompaniment of "hard rock stuff like AC/DC, Guns 'n' Roses and Metallica," and acknowledges that "Traditionally, the muses were women, but mine's a guy; I'm afraid we'll just have to live with that."[8] Jackson's New England milieu is very different, the Vermont academe of Bennington College which she shared with her husband, the critic Stanley Edgar Hyman; while King's writings articulate an ingrained suspicion of the critic predicated on grounds of class: "A good deal of literary criticism serves only to reinforce a caste-system that's as old as the intellectual snobbery which nurtured it."[9] In *On Writing*, he fears that his advice for aspiring writers will lead to accusations of "encouraging people who are 'just not our sort, old chap' to apply for membership to the country club."[10] During her lifetime, Jackson's best-selling works were *Life Among the Savages* (1953) and *Raising Demons* (1957), two volumes of domestic humor recounting the comic family travails of a "typical" 1950s housewife: although, as Bernice Murphy and others have suggested, these works are by no means categorically distinct from her works of horror fiction (their very titles, in fact, evoke the genre). The sense of entrapment, alienation and cultural disenfranchisement felt by many housewives in 1950s suburbia finds clear symbolic articulation in Jackson's depictions of haunted or otherwise disturbed houses enfolding the lives of young women—Gloria Desmond and Julia Willow, Eleanor Vance, the Blackwood sisters—unable to leave their confines.[11]

King's work, according to the vampire novelist Chelsea Quinn Yarbro, contains one "lamentable flaw": that he is "not able to develop a believable woman character between the ages of seventeen and sixty."[12] Yarbro's age parameters seem to us a little generous, as a good deal of King's writing seems predicated on a genuine fear and loathing of the female body as the site of a horrifying abjection, be that in the leaking form of Carrie White's menstrual blood or the disquisitions on women's feces in *The Stand* or *Dolores Claiborne* (or *Cujo*, which contains disquisitions on menstrual blood *and* feces).[13] *Dolores Claiborne*, in particular, is devastatingly scatological in its account of the abject female body. Here, Dolores recounts her days as paid companion and later nurse to the increasingly senile Vera Donovan:

> She was sittin up in bed, wide awake, covers thrown back, her rubber pants pushed down to her big old flabby knees and her diapers undone. Had she made a mess? Great God! The bed was full of shit, she was covered with shit, there was shit on the rug, on the wheelchair, on the walls. There was even shit on the curtains. It looked like she musta taken up a handful and *flang* it, the way kids'll fling mud at each other when they're swimmin in a cowpond.[14]

(Presumably, this is what King means by "the gross out," figured in *Danse Macabre* as a gesture of last resort, but one to which he turns at the very beginning of *Dolores Claiborne*.) Conversely, Paul Sheldon, King's alter ego in *Misery*, imagines Annie Wilkes as a terrifying embodiment of the taunt with which her classmates torment the menstruating Carrie White in *Carrie*: "Plug it *up*, plug it *up*, plug it *up*."[15] What Paul finds most horrifying about Annie is her seeming *absence* of orifices:

> She was a big woman who, other than the large but unwelcoming swell of her bosom ... seemed to have no feminine curves at all—.... There was a feeling about her of roadblocks rather than welcoming orifices or even open spaces, areas of hiatus.
> Most of all she gave him a disturbing sense of *solidity*, as if she might not have any blood vessels or internal organs; as if she might be only solid Annie Wilkes from side to side and top to bottom.[16]

Interestingly, Darryl Hattenhauer, in the most recent full-length critical study of Shirley Jackson, renders *her* body as abject, dwelling at some length on her physical repulsiveness. Hattenhauer reads Jackson's work in part psychobiographically, as the product of her oppressive relationship with her husband Stanley Edgar Hyman, who "controlled her."[17] There's no doubt that Hyman was a philanderer who often treated his wife appallingly: Jackson's biographer Judy Oppenheimer records the story (which Hattenhauer repeats) of a pregnant Jackson trudging up the driveway with armloads of groceries; Hyman rushed out of the house, took the newspaper from under her arm, and returned to his armchair to read it![18] Unquestionably, this uneasy domestic relationship contributed to Jackson's physical and psychological dissolution: she became an alcoholic, agoraphobic recluse, addicted to codeine, amphetamines and tranquilizers, and increasingly obese (she ate a pound of butter a day). Hattenhauer concentrates particularly on Jackson's increasingly unattractive physical appearance:

> Few know what she looked like because she appeared only on radio and released only two photographs of herself, ones that had been taken when she was young and not yet obese.... Those who met the real Jackson were shocked.... When *Time* published a photograph of what Jackson really looked like in 1962, even her mother was stunned ... [by] how unattractive [she] really looked.[19]

Jackson furthermore developed colitis, which gave her nausea and diarrhea. Jackson's neglect, her refusal of a conventional feminine persona, seems further adumbrated in her attitude to her enforced status as housewife: in a very telling phrase, Hattenhauer discusses Jackson's "less than anal-retentive grooming and housekeeping," which shocked her conformist mother.[20] In the very physical abjection of her monstrous-feminine body, Jackson becomes figured in terms discursively analogous to King's anal-excretive Vera Donovan, and his other "gross-out" women. It is difficult to imagine an academic critic rendering a *male* writer so completely in terms of his perceived disgusting physical appearance. The similarly obese Henry James, for example, does not have his great gut figured as a key to his work: when Judith Woolf closes her study of James with a physical description of her subject, the effect is rather touching: she concentrates on his piercing eyes, and quotes with approval Ezra Pound's poetic description from the *Cantos* of the ghost-James's "great domed head."[21] James's and Jackson's work is often compared, not least by Stephen King himself: "it seems to me that [*The Haunting of Hill House*] and James's *The Turn of the Screw* are the only two great novels of the supernatural in the last hundred years."[22] It is interesting that one great haunted house novel should be analyzed as the product of female abjection while the other is understood as springing from masculine genius.

In *Danse Macabre* King, looking back on *Carrie*, his first published novel, saw it as "an uneasy masculine shrinking from a future of female equality": "writing the book in 1973 and only out of college three years, I was fully aware of what Women's Liberation meant for me and others of my sex."[23] In *The Stand*, the rebarbative social politics of King's postapocalyptic new society have no place for feminism. The pregnant survivor Fran Goldsmith muses:

> Women's lib, Frannie had decided ... was nothing more nor less than an outgrowth of the technological society. Women were at the mercy of their

bodies. They were smaller. They tended to be weaker.... *Liberation,* that
one word said it all. Before civilization, with its careful and merciful system of protections, women had been slaves.... And the Women's Credo,
which should have been hung in the offices of *Ms* magazine, preferably in
needlepoint, was just this: *Thank you, Men, for the railroads. Thank you,
Men, for inventing the automobile and killing the red Indians who thought it
might be nice to hold on to America for a while longer, since they were here
first. Thank you, Men, for the hospitals, the police, the schools. Now I'd like to
vote, please, and have the right to set my own course and make my own destiny.... Thank you, Men.*[24]

These musings close with Fran's realization, "Oh God, she badly needed
a man."[25] The kindest thing that one can say about King's politics, sexual and otherwise, is that they are confused and ill-considered—a subject to which we shall return at some length later in the essay.

Jackson's real significance for King, though, is a matter of his own
specific cultural and aesthetic formation as part of a self-mythologizing
"baby boomer" generation growing up in the 1950s and '60s. The great
majority of King's major cultural referents thus date from this period:
Jackson herself, plus Forrest Ackerman, Ray Bradbury, Richard Matheson, Robert Bloch, Harlan Ellison; *The Outer Limits, The Twilight Zone,
Invasion of the Body Snatchers,* and Wise's *The Haunting*—one of the films
singled out for mention as part of his formative moviegoing years,
1958–66, in the Ritz cinema, Lewiston, Maine, "amid the pawnshops and
not far from Louie's Clothing, where in 1964 I bought my first pair of
Beatle boots."[26] These, and others like them, are the figures and texts
recurring again and again in King's work, both fiction and nonfiction.
As Hattenhauer has demonstrated most ably, it is easy to forget just how
visible a cultural presence Jackson really was during these decades, when
she won numerous awards and was regularly anthologized and cited as
a major living exponent of American letters.[27]

Kings' intertextual reliance on these predominantly 1950s models
also serves to explain his own valorization of the experience of childhood,
the many wise children—Gordon Lachance, Danny Torrance, Mark
Petrie and many others—who stand in opposition, in his novels, to an
uncomprehending and often brutal adult authority; what Nina Auerbach
calls King's "passionate allegiance to pre-adulthood."[28] Like the telling
reference to the Beatle boots, it is his own childhood and adolescence
that King's fictions are condemned perpetually to repeat; rather like the
heroines of Jackson's novels, unable to leave the confines of the houses
that contain and entrap them.

King's insistence on upholding traditional masculine roles and his
concomitant unease about "Women's Liberation" concealing a deeper
anxiety about sexuality, women, and their bodies, also serve to place him

historically within the ideological confines of his own formative years. Paradoxical though this may sound, what finally unites Jackson and King is that, in terms of their cultural and ideological positions, they are both fundamentally writers of the 1950s. However, we shall argue, while many elements of King's work borrow heavily from Jackson's, he not only ignores the subtlety and ambiguity for which she is justly renowned, but frequently gives meanings to images taken from her work that are precisely opposite to those of the originals.

## The Sundial

*The Sundial*'s apocalyptic concerns place it in the main stream of cultural enquiry during the 1950s. Famously, accepting his Nobel Prize for Literature in 1950, William Faulkner regretfully posited nuclear destruction as the only valid subject for Cold War literary-intellectual discourse: "Our tragedy today is a general and universal fear so long sustained by now that we can even bear it. There are no longer problems of the spirit. There is only the question: When will I be blown up?"[29] *The Sundial*, then, is hardly eccentric, but rather one of a great number of 1950s cultural documents operating in the shadow of impending total destruction that had become a real and seemingly imminent possibility in the wake of the discovery and testing of the hydrogen bomb. The H-bomb had been developed and tirelessly championed by Edward Teller, the ultra-hawkish Hungarian–American nuclear physicist who has entered popular demonology as the major model (alongside Wernher von Braun, the former Nazi rocket scientist who came to work for the American space program) for the archetypal nuclear mad scientist, Dr. Strangelove.

The first controlled thermonuclear explosion, codenamed "George," took place on May 9, 1951, on Eniwetok Atoll in the Pacific Marshall Islands, 3,000 miles west of Hawaii. The first full-scale bomb, codenamed "Mike," was tested on November 1, 1952; it completely vaporized Elugelab Island, leaving behind a crater a mile wide. Before the tests, many scientists had feared that that the U.S. was about to unleash a doomsday weapon that would set fire to the atmosphere and the oceans. In a joint declaration, Nobel Prizewinning physicists Enrico Fermi and Isidor Rabi described the Bomb as a weapon "of genocide.... The fact that no limits exist to the destructiveness of this weapon makes its very existence and the knowledge of its construction a danger to humanity, as a whole. It is necessarily an evil thing considered in any light"; while J. Robert Oppenheimer, formerly head of the Manhattan Project at Los Alamos, put it more succinctly: "This is the plague of Thebes."[30] On December 30, 1952, members of the outgoing Truman administration met to discuss the implications of the "Mike" test, concluding unanimously that "a weapon was in the offing which, in sufficient numbers, might have the power to destroy the world."[31] In 1955, the theoretical death toll from a U.S. thermonuclear strike on the Soviet Union was put at 500 million, many of these deaths being caused by radiation clouds blowing inexorably across Europe and Asia.[32]

Specifically, *The Sundial* belongs to a particular subgroup of Cold War cultural products: the shelter novel.[33] As Guy Oakes argues in his account of the American civil defense movement of the 1950s, for Americans under nuclear attack "survival would largely be a do-it-yourself enterprise," since the government would not fund a public civil defense program[34]—although, in the wake of the Cuban Missile Crisis, Teller urged President Kennedy to embark on a wholesale national project of shelter-building.[35] Consequently, Federal Civil Defense Administration chief Val Peterson argued in 1953 that the home front of the Cold War "actually exists in our houses, right in our living rooms": the preparation of the home as a shelter was the item of first priority in the FCDA's 1953 manual *Home Protection Exercises*.[36] In *The Sundial*, the novel's cast spend the last days before the projected catastrophe barricading themselves into the Halloran house, covering the windows with "blankets, bedspreads, tablecloths, sheets, and finally the huge canvas cover from the barbecue pit," and ensuring a proper supply of candles, cigarettes, sandwiches, and Thermos flasks "each filled and labeled 'Coffee,' 'Soup' or 'Tea'" (*S* 242–3). "Have you actually seen to it that [your families] know what to do in an atomic emergency?" Peterson asked in 1953. "Have you prepared a shelter or pointed out to them the safest refuge in the house?"[37] The Hallorans and their companions are, in other words, ostensibly a proper, and properly patriotic, 1950s nuclear family.

The Halloran house is itself the outward and visible symbol of the first Mr. Halloran's naive utopianism. Richard Pascal opens his account of *The Sundial* and postwar American society by quoting from A.J. Downing's *The Architecture of Country Houses*: the American home, writes Dowling, "must be a home built and loved upon new world, and not the old world, ideas and principles"[38]; and the first Mr. Halloran "could think of nothing better to do with his money than set up his own world."[39] "Humanity, as an experiment, has failed" (*S* 45), says Aunt Fanny; Richard Halloran retires to read that great classic of self-fashioning in a new world, *Robinson Crusoe*. The Halloran house itself is built on what appear to be rationalist principles, as a microcosm of the new society:

> Mr. Halloran had been a methodical man. There were twenty windows to the left wing of the house, and twenty windows to the right; because the great door was double, on the second floor there were forty-two windows across and forty-two on the third floor.... The lawn swept precisely around

the blue pool—which was square—and up in a vastly long movement to a summer house built like a temple to some minor mathematical god [*S* 14–5].

The Halloran house, then, constitutes what amounts to a caricature of neoclassical architecture and landscaping and thus the (re-)insertion of an imagined eighteenth century polity into a Cold War context: this is the social organization that is to survive apocalypse. Jackson herself looked back to the eighteenth century for a vision of social harmony now vanished, for, in her own words "the preservation of an insistence on a pattern imposed precariously on the chaos of human development."[40] *The Sundial* reiterates this imagined Augustanism parodically in Fanny Halloran's prophecy: "The imbalance of the universe is being corrected. Dislocations have been adjusted. Harmony is to be restored, imperfections erased" (*S* 49). As Hattenhauer notes, Samuel Richardson was a particular favorite for Jackson, who saw him as "an emblem of fairness and love."[41] Thus, in *The Haunting of Hill House*, Dr. Montague reads *Pamela* and attempts to read *Sir Charles Grandison* as a corrective to the supernatural chaos of the haunted house, whose very asymmetry bespeaks its evil: "every angle is slightly wrong. Hugh Crain must have detested other people and their sensible, squared-away houses, because he made his house to suit his mind."[42] *Grandison*, whose hero is the great eighteenth century exemplar of virtuous masculinity, is particularly interesting here for Grandison's management of his estate, Grandison Hall, which, as Edward Malins has suggested, bears all the hallmarks of Capability Brown's handiwork[43]:

> This large and convenient house is situated in a spacious park; which has several fine avenues leading to it....
> The park itself is remarkable, for its prospects, lawns, and rich-appearing clumps of trees of large growth; which must therefore have been planted by the ancestors of the excellent owner; who, contenting himself to open and enlarge many fine prospects, delights to preserve, as much as possible, the plantations of his ancestors; and particularly thinks it a kind of impiety to fell a tree, that was planted by his father.[44]

Furthermore, the presence of characters named Fanny and Julia, and most particularly Mrs. Halloran's remark, "I feel like Aunt Norris" (*S* 147), suggest another potent intertext at play here, Jane Austen's great "Condition of England" novel *Mansfield Park*. This novel is suffused with images of landscape and architecture as symbols for the state of the nation, and significantly containing, in the Bertrams, a depiction of a landed family collapsing in on itself through incest and its financial reliance on the slave trade—a novel, then, in which traditional forms of authority, and the polity they are taken to represent, break down.

The Halloran house, then, partakes of a characteristically eighteenth century complex of aesthetic, cultural and national discourses all of which cohere around one area of symbolic investigation and display, architecture and landscape, the house. Horace Walpole, a significant intertextual figure for *The Sundial*, we shall see, suggested in his *The History of the Modern Taste in Gardening* (1780), that it was William Kent's development of the ha-ha or sunken fence, allowing for uninterrupted vistas, that was the major development in the liberatory aesthetic of the English landscape garden:

> I call a sunk fence the leading step, for these reasons. No sooner was this simple enchantment made, than leveling, mowing, and rolling followed. The contiguous ground of the park without the sunk fence was to be harmonized with the lawn within; and the garden in its turn was to be set free from its prim regularity, that it might assort with the wilder country without.... [Kent] leaped the fence, and saw that all nature was a garden.[45]

In *The Sundial*, Gloria's envisaged postapocalyptic new Eden is imaged in terms of a classic English landscape garden: "There aren't any ... separations in it, that's what I'm trying to say. Nothing like walls or fences, just soft green countryside going off in all directions" (*S* 132). The greatest of eighteenth century landscape gardeners, Lancelot Brown, earned his distinctive nickname for his repeated belief that any landscape had "capabilities of improvement," but also the belief (or suspicion) that the function of the landscape gardener was that of correcting the defects of nature in what amounted to a discourse of power, of control and mastery. Carole Fabricant, seeing in this a model for some eighteenth century gender-theories, suggests that "There is little doubt who was the master, who the obedient and dismissive servant—though admittedly a servant well cared for, lavishly fed, and dressed in the finest money could buy.... Contemporary treatises on gardening all agree that the landscape designer should not only use nature intelligently but *make her better.*"[46]

As Peter Biskind argues, many Cold War and apocalyptic films of the 1950s—*Them, The Thing from Another World, Forbidden Planet, Invasion of the Body Snatchers,* all films that played a very large part in Stephen King's cultural formation—tended to resolve themselves ultimately into debates on nature versus culture.[47] *The Sundial* also stakes out its ideological position along this nature/culture binary. What the sundial itself symbolizes in Jackson's novel, with its striking asymmetry against the perfect Augustan balance of the Halloran house, is the persistence of nature in defiance of culture: "Intruding purposefully upon the entire scene, an inevitable focus, was the sundial, set badly off center and reading WHAT IS THIS WORLD?" (*S* 15) It is only at the imagined and prophesied apocalyptic close of the novel, when the sun turns black in the sky, that nature is, briefly, eradicated—although this is really a preamble to the return of a postapocalyptic natural pastoralism, a "soft untouched green world" (*S* 164). The perfectly symmetrical Halloran house, then, like the selfishly utopian 13-point plan that Orianna intends to impose upon her new society, stands Ozymandias-like as a futile emblem of the vanity of human wishes.

Its very distrust of Utopianism as a naive and potentially dictatorial fantasy situates *The Sundial* squarely as a cultural product of the 1950s, since, as Biskind puts it, "Utopians are ... extremists, and utopianism was worked over so thoroughly [in the 1950s] that *utopian* and *millennial,* like *ideological,* became epithets of abuse.... Utopians were not only foolish, they were dangerous. They had paved the way for Hitler and Stalin."[48] *The Stand,* Stephen King's 1978 novel of mass destruction and a depopulated world, written in the context of the energy crisis of 1970s, allows room for no such doubts or ambiguities. In her celebrated essay "The Imagination of Disaster," itself written in the wake of the Cuban Missile Crisis and the very real threat of nuclear annihilation, Susan Sontag suggested that "The lure of such generalized disaster as a fantasy is that it releases one from normal obligations," positing instead an economy of "extreme moral simplification—that is to say a morally acceptable fantasy where one can give outlet to cruel or at least amoral feelings."[49] King's distrust of critics is a manifestation of an ingrained anti-intellectualism, a recurring characteristic of American life which, as Richard Hofstadter has demonstrated, gained especial currency during the 1950s, where its most visible manifestation was in McCarthyism.[50] Where Jackson's work manifests a profound skepticism, articulated through satire, towards extremist thinking, *The Stand* submits absolutely to the tendency of naive utopianism to refashion the world along the lines of "extreme moral simplification," using apocalypse as a kind of cleansing process, and goes so far as to create a character, the retired New Hampshire sociology professor Glen Bateman, whose entire function in the novel is to articulate the practical requirements of a postapocalyptic polity. Conversely, in its suspicion of the anti-intellectual animus of Utopianism, *The Sundial* deploys the potent image of book-burning— the Halloran library, never more than an artifact of cultural display, provides the fuel for the barbecue that the Hallorans throw for the villagers on the eve of apocalypse—familiar from a number of nuclear dystopias of the period, for example Aldous Huxley's *Ape and Essence* (1949), in which books are used to bake bread in his Belial-worshipping postapocalyptic Los Angeles, and, most famously, Ray Bradbury's *Fahrenheit 451* (1953), a genuine document of intellectual terror whose future America (which, as ever with Bradbury, is really a grotesque fantasia of 1950s America) is entirely premised on the burning of books.[51]

The action of *The Stand,* King writes,

sounds terrible, *is* terrible, but to me the vision was also strangely optimistic. No more energy crisis, for one thing, no more famine, no more
massacres in Uganda, no more acid rain or hole in the ozone layer. *Finito*
as well to sabre-rattling nuclear superpowers, and certainly no more over-
population. Instead, there was a chance for humanity's remaining shred to
start over again in a God-centered world to which miracles, magic and
prophecy had returned.[52]

The central plank of American anti-intellectualism, privileging the intu-
itive and emotional over the rational and educated, folksy naivety over
urban sophistication, practical application over theoretical abstraction,
the plain man over the expert, nature over culture, is evangelical Protes-
tantism. King's musings here replicate precisely the ideological position
of the American religious right in its more extreme theological speculations—most particularly, it is an exact description of the premise underlying the hugely successful *Left Behind* series, Tim LaHaye and Jerry B.
Jenkins's apocalyptic thrillers of the "rapture."[53] In its McCarthyite and
Religious Right manifestations, American anti-intellectualism has always
stood in opposition to leftism or liberalism in even its most diluted forms.
It is therefore no accident that King's novel should offer as the leader of
the forces of goodness in his Manichean postapocalyptic America the
figure of Mother Abagail. A preposterous caricature, Mother Abagail is
a 108-year-old black woman, so allergic to technological modernity that
she does not even possess a flush toilet, and much given to the homeli-
est of religious sentiments. Mother Abagail is also, we are informed, a
lifelong Republican.

*The Stand* is, in other words, like *Left Behind*, a right-wing-revenge
fantasy that gleefully dispenses with liberal modernity. Hofstadter claimed
that 1950s America embraced anti-intellectualism as a response to culture shock:

> Within only two generations the village Protestant individualist culture
> so widely observable before the First World was repeatedly shocked by
> change. It had ... to submit in matters of taste and conscience to the lead-
> ership of a new kind of educated and cosmopolitan American.[54]

What *The Stand* does is to return America to this "village Protestant
individualist culture": the community at Boulder is governed by a village council, guided by the downhome evangelicalism of Mother Abagail, and lives without technology (unlike their Satanic counterparts holed
up in Las Vegas who, doomed to commit the inevitable mistakes of
modernity, eventually blow themselves up with a nuclear bomb). By far
the most effective section of King's novel is the description of the rapid
social breakdown that follows in the wake of the deadly superflu that
escapes from an American biological warfare installation. King ded-
icates a chapter to the unworthy dead, closing with the death by massive

heroine overdose of "Richard Hoggins ... a young black man who had lived his entire life in Detroit, Michigan. He had been addicted to the fine white powder he called 'hehrawn' for the last five.... No great loss."[55]

## The Haunting of Hill House

In spite of the relationship that King appears to believe his work has with *The Haunting of Hill House*, any attempt to relate the two soon exposes fundamental differences. In reality, King rereads (indeed, misreads) many of *Hill House*'s central issues. The most important of these are the problem of absolute reality and the related issue of cleanliness, both literal and figurative, as well as the extent of Eleanor's role in the events in the house, and the question of how to read the ending.

*Hill House* begins and ends with more or less the same much-quoted words:

> No live organism can continue for long to exist sanely under conditions of absolute reality; even larks and katydids are supposed, by some, to dream. Hill House, not sane, stood by itself against its hills, holding darkness within; it had stood so for eighty years and might stand for eighty more. Within, walls continued upright, bricks met neatly, floors were firm, and doors were sensibly shut; silence lay steadily against the wood and stone of Hill House, and whatever walked there, walked alone [*HH* 227].

As so many commentators, including King, have recognized, these lines are vital to an understanding of the novel as a whole. Some interesting interpretations become possible if one uses Gaston Bachelard's *The Poetics of Space* (first published in 1957, two years before *Hill House*) as a theoretical framework. According to Bachelard, "if a house is a living value, it must integrate an element of unreality. All values must remain vulnerable, and those that do not are dead."[56] In other words, it is the process of daydreaming within a house, of incorporating into one's conception of it elements that are not strictly part of its material structure, that keeps a house "alive." Hill House, in the absence of dreams, is not simply dead but mad and malignant.[57] Eleanor, driving up to the house and imagining smugglers and secret chambers, is pulled up short by the sight of the house, which "was vile. She shivered and thought, ... Hill House is vile, it is diseased; get away from here at once" (*HH*, 247). It does not merely lack unreality or dreams, but actively discourages them.

King, however, has an almost diametrically opposed conception of what constitutes a haunted house (or, to use his terminology, Bad Place), one that is carried into his misreading of Jackson's opening sentence. He states that Hill House "does *not* exist under conditions of absolute reality; therefore, it does not dream; therefore, it is not sane" (italics added).[58] This becomes significant if we interpret Bachelard as suggesting that a house that is viewed in figurative terms will be safeguarded from any excess of reality. King's Bad Places are essentially metaphors, in that their badness is the symbolic manifestation of something that has happened there, rather being innately *of* the house. In *'Salem's Lot*, the Marsten House is a kind of "psychic battery" or "sounding board,"[59] soaking up and re-emitting the residue of the terrible deeds performed by its former owner. Similarly, the Overlook Hotel in *The Shining* has had a series of greedy, crooked owners and was the site of several gangland-type killings and suicides.[60] In King's own words, "the truest definition of the haunted house would be 'a house with an unsavory history.'"[61]

This is not unequivocally the case with Hill House. Despite the deaths and bitter family feuds that have characterized its history, the dubious character of its original owner and the deliberate oddities of its construction, the text is committed to leading the reader to question whether any of this is directly responsible for the fact that no one has ever been able to live there for any length of time. Dr. Montague is convinced that it was "born bad," and that, while people have died and argued in all old houses, not all of them are so disturbed or disturbing (*HH*, 248, 272, 280). Indeed, the house's tragic history, from the death of the first Mrs. Crain onwards, seems to have been more the product than the cause of the evil resident there. The manifestations themselves, their multifarious nature, and the fact that they almost never take visible human form, all imply an amorphous malevolent force, without origin or motive. King, discussing Wise's *The Haunting,* rejects such undecidability which, in his phraseology, lets the door bulge but never opens it, preferring to rely upon specifics than upon unnamable dread.[62] Together with his misapprehension that it is a *lack* of absolute reality that renders Hill House insane rather than vice versa, this further confirms that King's horror aesthetics are based on presence and Jackson's on absence.

This dichotomy also permeates the content of both writers' work, manifesting itself particularly in the tensions and overlaps between notions of dirt and cleanliness. Jack Morgan asserts that "Housekeeping, in its deepest implications, is ... part of our warding off of abjection—of decay, rot, squalor."[63] However, as Mary Douglas points out, "It is part of our condition that the purity for which we strive and sacrifice so much turns out to be hard and dead as a stone when we get it."[64] Her thesis is that cleaning and purification rituals are a means of marking off certain parts of the world as sacred, and others as impure and dangerous. For several reasons, this has led anthropologists to confuse and conflate the sacred and the unclean in primitive religions. Furthermore, Douglas's ideas are very close to those of Mircea Eliade, who describes sacred space, significantly, as "absolute reality."[65]

These issues surface time and again in *Hill House*. Dr. Montague alludes to the "concept of certain houses as unclean or forbidden—perhaps sacred" and mentions the reference in Leviticus to a "leprous" or *tsaraas* house (*HH* 272). Moreover, the novel places great emphasis on the problematic nature of cleanliness and order, focusing primarily on Mrs. Dudley, who insists upon everything being put back where it belongs. This insistence rapidly causes her to be associated in the minds of the group with the tendency of doors to swing shut, even when they have been propped open. Theo suggests that Mrs. Dudley would "rather shut them herself than come along and find them shut by themselves because the doors belong shut and the windows belong shut and the dishes belong—" (*HH* 303–4). Eleanor's first impression of Mrs. Dudley is that "Her apron was clean, her hair was neat, and yet she gave an indefinable air of dirtiness" (*HH* 249). The house (though its house-*keeper*) is therefore dirty and leprous in spite of, or perhaps because of, its undeniable cleanliness and neatness, which in turn is related to its dreamless, psychically pure, overly real condition.

There is an interesting parallel here with *'Salem's Lot*. Margie Glick and Dud Rogers are both seized with sudden urges to clean after becoming vampires, and in both cases cleaning is associated with absence. Margie's cleaning is done "with a maniacal zeal that precluded all other thought," while Dud's empty shack is described as "astringently neat," "as deserted and sterile as the moon."[66] However, King, here as elsewhere, generally favors the defiled and the abject, the filthy, the smelly, and the residue of evil. Thus, the Marsten House exudes a smell reminiscent of "tears and vomit and blackness," and is, as Susan points out, a mess[67]; and after these early instances of disturbing tidiness, most vampire-converts appear half-dressed and unkempt. Thus, after giving a nod to Jackson's use of the inhumanly clean, King rejects it in favor of the tangible, physical horror of the abject and the soiled.

King is also determined not to see Hill House as clean in any sense. He asserts that the final paragraph leaves the reader

> with an unpleasant surmise: if Hill House was not haunted before, it certainly is now. Jackson finishes by telling us that whatever walked in Hill House walked alone.
> For Eleanor Vance, that would be business as usual.[68]

In Wise's *The Haunting*, Julie Harris's Eleanor closes the film by saying, off-camera, "and we who walk here, walk alone."[69] Similarly, King ignores Jackson's repeated use of the singular, and even the word "alone." Despite saying repeatedly that the bulk of the story concerns Eleanor's desire and inevitable failure to become part of something, anything, King applies his own vision of the horrific to Jackson's fairly unambiguous statement, a vision evident in *The Shining*'s relationship with *Hill House*. The Torrance family, the novel suggests, "could end up flitting through the Overlook's halls like insubstantial shades in a Shirley Jackson novel, whatever walked in Hill House walked alone, but you wouldn't be alone in the Overlook, oh no, there would be plenty of company here."[70]

Once the hotel finally gains control of Jack's body, what remains is described as "a strange, shifting composite, many faces mixed imperfectly into one."[71] The Overlook is thus a collective being, of which Jack's psyche is now a part, an idea nicely portrayed in Stanley Kubrick's film version, when Jack's face is shown as having taken its place in a group photograph in the lobby. King reiterates this image in the final episode of his series *Rose Red*, in which Joyce Reardon, the researcher who has been so fascinated by the house, is welcomed, screaming, into the group of putrefying women who have been absorbed by it.

Eleanor, conversely, does not belong anywhere or with anyone. In her youth, stones fell on the roof of her house, an event that her mother blames on the neighbors, with whom they never mixed and who had always been hostile towards them. Similarly, in "The Lottery," the rain of stones is the answer to the outsider status conferred on Tessie Hutchinson by the black spot on the slip of paper. It is thus the mark of the socially abject, of enforced individualism, isolation and persecution. King himself underlines this point through his use of the image in *Carrie* (the name of Eleanor's younger sister), once in the form of a rain of stones identical to Eleanor's, and later in the form of the pig's blood (a typical example of King's radical altering of Jackson's images, emphasizing the waste substances of the body over the frightening cleanliness of Jackson's own work). For Eleanor as for Tessie and Carrie, once marked, it is impossible to be anything other than an outsider, as we see in the way in which the sheer weight of the combined opinion of the rest of the group, saying that she must leave, leads directly to Eleanor's suicide.

To imagine that she becomes part of the house in the end is to ignore a vital element of her tragedy—that she has been tricked. She says at one point, "The sense was that it wanted to consume us, take us into itself, make us a part of the house, maybe—oh, dear. I thought I knew what I was saying, but I'm doing it very badly" (*HH* 320). The interruption introduces a doubt as to the validity of the statement, a doubt more than backed up by the ending of the novel, when Eleanor truly believes that Hill House wants her to stay, but again, her own thoughts seriously undermine this assurance. She goes from proudly thinking that she is really committing suicide all by herself, to demanding, too late, *why* she is doing it. Moreover, the book's ending on the repetition of the words "and whatever walked there, walked alone" settles it once and for all: Hill House, a place "without concession to humanity," is not interested in consuming or incorporating its inhabitants, merely in stripping them of all of their dreams and illusions, including the illusion that it can be a home, either for the living or for the dead (*HH* 248, 395). Hill House is clean, dreamless and utterly, horribly real; and, as repetition always suggests, that is not about to change.

## We Have Always Lived in the Castle

King is a writer who likes to "yank the door open at some point in the festivities," rather than to leave the reader guessing as to the nature of the source of fear.[72] He also, however, has major problems with unseen, and with hidden things in general, as the following comment on *'Salem's Lot* illustrates, in which he links the atmosphere of the novel to the political climate of the Watergate hearings:

> The thing that really scared me was not the vampires, but the town in the daytime, the town that was empty, knowing that there were things in closets, that there were people tucked under beds, under the concrete pilings of all those trailers.... During that time I was thinking about secrets, things that have been hidden and were being dragged out into the light.[73]

Indeed, the association of the secret with the dangerous pervades the novel. The town gossip, Mabel Werts, attempting to spy on the new occupants of the Marsten House, grumbles, "Now what kind of people is it that only opens up when a body can't catch a decent glimpse of them?"[74] One of the reasons why the town is so easily infiltrated by the vampires is that it is so secretive itself. As one character points out, "The secrecy concerning that aspect of Hubie and his wife and his house is almost tribal."[75] Furthermore, the killing of Barlow, the king vampire, is only accomplished by means of a succession of breaking-and-entering scenes. Nothing is permitted to lurk unseen in the dark, either on the level of form or of content.

Jackson's attitude to privacy and violation, on the other hand, might best be understood through a brief examination of Sigmund Freud's essay "The Uncanny," the argument of which famously hinges on the confluence between the terms *heimlich* and *unheimlich*. The definition of *heimlich*, Freud notes, is "intimate, friendlily comfortable; the enjoyment of quiet content, etc., arousing a sense of agreeable restfulness and security as in one within the four walls of his house." However, it also contains the second sense of "Concealed, kept from sight, so that others do not get to know of or about it, withheld from others." Under the entry for *unheimlich* on the other hand, is the extremely revealing definition of the word as "'*the name for everything that ought to have remained ... secret and hidden but has come to light*' (Schelling)." Thus, "*heimlich* is a word the meaning of which develops in the direction of ambivalence, until it finally coincides with its opposite, *unheimlich*. *Unheimlich* is in some way or another a sub-species of *heimlich*."[76]

According to Bachelard, an element of secrecy is necessary if a house is to avoid becoming overly real, and so "the oneirically definitive house, must retain its shadows."[77] He then goes on to say that "what is secret never has total objectivity."[78] A house into which outsiders are permitted to enter runs the risk of losing all of its shadows and becoming dangerously objective and real. Darkness, shadows, and privacy are all one and the same thing—the necessary condition for the psychic well-being of a house, the things that prevent, paradoxically, the house from becoming overwhelmed by darkness, shadows, and terrible secrets that should never have been brought to light. Matters are not as simple as this, however, as his musings on the effects of housework suggest:

> Objects that are cherished ... attain to a higher degree of reality than indifferent objects, or those that are defined by geometric reality. For they produce a new reality of being.... From one object in a room to another, housewifely care weaves the ties that unite a very ancient past to a new epoch. The housewife awakens furniture that was asleep.[79]

Housework is associated with the malignantly supernatural in *Castle*, not only in that it is Merricat (who has murdered her entire family and idly wishes that she had been born a werewolf) who is so constantly concerned with neatening the house, but more explicitly in her description of Constance and herself as "carrying our dust cloths and the broom and dustpan and mop like a pair of witches walking home" (*C* 461). However, it is not through this association, but rather when the house's seclusion is threatened, that it becomes like Hill House—personified because it is too real. The first instance of this is Charles's arrival, when Merricat watches him "looking up at a blank face of a house looking down because we always kept the shades drawn on the upstairs windows" (*C* 450). That the adoption of human characteristics by the house is the direct result of having its intimacy compromised is confirmed during the fire, which allows the villagers to storm the sanctum of the Blackwood home. Merricat tells how she and Constance

> watched the great feet of the men stepping across our door-sill, dragging their hoses, bringing filth and confusion and danger into our house. More lights moved into the driveway and up the steps, and the front of the house was white and pale and uncomfortable at being so clearly visible; it had never been lighted before [*C* 491].

Thus, what was homely and familiar and private, *heimlich*, has become *unheimlich* and frightening, simply by virtue of no longer being exclusively private, and the reaction of the house is to take on human characteristics as a defensive strategy. However, the novel also suggests that the status of a house as a Bad Place can be a relative quality, created by and frightening only to intruders, while keeping those inside—who are themselves considered to be strange and dangerous—safe from all those who might otherwise have wished to enter. The fire, after all, is not a wholly negative event for the Blackwood sisters. Baskets of food begin to be surreptitiously deposited on their front step and the villagers refer to them as "the ladies," describing them to their children as bad fairies or witches, a situation that assures the girls the isolation they have always cultivated and craved.

For King, on the other hand, although invading a home is also a frightening event for the invaders, there is no sense of the sanctity of the privacy of those being invaded. In 'Salem's Lot, Ben's entry into the room where, as a child, he saw the dead Hubie Marsten causes the door to give "a scream against the wood like a woman in pain," an image that is somehow supposed to elicit sympathy for Ben, rather than for the screaming house.[80] Moreover, the personification of the house, which is evoked in language more than a little reminiscent of that in Hill House, is the result of the psychic dirt left by its former owners and encouraged by Barlow. Jackson's frankly ambivalent attitude to housework and the resultant effects on the nature of a dwelling is rejected by King in favor of the straightforward equation of dirt and fear, a move that conveniently (since King's reaction to secrecy and privacy is one of fear) hints that the house is loved by no one and so may be invaded by anyone.

What is more, the kind of isolation valorized in Castle and to which The Sundial takes a distinctly ambivalent attitude, is, for King, never desirable. As Mark Jancovich points out, The Shining "highlights that the retreat from the social world into a self-contained domestic sphere is not only impossible, but also destructive."[81] This is even more pronounced in Carrie, a novel about a girl's doomed efforts to be accepted in the cutthroat world of the American high school. While we are encouraged to feel sympathy towards Carrie, to understand the social origins of her final pyromaniacal rage, and to take away with us a rather terrifying lesson about tolerance, it is during this mindless rampage that we come to realize that King is profoundly suspicious of those who do not conform to the standards of society. Her revenge turns her oppressors into victims, and the text's distancing from her as it progresses, into "factual" accounts and other points of view, serves to transform her into a monster. Precisely the same contradiction is latent in the quotation from Danse Macabre with which this essay began: "the horror story or horror movie says it's OK to join the mob, to become the total tribal being, to destroy the outsider." King evidently fails to see that he is saying that the only aim of acting like a deviant is to join a mob and stone the outsider, even though outsiders tend to become so because of socially deviant behavior. If horror divides readers into the stoners and the stoned, then while *Castle* and "The Lottery" are critical of mindless mob-mentality, King would most likely be out there with a torch and a pitchfork.

King's mistrust of those who do not partake in such displays of communal violence—and communal behavior in general, as *Carrie* implies—is coterminous with his dislike of hidden, indoor things. The two are conflated in his insistence upon the frightening nature of domestic space and its natural association with women. The case of Susan in *'Salem's Lot* is illustrative here. Ben somehow believes that she will be safer in her own home than chasing vampires with him, although the evidence of the narrative is flatly to the contrary, most of the vampire attacks taking place in people's homes, and the most frightening scenes being those in which characters enter the Marsten House. She "rebels," drives off to the Marsten House, is promptly turned into a vampire, and is henceforth part of the terror embodied by the house. This "rebellion" simply shunts her from one house to another. This transfer, it is implied, is her own doing, even though, having been incorporated into the Marsten House as Eleanor can never be into Hill House, Susan is never really permitted to rebel or leave home at all.

As might be expected, Jackson's views on such matters are rather more complex. She wrote in her diary, "I [sic] have been thinking of these pages as a refuge, a pleasant hiding place," only to apparently recant later, saying, "this is not a refuge, these pages, but a way through, a path not charted."[82] Such a fluid relationship between the concepts of geographical movement and refuge is also present in Eleanor's journey to Hill House, as she contemplates driving forever while fantasizing about finding a true home. A slightly different version of this is Merricat's strategy for coping with the ordeal of shopping in the village. She imagines her journey there and back as being like

> the children's games where the board is marked into little spaces and each player moves according to a throw of the dice; there were always dangers, like "lose one turn" and "go back four spaces" and "return to start," and little helps, like "advance three spaces" and "take an extra turn" [*C* 402].

This is similar to the way in which prison inmates are encouraged to create "a comfortable private space that they may figuratively 'put on' and go about in, thus suspending some of the harsher social pressures."[83] Merricat figuratively carries with her into the village the safe, square intimacy of her house, while at the same time breaking up the frightening outdoors into manageable chunks.[84]

King, who refers to the squareness of houses twice in *'Salem's Lot*,[85] also uses this imagery, with particular reference to Monopoly, a game about geographical movement, and settling down to building houses (and hotels). It emerges in *Carrie* as Carrie White begins to explore her powers: "She let the hairbrush down carefully. Good. Last night she had dropped it. Lose all your points, go to jail."[86] In *The Shining,* as her insane husband roams the hotel, Wendy sees her journey from the kitchen (where she feels inexplicably secure) to the bedroom in precisely the same terms: "(*Now back the way you came. Turn off the kitchen lights. Go through the inner office. Through the desk gate, collect two hundred dollars)*" (italics King's).[87] The differences between these two women serve to underline King's attitudes. Wendy, the obedient little wife, knows her place, and needs the imagery of Monopoly because she knows that, in the big bad unstable world of the Overlook, to leave the kitchen is to abandon a woman's proper position.

Carrie, on the other hand, both loves and hates her mother's ultra-repressive house. That such dark domestic space should be her defense against failure suggests again the suspicion latent in King's conception of the home and of women. It is with these emerging powers—metaphorically protected by the square shape of domesticity, about which Carrie is uncertain how she feels—that she kills her classmates, before killing her mother, destroying her house and dying herself. Her figurative traveling has only rendered her monstrous and, as Brian De Palma's film version makes explicit, she literally cannot live without the terrible house with which those powers are associated.

The Blackwood house, however, manages to be a refuge and a "way through" for Merricat precisely because of its status as a Bad Place. The more the house is a source of fear and superstition for the villagers, the more it is one of privacy and safety for the sisters: its *heimlichkeit* is made possible by means of its becoming *unheimlich* for everybody else. A recognition of the overlap between the two would appear to be impossible for King, however, and, opting characteristically for a simplistic association between two things that he finds disturbing, he would seem to saying, in true 1950s fashion, that a woman's place is in the home.

## Notes

ACKNOWLEDGMENT: While this is very much a joint effort for which we take joint responsibility, we wish to note that Darryl Jones is primarily responsible for the introduction and the section on *The Sundial,* while Dara Downey wrote the sections on *Hill House* and *Castle.* We would like to thank Dr. Bernice M. Murphy for her advice and encouragement.

1. Don Herron, "Horror Springs in the Fiction of Stephen King," in Tim Underwood and Chuck Miller, eds., *Fear Itself: The Horror Fiction of Stephen King (1976–1982)* (London, Sydney and Auckland: Pan Books, 1982), 62. Herron glosses

this as King "modestly" complaining, though it is worth noting that the "yet" in King's remark seems to foreshadow his later megalomania.

2. King, *Danse Mababre: The Anatomy of Horror* (London: Futura, 1982), 47.

3. Ibid. 466.

4. King, *Danse Macabre*, 315.

5. Ibid. 39, 325.

6. Ibid. 40.

7. King, *Firestarter* (1980; London: Warner Books, 1992), 5.

8. King, *On Writing: A Memoir of the Craft* (London: Hodder and Stoughton, 2000), 122, 111.

9. King, *On Writing*, 110. For a longer analysis of King's obsessive concerns with writing and with critics, see Darryl Jones, *Horror: A Thematic History in Fiction and Film* (London: Arnold, 2002), 137–43.

10. King, *On Writing*, 111.

11. Bernice Murphy, *"Do You Know Who I Am?" Contextualizing Shirley Jackson* (unpublished Ph.D. thesis, Trinity College Dublin, 2003).

12. Chelsea Quinn Yarbro, "Cinderella's Revenge: Twists on fairy tale and mythic themes in the work of Stephen King," in Underwood and Miller, op cit, 49.

13. Though there is no space to rehearse their arguments here, our thinking on the female body and abjection draws upon the following works: Barbara Creed, *The Monstrous-Feminine: Film, Feminism,* Psychoanalysis (London: Routledge, 1993); Mary Douglas, *Purity and Danger: An Analysis of the Concepts of Pollution and Taboo* (London: Routledge and Kegan Paul, 1984); and Julia Kristeva, *The Powers of Horror: An Essay on Abjection* (New York: Columbia University Press, 1982).

14. King, *Dolores Claiborne* (1992; London: Hodder and Stoughton, 1993), 32.

15. King, Carrie.

16. King, *Misery* (1987; London: Hodder and Stoughton: 1988), 8.

17. Darryl Hattenhauer, *Shirley Jackson's American Gothic* (Albany: SUNY Press, 2003), 17.

18. Judy Oppenheimer, *Private Demons: The Life of Shirley Jackson* (New York: Putnam's 1988), 115–6; Hattenhauer, 17.

19. Hattenhauer, 21, 24.

20. Hattenhauer, 23.

21. Judith Woolf, *Henry James: The Major Novels* (Cambridge: Cambridge University Press, 1991), 150.

22. King, *Danse Macabre*, 319.

23. King, *Danse Macabre*, 198.

24. King, *The Stand: The Complete and Uncut Edition* (1978, 1990; London: Hodder and Stoughton, 1992), 651–2.

25. Ibid. 652.

26. King, *On Writing*, 27.

27. Hattenhauer, 1–2.

28. Nina Auerbach, *Our Vampires, Ourselves* (Chicago and London: University of Chicago Press, 1995), 159.

29. William Faulkner, "Address upon Receiving the Novel Prize for Literature," in *The Portable Faulkner*, revised and expanded edition, ed. Malcolm Cowley (Harmondsworth: Penguin, 1977), 723.

30. Peter Goodchild, *Edward Teller: The Real Dr. Strangelove* (London: Weidenfeld and Nicolson, 2004), 151–2, 165.

31. Ibid. 210.

32. Ibid. 266–7.

33. For an account of the cultural products of "Sheltermania," see Kim Newman, *Millennium Movies: End of the World Cinema* (London: Titan, 1999), 63–70.

34. Guy Oakes, *The Imaginary War: Civil Defense and American Cold War Culture* (New York and Oxford: Oxford University Press), 105.

35. Goodchild, 298–9.

36. Oakes, 107, 109–10.

37. Ibid. p. 108.

38. Richard Pascal, "New World Miniatures: Shirley Jackson's *The Sundial* and Postwar American Society," *Journal of American and Comparative Cultures* 23:3 (fall 2000): 99.

39. Shirley Jackson, *The Sundial* (New York: Popular Library, 1958), 13. All further references to this edition will be incorporated into the main body of the text.

40. Oppeheimer, 125.

41. Hattenhauer, 24.

42. Jackson, *The Haunting of Hill House*, in *The Masterpieces of Shirley Jackson*, (London: Raven Books, 1996), 297. (Hereafter in main text as *HH*.)

43. Edward Malins, *English Landscaping and Literature 1660–1840* (London: Oxford University Press, 1966), 110.

44. Samuel Richardson, *The History of Sir Charles Grandison*, ed. Jocelyn Harris (Oxford: Oxford University Press, 1986), 7:272–3.

45. Horace Walpole, *The History of the Modern Taste in Gardening*, (New York: Ursus, 1995), 42–3

46. Carole Fabricant, "Binding and Dressing Nature's Loose Tresses: The Ideology of Augustan Landscape Design," *Studies in Eighteenth-Century Culture* 8 (1979): 113, 125–6.

47. Peter Biskind, *Seeing Is Believing: How Hollywood Taught Us to Stop Worrying and Love the Fifties* (1983; London: Bloomsbury, 2000), 101–60.

48. Ibid. 112–13. For a similar argument, see Mark Jancovich, *Rational Fears: American Horror in the 1950s* (Manchester: Manchester University Press, 1996), 19.

49. Susan Sontag, "The Imagination of Disaster," in *Against Interpretation* (New York: Octagon, 1978), 215.

50. Richard Hofstadter, *Anti-Intellectualism in American Life* (London: Jonathan Cape, 1964). We are indebted to Hosftadter's work for many of our comments on the nature of American anti-intellectualism here.

51. Book-burning continues to be a resonant postapocalyptic image: in Roland Emmerich's *The Day After Tomorrow* (2004), survivors of catastrophic climate change take shelter in New York Public Library and survive by burning books to keep warm.

52. King, *On Writing*, 161.

53. Tim LaHaye and Jerry B. Jenkins, *Left Behind* (Wheaton, Illinois: Tyndale, 2000).

54. Hofstadter, 42–3.

55. King, *The Stand*, 443–4.

56. Gaston Bachelard, *The Poetics of Space,* trans. Maria Jolas (New York: Orion Press, 1964), 59.

57. For a discussion of Hill House's failure—or refusal—to be a home, see Tricia Lootens, "'Whose Hand Was I Holding?': Familial and Sexual Politics in Shirley Jackson's *The Haunting of Hill House*," in Lynette Carpenter and Wendy K. Kolmar, eds., *Haunting the House of Fiction: Feminist Perspectives on Ghost Stories by Women* (Knoxville: University of Tennessee Press, 1991).

58. Stephen King, *Danse Macabre* (London: Warner, 1994), 301.

59. King, *'Salem's Lot* (London: Hodder and Stoughton, 1977), 135 and *Danse*, 297.

60. In Stanley Kubrick's 1980 film version, the hotel is built over an Indian burial ground, as is the house in King's television series *Rose Red* and the cemetery in *Pet Cemetery*.

61. King, *Danse*, 300.

62. King, *Danse*, 134.

63. Jack Morgan, *The Biology of Horror: Gothic Literature and Film* (Carbondale and Edwardsville: Southern Illinois University Press, 2002), 182, 186.

64. Mary Douglas, *Purity & Danger: An Analysis of the Concepts of Pollution and Taboo* (London: Ark, 1966), 161.

65. Mircea Eliade, *The Sacred and the Profane: The Nature of Religion,* trans. Willard R. Trask (New York and London: Harcourt Brace Jovanovich, 1959), 21.

66. King, *'Salem's Lot*, 249, 262.

67. King, *'Salem's Lot*, 322–23.

68. King, *Danse*, 330.

69. Quoted in Manuel Aguirre, *The Closed Space: Horror Literature and Western Symbolism* (Manchester and New York: Manchester University Press, 1990), 191.

70. King, *The Shining*, in *The Shining, Carrie and Misery*, (London: Chancellor Press, 1992), 202.

71. King, *The Shining* in *ibid,* 304.

72. King, *Danse*, 136.

73. Quoted in Tim Underwood and Chuck Miller, eds., *Bare Bones: Conversations on Terror with Stephen King* (New York: Warner, 1988), 5.

74. King, *'Salem's Lot,* 92.

75. King, *'Salem's Lot,* 233.

76. Sigmund Freud, "The Uncanny," in The Standard Edition of the Complete Works of Sigmund Freud: Volume XVII (1917–1919): *An Infantile Neurosis and Other Works,* trans. James Strachey (London: Hogarth and Institute of Psychosis, 1955), 222–26. All italics, insertions and inverted commas are Freud's.

77. Bachelard, ibid, 13.

78. Bachelard, ibid, 13.

79. Bachelard, ibid, 68.

80. King, *'Salem's Lot,* 43.

81. Mark Jancovich, *American Horror from 1951 to the Present* (Staffordshire: Keele University Press, 1994), 21.

82. Quoted in Darryl Hattenhauer, *Shirley Jackson's American Gothic* (New York: State University of New York Press, 2003), 27.

83. Carl Darryl Malmgren, *Fictional Space in the Modernist and Postmodernist Novel* (Lewisburg: Bucknell University Press, 1985), 26.

84. See Reginald G. Golledge, "Human Wayfinding and Cognitive Maps," in Mary Rockman and James Steele, eds., *Colonization of Unfamiliar Landscapes: The Archaeology of Adaption* (London and New York: Routledge, 2003), for a discussion of "chunking" as a means of coping with unfamiliar space.

85. King, *'Salem's Lot,* 146, 150.

86. King, *Carrie,* in ibid, 357.

87. King, *The Shining,* in ibid, 26.

# 12

# Chambers of Yearning: Shirley Jackson's Use of the Gothic

## John G. Parks

Mrs. Arnold of Shirley Jackson's story "Colloquy" (1944) feels driven to see a psychiatrist because of her confusion and bewilderment over her loss of "a world where a lot of people lived too and they all lived together and things went along like that with no fuss."[1] The psychiatrist tries to get her to accept "reality," which to him means to accept and adapt to a world with "cultural patterns rapidly disintegrating." Mrs. Arnold refuses to accept the doctor's "disoriented world" and leaves his office. But the reader senses that the price for her refusal to accept the doctor's, and the rest of society's, definition of reality will be loneliness and madness. This story is in many ways representative of the concern of most of Jackson's fiction, which is to reveal and chronicle the outrage, at times tempered with laughter, stemming from the violation of the self by a broken world. Through the effective use of gothic conventions Jackson reveals the contours of human madness and loneliness in a disintegrating world generally bereft of the meliorating power of love and forgiveness.[2]

The broken world depicted in Shirley Jackson's fiction, with its attendant madness and possibilities of evil, has been the subject of much analysis in recent years. Robert Jay Lifton writes of the breakdown of

*This essay originally appeared in* Twentieth Century Literature *30 (1984): 15–29 and is reproduced here with the permission of* Twentieth Century Literature.

fundamental human boundaries due to several major "psychohistorical" developments—a loss of a vital and nourishing connection with the cultural past, the flooding of imagery produced by the mass media, and the threat of nuclear disaster. These forces have brought about what he calls an "Age of Numbing."[3] Rollo May describes the contemporary experience as schizoid where people are out of touch with their feelings and thus avoid close relationships.[4] R.D. Laing argues that contemporary culture is schizophrenic and that schizophrenia is an understandable response to a mad world, a strategy for survival.[5] Similarly, the philosopher Lionel Rubinoff writes that "modern man has been so violated that he is virtually looking for an excuse to go mad, and he will seize every opportunity to do so."[6] Expanding on the arguments of Laing and using a phenomenological analysis of culture, John Vernon argues that schizophrenia is the defining characteristic of Western culture—it is a culture that polarizes and compartmentalizes reality, fragments experience into opposites, thus repressing the possibilities of unity between self and world. This kind of structure Vernon calls a "map"—"that schizophrenic structure whereby areas of experience are extricated from each other and arranged in discrete spaces from each other, often as opposites."[7] Twentieth century consciousness, Vernon argues, is undergoing a shift from the map to the garden—a structure that unites opposites, enabling all areas of experience to be accessible to each other, a shift from polarization to unity. For Vernon, as for others, our very survival may depend upon the success of that shift.

Feminist critics are also building on the radical psychology of R.D. Laing, seeing madness largely as a political event stemming from female oppression in a male-dominated culture. Phyllis Chesler, in her book *Women and Madness,* strongly criticizes traditional psychotherapy for reflecting and sustaining an image of woman that emphasizes her helplessness and dependency upon male authority figures. Accordingly, to enforce or expect compliance with rigid sex roles is more causative than curative of some forms of madness in women. Barbara Hill Rigney develops the insights of Laing and Chesler, among others, and applies them to an analysis of selected novels by Charlotte Brontë, Virginia Woolf, Doris Lessing, and Margaret Atwood. According to Rigney, the novels present

> a criticism of a patriarchal, political, and social system, a universe dominated by masculine energy, which, in itself, manifests a kind of collusive madness in the form of war or sexual oppression and is thereby seen as threatening to feminine psychological survival. Most of these novels depict a female protagonist who, in spite of such oppression, achieves a superior sanity and at least a relative liberty in the assertion of a self.[8]

While some of the novels by Shirley Jackson reveal a similar pattern, very few of her protagonists achieve much of a victory over oppression. Indeed most of Jackson's protagonists are emotionally violated and must struggle desperately to overcome their estrangement and dislocation, and most of them fail.

Appearing in the same year as her famous story "The Lottery," Jackson's first novel, *The Road Through the Wall* (1948), chronicles the collapse of a small community due to its own inner demonic contradictions. By focusing upon a whole neighborhood, rather than upon a single violated protagonist as in her other novels, the novel creates an effective metaphor or microcosm for the tensions inherent in the culture in the postwar period. Moreover, whether the protagonist is individual or collective, the novel adumbrates and begins exploration of one of Jackson's primary concerns throughout her career: the dark incomprehensible spot or stain upon the human soul and our continuing blindness and, hence, vulnerability to it. Jackson's fiction refuses to compromise with the glib psychologies of our therapeutic age.

The story takes place in Cabrillo, a fictitious suburb of San Francisco, in 1936. It concerns a group of families and single individuals who live side by side in relative privacy and in apparent harmony, a kind of cross section of middle-class and upper-class aspiring families. Their children attend school together and share the street in play. Some of the parents gather weekly for sewing, and less frequently for parties. The apparent security and equilibrium of this community are broken and destroyed by a series of events. The first important event is the tearing down of the wall in order to extend and join Pepper Street with the one beyond the wall. This serves as a kind of catalyst for the rest of the action and the climax of the story. A three-year-old girl is discovered missing from a party at one of the homes, necessitating an all-out search. Missing also is a 13-year-old boy who "acted funny." Panic and wild imaginings spread. The little girl is soon found dead, her head smashed in by a rock. The boy is accused of murder, but before anything is found out he hangs himself. The important thing about the novel is not the plot but, rather—as in most of Shirley Jackson's stories—the gradual unfolding of the layers of human personality, sometimes in response to, at other times causative of, events.

The novel operates on two complementary levels. On one level the novel presents an exposure and examination of the social morals and manners of a community. The presence of a Jewish family and the incipient and, at times, outright anti–Semitism of the community, and the hidden envies due to economic differences are instances of this. These are symptomatic of what is going on at a deeper level—the level of the inner workings of the personality; and this is ultimately what the novel is seeking to delineate. The real world of the novel is not the world of social realism. There are enough features about it to indicate otherwise. The way the novel begins gives it the quality of the fairy tale or fable: "The weather falls more gently on some places than on others, the world looks down more paternally on some people. Some spots are proverbially warm, and keep, through falling snow, their untarnished reputations as summer resorts; some people are automatically above suspicion." And the use of the old gothic convention of the old woman making prophecies is further evidence that the novel is not just concerned with social conflicts. Its concern is with the inner demonic cancer of the community and how it eats away and destroys not only individuals but families and the social unit as a whole. In short, beneath the mask of the ordinary lies unrecognized terror.

The Road Through the Wall exemplifies what Irving Malin calls the "new American gothic," in which the psyche is given priority over society, or, in Malin's words, "the disorder of the buried life must be chartered."[10] The new American gothic employs a microcosm, with love as a primary concern. The weakling characters struggle with narcissism, which often destroys others as well as themselves. Their narcissism leads them to make reality into a reflecting mirror of their own compulsions. The chief microcosm is the family, which "dramatizes the conflict between private and social worlds, ego and super-ego."[11] In the new American gothic, as in old gothic, there is often a confused chronology and dreamlike quality about the narrative. The old conventions of the gothic—the haunted castle or house, the voyage or flight, and the reflection—function now as images of narcissistic love and antagonism. Nearly all journeys end in failure or disaster. The narcissism of the characters intensifies their isolation and loneliness, creating a kind of vicious, self-destructive cycle.

Using the neighborhood as her microcosm, Jackson presents a series of short glimpses into the households on the street—the tangled relationships, the lovelessness, which produces its own poison that strangles and chokes off spontaneous life. The youngster accused of murdering the three-year-old girl is a victim of familial lovelessness. The evidence against him is circumstantial at best, but, with few exceptions, the street accepts his guilt. The crime or accident raises the larger issue of human responsibility. The novel depicts a community so fragile and sick that the ultimate responsibility is diffuse and all are implicated; no one is innocent. That few even glimpse this possibility betokens a community bereft of imagination and morally bankrupt.

Against this background of communal failure, Jackson moves in her second novel, Hangsaman (1951), into an initiation story tracing the descent into madness of an individual protagonist and her apparent return to a tenuous grasp upon reality. Natalie Waite, a college freshman, spends half her time in an imaginary world where she is being questioned by a detective regarding a murder; leaves family and home for college and faces loneliness, hostility, and rejection by most of her peers; encounters the duplicity of institutions and adult life; falls into a relationship with a strange girl named Tony, who may herself be wholly imaginary; and comes near to a loss of self through absorption or suicide before finally emerging from the woods, literally as well as figuratively, to a new self-understanding and a new approach to tangible reality. Natalie does, however, make the frightful transition from innocence of a sort to experience, to the beginning of adult life. Leslie Fiedler writes of the handling of this passage in much recent literature: "Most serious writers in the twentieth century ... have given up the notion of seduction as well as that of redemption; they are no more moved by the concept of corruption than they are by that of salvation, substituting for the more traditional fable of a fall to evil that of an initiation into good and evil."[12] While seduction and sex figure in Natalie's initiation, her final crossing is a kind of death and rebirth into a world solid but devoid of moral absolutes.

Natalie needs to escape from the heavy dominance of an egotistical and narcissistic father who seeks to create Natalie in his own image. Her mother has escaped from her dominating husband by fleeing into drink so that she offers no solace to Natalie in her time of need. Natalie's only outlet has been her rich imagination and fantasy life, to which she turns to escape the intrusive assaults of her father. At her college, Natalie becomes enamored of her literature instructor, but, as she gets to know him, she sees that he is selfish and cruel towards his wife and that his success is due more to his charm than to his intellect—in short, he is no better than her father. Thus, with the men in her life betraying her, and without any help or guidance from her mother, Natalie is ripe for a fall into madness.

Out of desperation and loneliness, Natalie retreats deep into herself and her rich fantasy life. Writing fervently in her secret journal, she dreams of a time when people will fear her and she will be revered and respected. She lives with the feeling that something momentous is about to happen to her. She develops a close relationship with Tony, another despised girl on campus. To Natalie, Tony is exotic, clever, intelligent, and self-possessed. However, it is not clear throughout the novel whether Tony is real or an imagined creation that fulfills Natalie's need. In any case, Tony functions as Natalie's Doppelgänger, and as such represents Natalie's own growing fragmentation and self-alienation. Together they read the Tarot cards and walk about the town like two Alices in a Wonderland of their own making. From the significantly named Paradise Park, the winter-abandoned recreation area, Tony leads Natalie into the woods for a decisive encounter. If Tony is real, the scene may suggest a

homosexual seduction or a kind of vampirism by her dark double, as in
some of Poe's stories, or possibly even suicide. As a fantasy projection,
the threat is psychic destruction through narcissistic nihilism. In either
case, Natalie loses self and retreats from reality. But at the last moment,
Natalie repels the dark other's embrace and returns to the school and to
a renewed sense of reality. Out of her own inner resources, Natalie is
able to repel the threat of her "dark lady" and make a successful, though
perilous, passage to the world of experience and the knowledge of good
and evil.

Shirley Jackson's fiction is filled with lonely, desperate women who
reflect the disintegrations of modern life. This is seen quite clearly in Elizabeth Richmond, the disintegrating protagonist of *The Bird's Nest* (1954),
Jackson's third novel. She is 23 years old when we first meet her in the
novel, and lives with her eccentric maiden aunt, Morgen Jones, in an ugly,
almost gothic, house. Her mother died when Elizabeth was 19, and since
that time she has not spoken intimately with anyone; her life has become
a virtual blank. She works in the upstairs office of the local museum
because her aunt felt the job would give Elizabeth a more definite identity. But when the museum begins to undergo renovation, Elizabeth's
precarious hold on reality slips, and she falls prey to a form of "possession" all too common in the modern world. As Rollo May describes it:
"Loneliness and its stepchild, alienation, can become forms of demon
possession. Surrendering ourselves to the impersonal daimonic pushes
us into an anonymity which is also impersonal; we serve nature's gross
purposes on the lowest common denominator, which often means with
violence."[13] The violence in which Elizabeth indulges, as her demons
come to the surface to haunt her, is a convoluted kind turned against her
own fragile self.

While Shirley Jackson was a lifelong student of mental illness, and
all of her novels explore some aspect of the inner life, *The Bird's Nest* is
doubtless her most overtly psychological novel. She got the idea for the
novel in part from reading Morton Prince's 1905 study entitled *The Dissociation of a Personality,* which records the case of a person with several
successive personalities. Besides the complex psychic struggles of the
patient, Jackson was also struck by the role of the psychiatrist, and how
oblivious he appeared to the possibility that the various personalities of
his patient might be creations of his own imagination. This same obtuse-
ness is made a part of the character of the novel's Dr. Victor Wright, the
rather oddball metapsychiatrist who patterns himself after Thackeray.
This purblind but essentially benevolent doctor treats Elizabeth for two
years with the use of hypnosis. When he discovers four competing personalities in Elizabeth, he gives each one a name and sets out to fulfill
the godlike role of creating a new person. He definitely likes some of the

personalities better than others; indeed, he recoils instinctively from the demonic aspects of Elizabeth's psyche and seeks to destroy them in the name of his self-declared superior judgment and goodness. Despite his benevolence, it is quite clear that the pretentious good doctor is not aware of the implications of his treatment. He is dividing being down the middle, separating evil from good, denying the one for the other, and thereby tampering with the wholeness of a human soul. The doctor may be operating on an ideal yet false understanding of human nature. In this regard, Dr. Wright—called "Dr. Wrong" by one of Elizabeth's personalities—is not unlike Carwin the Ventriloquist in Charles Brockden Brown's *Wieland*, a kind of obtuse psychologist who does not realize how serious the consequences of his experiments may be.

Unlike Natalie of *Hangsaman*, who had no adult guides to turn to on her journey, Elizabeth is aided by the eccentric Aunt Morgen, whose quick but masculine and coarse wit makes her a perfect foil for the pompous Dr. Wright. It is from Aunt Morgen that Elizabeth learns the truth about her mother's death—Elizabeth was not to blame for it as she had believed. With the release from guilt, Elizabeth is able to make the journey back to wholeness—her four personalities disappear and a new one emerges. At the end the doctor and Morgen assign her a new name, Victoria Morgen, thus making her a product of both their imaginations, an ending not without irony and ambiguity. The novel, as do Jackson's first two, employs several features of the gothic. While the gothic mansion is not given much prominence, it is described as an ugly monstrosity well suited to an eccentric maiden aunt. There is the journey or flight from imprisonment when Elizabeth escapes to New York in search of her mother; there is the reflection when the disintegrating Elizabeth sees her image in all the shiny surfaces of a room, symbolizing her growing schizophrenia and loss of control; and there are the split personalities that were always cropping up in Poe and the vampire novels.

The gothic house is a prominent feature of Jackson's last three novels. It serves not just as the focus of action or as atmosphere, but as a force or influence upon character or a reflection of character. In Irving Malin's terms, the house stands as "the metaphor of confining narcissism, the private world."[14] The house not only reflects the insanities of its occupants, but serves as a fitting microcosm of the madness of the world.

One is used prominently in *The Sundial* (1958), which employs all the gothic conventions for comic and satiric purposes. Susan Sontag, in her essay "The Imagination of Disaster," which explores the cultural significance of fantasy and science fiction films, writes: "Ours is indeed an age of extremity. For we live under continual threat of two equally fearful, but seemingly opposed destinies: unremitting banality and inconceivable

terror."[15] When both of these elements are combined in one novel, you
have the makings of what Richard Poirier refers to as "the comic apocalyptic,"[16] a term providing an apt description for Shirley Jackson's fourth
novel.

Showing her ability to find pity and terror in the ludicrous and the
ludicrous in terror, Jackson created a fantasy of the end of the world that
parodies the apocalyptic imagination while at the same time portraying
it. The novel is a full exposition of the poem by William Empson titled
"Just a Smack at Auden."

At the end of the novel 11 self-elected survivors of the imminent end
of the world are all there waiting, with Mrs. Halloran dead and propped
up against the sundial on the lawn of the great Halloran estate, the windows and doors battened down from the inside as protection against the
growing winds of doom. Some play bridge. Others talk of the realism of
a recent movie. A few drink Scotch and yawn in anticipation. "'My.'
Mrs. Willow stretched, and sighed. 'It's going to be a long wait,' she
said."[17] Indeed it is, for we leave them feeling that they will still be waiting to enter their hoped for brave new world when the supplies they have
stored in the library have been used up. The disconfirmation of apocalypse will doubtless lead only to new "revelations" and to new calcula-
tions for their waiting game. No matter, for they have already sealed their
doom, which this grisly tale of comic horror and fantasy reveals.

The novel is concerned with the nature of belief, with the way desperate people grasp a belief and make it their truth; with how belief
and madness combine, in turn, and lead to more desperate behavior;
with how belief can be a form of madness itself, making people into
grotesques. Jackson portrays 12 people who become grotesques because
they need, and desperately want, to believe in the apocalyptic revelations
of the mad spinster Aunt Fanny, who herself is in a desperate contest, a
power struggle for control of the massive Halloran estate with the matriarch Mrs. Halloran. Before Mrs. Halloran can gain total control of the
estate and carry out her threatened banishments, Aunt Fanny has a "revelation" from her dead father of the impending end of the world. The
only survivors, he reveals, will be the residents of the Halloran mansion,
who will enter a new and better world. Because everyone else longs to
accept the revelations as fact, Mrs. Halloran is forced to accede to their
belief and attempts to control a household of people who now regard
themselves as a new chosen race.

In preparation for the new day, the Halloran clan burn all the books
in the library and stock it with tons of food and supplies, and, remembering Robinson Crusoe, a grindstone, several shotguns, and hunting
knives. Mrs. Halloran draws up a list of rules for conduct in the new era,
setting herself as the sole monarch. But Mrs. Halloran fails in her attempt

to control both present and future, for on the night before the expected new day, she falls or is pushed down the stairs, and her corpse is propped up against the sundial on the lawn.

The insane revelations of Aunt Fanny speak to a sense of loss and of the possibility of recovery that each within the house feels. Each is filled with what one of the characters calls "a kind of unholy, unspeakable longing." It takes over the self: "It is a longing so intense that it creates what it desires, it cannot endure any touch of correction" (*S* 62). This longing feeds the need to believe, no matter how bizarre the belief. And yet, at one point in their preparations, Mrs. Halloran remarks, "I wonder what nonsense we would be engaged in, if we were not doing this," to which her courtier, Essex, replies, "It is probably just as well that we have some nonsense to occupy us; just think of the harm we could do if we were bored" (*S* 100). Mrs. Halloran and Essex, on one level at least, still realize that what they are engaged in is a fiction, a masquerade, a game, and can indulge in irony about it. But as they continue to play, the game becomes reality, each player acts in deadly earnest, and they become trapped in their own fiction and lose the capacity to change it. What begins as "harmless nonsense" evolves into a game involving unimagined consequences. The novel satirizes a human condition in which gullibility, cupidity and culpability reign virtually unrestrained by moral principle, and create a community of the survival of the worst.

In *The Sundial* Shirley Jackson portrays the elitism of the apocalyptic mind that sees only itself as being worthy of survival and salvation. It is an imagination that accepts powerlessness and surrenders human responsibility to what it regards as an overpowering destiny, in the name of which any crime is possible. To the Halloran household the world will end and begin again with itself as the inheritor. This is an example of what John R. May calls "presumptive eschatology" of a secular imagination that sees a simple continuation of history after the cataclysm.[18] Here, there is no sense of judgment and renewal in connection with the cataclysm as in traditional apocalypse.[19] A new world is expected, but no personal renewal is promised or demanded, implying no change at all in the human condition.

The Halloran clan do not even shrink from murder on the eve of their new day. Their self-deception begins as a potentially humorous masquerade party, but in their desperate belief it quickly leads to the burning of books, the disengagement from life, and to the declaring of themselves as a new race of men. For the rest of mankind they feel little more than pity, or, more than likely, contempt. To theologians, apocalypse, properly conceived, is a message of hope for a people in stress and crisis, for it provides a context for the faithful to understand themselves and to act. But this understanding of apocalypse, essentially a biblical one, contrasts sharply with the pretensions of the Halloran party. They long for a revelation without judgment, and thus without renewal as well. Because they lack courage to live responsibly in the present world and because they lack hope for the future, they abdicate their humanness for the apocalyptic visions of a madwoman, and choose to substitute appearance for reality, a dangerous fiction for life. They should have been listening when the nurse read from *Robinson Crusoe* to Mr. Halloran: "A little after noon I found the sea very calm, and the tide ebbed so far that I could come within a quarter mile of the ship, and here I found a fresh renewing of my grief; for I saw evidently, that if we had kept on board, we had been all safe" (*S* 41). Believing themselves to have escaped time, history, and death, they fail to see that the question on the sundial is still their riddle: "WHAT IS THIS WORLD?"

While a setting for what begins as a mad masquerade party in *The Sundial*, the gothic house in a real sense is the chief character of *The Haunting of Hill House* (1959), Jackson's fifth and probably most popular novel. Its presence is felt on nearly every page. The house is over 80 years old and carries the unsavory reputation of death, madness, revenge, and suicide. It is marked by "clashing disharmony," everything off center, made entirely at "wrong angles," all the small aberrations adding up to a rather large distortion. Its basic structure is laid out in concentric circles, with rooms surrounded by other rooms—a "mother house." It is a fitting metaphor for madness, for the irrational, for an illogic that perversely coheres. In classic gothic fiction, as Devendra P. Varma reminds us, "the element of terror is inseparably associated with the Gothic castle, which is an image of power, dark, isolated, and impenetrable." To the Romantic movement and in gothic fiction "the castle stands as a central image of the lonely personality."[20] It is this house that welcomes home the utterly guilt-ridden, lonely, and loveless protagonist, Eleanor Vance, who surrenders willingly to its dark embraces, her own fragile self dissolving and fusing with the substance of Hill House.

Eleanor Vance, another of Jackson's violated women, is brought to Hill House as part of a scientific experiment into psychic phenomena. She is so fragile and vulnerable that her survival is questionable from the beginning. Her chief foil, reminiscent of Dr. Wright of *The Bird's Nest*, is Dr. Montague, a pompous academic representing scientific rationalism and logic. He is little more than an intellectual voyeur, knowing very much but really understanding very little, especially when it comes to the mysteries of the human personality and the human heart. Terror and fear, the fatuous doctor believes, can be explained and controlled in terms of logic and will: "Fear ... is the relinquishment of logic, the *willing* relinquishment of reasonable patterns. We yield to it or we fight it, but we cannot meet it half way."[21] This militant rationalist shows little compassion for Eleanor's loss of sanity and banishes her from the house to protect his so-called experiment.

The character Theodora is another of Jackson's "dark ladies," recalling the figure of Tony in *Hangsaman*. She is the opposite of Eleanor. She is secular and much experienced, exotic and exciting, representing, in part, what Eleanor might have been if her life had not been so restricted and inhibited. At times Theodora's ministrations to Eleanor verge on the lesbian. At other times she ridicules Eleanor, and when Eleanor desperately reaches out for help, Theodora turns away, abandoning her to her lonely dissolution. If Theodora functions partly as Eleanor's Doppelgänger, she does so in the sense of representing what Barbara Hill Rigney refers to as "the tragedy of one's own fragmentation and alienation from the self."[22]

There is no place in the world for Eleanor. Unlike the Apollonian Dr. Montague, the Dionysian and cynical Theodora, Eleanor has no resources to call upon for survival. Her loneliness and schizophrenia find a welcome in the chaos of Hill House. If Eleanor is abandoned to suicide, the house remains unconquerable, eluding the vain assaults of rationality and pointing to the mysterious and incomprehensible.

The gothic mode serves well Jackson's purpose to explore the depths and contours of female violation in the modern world. Alfred Kazin writes that "'woman's fiction' exists not as writing by women but as inordinate defensiveness against a society conceived as the special enemy of the sensitive."[23] In Jackson, he says, the stories reveal a pattern of "assault, deception, betrayal," where a woman as victim is the protagonist and her defenselessness is the story. While we may disagree with his assessment of "woman's fiction," his suggested pattern applies well to most of the protagonists of Jackson's novels.

Violation, in the sense of assault, deception, and betrayal, is the concern of Jackson's sixth and last complete novel, *We Have Always Lived in the Castle* (1962). Here also, as in so much of Jackson's work, there is a sense of primal sin and darkness pervading a world where forgiveness is lacking, where love is ambiguous, where hatred and hostility are all too ready to surface into action.

In contrast to the dark despair of the fifth novel, the movement of this one is from a precarious and volatile form of order through chaos to a new order of things, also fragile and precarious, but perhaps enduring. It moves from a situation where the Blackwoods are caught between internal fear and external anger, through the chaos of terror and violence, during which time the top story of the Blackwood mansion is gutted by fire and the house ravaged by hostile villagers, to a new order, not wholly of this world, which is referred to as "life on the moon."

For the first time in Jackson's novels, the tale of violation and defenselessness is told by a first-person narrator, the mad 18-year-old Merricat Blackwood, who murdered four members of her family with arsenic six years before the story starts. Merricat's older sister, Constance, was accused but acquitted for lack of evidence. For six years they have lived in constant tension with the villagers, who resent the Blackwoods for their wealth and for the fact that mass murder went unpunished. To Merricat the village is a wasteland filled with gray, drab, and hateful people, while her "castle" is a place of peace, light and harmony. Constance is a virtual handmaiden of nature, raising and canning fruits and vegetables, and tending flowers all over the estate.

The volatile tension between the lovely, pastoral Blackwood home and the hostile, resentful village wasteland breaks into violence soon after cousin Charles Blackwood comes to visit. Ostensibly coming to help Constance, it is clear that he is really after the Blackwood fortune. Merricat senses his threat to their idyllic existence and seeks to purge the estate of his presence. When a fire breaks out, cousin Charles brings in the villagers to help. In a scene of terror reminiscent of Hawthorne's witches' Sabbath in "Young Goodman Brown," the villagers go on a rampage through the house and Merricat and Constance flee to the woods. When they return the next morning their proud mansion is a gutted ruin, but the two women close themselves in to create a new life in the remaining rooms. Some people come to help but are not received. Many of the villagers return at night and leave baskets of food with notes of apology.

The novel closes with the image of a ruin nearly completely covered with vines with two sisters huddled in fragile happiness within it. In old gothic literature, as Devendra P. Varma reminds us, "a ruin is not only a thing of loveliness but also an expression of Nature's power over the creations of man.... Ruins are proud effigies of sinking greatness, the visual and static representations of tragic mystery"[24] and are perhaps all that can survive in the gothic vision. There is indeed a sense of tragic mystery about the fall of the Blackwood house. However, one feels that it is not so much the triumph of nature over human arrogance and pride that the vine-covered ruin represents. Rather, it can be seen as nature covering and protecting her own against the assaults of a vengeful and violent world. In a very real sense, the Blackwood sisters are children of nature, though not in perfect harmony with it because of the lingering guilt-burden of the murders. The ruin symbolizes not only their crime, but also the crime of dark retribution perpetrated against them in anarchic passion by the maddened villagers. The real horror of the novel comes not so much from the unpunished murders by a 12-year-old child, but largely from the inexplicable madness and violence of the so-called normal and ordinary people of the world outside the Blackwood home.

Like her story "The Lottery," *We Have Always Lived in the Castle* has to do with a kind of primordial sense of sin and defilement, which casts an ambiguous character upon love and forgiveness. The novel explores the dark dynamics of a virtually pre-ethical level of human experience—defilement, dread, retribution, revenge. This is the level where evil and personal suffering are still connected. Fault gives rise to the anticipation of punishment, which strengthens the bond between doing evil and suffering ill. This pre-ethical sense of defilement and vengeance is opposed in the novel by an ethical order of innocent sacrificial love and forgiveness, as seen in the figure of Constance and the world she creates. The villagers, representative of the world, cannot or will not forgive without an act of vengeance or retribution—hence, the mindless outbreak of violence and rage against the helpless Blackwood sisters. Perhaps this violence is somehow necessary; it has its role, its part to play in the mysterious dynamics of forgiveness and atonement. It does lead to a new order of love, though a fragile and precarious one because the world about it is still uncomprehending and unable to accept forgiveness obviating retribution. Love seeks to bring order out of chaos and strength out of weakness, and perhaps the ruin of the castle will symbolize that, as well as the shame of lovelessness.

Shirley Jackson's gothic fiction is an effective mode for her exploration of the violations of the human self—the aching loneliness, the unendurable guilt, the dissolution and disintegrations, the sinking into madness, the violence and lovelessness. Her fiction fits well the description John Hawkes gives of several modern authors:

> There is a quality of coldness, detachment, ruthless determination to face up to the enormity of ugliness and potential failure with ourselves and in the world about us, and to bring to this exposure a savage or saving comic spirit and the saving beauties of language. The need is to maintain the truth of the fractured picture; to expose, ridicule, attack, but always to create and to throw into new light our potential for violence and absurdity as well as for graceful action.[25]

This applies well to many of Jackson's fictions, especially to *We Have Always Lived in the Castle,* where disorderly or mad love summoned up evil darkness, setting in relief the bright light of forgiveness. As Paul Ricoeur declares: "The fear of not loving enough is the purest and worst of fears."[26] In the tales of Shirley Jackson, poetic justice and moral virtue do not win out as in many popular gothics and fairy tales, for she is true to her vision of the evil of our time. And she places her trust in the fact that if a tale is good and powerful, one need not explain or defend it; one need only tell it.

# *Notes*

1. Shirley Jackson, *The Lottery* (New York: Avon, 1971), 110.

2. Lenemaja Friedman's *Shirley Jackson* (Boston: Twayne, 1975) discusses Jackson's use of gothic conventions in a context and focus different from mine.

3. Robert Jay Lifton, *Boundaries* (New York: Vintage Books, 1970), 43 ff.

4. Rollo May, *Love and Will* (New York: Norton, 1969), 16.

5. R.D. Laing, *The Politics of Experience* (New York: Ballantine Books, 1967), 114–15, and passions.

6. Lionel Rubinoff, *The Pornography of Power* (New York: Ballantine Books, 1968), 83.

7. John Vernon, *The Garden and the Map: Schizophrenia in Twentieth Century Literature and Culture* (Urbana: University of Illinois Press, 1973), xi–xii.

8. Barbara Hill Rigney, *Madness and Sexual Politics in the Feminist Novel* (Madison: University of Wisconsin Press, 1978), 7.

9. Shirley Jackson, *The Road Through the Wall* (New York: MacFadden, 1969), 7.

10. Irving Malin, *New American Gothic* (Carbondale: Southern Illinois University Press, 1962), 5.

11. Ibid. 8.

12. Leslie Fiedler, *No! In Thunder* (Boston: Beacon Press, 1960), 279.

13. May, *Love and Will*, 162.

14. Malin, *New American Gothic*, 80.

15. Susan Sontag, *Against Interpretation* (New York: Farrar, 1966), 224.

16. Richard Poirier, *A World Elsewhere* (New York: Oxford University Press, 1966), 251.

17. Shirley Jackson, *The Sundial* (New York: Ace Books, 1958), 192. Future quotes from this novel appear parenthetically in the text, cited as *S*.

18. John R. May, *Toward a New Earth: Apocalypse in the American Novel* (Notre Dame: University of Notre Dame Press, 1972), 37.

19. Ibid. 24.

20. Deveandra P. Varma, *The Gothic Flame* (London: Arthur Baker, 1957), 18–19.

21. Shirley Jackson, *The Haunting of Hill House* (New York: Popular Library, 1959), p. 113.

22. Rigney, *Madness and Sexual Politics in the Feminist Novel*, 10.

23. Alfred Kazin, *Bright Book of Life* (Boston: Little, Brown, 1973), 174.

24. Varna, *The Gothic Flame*, 204.

25. Quoted in Tony Tanner, *City of Words* (New York: Harper, 1972), 204.

26. Paul Ricoeur, *The Symbolism of Evil*, trans. Emerson Buchanan (Boston: Beacon Press, 1969).

# 13

# Steven Spielberg's *The Haunting*: A Reconsideration of David Self's Script

## DARRYL HATTENHAUER

Filmmakers have produced two adaptations of Shirley Jackson's novel *The Haunting of Hill House*. The first adaptation, which appeared in 1963, is almost universally acclaimed. The second adaptation, which appeared in 1999, is almost universally condemned.[1] It received four Razzie nominations: worst picture, worst director (Jan de Bont), worst actress (Catherine Zeta-Jones), and worst screenplay (David Self). Most reviewers and critics find that the screenwriter is as blameworthy as everybody else. But David Self's screenplay reveals that the worst of the movie is not in his screenplay; rather, the best of the movie is in his screenplay, and the parts of his screenplay that are not in the movie would have made for a much better production.[2]

David Self is a very successful screenwriter who rose to the top in just four years. After *The Haunting*, which was his first produced screenplay, his next produced screenplay was *Thirteen Days*, the financially and critically successful treatment of the Cuban missile crisis. His third produced screenplay was the even more successful *Road to Perdition*, which was directed by Sam Mendes (who also directed *American Beauty*) and starred Tom Hanks and Paul Newman. He also did an uncredited rewrite of *The Bourne Identity*. Recent reports have him rewriting *Gates of Fire* for Universal. He has now been entrusted with another high-visibility project, *The Sub-Mariner*. This time he is both a screenwriter and an executive producer—for seven figures ("The Sub-Mariner"). Whatever

251

the faults of Hollywood producers, they evidently recognized that the strengths and not the weaknesses of *The Haunting* were attributable to David Self.

His life and education prepared him for success. He has a B.A. and an M.A. in English from Stanford, which has produced many success-ful writers—for example, Ken Kesey. His interview in *Creative Screen-writing* reveals his knowledge of not only the novel and classical drama, but also film—especially the historical and crime genres. But if the review-ers had had their way, Self would have gone through life with only one of his scripts produced—a fate not uncommon in an industry where incompetent reviewers often sink the best talents and buoy up the worst.

However, the reviewers of this film simply do not know what they're talking about. Those who assume that the screenwriter is responsible for the finished product's plot, characters, dialogue, sets, stage directions, and theme simply do not know how movies get made. Once the writer submits the screenplay, it gets changed by other writers, the producers, the director, and sometimes even the actors.[3] Self's screenplay was rad-ically revised by Michael Tolkin, and Tolkin's revision in turn is very different from the film. Another common assumption is that a screen-play can and should reproduce a novel. For example, Laura Clifford asks, "Why mess with a story by one of America's greatest, Shirley Jackson?" (7). The most common theory informing the reviews is the fallacy that if the movie does not scare the reviewer, it is a bad movie. Such reviews bypass the mind and report on the glands. Many reviewers comment that the cherubs were not scary, but by definition, cherubs are not scary. Similarly, Joe Mauceri states that it is easy to tell that the 1999 adapta-tion was bad and the 1963 adaptation was good because his 12-year-old nephew laughed at the new film and shuddered at the old one (2). Mauceri does not wonder if the new version is over the child's head while the old version is suitable for children. Some of the reviews are so lame that it makes one reconsider the right of free speech. For example, Ted Prigge complains that a character who gets killed is played by a good actor (2). Apparently Prigge assumes that all characters who are killed should be played by bad actors.

If the reviewers often do not understand the concept of what nov-els and movies are, they also fail to report even the simplest facts accu-rately. Luther Manning and Mike Oliveri not only misspell Luke Sanderson's last name, but they misspell it the same way: "Sannerson" (2; 2). This coincidence suggests that one of these writers plagiarized the other. Indeed, so many commentators say the same things that it seems they not only plagiarized each other but also skipped watching the film. For example, many object that the characters can unlock the front gate at the start of the movie yet not at the end. But the characters who leave in the beginning take the only key with them. Another reviewer who does not get his facts straight is Richard von Busack. He calls Jackson "a San Francisco author" (1). Apparently the only research he did on her was to look up her birthplace. Other reviewers make similar errors. Ed Kelleher refers to *The Haunting of Hill House* as a "novella" (1), and Eddie Cockrell calls it a "short story" (2).

If most of the reviewers do not understand the genres of film and novel, neither do they understand the subgenres of gothic and horror.[4] They seem to judge this film by the standards of realism (that most unrealistic of modes). For example, John J. Puccio complains that there is no explanation of where Dr. Marrow gets the money to rent the house, and how it can be vacant. If Puccio had paid more attention to the film than the popcorn, he would have noticed that research funds paid the rent, and the house is vacant because—duh—it is haunted. More importantly, most films should not have to explain the obvious, and reviewers who think they do need another vocation—or, more accurately, avocation. Also, a reviewer should not ask questions impertinent to the genre at hand. Asking such realistic questions about nonrealist genres is tantamount to asking Captain Ahab what he would do if he caught the whale. Such reviewers show no awareness that gothic and horror, especially in film, have a general set of conventions, and that these conventions condition audience expectations and responses. For example, Dan Craft claims that this movie calls for "understatement" (3). Gothic calls for understatement? Horror exemplifies understatement? Poe relied on understatement? Similarly, Rob Blackwelder complains about "such shopworn gimmicks as slowly creeping doorknobs" (2). But these are definitive conventions of gothic and horror. He might as well complain about a Western because it has a sheriff. Moreover, such complaints miss the intertextuality of the film. The slowly turning doorknob is a motif not only in the novel and first adaptation, but also of gothic and horror in general. The film keeps too few of Self's allusions to *Aliens, Citizen Kane, Cool Hand Luke, Ghostbusters, Labyrinth, The Omen, Poltergeist,* and *The Shining*. But the reviewers would have missed them anyway.

If the reviewers do not understand novels and films, it is not surprising that they fault David Self for the film's ruinous dénouement because they assume (incorrectly) that he is the one who wrote it. For example, Matt Easterbrook states, "Whoever wrote the final fifteen minutes, namely David Self, should be tossed head first into an iron maiden" (2). The ending is indeed deplorable. The decapitation is gratuitous, and the scene's special effects are not at all special—and this in a film that otherwise emphasizes technology. Almost as bad is that the film has a skeleton pop out of the ashes. Self's version is more significant. Eleanor pulls the poker out of the ashes, and two skulls are stuck to it. One is a

Shirley Jackson

child's, and the other is Crain's with his cranium bashed in. Mrs. Crain killed him to prevent him from killing their last child. I'd like to think that she also wanted to prevent Hugh Crain from writing film reviews.

Departing from Self's script, the film shows Eleanor transforming first into a soldier and then into a savior. Swinging her mighty sword, she fends off an attacking gargoyle. She is also a young tough when, in effect, she challenges Hugh Crain's ghost to put up his dukes. Moreover, she announces piously, "The children need me, and I'm going to set them free." In one of the worst lines ever inflicted on a movie audience, Eleanor declares, "It's about family!" And in one of the worst plot resolutions ever inflicted on a movie audience, Eleanor releases the souls of the children from purgatory, who then ascend to heaven, taking Eleanor with them. After shouting to Crain, "You go to hell," she deploys her supernatural powers in a kind of prisoner exchange and gets the demons of purgatory to take Crain's ghost and release the souls of the children. After she is martyred as a result of freeing the children from the slavery of purgatory and delivering them to the promised land, one almost expects her to morph into Abraham Lincoln. Instead, she looks like Jesus (with Dr. Marrow and Theo at the Crucifixion, the Pietà, and the Ascension all compressed into seconds). Although the critics overlook the weak ending in both the novel and first adaptation, they are right about the second adaptation's deplorable conclusion. Likewise, they are right about the second adaptation's weak beginning, which is unnecessarily slow and contains two unnecessary characters who leave due to a medical emergency and are not heard from again, even though Dr. Marrow tells them to call as soon as they talk to a doctor. Maybe they are not heard from again because they are so superfluous that somebody (the producers? the director?) forgot about them.

But none of that is in Self's screenplay. Abbie Bernstein reports that reshooting resulted in the ridiculous ending (2). And according to Edward Johnson-Ott, it was "the studio" that ordered de Bont to reshoot the ending, which could mean that any one or more of the producers are to blame (1). Andy Dursin states it was Steven Spielberg himself who ordered the "tampering" (3). At any rate, the result is that a bad turning point and denouement overshadow what is otherwise a good movie. As James Berardinelli notes, "The first half of *The Haunting* is surprisingly absorbing" (2). Similarly, James Kendrick writes of "the better, more restrained work that went into the first half of the film" (3).

Most commentators give Self no credit for imagining the house, even though it is one of the best things about the movie. Disparagements of the house range only from the uninformed to the ill-informed. Bill Chambers states, "Nobody would spend a night here" (5). While that is true of real life and realistic attempts to represent it, gothic and horror have long employed the convention of people staying in what a James Purdy character calls "a not-right house" (134). A not-right house implies a not-right character. Self uses that locution to describe Eleanor: she is "not right" (98). A haunted house that is a trap for children is related to not just literal texts such as Neverland in *Peter Pan* and the ginger-bread house in "Hansel and Gretel," but also with the social text of child exploitation. Puccio grumbles that the house looks "like the imperial courts of the French kings or Russian czars" (2). But that is exactly what it should look like, not only because of the gothic's anxiety about aristo-cratic and monarchical privilege, but also because of the movie's refer-ence to the abuses of privilege. Likewise, Self describes the house in both representational and historical terms. The house appears to have "human heads from a Picasso. Distorted. Features out of place, wrong. All wrong. And if the house is a Picasso ... it is terror. It is despair. It is *Guernica*" (14).

If commentators miss the general conventions of the haunted house, they also miss some of the specific turns on that convention. For exam-ple, some reviewers did not appreciate this film's complication of Hill House's aesthetics: the arches, banisters, balustrades, carvings, columns, filigrees, fountains, friezes, giant doors, headboards, high ceilings, mar-ble floors, merry-go-round, newel posts, ornaments, scroll work, settees, statuary, stepping stones resembling books, wainscoting, walls of mir-rors, water course, etc. Joe Baltake claims, "The house is so ornate and overdone that it's ridiculous" (2). But this complication is exactly right. It hardly outdoes the preposterous homes built by Hugh Crain's cohort of other robber barons, such as William Randolph Hearst, J.P. Morgan, and Andrew Carnegie. Rather, it quite rightly develops the haunted house in a way that historicists appreciate. Self's description of the fence and gate suggest that he visited the estate (15 minutes from Stanford) that looms down the road from Jackson's childhood home—which she describes in her first novel, *The Road Through the Wall*. More impor-tantly, the aesthetics in Self's screenplay (and, thankfully, the film) fol-low not only the conventions of the gothic and baroque, but also the grotesque by emphasizing Islamic aesthetics. One of the great ironies of history is that gothic representation was influenced by forms brought back by Europeans during the Crusades. It is also ironic that critics over-look Islam's influence on the gothic. So it is fitting that when Mrs. Dud-ley guides Nell to her bedroom, Self's stage directions call for the hallway to be covered with "aged Persian carpets" (16). And just as the review-ers miss the historical referentiality, they also miss the allusions. For example, the walk-in fireplace recalls the one in *Citizen Kane*.

Since the reviewers do not understand the conventions of set-ting, it is not surprising that they make little sense when discussing the technology used for setting the house in motion. On the one hand, they complain that the computer-generated images are "not realistic enough" (Haflidason 1). For example, Dustin Putman says the effects are "never actually real looking" (2). This is just literal mindedness. How realistic looking were Rodan, King Kong, and the creature from the black lagoon? The point is not how believable the unbelievable looks. The point is that even unbelievable representations of the unbelievable are nonetheless powerful. The makers of this film are trapped between those who want it literal and those who do not. An example of the latter is John Larson, who complains that "nothing is left to the imagination" (2). This notion is reminiscent of the cliché that television and movies are inferior to radio because nothing is left to the imagination.

While giving Self no credit for the house, the reviewers give him no credit for the strengths in characterization and all of the blame for the weaknesses. As mentioned, Nell's pious shenanigans in the end do not appear in Self's script but were added on during reshoots. Critics rightly point out that despite her psychic disintegration, she solves the mysteries—the most irrational character, then, is the most rational. She comes off as a scatter-brained Sherlock Holmes. But Self's screenplay manages this problem not as contradictory but as ironic, partly by giving Luke more of the detective duties than he has in the movie. And Self's screenplay does not contain the film's cliché of having Nell find the clues in a room behind a bookcase. Some reviewers complain that the Nell of 1999 is not as interesting as the Nell of 1963. They forget that the Nell of the first adaptation was annoyingly insipid, passive, and weak. She spends most of her time wringing her hands and trembling. Neither movie catches the psychological complexity of the novel, but Self's Nell is much more complex and significant than the Nell of either movie.

The most common criticism of the film is that the other characters are too flat. The reviewers do not remember from their primers on film that a flat character is not necessarily a bad character. Many flat characters appear in the greatest of narratives. Moreover, the reviewers ignore just how flat the professor, Theo, and Luke are in the 1963 adaptation and even in the novel. When they first meet, their patter is a lame attempt at wit. One of Jackson's masterful achievements (in this text and others) is that she can show the painful comedy of conversations that aim at wit but miss. Almost all studies of the novel overlook this aspect of it and thus are dissatisfied with the ending when the professor's wife arrives and inconveniences the literal belief in ghosts and the supernatural. By contrast, the 1963 adaptation is utterly humorless. But the 1999 version has its comic moments, such as Marrow's several embarrassments and the undercutting of Mrs. Dudley. But Stephanie Zacherek writes, "It's audacious of De Bont and screenwriter David Self to even *try* to give *The Haunting* "a sense of humor" (2).

Many reviewers complain that the character of Professor Marrow is unbelievable on the grounds that he is unethical. Bill Chambers asks, "Why was this nice, helpful, and immediately redemptive researcher so absent of ethics at the start?" (5). Similarly, Marty Mapes writes, "Marrow's character is badly researched and poorly thought out. His study on fear is completely unethical" (2). Maybe Chambers and Mapes think professors are ethical because their professors told them what deep thinkers and writers Chambers and Mapes are. Maybe such reviewers have not figured out that their professors were just selling admission tickets and the A's were part of the hustle. If Chambers and Mapes do not know that academia in America is as cheesy as any crooked law firm or used car lot, if they are oblivious to what was happening at the university. Perhaps Jeremy Hughton never attended. He complains, "Neeson has never been so dull" (2). Maybe Neeson never played a professor before. But as a Stanford graduate, Self would know just how gothic academics can be. For it is Stanford that has given us Condoleezza Rice and the Hoover Institute. And like Hugh Crain and Andrew Carnegie, Leland Stanford built mansions and a university from the money made by literally working laborers to death.

More specifically, Self's version of the college psychology department illustrates Joyce Carol Oates's statement that "Gothicism ... is ... a fairly realistic assessment of contemporary reality" (108). His script pointedly includes the cruel experiments by two actual psychology professors, Stanley Milgram and Phil Zimbardo, going so far as to contextualize them with Adolph Hitler. Some of these experiments were done at Stanford. So it is fitting that Neeson (in Self's screenplay and the film) plays not the anthropologist from the novel but a psychology professor who treats his subjects like rats in a maze. For Self has kept the inept foolishness of Jackson's original professor and made him more complex by making him also a turn on the gothic mad scientist. Self thereby achieves not just intertextual complexity but referential significance. Postmodern narratives are replete with the mad psychotherapist as mad scientist—for example, Ken Kesey's Big Nurse and Thomas Pynchon's Dr. Hilarius. As for additional clownish psychologists, there was a psychology professor at an American university who advised that people should emulate his way of pursuing happiness: he drove a new car. And today there is another psychology professor at an American university who keeps dozens of monkeys in cages, and for years he has been cutting out their cerebral cortex while they are still alive. The number of brainless monkeys must be a thousand by now. Or a thousand and one, if you count the professor.

The reviewers also charge that Luke is too flat. But he is not as flat in Self's manuscript as he is in the film. And again, the commentary overlooks the flatness of Luke in Jackson's novel. The original Luke stands to inherit the house, which is an important Gothic motif and political theme that perhaps Self should have kept. But Luke's psychology is essentially the same. Both Jackson's and Self's are feckless ne'er-do-wells. Just as the group is funny because it is not, both Lukes are fascinating because they are so uninteresting. Self updates the vacuous Luke by making him a creature of the media. Much of his dialog consists of ideas, even quotations, gleaned from television. For example, he sarcastically refers to Crain as "a regular Captain Kangaroo." But he is not ironic when his sentences consist of one-word clichés such as "Chill" (57; 32).

The commentators also regard Theo as too simplistic. First, they want her motivation explained (at least they retain something from high school English). For example, they say it is gratuitous to make her bisexual, and they are right, but the issue does not appear in Self's script. Nor does a particularly bad special effect: Theo jumping off the floor, turning a midair summersault with a 180-degree twist, and then landing in the bed on her back. Also absent from Self's manuscript is her shallow, self-important dismissal of the cerebral Marrow: "You don't feel." But like Jackson's novel, Self's screenplay gives her some knowledge of psychology, something she lacks in the movie. Theo recognizes that Nell is "passive-aggressive" and that Theo is her opposite, a "cat-fighter" (12). And to indicate that (as in the novel) Theo is Nell's double, Self describes Theo's bedroom as "a mirror-image twin of Nell's room," something else the film would have done well to retain (20). Reviewers also claim that Theo does not grow (as if most real people do). There is some truth to that accusation. She is indeed flatter in the film than in the screenplay. But in each, she goes from cocksure to chastened. In the screenplay, she arrives making insulting remarks to Mrs. Dudley about her "gorgeous hunk of husband" (20). Then in Mrs. Dudley's absence, she makes catty speculations on the Dudleys' sex life. But she eventually takes on some of Nell's humility. Self's script ends with a humble Theo hesitantly returning to the house and softly calling, "Nell?" (124).

Unfortunately, the film foregoes Self's complex development of Mrs. Dudley by presenting her only as an ogre, and a not very commanding one at that. Self makes her more daunting, but he also manages to add a trait found in Jackson's treatment of Marrow's wife. Self develops her as a comic parody of the evil mother. In addition, Mrs. Dudley is the product of impoverished domesticity. She thereby becomes threatening, comic, and sympathetic all at once. Likewise, the movie wastes Bruce Dern by simplifying Mr. Dudley. Self develops him as not only threatening but also comic. He is a parody of not only the gothic villain, but also the supernatural guardian-of-the-gate and mythic guide to the underworld.

For example, in a send-up of Poseidon and his trident, Dudley carries a three-pronged "weed spear" (12).

Self's script goes beyond even Jackson's development of doubles. Eleanor has several doubles. In Self's script, as in the novel and the movie, the house is Nell's mirror double. She merges with it, or rather it imbibes her. The script repeatedly mentions the house breathing and Nell breathing. The movie's attempt to render the sound of this breathing is unclear. In addition to the house, Eleanor has another double, Mrs. Dudley, who exemplifies what Nell will become after a couple more decades of servitude. But the movie abandons Self's unsettling theme that the bourgeois individual cannot free herself from the repetition of history. So the movie develops Nell as heroic and salvific, which merely reinscribes what Jackson and Self deconstruct. Self underscores this deconstruction by mentioning a gothic mansion that Jackson knew about, the Winchester House, which resembles Hill House. Self points out that Sara Winchester built the monstrosity on money made from mass death— the many people killed by her husband's rifles (the Winchester rifle was instrumental in the so-called settling of the west).

In addition, Eleanor and Mrs. Crain are doubles. Thankfully, the movie keeps Self's emblem of this doubling: Nell wears a French twist in her hair and then finds that Mrs. Crain also wore one. The French twist is appropriate not only for the brutal sound of the word but also for the circular shape. The robber baron's wife must kill her husband to save her child; she must commit the mortal sin that her husband commits on many children in order to save her own. The cost is her own life, for Crain's ghost returns and murders her, making her look like a suicide. Self makes the French twist as a metonymy of Mrs. Crain repeat itself in the circularity of the double helix staircase. And to underscore the motif of history repeating itself, he makes it clear that Nell might hang herself at the top of the stairs as Mrs. Crain did. But the movie uses only Self's harrowing scene of Marrow climbing the double staircase to retrieve Nell after she climbs it in search of Mrs. Crain's ghost.

In addition, Mrs. Crain and Nell's mother are doubles. Despite being dead, both of these women drive Nell's motivation. In the beginning, the long servitude to her mother gives Nell her identity, and then the secrets Mrs. Crain has left behind appear to offer Nell an escape. In Self's manuscript, this way out is simply the way back in to the domestic trap. Eleanor not only dies, but her death accomplishes nothing. In the movie, however, her death not only frees the souls of the children from purgatory but also earns her a place in heaven.

And of course Eleanor doubles her mother. Eleanor's domestic role as her mother's attendant grows out of a patriarchal tradition that in the past made her a symbol of Crain's exploited wife, in the present her

mother's attendant, and in the future (if her sister and brother-in-law have
their way) an attendant to them.

Dr. Marrow doubles Hugh Crain. He is an apologist for his fellow
man of the house:

> "All the lurid history is just gossip, the stuff that the local oppressed
> underclass heaped on the rich guy with the big house. These people lost
> their kids in Crain's mills and projected this ... bullshit on him.
> (beat)
> "You see, there has to be a Monster in the labyrinth. We make them up.
> That's how we deal with the things about everyday life that are too terrible
> to deal with" [82].

Marrow is right in one sense. We make up supernatural monsters so we
can dismiss the truth of literal exploitation. One of the most common
motifs in the social text is encapsulated in the phrases "conspiracy theory" and "class resentment." Such phrases imply that conspiracies cannot truly exist and that class is natural. Concomitantly, the empowered
and privileged appear as if they are heroic scapegoats. In Self's manuscript but not the movie, Marrow's position as the new Hugh Crain
emerges when Nell wears the French twist for him.

Although the reviewers complain about the film's plot, they overlook the many unifying techniques, especially the strategic repetitions.
In addition to the circularity of the doubling, Self also uses the repetition of incident to create an uncanny allegory of the eternal return of the
repressed. Like Self's script, the movie begins with the flapping of sheets
and the wafting of curtains. By showing the mother's sickroom in the
end as it is in the beginning, he underscores the inescapability of Nell's
situation and the repetition compulsion of her personality. The recurrence of white sheets and gauzy curtains blowing ghostlike into the house
underscores Eleanor's entrapment in death.

His characterization of Luke, Jackson's usurper of the inheritance,
shifts that trait from Luke to Nell's sister and brother-in-law. This move
highlights the theme of the repetition of history. In Self's version, contemporary society reproduces patriarchy even more clearly than it does
in the novel. By having the sister offer to let Eleanor continue as a servant of the sister's family, Self even more fully develops the theme of
Eleanor as a reproduction of patriarchy and class. Furthermore, the
mother is complicit, for it is she who has made out a will that allows the
sister to take the entire estate. And the sister is also complicit in this
exploitation. Despite their calls for realism, some viewers are undoubtedly displeased with a representation of women exploiting other women.
They would fault Self's screenplay because it contains no role models—
it is not politically correct propaganda.

The film wisely adheres to Self's sense of inescapable repetition by revisiting scenes. The mother's sickroom appears twice; the watercourse with book-shaped stepping stones appears twice; the mirrored merry-go-round appears twice. But the film diminishes Self's most significant repetitions. Repeatedly, the characters find that no matter what path they take through the house, it leads to the same room. Repeatedly, characters start out on the first floor but wind up on the second floor without having climbed any stairs or ramps. Repeatedly, the characters return to the ominous locked room without intending to. Similarly, Self calls for repeating the convention of red as the color of carnality, such as Nell feeding Marrow a tomato. But the film sacrifices these in favor of clichés such as the bloody footprints. In Self's screenplay, Nell's breathing is as repeatedly audible as that of the house, but the film does not capture this repetition clearly. Overall, the film's repetitions tend to achieve not a sense of the cyclical history and the eternal return of the repressed, but just redundancy and gratuitousness.

In another plot complication that the movie excludes, Self presents a fifth character, David Watt, who is a no-show. The plot returns to the mystery of his whereabouts when car keys are found in the house (even though he apparently did not arrive there). Later, Self raises the tension in this subplot when the missing man's identification is found in the house. The addition of this character creates a possible realistic explanation—for the characters and the audience—of the mysterious events. So this character helps maintain tension by keeping the possibility that the seemingly supernatural events (such as the writing on the portrait) could be caused not only by Marrow or Dudley, but also by Watt. Not until the turning point does Self's script clearly establish that the events are supernatural. By maintaining undecidability until the end, he adds to the suspense. He accomplishes this ambiguity by suggesting that the seemingly supernatural events could be imagined.

There are many other plot developments that the movie unwisely excludes. First, Self gets the mysterious and threatening house in motion sooner than the movie does. He quickly develops Jackson's description of the house as irrational and unpredictable. As soon as Nell arrives, he has optical illusions and doors slamming inexplicably.

The movie also excludes a significant thematic motif in the script; that Crain could have been exploiting the children sexually. Luke says of the child laborers, "They died by the thousands to make America rich. You can imagine what else went on" (45). And when Nell visits the locked double doors that apparently hide dead children, a giant tongue extends towards her. Also, when the ceiling descends toward her as she lies in bed, it is "THRUSTING at her rhythmically" (capitalization in original, 96). The sheer size of Crain depicts him as the giant that he was in the viewpoint of the children. As he stalks out of the painting and down the stairs to kill Nell, he is almost two stories high. And the metonyms of Crain that foreshadow this turning point are also huge— for example, the hands grasping for her, the statues that come to life, and the eye watching her. By contrast, the images of children—statues, carvings, outlines under sheets,—are almost all small.

Also worth noting is that the film does not include Self's retention of an important scene from the novel: the little girl in the diner who wants her cup from home because it has stars on the bottom. Self calls for an ominous transition from that scene to a run-in with a foreboding waitress, a harbinger of not only Mrs. Dudley but also the future Nell if she remains trapped as a domestic laborer.

In addition, Self's ending features Crain's ghost, not Eleanor, as the winner in the power struggle. Eleanor is the latest round in domestic vic-timhood. And Marrow is rewarded for reproducing the patriarchy. He gains an endowed chair because of his dishonest publications about Hill House, which contradict everything he has experienced there. Rather than write the truth, he tells the profession what it wants to hear.

If the film leaves out a lot of Self's plot, it also forsakes a lot of his gothic techniques. For the plotting, Self uses a technique that Jackson used in may of her narratives: a scene changes as the protagonist's state of consciousness changes. For example, the transition from scene to scene repeatedly occurs when Nell falls asleep or awakens, thus suggesting that the previous or following scene—and perhaps both—are dreams or delu-sions. Self uses another of Jackson's techniques for changing scenes with the character's change in consciousness. In the script, Nell takes codeine, and in the next scene is awakened by a phone call that tells her about the research study at Hill House. This technique ambiguates the decidabil-ity of how she received the call; it even suggests that she did not actually receive it. The undecidability increases when the scene jumps to a psy-chology department. In other scenes, Nell is reminiscent of several of Poe's characters when wine might be the explanation of her perceptions.

For the setting, Self thoroughly develops the gothic convention of the house as the self. He recurrently describes the house anthropomor-phically: "tortured," "eye-like windows," "stonework like muscle under skin," "a mouth full of black, twisting, snake tongues," "finger-like pil-lars," "screaming" (14). Another technique that Jackson uses in many of her narratives is the unreliability of representation, particularly mirrors. When Nell's hair divides as if invisible fingers are running through it, Self depicts this as visible in the mirror; he does not show whether or not it would actually happen if the camera were directly on Nell's hair instead of the mirror's representation of it. So he treats this event as if it could be either a trick by the house or a delusion of Eleanor's.

Self also includes a lot of interesting techniques from the mystery and detective modes—gothic's closest family members. As soon as Nell is in her room, she notices something out her widow. The scene directions state, "At the very edge of the woods is a faded white picket fence with a gate surrounding a small plot of some sort. No way to tell what it is from here" (18). In Self's version, this is the place where Crain's children are buried, and Nell discovers that they all died at age seven, a fact suggesting that he killed them all.

Self's intertextual allusions escaped the reviewers. Following Jackson's many Elizabethan allusions, Self names Marrow's department chair "Malcolm." In a script that treats academia as gothic, this name compares the head of the department to a medieval king—an autocrat, not a democrat. The movie excludes the script's allusion to William Faulkner's gothic classic "A Rose for Emily." As in Faulkner's story, the script describes the dead person's pillow as still showing the impression of a head. The movie is a little heavy handed with its direct reference to *Citizen Kane*. Self calls only for the fireplace and a cane on the dead mother's bed. Also, Dr. Marrow works at Amherst College, the perfect association for a gothic story about a sensitive woman badly served by the patriarchy. The film excludes Self's allusion to another gothic text about exploited labor, Herman Melville's "The Bell-Tower." Where Melville has a worker die in the construction of a megalomaniac's grandiose bell-tower, Self has four workers die in the construction of Crain's grandiose chimney. And where Melville's "The Bell-Tower" has the secret of repeated history revealed by falling mortar, Self's manuscript has the secret of repeated history revealed by the falling mortar that Nell hears in the large fireplace. The pun on the root word of mortar—"mort"—is just one suggestion of Self's sophistication. Also, another allusion to one of Melville's stories satirizing phallocentrism, "I and My Chimney," foreshadows the later revelation that the children were cremated in the fireplace. And like the eye with a cataract in "The Tell-Tale Heart," when Crain's ghost stares through a window at Eleanor, the window looks "like an eye with a cataract in a face howling in horror" (67). This allusion is particularly apt because in this story (as elsewhere) Poe uses the house to figure not just the self, but also the self that appears to be two characters yet is really one character with a schizoid mind.

David Self also contextualizes his narrative in painting. The house, as you have seen, looks like *Guernica*. The film unfortunately excludes Self's scene direction for Crain's portrait. Self wanted it to look like a vaulted room—another architectural pun referring to death. And if the film had followed Self's scene directions, the writing on the wall calling Eleanor to come home could have leaked from Crain's portrait, thus implying both a possible realistic explanation and a supernatural one.

This image also develops the gothic motif that Jackson used of representations such as statues and paintings coming to life. Thankfully, the film retains Self's updating of representation coming to life when Nell listens to Marrow's tape of himself discussing Nell's symptoms. In addition, Self repeats the motif of sheets both masking and marking the movements of the self. The original screenplay shows not just the ghosts of the children and Crain coming through bedsheets and sheet-like curtains. A sheet covers Crain's portrait after it is defaced—rather like a curtain over a window. Likewise, Crain's ghost breaks through the sheet at the turning point.

A fuller analysis would situate this script in other contexts and approach it with different theories and methods. Further formal analysis of both adaptations would be valuable. For example, a study of just the sound and music of both films—let alone the sets and cinematography—would be a boon. Like the gothic in general, the adaptations would be excellent objects for psychoanalytic and feminist studies. But historicism might be the most productive turn for Jackson studies. (Indeed, the most important article ever written about Jackson may well be Rich Pascal's historicist analysis of *The Sundial.*) A historicist analysis could situate this film's emphasis on Islamic form in current anxieties about Islamic fundamentalism. The impulse to make Nell a savior and detective would be amendable to historicist methods in tandem with feminism. And historicism coupled with reader response could gauge how the studio made certain decisions, and how the reviewers and audiences made—and failed to make—certain responses. Indeed, a book could and should be written about the dialogue between this film, the 1963 adaptation, the novel, gothic representation, and the social text.

Self's screenplay, then, pays intertextual homage to the gothic in general and Shirley Jackson in particular. Like a musician developing variations on a tune, Self takes one of the greatest gothic novels and shows what else can be done with it. So this script is not a desecration; it is a consecration. It honors Jackson and the gothic by extending their forms and themes. Shirley Jackson would have appreciated this screenplay.

## Notes

1. For discussions of the first adaptation, see Bunnell; Morrison. For a discussion of the second adaptation, see Smith. For discussions of both adaptations, see Duvall; Schneider.
2. For a study of adaptations of postwar novels, see Hendler.
3. For a discussion of the complexities and vagaries of the revising process, see Friend.
4. For a study of gothic fiction and cinema, see Morgan.

## *Works Cited*

Baltake, Joe. "Frightful Waste of Talent." *The Sacramento Bee's Movie Club,* 23 July 1999. *ng/haunting.html.*

Bernstein, Abbie. *"The Haunting."*

Berardinelli, James. *"The Haunting:* A Film Review." *g.html.*

Blackwelder, Rob. "Top-Shelf F/X So Distracting You'll Forget to Be Scared." *ml.*

Chambers, Bill. *"The Haunting." Film Freak Central.auntdvd.html.*

Clifford, Laura. "Laura's Review of *The Haunting." Reeling: The Movie Review Show with Robin & Laura Clifford.*

Cockrell, Eddie. *"The Haunting." Nitrate Online Review.*

Craft, Dan. "At the Movies." *Pantagraph.com: Connecting Central Illinois on the Web.* 30 July 1999. *ing.html.*

Dursin, Andy. "Of Haunted Houses and Killer Sharks." *Film Score. http://www.filmscoremonthly.com/articles/1999/02_Aug—Of_Haunted_Houses.*

Duvall, Daniel S. "Flawed Protagonists and Haunted Houses in *The Haunting* and *The Shining." Creative Screenwriting* 6.4 (1999): 32–37.

Easterbrook, Matt. *"The Haunting."*

Friend, Tad. "Credit Grab: How Many Writers Does It Take to Make a Movie?" *The New Yorker,* 20 October 2003: 160–69.

Haflidason, Almar. *"The Haunting."* British Broadcasting Corporation. *_1999_review.shtml.*

*The Haunting.* Dir. Jan De Bont. Perf. Bruce Dern, Liam Neeson, Lili Taylor, Owen Wilson, and Catherine Zeta-Jones. DreamWorks, 1999.

Hendler, Jane. *Best-Sellers and Their Film Adaptations in Postwar America.* New York: Peter Lang, 2001.

Hughton, Jeremy. *"The Haunting:* A Movie Review." *AllMoviePortal.com.28.html.*

Johnson-Ott, Edward. *"The Haunting."*

Kelleher, Ed. *"The Haunting." The International Film Journal.* http://www.film-journal.com/Article.cfm/PageID/611260094.

Kendrick, James. *"The Haunting." QNetwork.com. http://ofcs.rottentomatoes.com/click/movie1090789/reviews.php?critic=movies&sortby=default&page=5&rid=193082.*

*Larson, John. "The Haunting."* http://www.celebritywonder.com/movie/1999_The Haunting71.html.

Manning, Luther. *"The Haunting." DVD Cult.*

Mapes, Marty. "The Haunting." *Movie Habit: The Boulder Film Scene.*

Morgan, Jack. *The Biology of Terror: Gothic Literature and Film.* Carbondale: Southern Illinois University Press, 2002.

Morrison, Michael. "Journey's End: *The Haunting* from Book to Film." *Studies in Weird Fiction* 12 (1993): 25–30.

Oates, Joyce Carol. "Writing as a Natural Reaction." *Time,* 10 October 1969: 108.

Oliveri, Mike. *"The Haunting." Feomante's Horror HomePage. http:www.feomante.com/Movies/GHI/haunt99.html.*

Pascal, Rich. "New World Miniatures: Shirley Jackson's *The Sundial* and Postwar American Society." *Journal of American and Comparative Cultures* 23.3 (2002): 99–111.

Prigge, Ted. *"The Haunting:* A Film Review." *ting99.html.*

Puccio, John J. "DVD Review: *The Haunting." DVD Town. 3290/374/htm.*

Purdy, James. "63: Dream Palace." 1956; *The Color of Darkness* and *Children Is All.* New York: Avon, 1965.

Putman, Dustin. *"The Haunting." Celebrity Wonder.* http://www.celebritywonder.com/movie/1999_The_Haunting3.html.

Schneider, Steven Jay. "Thrice Told Tales: *The Haunting,* from Novel to Film ... to Film." *Journal of Popular Film and Television* 30.3 (2002): 165–176.

Self, David. *The Haunting*. 30 July 1998.

Smith, B.R. "*The Haunting*: Jan De Bont Reinterprets a Robert Wise Classic." *Popular Culture Review* 12 (2001): 127–33.

Tolkin, Michael. Revision of *The Haunting* by David Self. 10 November 1998. *http://www.dailyscript.com/scripts/the-haunting_production.html*.

Shewman, Den. "*Road to Perdition*: Interview with David Self." *Creative Screenwriting* July/August 2002: 39–46.

"The Sub-Mariner." *http://www.ez-entertainment.net/script/may02scriptsales.htm*.

Von Busack, Richard. "CGI Glut Swamps the Poetry out of the Remake of *The Haunting*." *Metroactive. aunting-9930.html*.

Zacherek, Stephanie. "*The Haunting*." *Salon. haunting/index.html*.

# 14

# Life Lessons in Shirley Jackson's Late Fiction: Ethics, Cosmology, Eschatology

## DIANE LONG HOEVELER

*...a rather haunted woman. She was a very strange lady and she had all kinds of very strange ideas. She lived with a lot of bad dreams.... She had all kinds of chips on her shoulder about life and about people and about things.*

—Roger Strauss on Shirley Jackson

Not many people who knew her during her lifetime would dispute the editor Roger Strauss's opinion of his client, Shirley Jackson. As a reading of her biography, *Private Demons*, makes painfully evident, this was a woman who suffered all her life from the chill she received from her mother from birth. Never pretty enough, never friendly enough, never appropriately feminine enough, Jackson suffered from depression, and as an adult she self-medicated with a frightening array of drugs, food, alcohol and tobacco, and finally landed herself in a very early grave.[1] But many writers suffer from such personal problems, and their writings reveal very little of them. One can think, for instance, of someone like Jackson's contemporary Flannery O'Connor, whose personal sufferings are transmuted in her fiction into something beyond the self, and in doing so, transcend the personal pain of the author. The same cannot be said of the very visible anguish in Jackson's fiction. This is fiction written by a woman who wore her heart on her sleeve, or rather, whose fiction bore the very strong impress of her angst, her rage, her frustration. That dark fury is more than evident in the very bleak cosmology that she constructs story by story, about some sort of sadistic deity, in her works. Jackson's fictions create a new and different world, a realm chilly and strange and ugly, and finally we have to conclude that these works have recreated the cosmos as Jackson experienced it and believed it to be. There were, apparently, no ordinary evenings in Bennington.

Setting aside her life and the sort of mythic status that it has assumed in regard to interpreting her fiction, the other issue that requires attention in any discussion of Jackson's works is her style and its connection with her fictional vision. Jackson herself observed, "I have had for many years a consuming interest in magic and the supernatural. I think this is because I find there so convenient a shorthand statement of the possibilities of human adjustment to what seems to be at best an inhuman world." Later she noted that she loved eighteenth century novels because they "preserv[ed] and insist[ed] on a pattern superimposed precariously on the chaos of human development."[2] But in spite of Jackson's insistence on the importance of the gothic for her style and vision, literary critics have been wont to see in her works something very different, very "proto-postmodern" (Hattenhauer 2).

In fact, if one were to recognize a constant refrain in the literary criticism of Shirley Jackson it is that she deserves to be appreciated as something other than a writer of horror tales, or stories about witchcraft, or gothic fiction.[3] One would think, in fact, that these critics are embarrassed by that particular strain in Jackson's work, or that if they could only absolve her of gothic tendencies, they could rehabilitate her reputation as a serious writer of contemporary fiction. This antigothic tendency in the criticism of Jackson's works has been countered most effectively by the recent publication of Darryl Hattenhauer's *Shirley Jackson's American Gothic* (2003), a critical study that places the gothic impulse at center stage in Jackson's life and works. This brief essay will take yet another angle on Jackson's work; it will embrace the gothic quality of her late fiction and argue that it actually informs the quasi-theology that begins to emerge in her late works. Even though she clearly admitted to writing some of her more sensational (or "gothic") short stories for the magazine market, she also held a worldview that was informed by her beliefs in magic, the occult, or could be called "gothic ethics." As she herself observed, everything that she wrote was concerned with the struggle between chaos and pattern: "the sense which I feel, of a human and not very rational order struggling inadequately to keep in check forces of great destruction, which may be the devil and may be intellectual enlightenment." By examining a few of her late short stories—"The Missing Girl," "Nightmare," "My Uncle in the Garden," "The Possibility of Evil," "One Ordinary Day, with Peanuts," and "Home"—it can be seen that Jackson worked out her ethical scheme, her program for living and dying, in a highly coded fashion in these short works.[4] As she herself noted, her recurrent concern was "an insistence on the uncontrolled, unobserved wickedness of human behavior" (qtd. Oppenheimer 125).

## Invisibility or Worse: "The Missing Girl"

Published in *Fantasy and Science Fiction* magazine (1957), *The Missing Girl* is neither science fiction, nor is it fantasy, except in the most perverse use of the terms. The protagonist is an adolescent girl, lonely, ignored, and victimized. Martha Alexander, the story's protagonist, says very few words at the beginning of the story, only that she has "something to do" (339), and then she promptly disappears one evening while on a walk at the Philips Education summer camp for girls. This "something" that she has to do suggests that she was not out on an aimless walk, but was actually going to meet someone, and the suggestion of a sexual tryst that ended in her death is present as a subtext throughout the tale. But rather than dwell on the act of murder, the story reveals a more chilling truth: as the police and various authorities attempt to trace the girl, it becomes obvious that no one seems to know much about her at all. Her roommate Betsy stumbles when identifying her age and group in the camp; the camp director seems to be unable to produce a picture or describe her accurately; while the painting instructor remembers only that Martha did "vague stuff ... no sense of design, no eye" (345). Apparently, no one else had an eye for seeing another human being, a girl who seemed to paint pictures that revealed her own sense of "rejection" (345). When an uncle (and uncles will take on an increasingly sinister status in Jackson's fiction) is called in to help with the search, he is hard pressed to even account for Martha's existence. After consulting with his sister, presumably Martha's mother, he explains that all her children are present and accounted for, and no one really seems to remember a child fitting Martha's description. In fact, the mother does not even remember having Martha, and can recall nothing about sending a child to a summer camp. In conclusion, we are told that "a body that might have been Martha Alexander's was found something over a year later" and was buried with little ceremony and even less grief (349).

We can assume that for Jackson, the horror of the story lies not simply in the random nature of the violence that is, after all, an everyday occurrence for young women. The true evil can be found in the way a young life is thrown away, discarded, snuffed out with absolutely no consequences at all. Clearly, the story is meant to suggest the first phase in Jackson's portrait of the female life cycle, the intense sense of rejection and abandonment by the mother. It is no coincidence, I think, that Jackson suffered her first complete depressive break during her freshman year at college, a particularly vulnerable age and very close to that of the missing and then murdered Martha Alexander. The female adolescent lives in Jackson's universe in a violent, chaotic world where at any moment she could simply disappear and no one—not even her mother—would know the difference. What is particularly poignant in the story, however, is the conversation with the art instructor at the camp. This instructor's dismissal of Martha's art work is telling, given the young Jackson's own attempts to write, with little if any encouragement from her mother, at a very early age. Not ever truly seen by anyone, the female adolescent as struggling artist—struggling, that is, to express her pain and experience thereby some sort of artistic catharsis—is simply extinguished and left on a deserted trail like so much road-kill.

## *Young Adulthood, or Growing Paranoia*

"Nightmare" is one of Jackson's signature stories, typical in its method of beginning a work in the realm of the ordinary and mundane and then shifting all of us—characters and readers—into a world that is something else altogether. This move into the bizarre is the first, most elemental position in the Jacksonian universe: the child's paranoia of being betrayed by authority figures and then being punished, watched, and exploited. Even though the protagonist is a 20-something woman, "Nightmare" is written from a dependent and frightened child's point of view, a child who is powerless to do anything other than obey commands and follow orders she does not understand. On a pleasant March day, the very "precise" Miss Toni Morgan, presumably in her mid-twenties, dressed in a red, white, and blue outfit, sets out for the office where she has ably assisted Mr. Lang, her boss, for the past six years (37). Asked to deliver a package to a downtown address, Miss Morgan enters the twilight zone, where the entire city's panopticon-like advertising forces appear to be pursuing her as the missing "Miss X." Dressed exactly the way Miss X is described as dressing, carrying the same package, Miss Morgan quickly settles into a posture of paranoia, actually fearing at one point that she will be sued for dressing like Miss X, "impersonating her" (42). Light hearted in a strange way, the style of this story exposes the disjunction between chaos and pattern Jackson suggested in her comments on her fictional vision.

Despite the external illusion of order and pattern (the red, white, and blue suit), despite the precise actions (the determined route to deliver the package), Miss Morgan is a seething, frightened, paranoid child, forced to navigate an urban environment in which she is stalked and yet guiltily sees herself as somehow to blame. After only a few blocks of being followed, instead of being filled with righteous indignation, Miss Morgan instead has assumed the posture of the victim, musing, "they can't blame me" (43). The dénouement occurs when the haggard Toni Morgan begs for an explanation of the parade that is trailing her and is told cryptically that it is all about "Advertising" (50). Advertising for what? The implication is that the purpose of this sadistic foray has been the spectralization, exhibition, objectification, and victimization of the female body, and more specifically, the female who seeks employment in the public, urban realm. Told that she will have to face the same humiliation tomorrow in Chicago (51), Miss Morgan smiles, takes her orders, and sinks into sleep, having failed to deliver Mr. Lang's package.

To understand this gothic universe we must note that Miss Morgan is a very brief portrait of the young professional woman who takes a beating from Jackson. Inept, gullible, naive, childlike in her trust and simplicity, Miss Morgan should understand that the universe she has slipped into is a world where she will never be anything other than an object or a workhorse for the patriarchy. And as an object she can only expect to be waved by the capitalist machine like a human flag, a symbol of the fruits of a prosperous military-industrial complex and the American public educational system. But clearly she is not intended to have a responsible role or identity apart from the one this consumer-driven world has constructed for her. And certainly it is Jackson's little joke that Miss Morgan is condemned to carry Mr. Lang's "package" (slang for sexual parts) all over town. Allowed for a brief time period to have a supposedly responsible position, the young woman is really nothing other than a womb in waiting, a young woman who will be punished and humiliated for seeking employment outside of the home. Again, the target of anger in the story is not the woman, who has been placed in the position of a beating victim, but the system that has propped her up and then relegated her to meaningless trophy status. And lurking not so slightly below the fictional surface is rage at the realization that any other role apart from decorative display object would never have been permitted by a society that positions women as either consumers or consumed.

## Consorting with the Devil, or the Fear of Fertility

In Jackson's universe, the first steps out of the innocence of the garden are fraught with peril and potential disaster. Indeed, Martha Alexander did not make it out alive, and Miss Morgan is left stranded as one of the walking wounded. But other characters do attempt to negotiate their way out of the quagmire of early adulthood, only to find themselves in a sort of limbo of perversion and evil. In Jackson's version of the fall, "My Uncle in the Garden," two bachelor uncles exude eccentricity;

indeed, one of them admits to dancing with the devil in the garden at night. But perhaps this is just one of the strange acts they have committed. Narrated by a naive innocent who in fact is not related by blood to the two men, the story presents Uncle Oliver and Uncle Peter as brothers who have lived together all their lives, except for the one year Oliver spent married to Mrs. Duff. An odor of perversion fills the air as the two old men fuss over Peter's gray cat, Sandra Williamson, in their static, perpetually frozen little rose-covered cottage (209). One evening, over dinner, the brothers lapse into a quarrel over the absence of tomatoes on the table, and Oliver confides to his young visitor that Peter has "been consorting with the devil" in the garden at night (211). But in addition to these nocturnal visits, the devil has also been invited to lunch and over this cozy repast the devil has requested a "tribute," and the tomatoes have been offered. After an absence of several weeks, the tomatoes suddenly reappear, the offering of "a little boy" (214).

Now all this could be read as a harmless and inconsequential matter, a tale about nothing much and certainly nothing very important. But in the last few paragraphs the other shoe drops, and we realize, with a sickening thud, that the men are something other than innocent bachelor uncles. As they turn to each other, reconciled by the reappearance of ripe tomatoes at their table, they wax nostalgic by musing about a trip into the city that they have never made. Talking about making this trip, leaving their sheltered abode for an adventurous foray into the urban unknown, has always been "their favorite mutual whimsy" (214). But now we hear the ominous suggestion, that this "whimsy" is second only to talking about "the death of Mrs. Duff," Oliver's bride for only one year. The implication is that the brothers conspired to kill Mrs. Duff for her inheritance and have been happily living off of it—perhaps even as pedophiles—ever since. In fact, it would appear that the devil had appeared to the insane Peter earlier and had requested a "tribute" then as well, and that the "tribute" offered earlier had been the life of Mrs. Duff. It would appear that Mrs. Duff had been an inconvenient woman who had stood in the way of primal male-bonding and the earlier, intense, perhaps even homoerotic relationship between the brothers. These men, so pleasant and mild that generations of neighbors entrust their children to them for strolls in the park and zoo, appear to be members of some sort of ancient fertility and satanic cult that practices human sacrifice and when humans are not readily available, offers crops.

And what of Mrs. Duff, the next female victim in a long line of female sacrifices in Jackson's world? Mrs. Duff had done nothing other than marry a man who had a somewhat close relationship with his brother. In fact, she is described in the story as "semi-mythical," her only role to have been the "planning and arranging of a rose-covered bower" for her husband of one year (209). The two men, it would appear, live out their lives in some sort of anti–fairy tale universe. They exist as if they were two male sleeping beauties, held in a cottage in the woods, purchased by the funds of the elderly woman they have murdered. This mild-mannered tale presents a hyperbolic version of the capitalistic and patriarchal logic that operates in so many of Jackson's stories, for this tale presents men as vampiric, homoerotic, murderous, satanic worshippers of an ancient fertility that produces life forms that they do not need or want. And the major female character, this time mature and wealthy, is once again offered up as expendable and consumable by the man she has foolishly admitted into her life.

But, to ask the autobiographical question: why uncles? According to biographer Judy Oppenheimer, Jackson had a peculiar relationship with her own uncle, an eccentric sort to be sure. Although their relationship is murky, Oppenheimer has suggested that Jackson herself was sexually molested when she was a child by her maternal uncle Clifford Bugbee, an eccentric bachelor uncle who spent his time inventing hopelessly impractical and gigantic radios. The only evidence we have for such a claim is the memory of Shirley's childhood friend Dorothy Ayling, who spent time at the Jackson home and particularly remembered Uncle Clifford: "Sometimes he bothered me. He would call me endearing names and kind of touch me sometimes and I didn't know quite how to handle that. It bothered me ... he'd put his arm around you. I got so I realized that I better just keep a distance. I pretty quick figured out I didn't want to be near him—the way he talked to you, and the hands" (Oppenheimer 27). As Oppenheimer notes, a man who will touch one child will touch another, and Shirley would have been within easy and continuous reach of her eccentric uncle. As Oppenheimer queries, "Was Shirley sexually abused as an adolescent?... It is hard not to conclude that something terribly evil happened there, something that cast a long shadow over the rest of her life. The dark current of awareness of evil that runs through her life and work seems too strong to have as its sole root the observance of suburban hypocrisy" (27).

Why would Jackson invent *two* uncles, one murderous and one an accomplice? One possible way of explaining this is to understand that when a psychological trauma occurs, it is very typical for the victim to process the event by "splitting" the perpetrator into two figures, one "good" and one "bad." Again, such a strategy places us in a fairy tale universe. But one way of getting at the coded fairy tale nature of the tale is to query whether or not Jackson was conveying to us a hint about the victimization she suffered at the hands of dear Uncle Cliff. Child sexual assault becomes murder in this version of the story, and the child psyche that would have seen the kind, public face of her uncle would have seen a devilish, evil face as well; hence the two figures. The literary critic playing psychoanalytical sleuth is perhaps not an attractive figure, but the texts fairly scream to be understood within the context of a lifetime of pain.

## Doing Battle with the Devil Within: "The Possibility of Evil"

When Miss Adela Strangeworth sits down at night to compose her many venomous, slanderous, shocking letters to her neighbors, sent under cover as an anonymous voice of warning to the community, she comes closest to expressing what many believe was Jackson's sense of herself as an artist. Oppenheimer has called this story "the most nakedly revealing" of all of Jackson's works: "Certainly nothing she ever wrote came as close to defining her own conception of herself" (271). Winner of the Edgar Allan Poe Award for 1965, the story is worthy of Poe himself, or perhaps Flannery O'Connor in a very angry mood. If, as John G. Parks has asserted, the story is "a key to much of her fiction" (320), then it is important to position it within the corpus of the short, late work.[5] Parks's analysis, while useful for bringing the story into focus, never explores the deeply autobiographical self-loathing that clearly inscribes itself throughout the text. Miss Adela Strangeworth is a masochistic self-portrait, an indictment of a creative self who does not find any artistic or cathartic redemption, only destruction and rejection. It is an extremely dark tale to leave as a legacy to oneself, and it could only have been written by a woman who understood herself as possessing a "strange" "worth" to her community.

In order to place the story in its autobiographical context, let us consider an issue that has received surprisingly little attention in Jackson's life, namely her curious ancestor Edward Henchall. Edward was Shirley's paternal grandfather, born in England and the very well-to-do school classmate of Prime Minister Herbert Asquith. After a lifetime of prosperity, the man suddenly lost his entire fortune, changed his name to "Jackson" and fled to America, leaving his wife and three children in England for many years. Shirley's father Leslie was himself never able to find out what had caused the family disaster, or at least he never passed the information on to anyone in the family (Oppenheimer 13). This incident, impossible now to unravel, must have sent a chilling message to the sensitive Shirley, who told others that she could see and hear things and people that others could not (Oppenheimer 20–21). The strange family history suggests that disaster—complete financial ruin, desertion, and loss of identity—can occur overnight and can arrive suddenly, with no warning, out of nowhere.

Viewing the Henchall-Jackson family disaster within the context of Jackson's work, it seems reasonable to wonder if Jackson wrote "A Possibility of Evil" as some sort of reenactment of the family's trauma. The letters written by Adela, for instance, all concern either financial malfeasance or sexual misconduct, the only two areas that could have been serious enough to cause a man like Henchall to disappear. In writing her story Jackson may be suggesting that being the bearer of bad tidings is not something she wanted to do as a writer, but something she was compelled to do because of her own personal history. Did someone write a letter, making an accusation, that forced her grandfather to disappear? Or could she be suggesting that even at this late date she wishes someone, anyone, had written such a letter of warning, of suspicion, to her own parents about her uncle Clifford?

In "A Possibility of Evil," the first letter described is addressed to Don Crane, and it mocks his child as "an idiot" and concludes with the kicker, "Some people just shouldn't have children, should they?" (424). Is she not here virtually screaming at her own mother? The second letter, sent to Mrs. Harper, warns her that she is being laughed at behind her back because "the wife really always [is] the last one to know" (424). Surely this must have been painful to write, given Stanley Hyman's flagrant affairs with students, some conducted while Shirley was in the next room, pounding on the walls (Oppenheimer 172–73). The third letter to an elderly Mrs. Harper suggests that she will be "accidentally" killed while on the operating table because her nephew has paid a doctor to get rid of the aunt so that he can inherit her estate. Again, fantasies about outliving her own parents and being relieved of the financial pressure of supporting the family must have played into this one. We learn that other vicious letters have been sent to townsfolk over the years, and Adela has justified such actions by noting that frequently her suspicions have actually been proven true: "Mr. Lewis would never have imagined for a minute that his grandson might be lifting petty cash from the store register if he had not had one of Miss Strangeworth's letters" (424).

But this is where the split occurs. On one hand, the letters that Adela writes are hidden or cryptic and express Jackson's own suspicions, frustrations, and desires. On the other hand, she needs to mock Adela in order to distance herself from what she knows is evil itself. Yes, Adela has an important role to fill. Styling herself as a rear-guard vigilante of Puritan values, she is a one-woman crusader for sexual repression and financial accountability. If she does not warn her neighbors that "possible evil [is] lurking nearby," then evil will triumph unchecked and unabated, and all of us will be powerless to confront and defeat it. Such a system of ethics presupposes a powerful fall from grace into a world of unremitting original and everlasting sin: "as long as evil existed unchecked in the world, it was Miss Strangeworth's duty to keep her town alert to it.... There were so many wicked people in the world and only one Strangeworth left in town" (424).

Discovered after she accidentally drops one of her poison pen letters at the post office, Adela wakes up to a new day and new era in town. No longer viewed as the respected and kindly maiden lady, she is recognized for who and what she is and the townspeople take out their fury on her beloved roses (428). When she realizes her secret is known, she weeps "silently for the wickedness of the world" (428). The irony is that Adela, even at this point, is incapable of recognizing that a large part of the wickedness she has attributed to others is, of course, within herself. But Jackson might very well say that such evil, and certainly the possibility of evil, is within us all. Jackson clearly suspected the motives of everyone she interacted with, for, from her own bitter experience, she knew well that people are motivated either by greed or sexual drives that verge on the perverse. Jackson's world is a primitive one at best, not one in which highly bred roses, artificial stock, and genetically freak blossoms, deserve to have a special place of prominence.

## Manicheanism and the Duality of God/s: Or, Is There Anything Ordinary About Life?

Jackson seems to suggest that we live in a world that is Manichean in nature, a roller-coaster ride that brings us into contact with wildly fluctuating forces of good and evil. Manicheanism was founded by Mani in the early second century after Christ's death, and as a form of syncretism, Manicheanism attempted to merge the great religions of the day, Christianity and Zoroastrianism, together. The central theological puzzle of the day was what to do with evil, how to explain the power and persistence of evil in the world. For Manicheans, the universe is a contested battlefield in which the powers of evil materialism struggle constantly against the forces of spiritual good. While Christians accept the evil nature of Satan, they do not believe that Satan has the same power as God, nor that he is an equal or balancing force, the way Manicheans do. This might seem distant to the interests of Jackson were it not for her extensive reading in the history of fertility cults, magic, and the supernatural. She clearly knew that other religions had struggled with the question of evil, its power and nature. Jackson seems to have thought of the abstractions of good and evil as almost distant parent-figures who dole out rewards or punishments randomly.

Consider the strange central character in "An Ordinary Day, with Peanuts," included in *Best American Short Stories*, 1956. In this odd story

Mr. John Philip Johnson wakes up one morning and goes about his business of dispensing one beneficent deed after another to total strangers. But when he comes home that evening he meet his double, his wife, who has spent the whole day doing just the opposite, doling out evil and misery to some of the same total strangers. As in most of Jackson's stories, the kicker comes at the conclusion when the husband hears about all the misery his wife has caused during the day, sometimes to the very same people whom he had been helping, and he calmly asks, "Want to change over tomorrow?" Her response: "I would like to, ... I could do with a change"(338).

Both of these people are each equally uncommitted to the actions they perform, whether doling out good or ill. Neither has any stake in feeding the hungry or persecuting the innocent; each is simply performing a role, a function, that randomly alternates depending on the other's mood. This sort of split personification is very similar to a child's conception of the godhead: kind, rewarding, or vengeful and punishing. Enhancing cosmological reading of the story, Jackson has provided her readers with the cues to set the tale in a religiously primitive context: wagering on a "horse named Vulcan," or avoiding "fire signs on a Wednesday," or betting on a horse named "Tall Corn," all of which references place us back in the pagan world of "The Lottery" (337). Vulcan is the Roman god of fire, especially associated with destructive power and craftsmanship, while Wednesday is associated with the Norse god Woden or Odin, god of war and death, but also the god of poetry and wisdom. According to legend, Odin hung for nine days, pierced by his own spear, on the world tree. Here he learned nine powerful songs and 18 runes. And like a powerful poet, Odin can make the dead speak to question the wisest amongst them. The presence of Woden/Odin at this point in the story provides us with a clue as to the pagan religious origins of a seemingly slight tale about two people wandering around a city.

Past critical impulse has been to read the fluctuation between good and evil in the story as operating within the normative Judeo-Christian tradition. In fact, Parks quotes Heinrich Zimmer, a Jungian, to make sense of this story's Jacksonian spin on evil:

> The function of evil is to keep in operation the dynamics of change. Cooperating with the beneficent forces, though antagonistically, those of evil thus assist in the weaving of the tapestry of life; hence the experience of evil, and to some extent this experience alone, produces maturity, real life, real command of the powers and tasks of life. The forbidden fruit— the fruit of guilt through experience, knowledge through experience—had to be swallowed in the Garden of Innocence before human history could begin. Evil had to accepted and assimilated, not avoided.[6]

Certainly there is some validity in reading the story within a Jungian framework, but it does a certain amount of violence to Jackson's outré sensibilities. This is not to assert that she was a literal believer in Manicheanism; but it does make more sense to see these two characters as a male/female divinity, a dyadic force of good and evil spinning around the vortex of our everyday lives. Such a reading allows us to see that Jackson actually presents a theology, a system of ethical beliefs, in her fiction. Rather than being merely macabre or trivial or quotidian, her fiction is theological much in the same way that Flannery O'Connor's fiction is spiritual—gothically spiritual, that is.

## Ghosts of Our Own: "Home"

The afterlife is not a particularly attractive place in the universe of Jackson's fiction, although there is biographical evidence to suggest that she may have believed, or desperately tried to believe, that there was an afterlife that was positive and healing rather than frightening and ghastly. The last letter that Jackson wrote before her sudden death at the age of 47 described a "wonderful voyage" she was soon to take alone, where she would meet many new people (Oppenheimer 271). Whether she had a premonition of her death and actually believed the scenario that she crafted for her literary agent Carol Brandt is open to speculation. Given the scathing critique of the apocalyptic mind that she undertook in *The Sundial* (1958), Jackson cannot be assumed to describe a consistent or coherent vision of the afterlife in her fictions. What is not open to speculation, however, is the fictional presentations of the dead in her short works, most frighteningly in "Home."

Ethel Sloane, the story's protagonist, is a recent transplant to country living. After one day she considers herself "acquainted with most of the local people" through her numerous trips to the hardware store. But Ethel, like all of Jackson's smug female characters, has more than a little to learn before the day is finished. In Ethel's case, she is unaware of the fact that there are also "local people" who are not living and who she has not met in the hardware store. Indeed, she and her husband have just bought a house that is considered by the locals to be haunted. The old Sanderson place was the site of a kidnapping and double drowning some 60 years before, and local legend has it that on rainy days it is best to avoid the creek where the disaster occurred. But Ethel has no time to hear warnings or village history from the owner of the hardware story, who tries in vain to warn her to avoid the route. So she proceeds to take the haunted road and even stops to pick up two mysterious and bedraggled "figures standing silently in the rain by the side of the road" (400).

An old woman and little boy are shivering, and the "child was sick with misery, wet and shivering and crying in the rain" (400). Although the old woman speaks only to ask for directions to "the Sanderson place," she clearly is controlling the child and putting him in harm's way. Ethel is shocked when she sees the condition of the boy, barefoot, wearing "thin pajamas," and wrapped in a wet and dirty blanket (400). The boy never speaks, but the old woman informs Ethel that "he wants to go home" and home is the Sanderson place (401). Ethel can hardly imagine how these two can intend to visit her and her husband, and she "felt oddly feudal with pride. We're the lords of the manor" (401). But when she arrives at the home, the woman and boy have vanished from the back seat of her car.

Ethel receives the explanation she seeks from her husband Jim, who has heard the legend about a "crazy old woman" who kidnapped and disappeared with the little Sanderson boy. As the night was rainy and the creek had risen, it was believed that the two had drowned. Pride, elation, and ownership of the "ghosts" initially fills Ethel with happiness, and she intends to tell the story of her recent encounter with her very own ghosts in town the next day. But when she next enters her car she once again has company, for the ghosts are back and are complaining that they could not go home because there "were strangers in the house" (403). Desperate, Ethel proposes to take the two back to where she found them yesterday, next to the creek. But her passengers have another idea. As the car skids on the wet road and almost plunges into the creek, Ethel hears the young boy's "horrible laughter," and she realizes that the two of them want to take her with them into the dark waters (404).

We might recall here the Nietzchean or Kierkegaardean theory of the "eternal return," the notion that we will return over and over again to certain moments within our lives. For the boy and the old woman the eternal return will be to the site of the betrayal, the kidnapping, and its violent dénouement in drowning. Forever kept out of a home the boy can never return to, the two of them seek to dispossess others as they were dispossessed, by poverty and victimization. For Jackson there is an afterlife, but it is just like "home," a place where we will return in order to be wounded and betrayed once again. And there are no parents at "home," only a crazy old woman who takes us with her into the dark waters of death. Jackson's eschatology is predicated on the dysfunctional family, a site where victimization, abandonment, disappointment, and abuse lurk around every corner. "Home" is not a cheery vision of families gathered around their fireplaces, providing moral and emotional support to one another; Jackson's vision of the afterlife, suggests that if there cannot be good parents in this life, what hope can we have that they will exist in the next?

Shirley Jackson wrote a highly coded autobiography of sorts in much of her short fiction, and her later works are particularly rife with unresolved familial traumas and personal disappointments. This is not to argue that Jackson's fiction can only be appreciated if one knows her biography, or if one is willing to ascribe psychoanalytical categories of meaning to her works. But it seems clear that Jackson was a gothicist with a personal agenda. She wrote out of deep personal pain, but she presented that pain as universal, as the lot of all people who are born into a world where they are unwanted, imperfect, and condemned to rail at those facts.

## Notes

1. See Strauss's full commentary on Jackson in Judy Oppenheimer, *Private Demons: The Life of Shirley Jackson* (New York: Putnam, 1988), 125–6. Oppenheimer is particularly good on Jackson's conflicted relationship with her mother, see especially pp. 11–17. Darryl Hattenhauer also discusses in some detail her extensive drug use in *Shirley Jackson: American Gothic* (Albany: SUNY Press, 2003), 19–21. Moving out of the realm of the personal, John G. Parks notes that "Jackson's gothic fiction is an effective mode for her exploration of the violations of the human self—the aching loneliness, the unendurable guilt, the dissolution and disintegrations, the sinking into madness, the violence and lovelessness" (28). See his "Chambers of Yearning," *Twentieth Century Literature* 30 (1984), 15–29; rpt. in this volume.

2. Jackson quoted in Oppenheimer 125.

3. See, for instance, how Lenemaja Friedman discounts Jackson's gothic strain in the comprehensive *Shirley Jackson* (Boston: Twayne, 1975). Analyzing her humor or her protofeminist tendencies are approaches taken by yet another large number of critics, most notably Lynette Carpenter, "Domestic Comedy, Black Comedy, and Real Life: Shirley Jackson, a Woman Writer," in *Faith of a (Woman) Writer*, eds. Alice Kessler-Harris and William McBrien (Westport, Conn.: Greenwood Press, 1988), 143–48; Gayle Whittier, "'The Lottery' as Misogynist Parable," *Women's Studies* 18 (1991), 353–66.

4. All quotations from Jackson's stories taken from Shirley Jackson, *Just an Ordinary Day*, ed. Laurence Jackson Hyman and Sarah Hyman Stewart (New York: Bantam, 1998). Citations from the stories will be provided in parentheses in the text.

5. See John G. Parks, "The Possibility of Evil: A Key to Shirley Jackson's Fiction," *Studies in Short Fiction* 15 (1978), 320–23.

6. *The King and the Corpse: Tales of the Soul's Conquest of Evil*, ed. Joseph Campbell (Princeton: Princeton University Press, 1971), 49; qtd. Parks, "Possibility," 322.

# Appendix:
# Shirley Jackson
# Bibliography

## Book-Length Works

*The Road Through the Wall* (1948).
*The Lottery and Other Stories or, The Adventures of James Harris* (1949).
*Hangsaman* (1951).
*Life Among the Savages* (1953) [family memoir].
*The Bird's Nest* (1954).
*The Witchcraft of Salem Village* (1956) [children's history text].
*Raising Demons* (1957) [family memoir].
*The Sundial* (1958).
*The Haunting of Hill House* (1959).
*We Have Always Lived in the Castle* (1962).
*The Magic of Shirley Jackson* (1966). Ed. Stanley Edgar Hyman.
*Come Along With Me: Part of a Novel, Sixteen Stories and Three Lectures* (1968). Ed. Stanley Edgar Hyman.
*Just an Ordinary Day* (1996). Ed. Laurence Jackson Hyman and Sarah Hyman Stewart.

## Short Stories with Dates of Initial Publication

"About Two Nice People." *Ladies Home Journal*, July 1951.
"Account Closed." *Good Housekeeping*, April 1950.
"After You, My Dear Alphonse." *New Yorker*, Jan. 1943.
"Afternoon in Linen." *New Yorker*, Sept. 4, 1943.
"All the Girls Were Dancing." *Collier's*, Nov. 11, 1950.
"All She Said Was Yes." *Vogue*, Nov. 1, 1962.
"Alone in a Den of Cubs." *Woman's Day*, Dec. 1953. "An International Incident." *New Yorker*, Sept. 12, 1943. "Arch-Criminal." *Just an Ordinary Day*, 1996.

"Aunt Gertrude." *Harper's*, April 1954.

"The Bakery." *Peacock Alley*, Nov. 1944. "Before Autumn." *Just an Ordinary Day*, 1996.

"Birthday Party." *Vogue* Jan. 1, 1963.

"The Box." *Woman's Home Companion*, Nov. 1952.

"Bulletin." *Magazine of Science Fiction and Fantasy*, Mar. 1954.

"Call Me Ishmael." *Spectre* 1, no. 1 (fall 1939).

"A Cauliflower in Her Hair." *Mademoiselle*, Dec. 1944.

"Charles." *Mademoiselle*, July 1948.

"The Clothespin Dolls." *Woman's Day*, Mar. 1953.

"Colloquy." *New Yorker*, Aug. 5, 1944.

"Come Dance with Me in Ireland." *New Yorker*, May 15, 1943. "Come to the Fair." *Just an Ordinary Day*, 1996.

"Concerning ... Tomorrow." *Syracusan* 4, no. 6 (Mar. 1939).

"The Daemon Lover ['The Phantom Lover']," *Woman's Home Companion*, Feb. 1949.

"Daughter, Come Home." *Charm*, May 1944.

"Day of Glory." *Woman's Day*, Feb 1953. "Deck the Halls." *Just an Ordinary Day*, 1996.

"Devil of a Tale." *Just an Ordinary Day*, 1996.

"Dinner for A Gentleman." *Just an Ordinary Day*, 1996.

"Don't Tell Daddy." *Woman's Home Companion*, Feb. 1954.

"Every Boy Should Learn to Play the Trumpet." *Woman's Home Companion*, Oct. 1956.

"Family Magician." *Woman's Home Companion*, Sept. 1949.

"A Fine Old Firm." *New Yorker*, Mar. 4, 1944.

"The First Car is the Hardest." *Harper's*, Feb 1952.

"The Friends." *Charm*, Nov. 1953.

"The Gift." *Charm*, Dec. 1944. "Gnarly the King of the Jungle." *Just an Ordinary Day*, 1996. "The Good Wife." *Just an Ordinary Day*, 1996.

"A Great Voice Stilled." *Playboy*, Mar. 1960.

"Had We but World Enough." *Spectre*, Spring 1940 v1 n3.

"Happy Birthday to Baby." *Charm*, Nov. 1952.

"Home." *Ladies' Home Journal*, Aug. 1965.

"The Homecoming." *Charm*, April 1945. "The Honeymoon of Mrs. Smith" (versions I and II). *Just an Ordinary Day*, 1996.

"The House." *Woman's Day*, May 1952. "I Don't Kiss Strangers." *Just an Ordinary Day*, 1996. "Indians Live in Tents." *Just an Ordinary Day*, 1996.

"The Island." *New Mexico Quarterly Review*, 1950 vol. 3.

"It Isn't the Money." *New Yorker*, Aug. 25, 1945.

"It's Only a Game." *Harper's*, May 1956. "Jack the Ripper." *Just an Ordinary Day*, 1996.

"Journey with a Lady." *Harper's*, July 1952.

"Liaison a la Cockroach." *Syracusan* 4, no. 7 (April 1939).

"Little Dog Lost." *Charm*, Oct. 1943.

"A Little Magic." *Woman's Home Companion*, Jan. 1956.

"Little Old Lady." *Mademoiselle*, Sept. 1944.

"Lord of the Castle." *Just an Ordinary Day*, 1996.

"The Lottery." *New Yorker*, June 26, 1948.

"Louisa, Please." *Ladies' Home Journal, May 1960.*

"The Lovely Night." *Collier's*, April 8,*1*950.

"Lovers Meeting." *Just an Ordinary Day, 1996.*
"Lucky to Get Away." *Woman's Day,* Aug. *1953.*
"Maybe It Was the Car." *Just an Ordinary Day, 1996.*
"Men with Their Big Shoes." *Yale Review,* Mar. 1947
"The Missing Girl." *Magazine of Fantasy and Science Fiction,* Dec. 1957.
"Monday Morning." *Woman's Home Companion,* Nov. 1951.
"The Most Wonderful Thing." *Good Housekeeping,* June 1952. "The Mouse." *Just an Ordinary Day,* 1996.
"Mother is a Fortune Hunter." *Woman's Home Companion,* May 1954.
"Mrs. Anderson." *Just an Ordinary Day,* 1996.
"Mrs. Melville Makes a Purchase." *Charm,* Oct. 1951.
"My Friend." *Syracusan* 4, no. 4 (Dec. 1938).
"My Grandmother and the World of Cats." *Just an Ordinary Day,* 1996.
"My Life in Cats." *Spectre* 1, no. 4 (summer 1940).
"My Life with R.H. Macy." *New Republic,* 22 Dec. 1941.
"My Son and the Bully." *Good Housekeeping,* Oct. 1949. "My Recollection of S.B. Fairchild." *Just an Ordinary Day,* 1996. "My Uncle in the Garden." *Just an Ordinary Day,* 1996.
"Nice Day for a Baby." *Woman's Home Companion,* July 1952. "Nightmare." *Just an Ordinary Day,* 1996.
"Night We All Had Grippe." *Harper's,* Jan. 1952.
"Nothing to Worry About." *Charm,* July 1953.
"The Omen." *Magazine of Fantasy and Science Fiction,* Mar. 1958.
"On the House." *New Yorker,* Oct. 30, 1943.
"One Last Chance to Call." *McCall's,* April 1956.
"One Ordinary Day, with Peanuts." *Magazine of Fantasy and Science Fiction,* Jan. 1955.
"The Order of Charlotte's Going." *Charm,* July 1954. "Party of Boys." *Just an Ordinary Day,* 1996.
"Pillar of Salt" *Mademoiselle,* Oct. 1948.
"Portrait." *Just an Ordinary Day,* 1996.
"The Possibility of Evil." *The Saturday Evening Post,* Dec. 18, 1965.
"Queen of the May." *McCall's,* April 1955.
"The Renegade." *Harper's,* Nov. 1949.
"Root of Evil." *Fantastic,* March–April 1953.
"The Second Mrs. Ellenoy." *Reader's Digest,* July 1953.
"Seven Types of Ambiguity." *Story,* 1943.
"Shopping Trip." *Woman's Home Companion,* June 1953.
"The Sister." *Just an Ordinary Day,* 1996. "The Smoking Room." *Just an Ordinary Day,* 1996.
"The Sneaker Crisis." *Woman's Day,* Oct. 1956.
"So Late on Sunday Morning." *Woman's Home Companion,* Sept. 1953.
"The Strangers." *Collier's,* May 10, 1952.
"Strangers in Town." *Saturday Evening Post,* May 30, 1959.
"The Story We Used to Tell." *Just an Ordinary Day,* 1996.
"Summer Afternoon." *Just an Ordinary Day,* 1996.
"The Summer People." *Charm,* 1950.
"The Third Baby's the Easiest." *Harper's,* May 1949.
"The Tooth." *The Hudson Review* 1, no. 4 (1949).
"Trial by Combat." *New Yorker,* Dec. 16, 1944.
"The Very Hot Sun in Bermuda." *Just an Ordinary Day,* 1996.

"The Villager." *The American Mercury,* Aug. 1944.
"Visions of Sugarplums." *Woman's Home Companion,* Dec. 1952.
"What a Thought." *Just an Ordinary Day,* 1996.
"When Things Get Dark." *New Yorker,* Dec. 30, 1944.
"Whistler's Grandmother." *New Yorker,* May 5, 1945.
"The Wishing Dime." *Good Housekeeping,* Sept. 1949.
"Worldly Goods." *Woman's Day,* May 1953.
"Y and I." *Syracusan* 4, no. 2 (Oct. 1938).
"Y and I and the Ouija Board." *Syracusan* 4, no. 3 (Nov. 1938).

## Essays

"Biography of a Story." In *Come Along with Me.* New York: Penguin, 1968.
"The Case for Dinner-Table Silence." *Good Housekeeping,* March 1960.
"Comment" (upon the death of Leonard Brown [1904–1960]). *Syracusan,* March 1960, 18.
"Experience and Fiction." From *Come Along with Me. The Writer* 82, no. 1 (Jan. 1969).
"Fame." *Writer,* August 1948.
"Go Down, Faulkner (in the Throes of William Faulkner's *Go Down, Moses)."* In *The Best of Bad Faulkner.* Ed. by Dean Faulkner Wells. San Diego: Harcourt, 1991.
"How to Enjoy a Family Quarrel." *McCall's,* Sept. 1957.
"Karen's Complaint." *Good Housekeeping,* Nov. 1959.
"The Life Romantic." *Good Housekeeping,* Dec. 1949.
"List Found in Coat Pocket." *Vogue,* April 15, 1953.
"A Little Test for Mothers." *Good Housekeeping,* Oct. 1960.
"Look Ma, We're Moving!" *Good Housekeeping,* Feb. 1952.
"The Lost Kingdom of Oz." *Reporter,* Dec. 10, 1959.
"Mother, *Honestly!" Good Housekeeping,* Sept. 1959.
"No, I Don't Want to Go to Europe." *Saturday Evening Post,* 6 June 1964.
"Notes for a Young Writer." *Come Along with Me.* New York: Penguin, 1968.
"On Being a Faculty Wife." *Mademoiselle,* Dec. 1956.
"Out of the Mouths of Babes." *Good Housekeeping,* July 1960.
"The Pleasures and Perils of Dining Out with Children." *McCall's,* March 1957.
"Questions I Wish I'd Never Asked." *Good Housekeeping,* March 1961.
"Santa Claus, I Love You." *Good Housekeeping,* Dec. 1956.
"What I Want to Know Is, What Do Other People Cook With?" *Good Housekeeping,* July 1961.

## Published Letters

Letters from Shirley Jackson to Leslie and Geraldine Jackson dated 18 December 1948, 11 April 1949, 13 June 1949, and 9 November 1949. In *Shirley Jackson: The Short Fiction* by Joan Wylie Hall. New York: Twayne, 1993.

## Jackson Interviews

Rogers, W.G. "Author Shirley Jackson is 'Sure Nuff' Witch." Indianapolis Star, May 22, 1949.

Breit, Harvey. "Talk with Miss Jackson." *New York Times Book Review*, June 26, 1949.

Hutchens, John K. "On the Books." *New York Herald Tribune Book Review*, May 8, 1949.

"On an Author." *New York Herald Tribune Book Review*, July 5,1953.

Roseberry, C.R. "'Life Among the Savages' Wins Acclaim For Area Author." *Albany Sunday Times-Union*, November 29, 1953.

Kunitz, Stanley J., ed. "Shirley Jackson." *Twentieth Century Authors*. New York: Wilson, 1955.

Meras, Phyllis. "Her Husband Turned Green" *Providence Sunday Journal*, August 14, 1960.

Nicholas, Lewis. "Demonologist." *New York Times Book Review*, October 7, 1962.

Ciccolella, Cathy. "Jackson Credits SU with Writing Start." Syracuse University *Daily Orange*, April 28, 1965.

## *Jackson Bibliographies*

Hall, Joan Wylie. "Shirley Jackson." *Facts on File Bibliography of American Fiction: 1919–1918*. Edited by Matthew Bruccoli et al. Vol. 1. New York: Facts on File, 1991, 266–67.

Herrick, Casey. "Shirley Jackson's 'The Lottery'." *Bulletin of Bibliography* 46, no. 2. (June 1989): 120–21.

Phillips, Robert S. "Shirley Jackson: A Checklist." *Papers of the Bibliographical Society of America* 56, no.1 (January–March 1962): 110–13.

_____. "Shirley Jackson: A Chronology and Supplementary Checklist." *Papers of the Bibliographical Society of America* 60, no. 2 (April–June 1966): 203–13.

Reinsch, Paul N. *A Critical Bibliography of Shirley Jackson, American Writer (1919–1965): Reviews, Criticiscm, Adaptations*. Lewsiton: The Edward Mellen Press, 2001.

## *Film Adaptations*

*Lizzie*. 1957. Directed by Hugo Hass, screenplay by Mel Dinelli.

*The Haunting*. 1963. Directed by Robert Wise, screenplay by Nelson Giddings.

*The Lottery*. 1996. Directed by Daniel Sackheim, television story by Anthony Spinner.

*The Haunting*. 1999. Directed by Jan. De Bont, screenplay by David Self.

# About the Contributors

**Lynette Carpenter**, professor of English at Ohio Wesleyan University, has published two previous books on women's ghost stories, both with Wendy Kolmar, in addition to essays on American literature and film. She also writes mysteries under the names D. B. Borton and Della Borton, most recently *Six Feet Under* and *Seventh Deadly Sin*.

**Dara Downey** is a post-graduate student in the English department at Trinity College, Dublin. She is currently engaged in research for a thesis on the importance of the concepts of space, movement and gender in the representation of haunted and "bad" houses in American literature and popular culture from the Salem witch trials to the present. She gave a paper titled "Doubles, Evil, and the Subjectivity of the Other" at the Fifth Annual Conference on Evil and Human Wickedness in Prague.

**James Egan** is professor of English at the University of Akron (Ohio) and has published widely on seventeenth century English literature and twentieth century fantasy, science fiction, and gothic, including essays on John Milton, Andrew Marvell, John Donne, Joyce Carol Oates, Shirley Jackson, H.P. Lovecraft, and Stephen King. He is currently completing several projects on the aesthetics of Milton's prose.

**Joan Wylie Hall** is an instructor in the University of Mississippi's English Department. She is the author of *Shirley Jackson: A Study of the Short Fiction* and editor of the recent interview collection *Conversations with Audre Lorde*. A specialist in literature of the southern United States, she has published articles on Ann Patchett, Josephine Humphreys, William Faulkner, Tennessee Williams, Eudora Welty, Lee Smith, and others and is currently writing a book about the 1890s local colorist Ruth McEnery Stuart.

**Darryl Hattenhauer** is associate professor of English at Arizona State University in Phoenix and specializes in American literature, especially gothic, grotesque, and fantastic fiction since 1850. His publications include articles on Nathaniel Hawthorne, Herman Melville, Stephen Crane, Jack London, Charles Chesnutt, F. Scott Fitzgerald, Ernest Hemingway, Edith Wharton, Sinclair Lewis, William Faulkner, Nathanael West, Zora Neale Hurston, Eudora Welty, James

Baldwin, Saul Bellow, Cynthia Ozick, Kurt Vonnegut, and Leslie Marmon Silko. His book on Shirley Jackson, *Shirley Jackson's American Gothic* (2003) was published by SUNY Press, and his next book will be about James Purdy.

**Diane Long Hoeveler** is professor of English and coordinator of Women's Studies at Marquette University, Milwaukee, Wisconsin. She is author of *Romantic Androgyny* (1990) and *Gothic Feminism* (1998), and is coauthor of *Charlotte Brontë* (1997) and the *Historical Dictionary of Feminism* (1996; 2004). Edited or co-edited works include *Comparative Romanticisms* (1998), *Women of Color* (2001), *Approaches to Teaching "Jane Eyre"* (1993), *Approaches to Teaching Gothic Fiction* (2003), and *Wuthering Heights* (2001). In addition, she has published over 35 articles on a variety of topics, including the gothic, melodrama, women writers, and romanticism and gender. She is also past president of the International Conference on Romanticism (2001–2003), and serves on the editorial board of a number of journals in the field of Romanticism.

**Darryl Jones** is lecturer in English and codirector of the School of English M.Phil. program in popular literature at Trinity College, Dublin. His books include *Horror: A Thematic History in Fiction and Film* (2002), *Jane Austen* (2004) and the forthcoming *Robert Emmet: Bicentenary Essays* (2005). He has also written numerous articles on nineteenth century literature and on aspects of popular literature. His current research is on mass death and catastrophe fiction.

**S.T. Joshi** is a leading authority on H.P. Lovecraft, Lord Dunsany, Ambrose Bierce, and other authors of supernatural fiction. He is the author of *The Weird Tale* (1990), *The Modern Weird Tale* (2001), and other critical and biographical studies. He is currently preparing editions of Ambrose Bierce's collected short fiction, H. P. Lovecraft's collected essays and the collected works of Clark Ashton Smith.

**Tricia Lootens** is associate professor of English at the University of Georgia in Athens and specializes in nineteenth century poetry and feminist criticism. The author of "Hemans and Home: Romanticism, Victorianism, and the Domestication of National Identity" (*PMLA* 1994; rpt 1995, 1999), Lootens is currently completing a book-length study of national sentimentality, Second Wave feminist criticism, and the "poetess tradition." In 1996, she published *Lost Saints: Silence, Gender, and Victorian Literary Canonization*, which was awarded the University of Georgia's creative Research medal in 2000. More recent writing has focused on Victorian patriotic poetry (in the *Cambridge Companion to Victorian Poetry*, 2000) and on transatlantic connections among female political poets (in *Women's Poetry, Late Romantic to Late Victorian*, 1999). Her essay on Letitia Elizabeth Landon, in *Romanticism and Women Poets* (1999), won the Keats-Shelley Association of America Award. She has also published on Victorian appropriations of Shakespeare, as well as on gothic modes of social criticism.

**Bernice M. Murphy** completed her Ph.D. thesis, titled *"Do You Know Who I Am?": Contextualising Shirley Jackson*, at Trinity College Dublin in 2003. Her article on Peter Carey and postcolonialism appeared in *The Essentials of Modern Literature in English* (2004), and she is contributing an essay on Stephen King to the *Dictionary of Literary Biography* volume on American Gothic and Romance Writers. She has also written entries on Shirley Jackson, Peter Straub, Stephen King, Richard Matheson, H.P. Lovecraft and the horror genre itself for the online *Literary Encyclopedia* (www.litencyc.com).

**Judie Newman** is professor of American Studies at the University of Nottingham, and the author of *Saul Bellow and History, John Updike, Nadine Gordimer, Harriet Beecher Stowe's Dred; A Tale of the Great Dismal Swamp* (editor), *The Ballistic Bard, Alison Lurie* and *Nadine Gordimer's Burger's Daughter: A Casebook*. She is currently researching *Fictions of America*, a critical study of transnational narratives for Routledge.

**John G. Parks** completed 32 years of teaching in 2004, and is professor of English at Miami University (Ohio), where he specializes in twentieth century American literature, especially contemporary fiction. In addition to several essays on Shirley Jackson's fiction and other novelists writing in the post–World War II period, Parks has published a book on the fiction of E.L. Doctorow. He has also edited an anthology of American short stories since World War II. He has a forthcoming essay on the fiction of Edward Lewis Wallant for a volume on the Holocaust novel in the *Dictionary of Literary Biography*, and an essay on John Updike coming out in *Renascence: Essays on Values in Literature*. He is working on essays on Robert Stone and Richard Power.

**Rich Pascal** has taught at several universities in the United States, New Zealand and Australia. Currently he is a senior lecturer in the School of Humanities at the Australian National University. Publications in recent years include articles on Jackson, Whitman, Zane Grey, Oliver La Farge, and "Ishi," as well as several on Australianist topics.

**Roberta Rubenstein** is professor of literature at American University in Washington, D.C., where she teaches courses in fiction by women, feminist theory, and modernism. She is the author of *The Novelistic Vision of Doris Lessing: Breaking the Forms of Consciousness* (1979); *Boundaries of the Self: Gender, Culture, Fiction* (1987); and *Home Matters: Longing and Belonging, Nostalgia and Mourning in Women's Fiction* (2001). In addition, she has published over 30 scholarly essays on twentieth century and contemporary writers, including Virginia Woolf, Shirley Jackson, Doris Lessing, Margaret Atwood, John Fowles, Margaret Drabble, Toni Morrison, Angela Carter, Barbara Kingsolver, and Paul Auster. Currently, she is working on the language of negation in Virginia Woolf's fiction.

**Marta Caminero-Santangelo** is assistant professor in the Department of English at the University of Kansas in Lawrence and is affiliated with the Department of African and African-American Studies. She has previously taught at DePaul University in Chicago. Her research interests cover U.S. Latino/a fiction, twentieth century American women's literature, feminist criticism, African-American fiction, and twentieth century American literature.

# Index